I'm extremely interested in Japanese-style clothes. That's why I like to watch historical dramas so much. I absolutely love the *dotera* (a traditional kind of Japanese garment like a nightgown for use in winter) I got from my mother and wear it almost every day! My cat, Coro, seems to really like it too… so we fight over it.

—**Katsura Hoshino**

Shiga Prefecture native Katsura Hoshino's hit manga series *D.Gray-man* has been serialized in *Weekly Shonen Jump* since 2004. Katsura's debut manga, "Continue," appeared for the first time in *Weekly Shonen Jump* in 2003.

Katsura adores cats.

D.GRAY-MAN
VOL. 15
SHONEN JUMP ADVANCED
Manga Edition

STORY AND ART BY
KATSURA HOSHINO

English Adaptation/Lance Caselman
Translation/John Werry
Touch-up Art & Lettering/HudsonYards
Design/Matt Hinrichs
Editor/Gary Leach

VP, Production/Alvin Lu
VP, Publishing Licensing/Rika Inouye
VP, Sales & Product Marketing/Gonzalo Ferreyra
VP, Creative/Linda Espinosa
Publisher/Hyoe Narita

Published by VIZ Media, LLC
P.O. Box 77010
San Francisco, CA 94107

10 9 8 7 6 5 4 3 2 1
First printing, November 2009

THE WORLD'S MOST
CUTTING-EDGE MANGA

SHONEN
JUMP
ADVANCED

www.viz.com

(www.shonenjump.com)

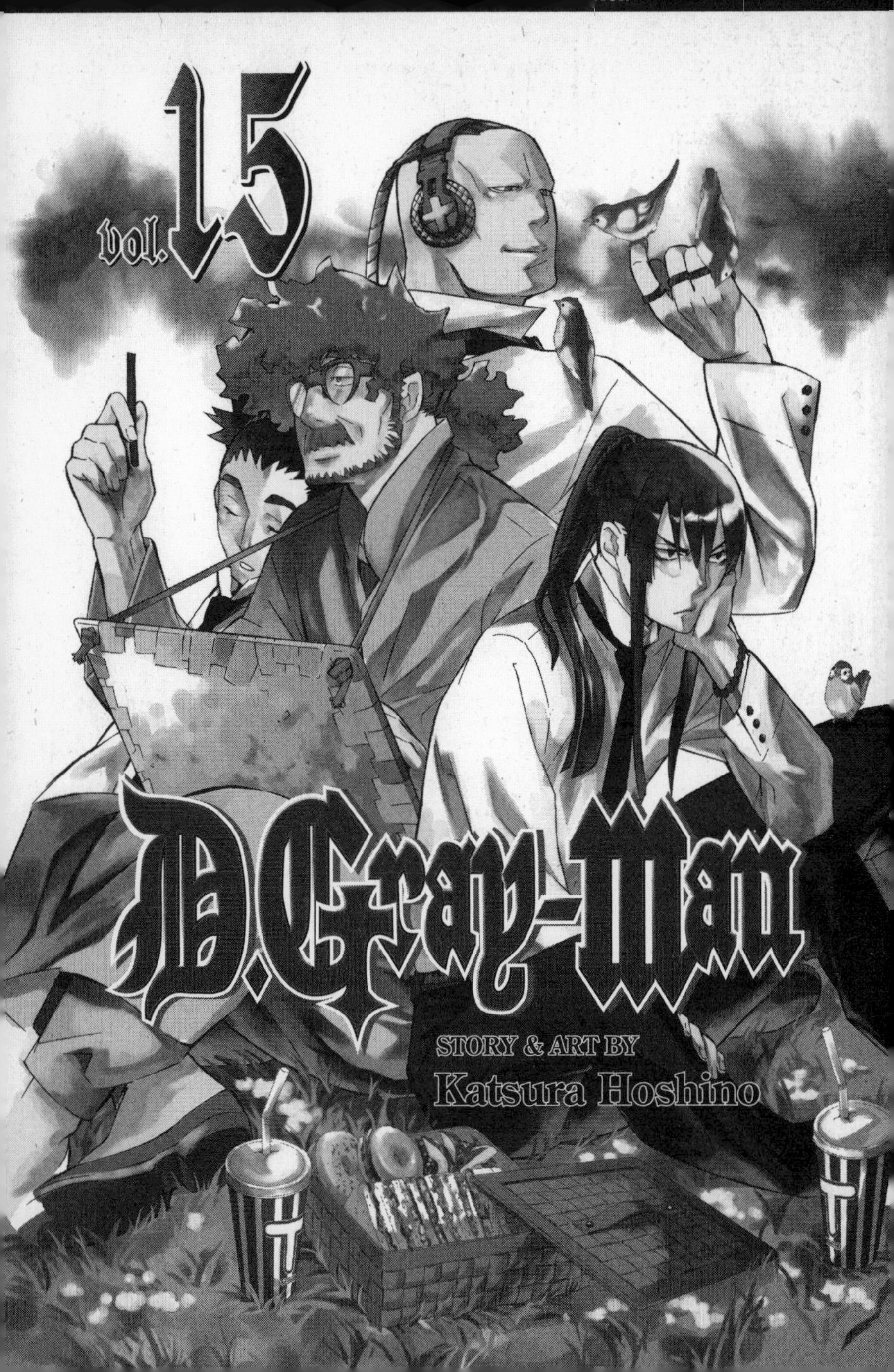
vol.15
D.Gray-man
STORY & ART BY
Katsura Hoshino

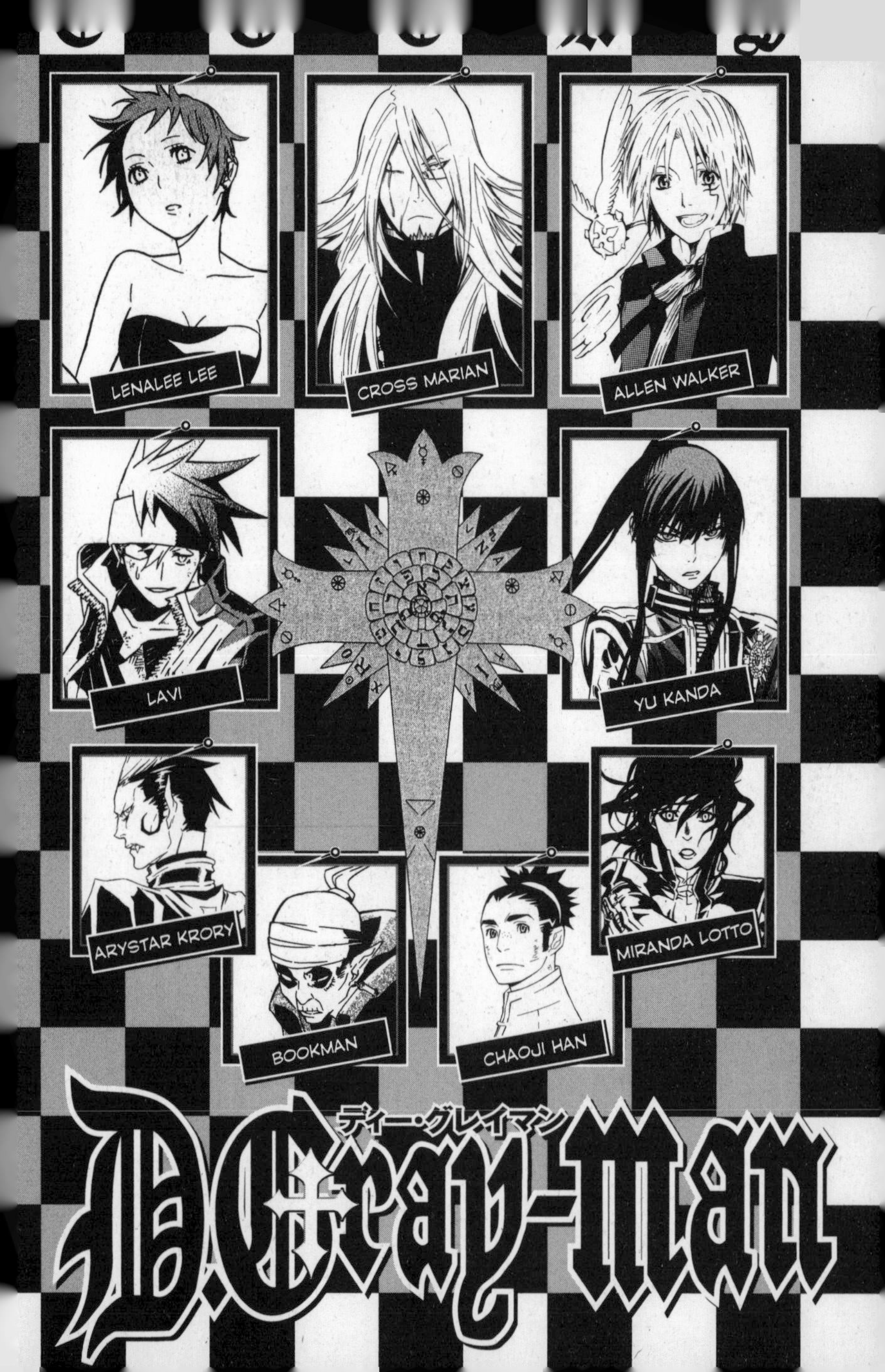
ALLEN WALKER
CROSS MARIAN
LENALEE LEE
YU KANDA
LAVI
MIRANDA LOTTO
ARYSTAR KRORY
CHAOJI HAN
BOOKMAN
ディー・グレイマン
D.Gray-man

JOHNNY GILL

BAK CHAN

KOMUI LEE

LEVEL 4

MALCOLM C. ROUVELIER

REEVER WENHAM

THE MILLENNIUM EARL

LULU BELL

HOWARD LINK

S T O R Y

IT ALL BEGAN CENTURIES AGO WITH THE DISCOVERY OF A CUBE
CONTAINING AN APOCALYPTIC PROPHECY FROM AN ANCIENT CIVILIZATION
AND INSTRUCTIONS IN THE USE OF INNOCENCE, A CRYSTALLINE
SUBSTANCE OF WONDROUS SUPERNATURAL POWER. THE CREATORS
OF THE CUBE CLAIMED TO HAVE DEFEATED AN EVIL KNOWN AS THE
MILLENNIUM EARL BY USING THE INNOCENCE. NEVERTHELESS,
THE WORLD WAS DESTROYED BY THE GREAT FLOOD OF THE OLD
TESTAMENT. NOW, TO AVERT A SECOND END OF THE WORLD, A GROUP
OF EXORCISTS WIELDING WEAPONS MADE OF INNOCENCE MUST BATTLE
THE MILLENNIUM EARL AND HIS TERRIBLE MINIONS, THE AKUMA.

HAVING DEFEATED THE EARL'S MINIONS AND TAKEN CONTROL
OF THE ARK, ALLEN AND HIS COLLEAGUES RETURN TO BLACK ORDER HQ,
WHERE, INSTEAD OF BEING RECEIVED AS A HERO, ALLEN IS PLACED
UNDER GUARD BY INSPECTOR ROUVELIER. BUT HE'S SOON FACED
WITH FAR MORE PRESSING MATTERS.

D.GRAY-MAN
Vol. 15

CONTENTS

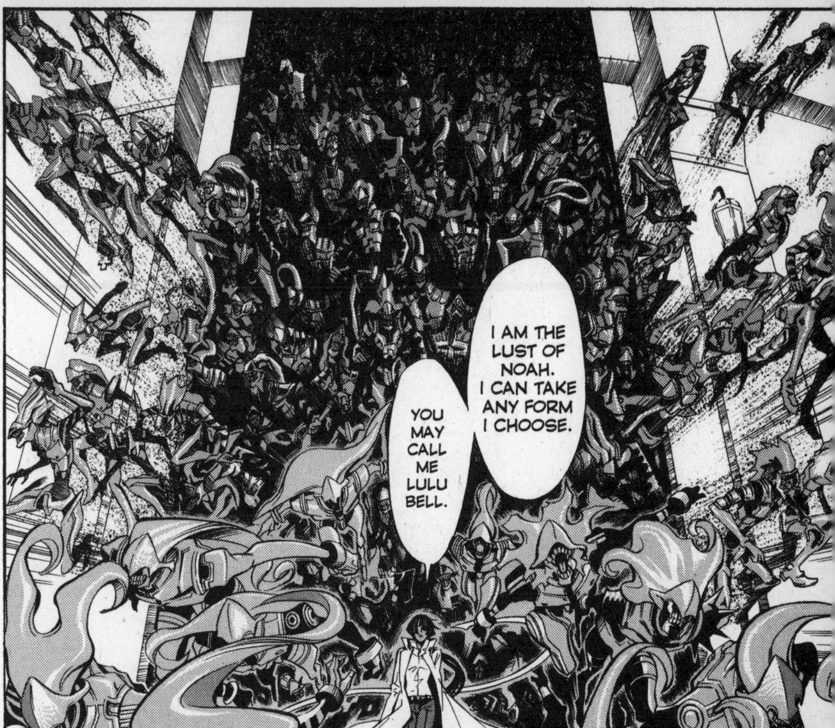
I AM THE LUST OF NOAH. I CAN TAKE ANY FORM I CHOOSE.
YOU MAY CALL ME LULU BELL.
THE 139TH NIGHT: ATTACK ON HEADQUARTERS

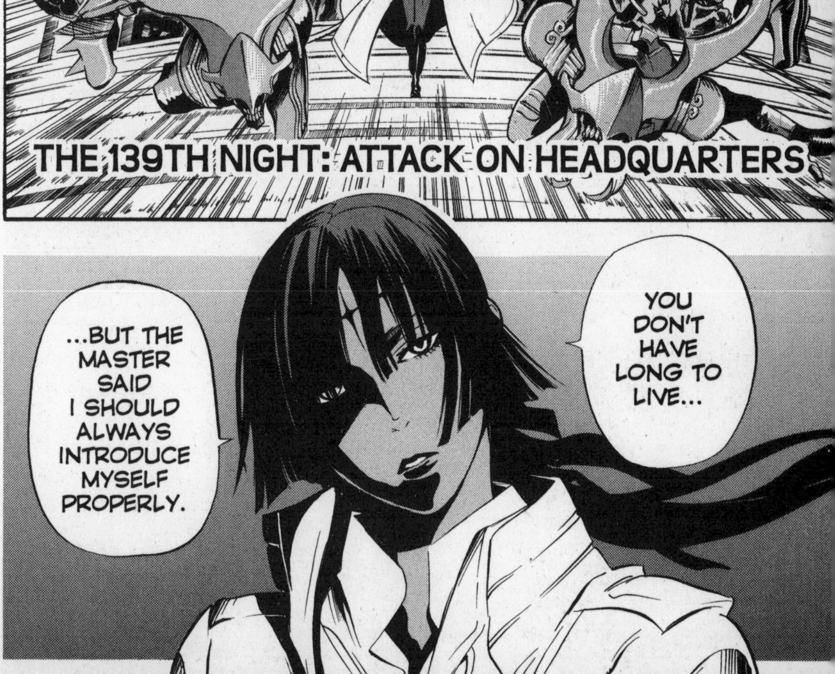
YOU DON'T HAVE LONG TO LIVE...
...BUT THE MASTER SAID I SHOULD ALWAYS INTRODUCE MYSELF PROPERLY.

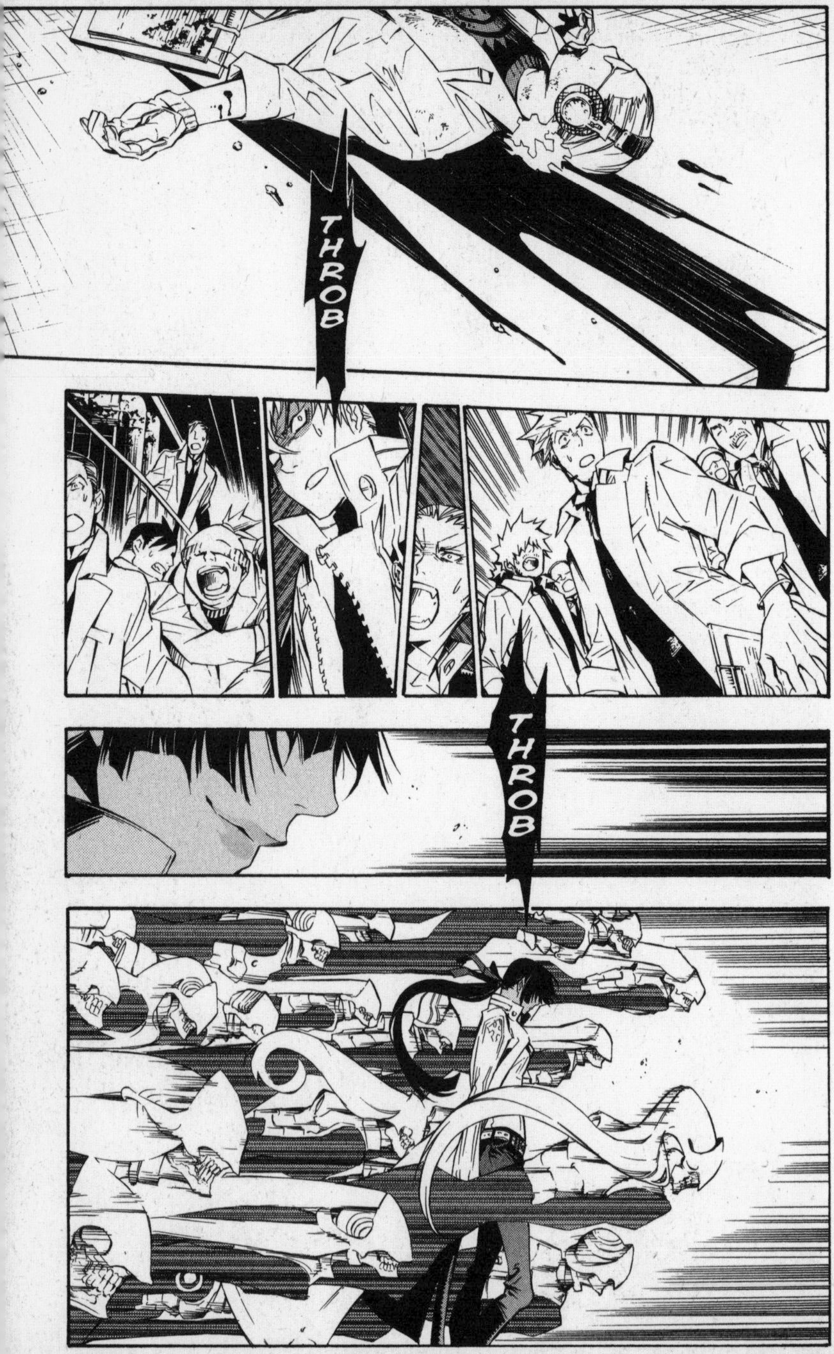
THROB
THROB

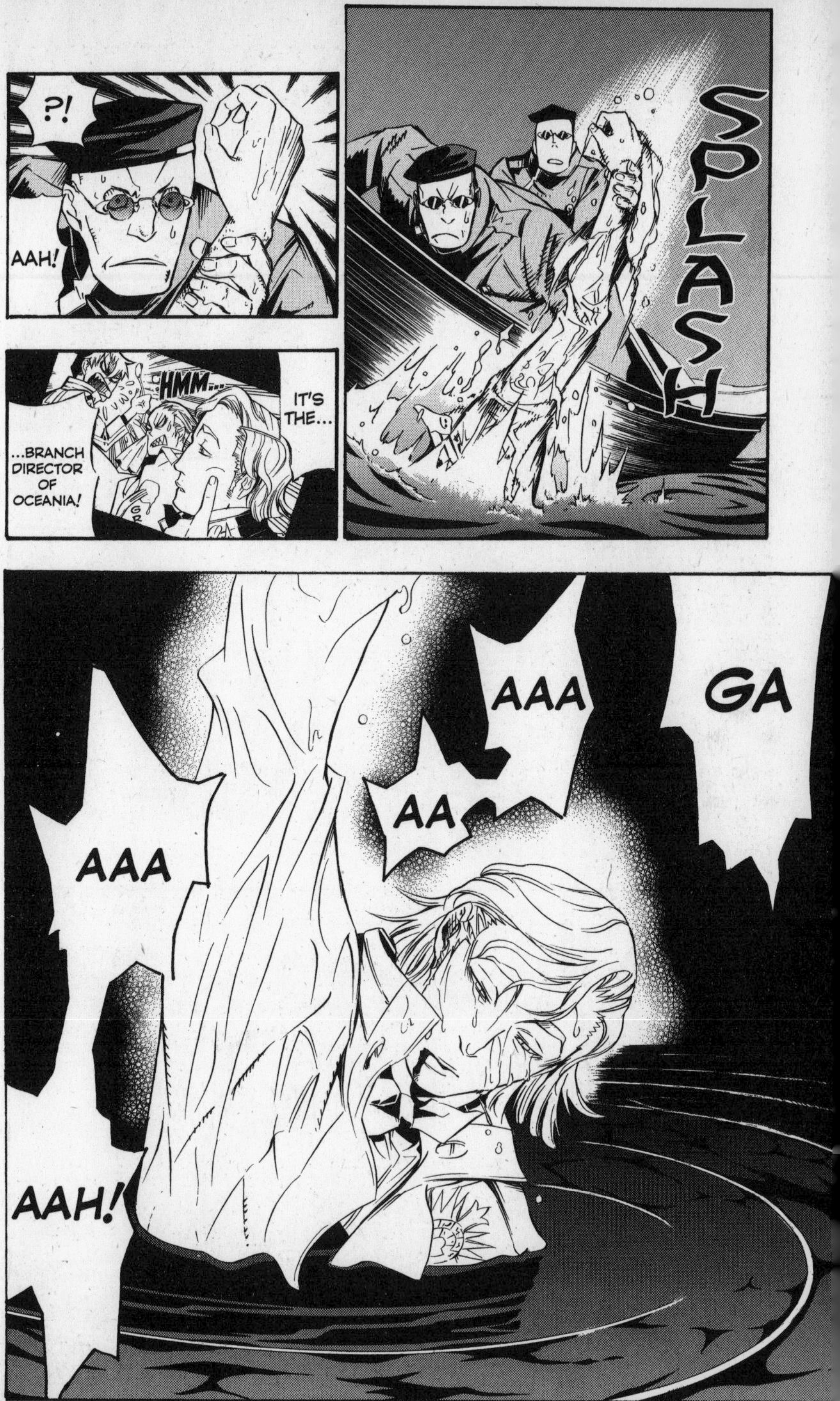
SPLASH
?!
AAH!
IT'S THE...
HMM...
...BRANCH DIRECTOR OF OCEANIA!
GA
AAA
AA
AAA
AAH!

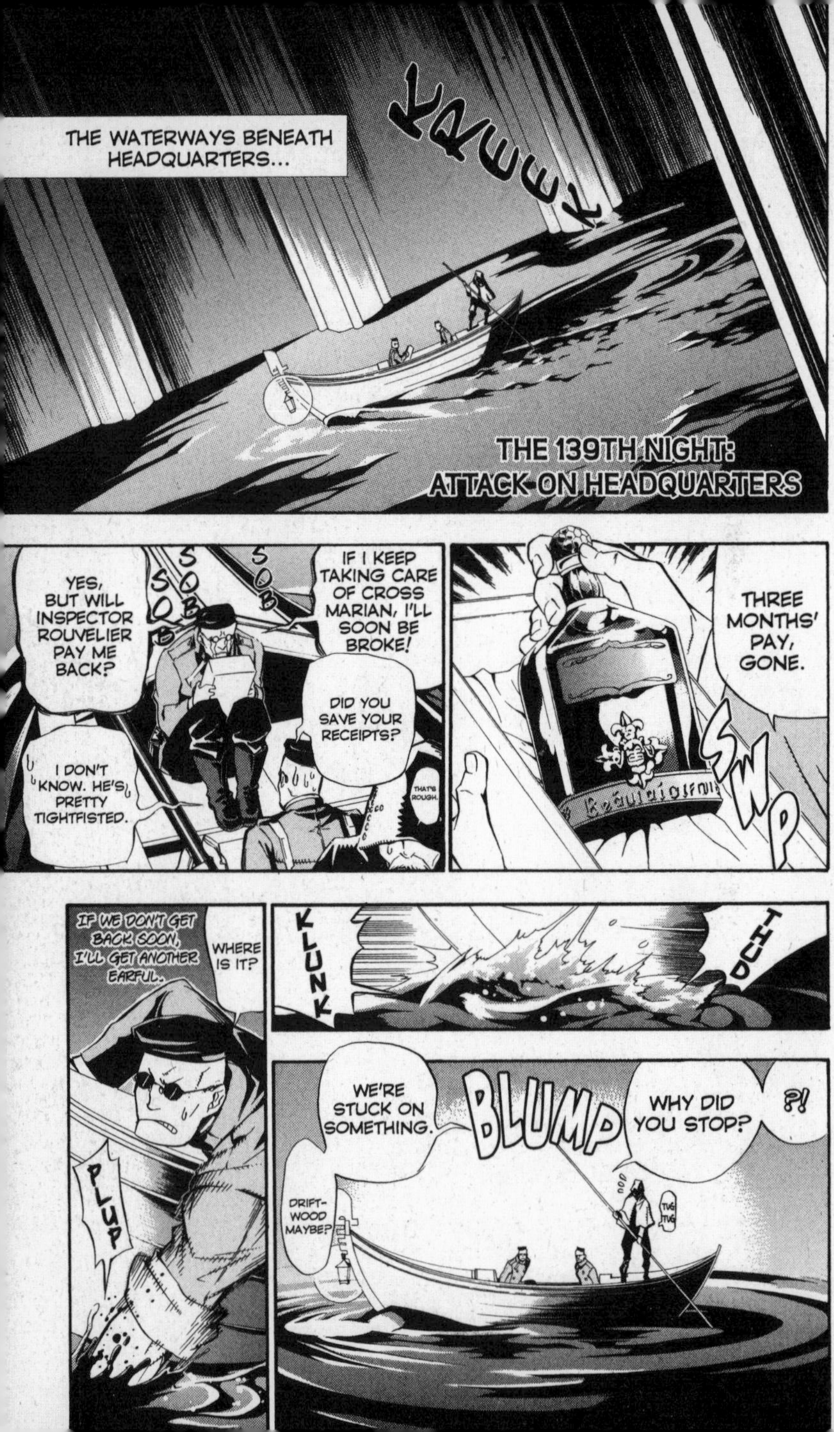
THE WATERWAYS BENEATH HEADQUARTERS...
KRAWK
THE 139TH NIGHT: ATTACK ON HEADQUARTERS
THREE MONTHS' PAY, GONE.
SWP
IF I KEEP TAKING CARE OF CROSS MARIAN, I'LL SOON BE BROKE!
SOB SOB
YES, BUT WILL INSPECTOR ROUVELIER PAY ME BACK?
DID YOU SAVE YOUR RECEIPTS?
I DON'T KNOW. HE'S PRETTY TIGHTFISTED.
THAT'S ROUGH.
THUD
KLUNK
?!
WHY DID YOU STOP?
BLUMP
WE'RE STUCK ON SOMETHING.
TUG TUG
DRIFT-WOOD MAYBE?
WHERE IS IT?
IF WE DON'T GET BACK SOON, I'LL GET ANOTHER EARFUL.
PLUP

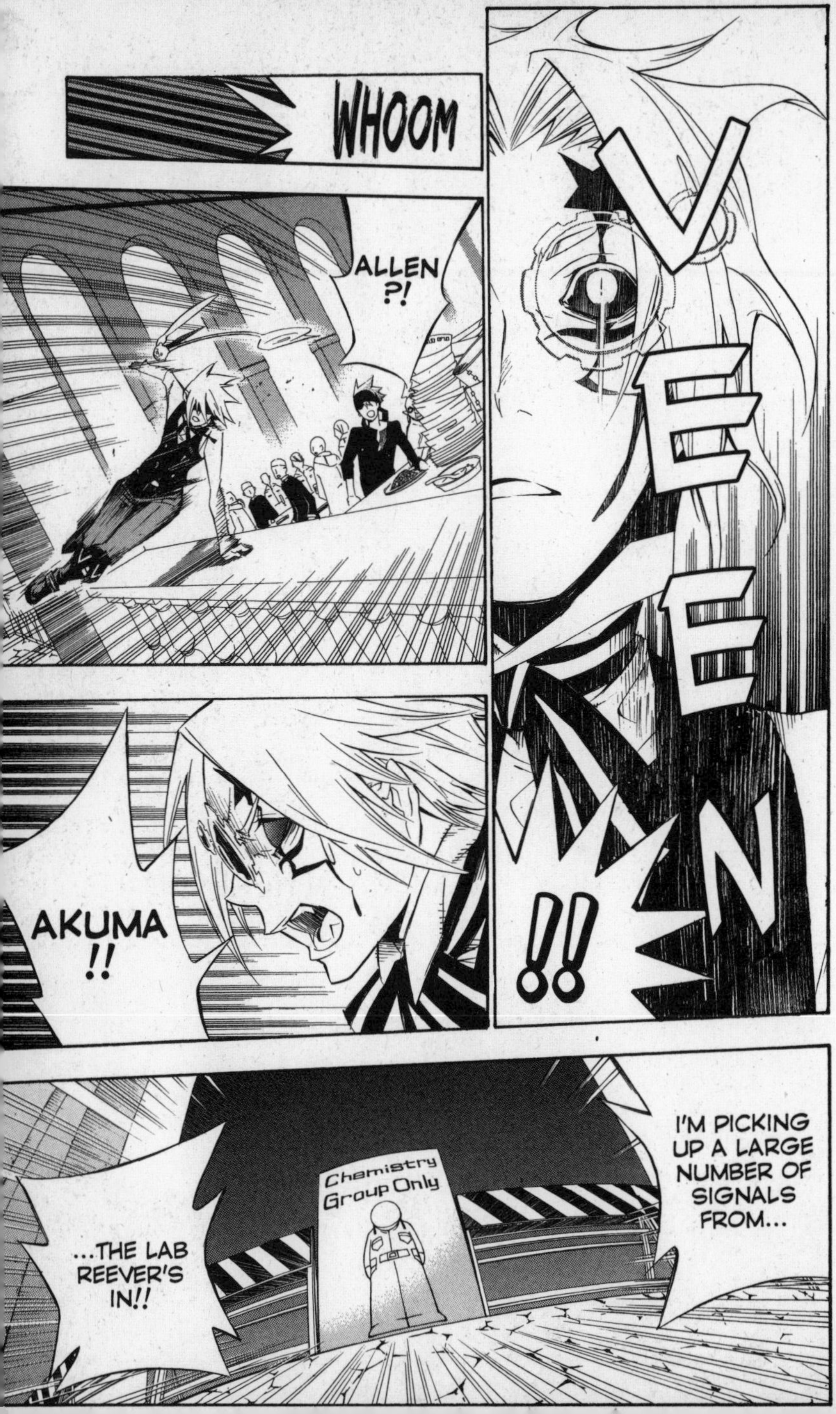
VEEEN!!
WHOOM
ALLEN ?!
AKUMA !!
I'M PICKING UP A LARGE NUMBER OF SIGNALS FROM...
Chemistry Group Only
...THE LAB REEVER'S IN!!

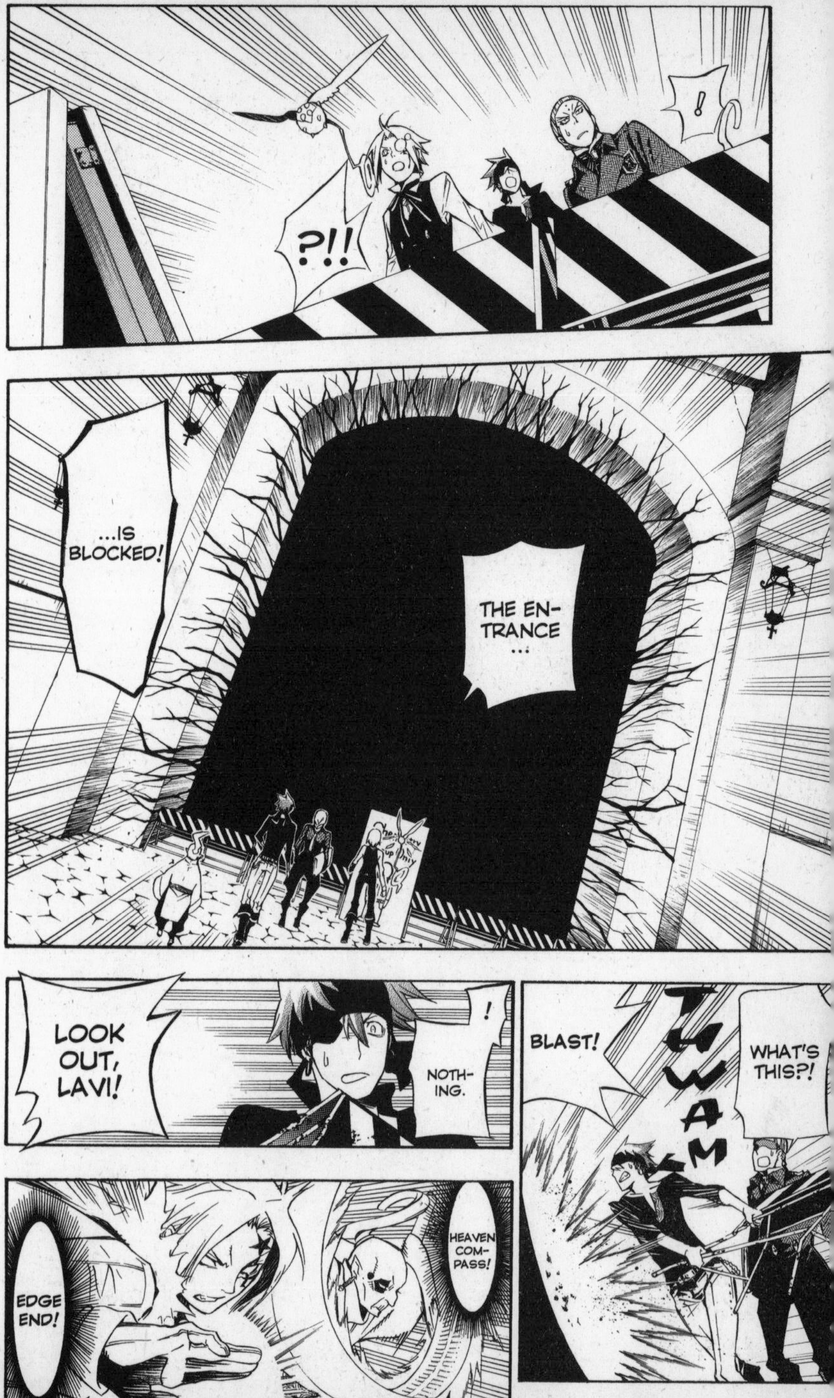
!
?!!
THE EN-TRANCE...
...IS BLOCKED!
WHAT'S THIS?!
TWAM
BLAST!
!
NOTH-ING.
LOOK OUT, LAVI!
HEAVEN COM-PASS!
EDGE END!

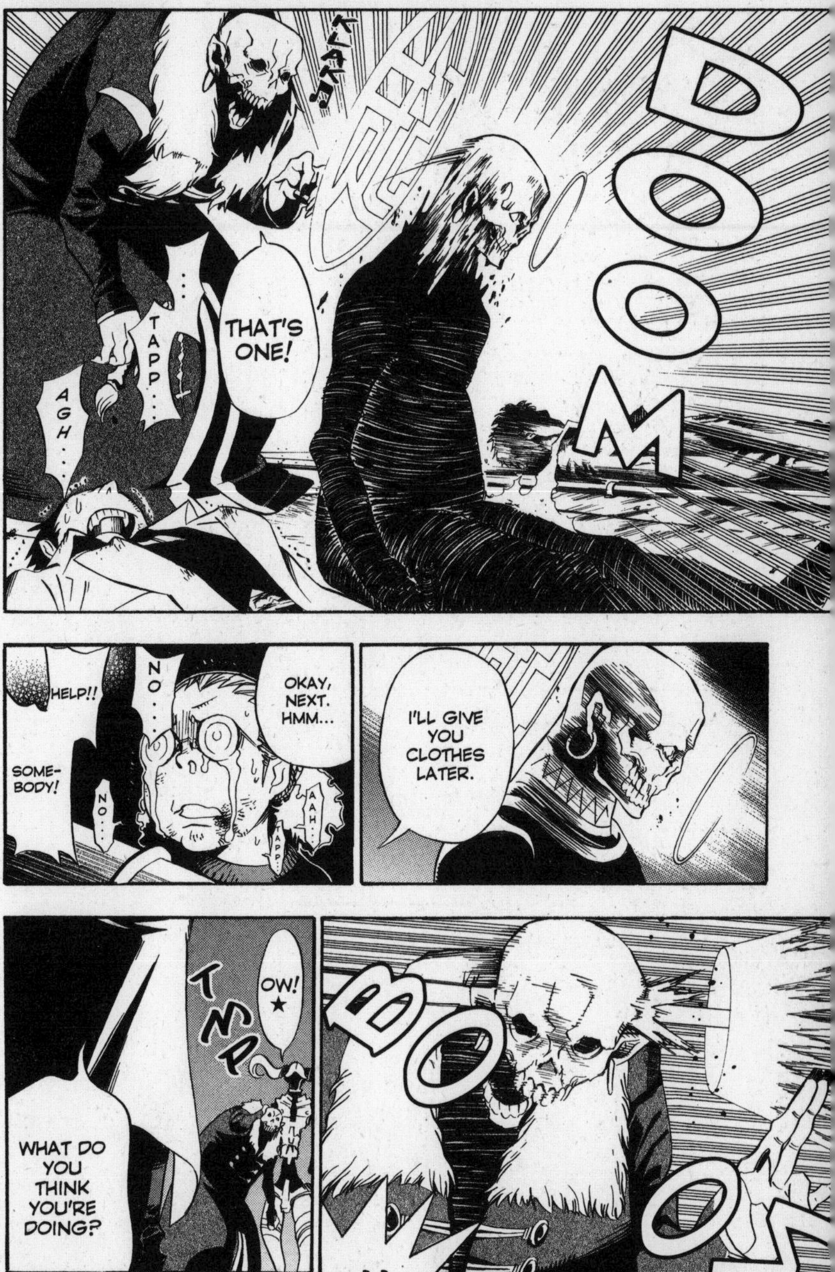
DOOOM
KLAK!
THAT'S ONE!
TAPP...
AGH...
I'LL GIVE YOU CLOTHES LATER.
OKAY, NEXT. HMM...
NO...
HELP!!
SOMEBODY!
AAH...
TAPP...
NO...
BOOM
!!
OW! ★
WHAT DO YOU THINK YOU'RE DOING?

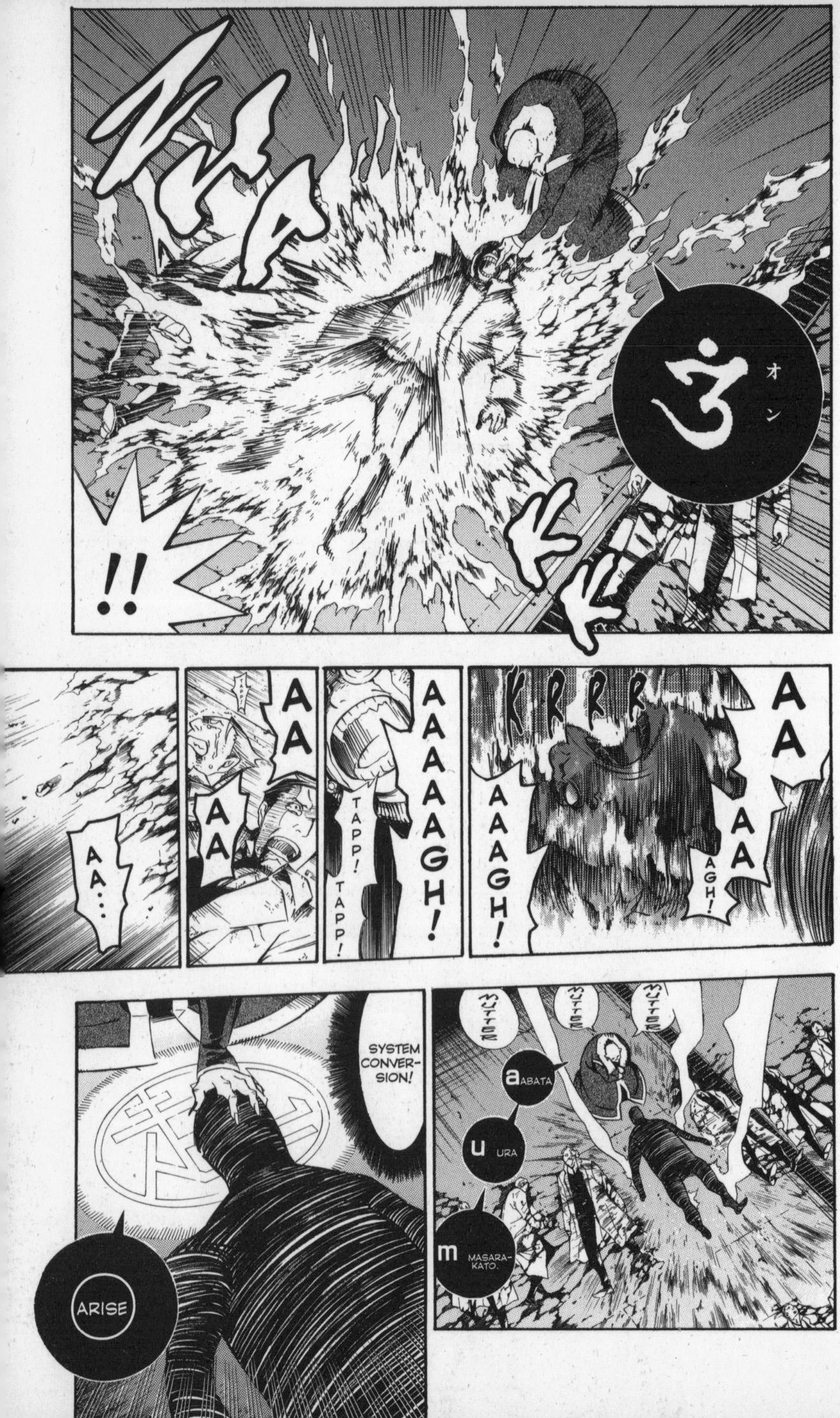
オン
!!
AAAAAGH!
KRRRR
AAAAAGH!
AAAAAAAGH!
TAPP! TAPP!
AAAA
TAPP!
AA...
MUTTER
MUTTER
MUTTER
a ABATA
u URA
m MASARA-KATO.
SYSTEM CONVERSION!
ARISE

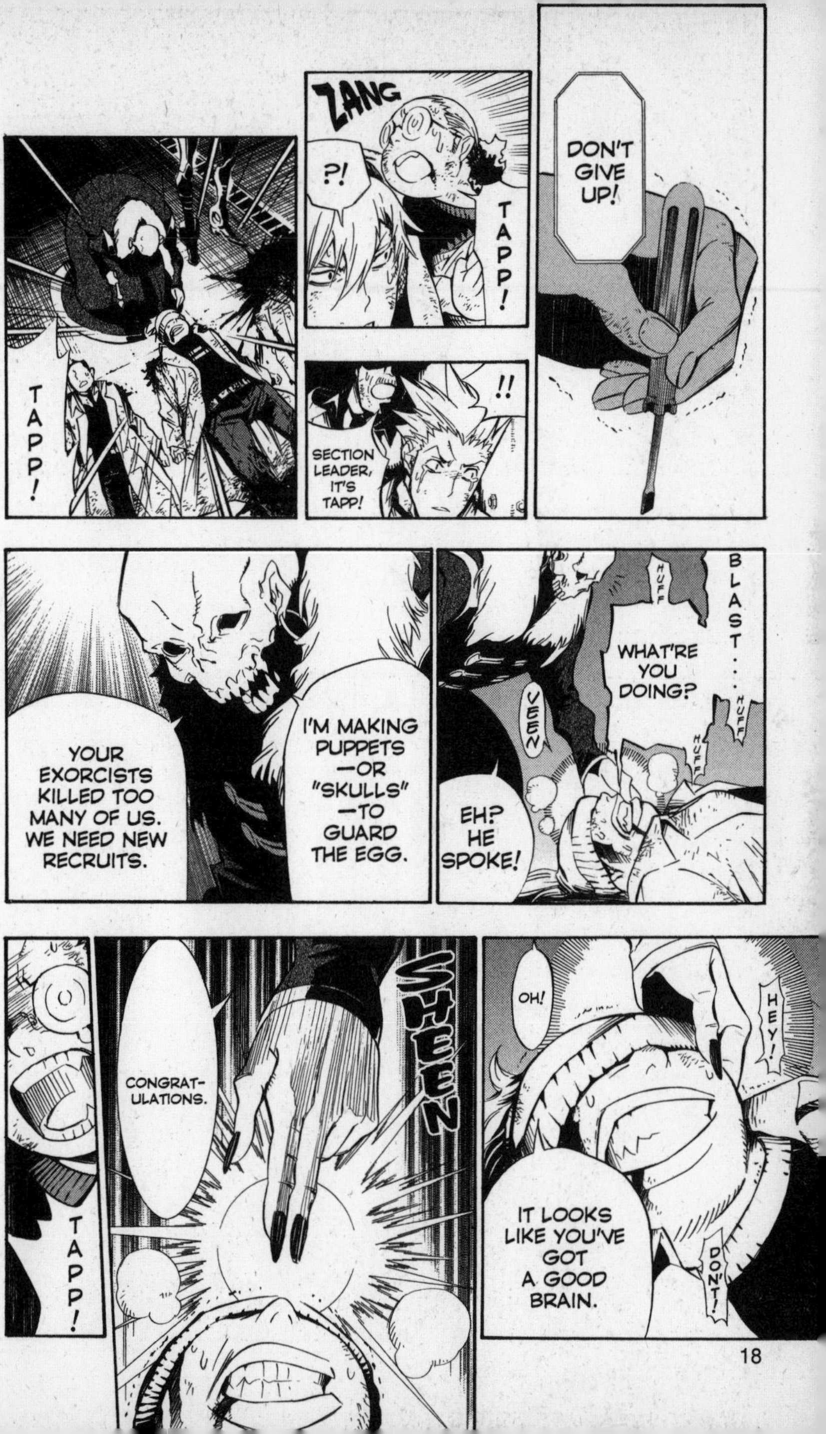
DON'T GIVE UP!
ZANG
?!
TAPP!
!!
SECTION LEADER, IT'S TAPP!
TAPP!
BLAST...
HUFF
HUFF
HUFF
WHAT'RE YOU DOING?
VEEN
EH? HE SPOKE!
I'M MAKING PUPPETS —OR "SKULLS" —TO GUARD THE EGG.
YOUR EXORCISTS KILLED TOO MANY OF US. WE NEED NEW RECRUITS.
HEY!
OH!
IT LOOKS LIKE YOU'VE GOT A GOOD BRAIN.
DON'T!
SHEEN
CONGRAT-ULATIONS.
TAPP!

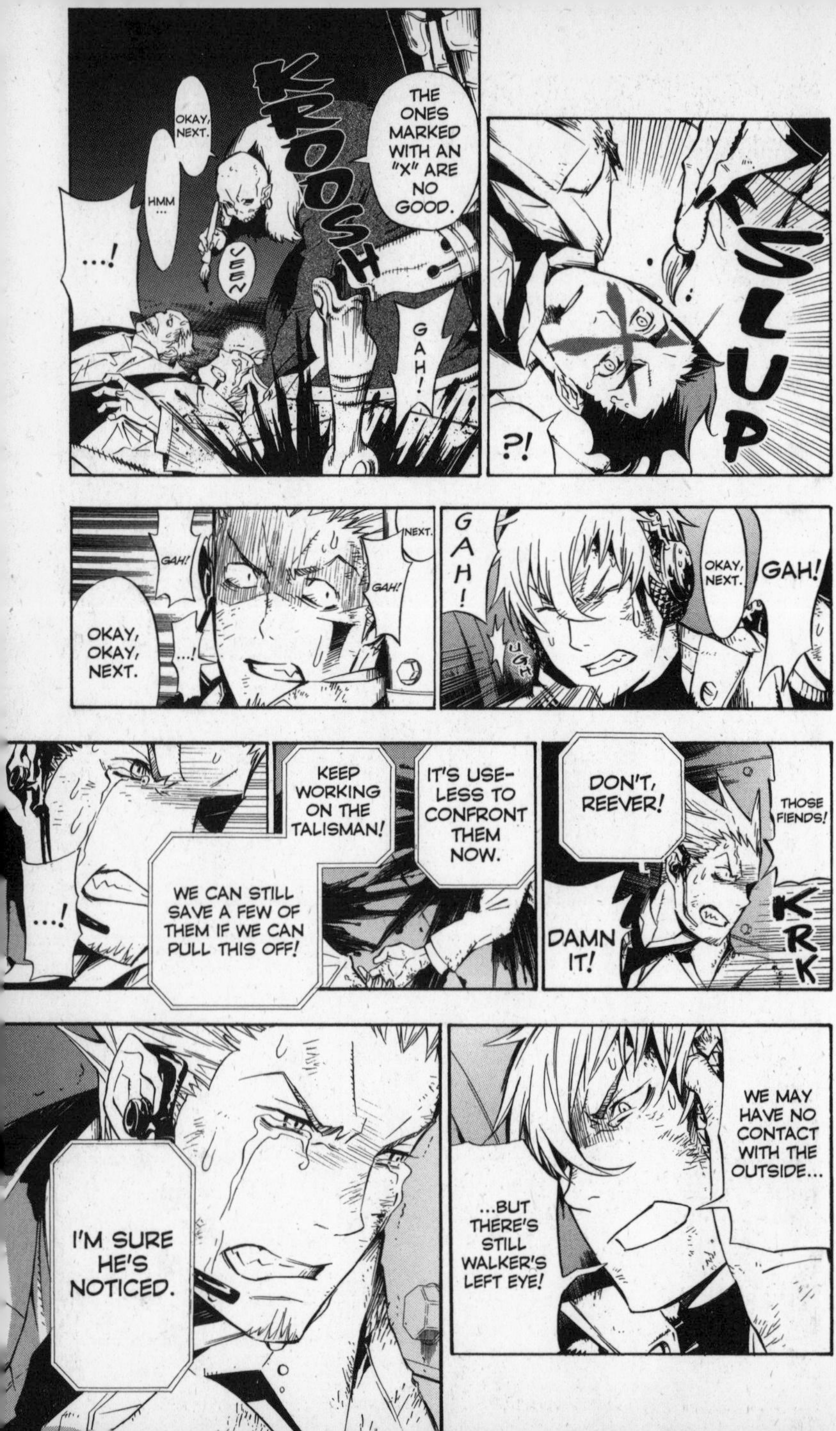
KSLUP
?!
THE ONES MARKED WITH AN "X" ARE NO GOOD.
KROOSH
OKAY, NEXT.
HMM...
GAH!
JEEN
...!
GAH!
OKAY, NEXT.
GAH!
UGH
NEXT.
GAH!
GAH!
OKAY, OKAY, NEXT.
...!
THOSE FIENDS!
DON'T, REEVER!
KRK
DAMN IT!
IT'S USE-LESS TO CONFRONT THEM NOW.
KEEP WORKING ON THE TALISMAN!
WE CAN STILL SAVE A FEW OF THEM IF WE CAN PULL THIS OFF!
...!
WE MAY HAVE NO CONTACT WITH THE OUTSIDE...
...BUT THERE'S STILL WALKER'S LEFT EYE!
I'M SURE HE'S NOTICED.

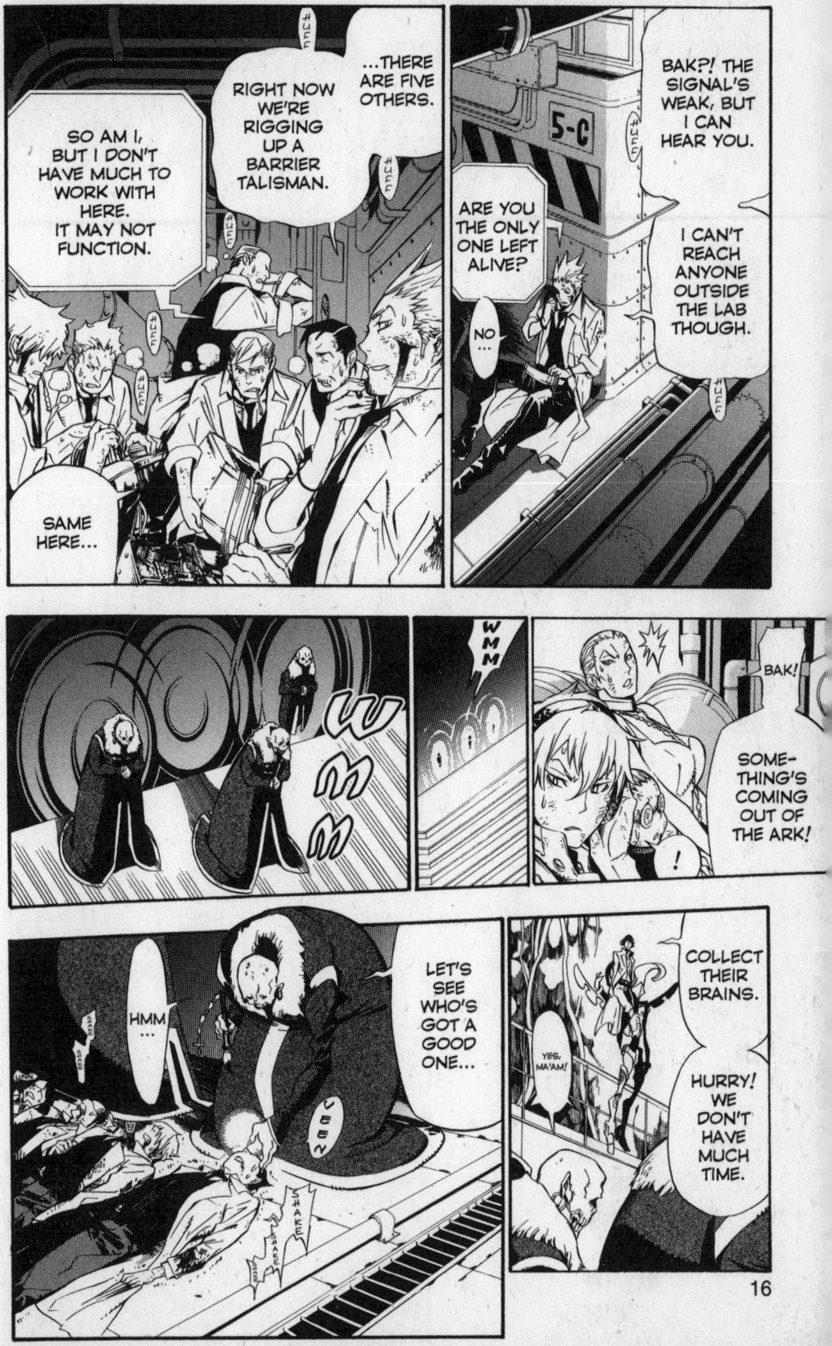
BAK?! THE SIGNAL'S WEAK, BUT I CAN HEAR YOU.
HUFF
I CAN'T REACH ANYONE OUTSIDE THE LAB THOUGH.
ARE YOU THE ONLY ONE LEFT ALIVE?
NO...
HUFF
...THERE ARE FIVE OTHERS.
HUFF
RIGHT NOW WE'RE RIGGING UP A BARRIER TALISMAN.
HUFF
HUFF
SO AM I, BUT I DON'T HAVE MUCH TO WORK WITH HERE. IT MAY NOT FUNCTION.
HUFF
HUFF
SAME HERE...
BAK!
SOME-THING'S COMING OUT OF THE ARK!
!
WMM
WMM
COLLECT THEIR BRAINS.
HURRY! WE DON'T HAVE MUCH TIME.
YES, MA'AM!
LET'S SEE WHO'S GOT A GOOD ONE...
VEEN
HMM...
SHAKE
SHAKE

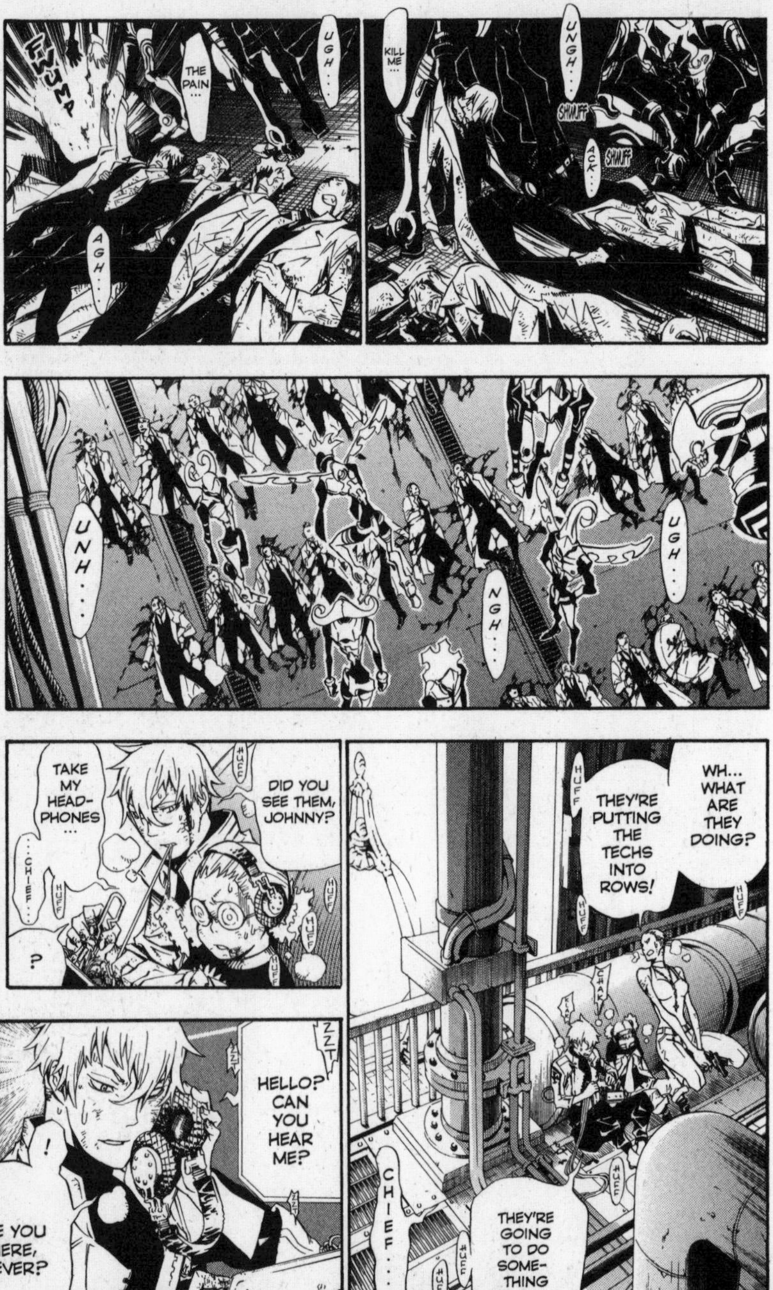
UNGH...
SHUFF
ACK...
SHUFF
KILL ME...
UGH...
THE PAIN...
FWUMP
AGH...
UGH...
NGH...
UNH...
WH... WHAT ARE THEY DOING?
HUFF
THEY'RE PUTTING THE TECHS INTO ROWS!
HUFF
HUFF
CHAK
HUFF
THEY'RE GOING TO DO SOME-THING TO THEM.
CHIEF...
HUFF
HUFF
DID YOU SEE THEM, JOHNNY?
TAKE MY HEAD-PHONES...
HUFF
HUFF
HUFF
...CHIEF...
HUFF
?
ZZT
ZZT
HELLO? CAN YOU HEAR ME?
ZZT
!
ARE YOU THERE, REEVER?

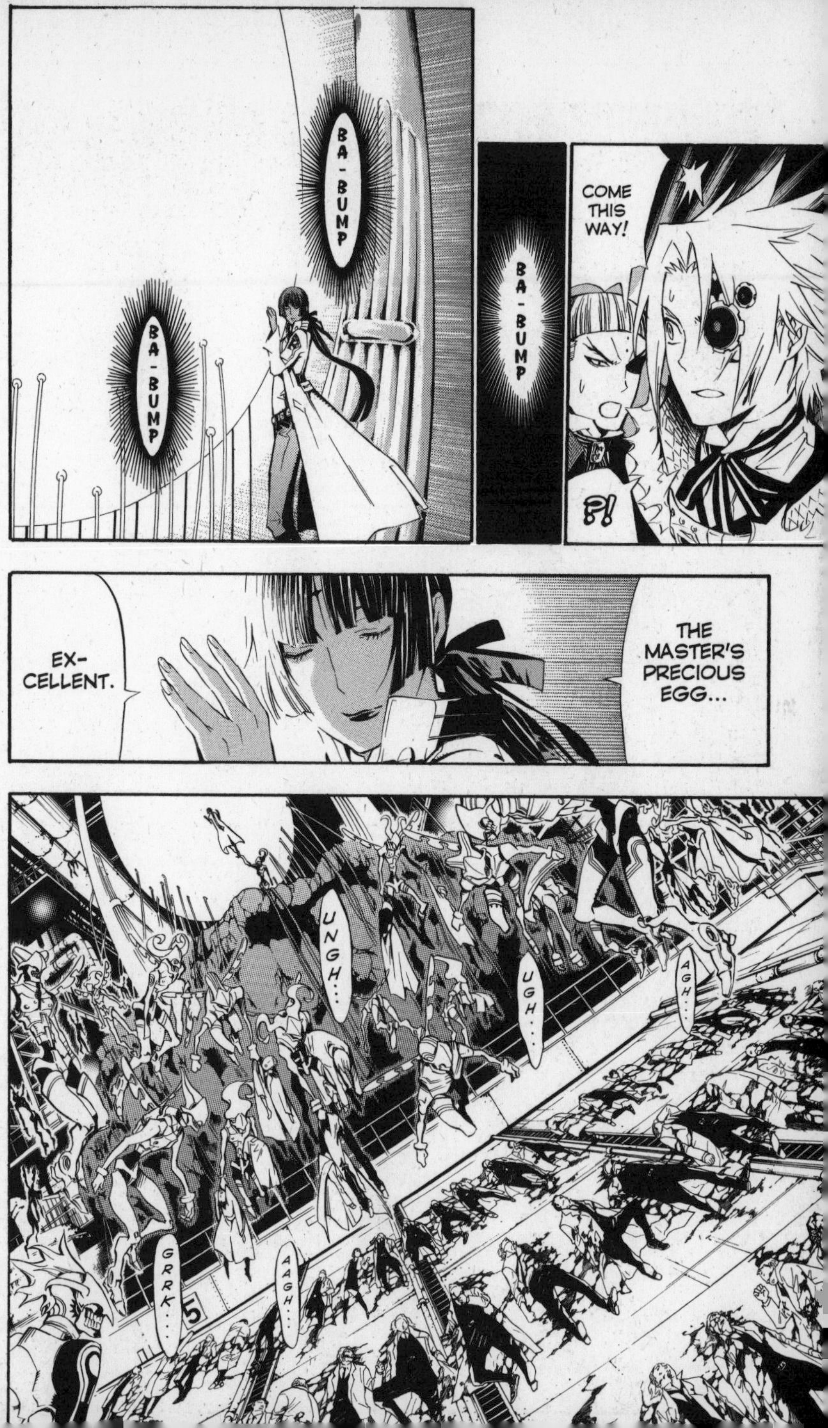
COME THIS WAY!
?!
BA-BUMP
BA-BUMP
BA-BUMP
THE MASTER'S PRECIOUS EGG...
EX-CELLENT.
AGH...
UGH...
UNGH...
AAGH...
GRRK...

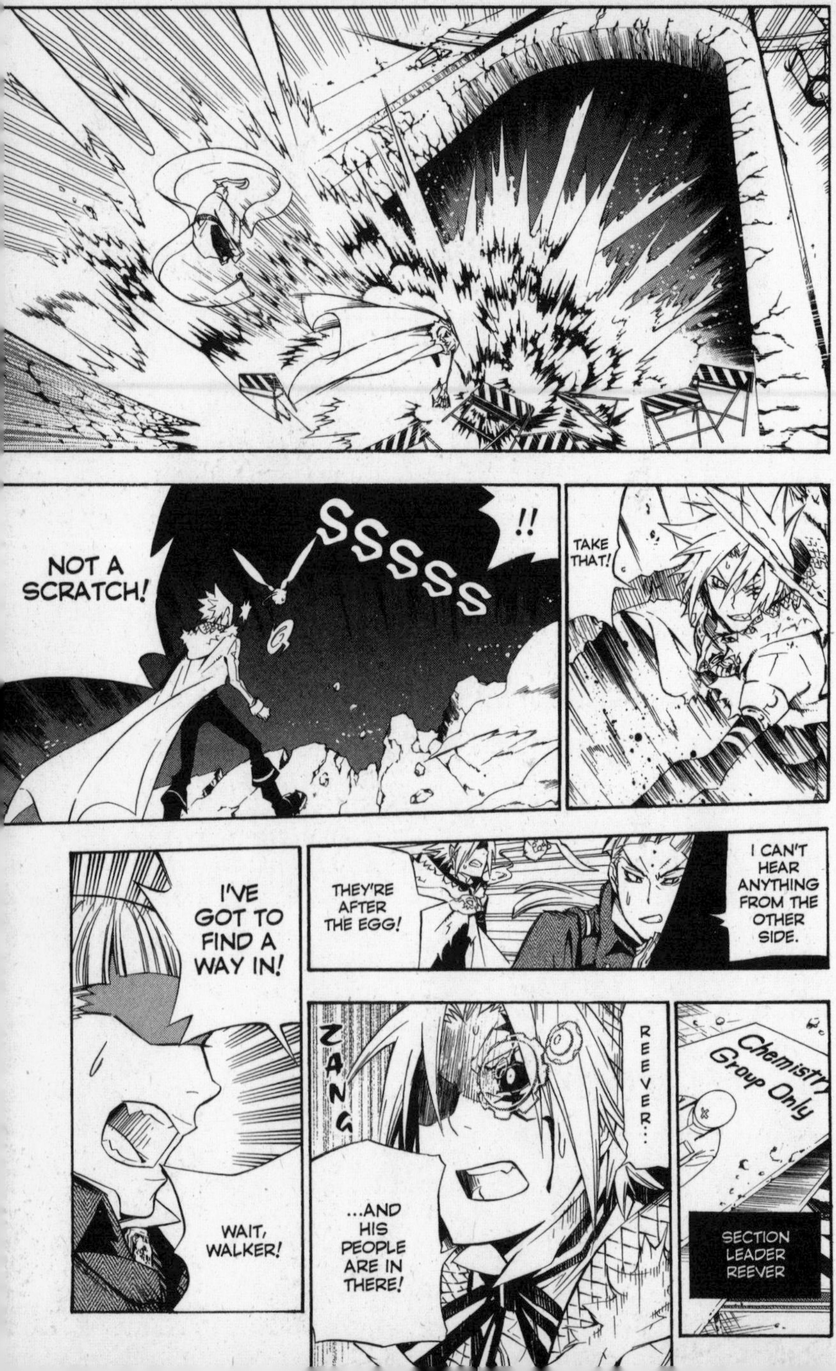
TAKE THAT!
!!
SSSSS
NOT A SCRATCH!
I CAN'T HEAR ANYTHING FROM THE OTHER SIDE.
THEY'RE AFTER THE EGG!
Chemistry Group Only
SECTION LEADER REEVER
REEVER...
ZANG
...AND HIS PEOPLE ARE IN THERE!
I'VE GOT TO FIND A WAY IN!
WAIT, WALKER!

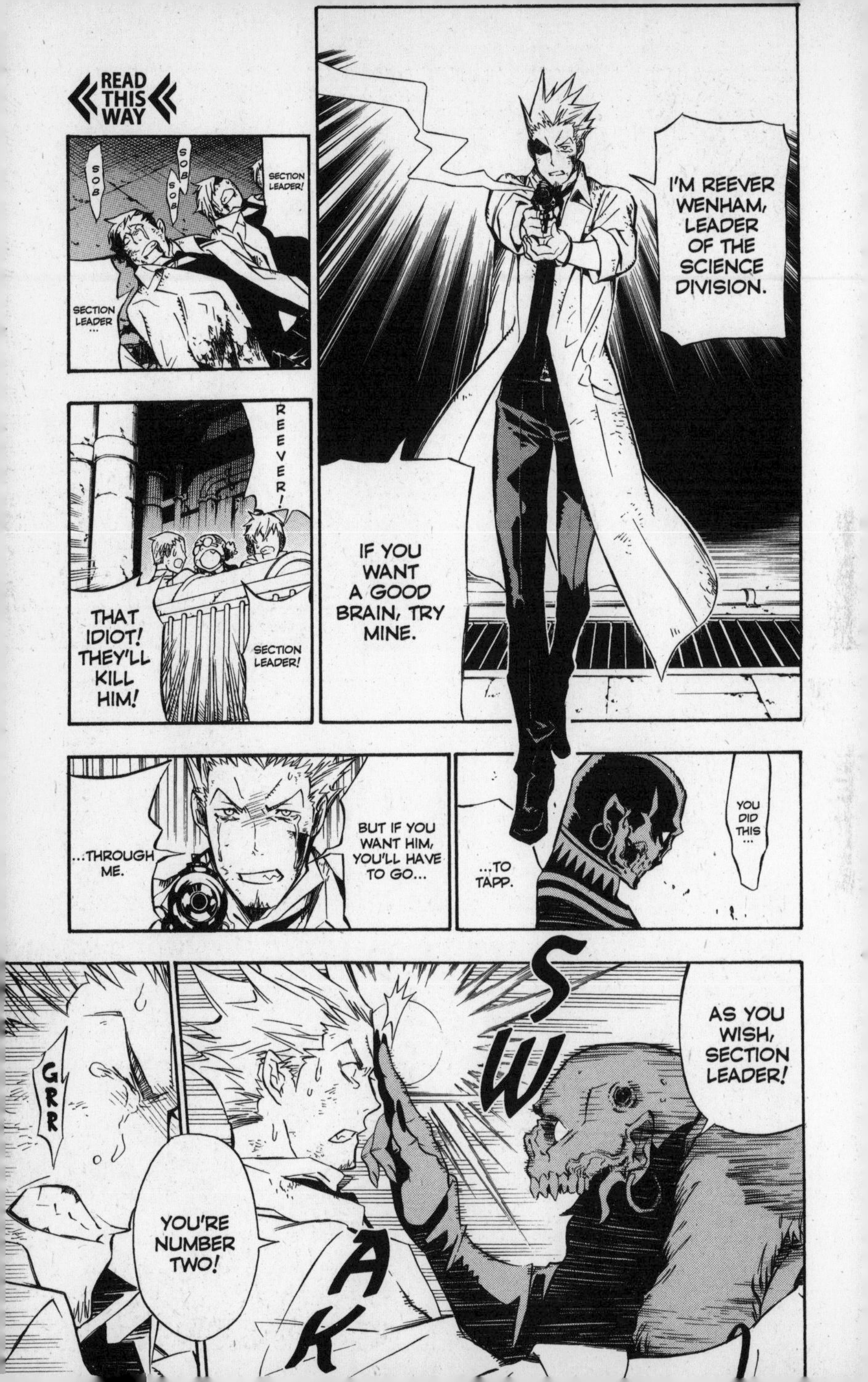
READ THIS WAY
I'M REEVER WENHAM, LEADER OF THE SCIENCE DIVISION.
IF YOU WANT A GOOD BRAIN, TRY MINE.
SOB SOB
SOB
SECTION LEADER!
SECTION LEADER...
REEVER!
SECTION LEADER!
THAT IDIOT! THEY'LL KILL HIM!
YOU DID THIS...
...TO TAPP.
BUT IF YOU WANT HIM, YOU'LL HAVE TO GO...
...THROUGH ME.
AS YOU WISH, SECTION LEADER!
SWAK
YOU'RE NUMBER TWO!
GRR

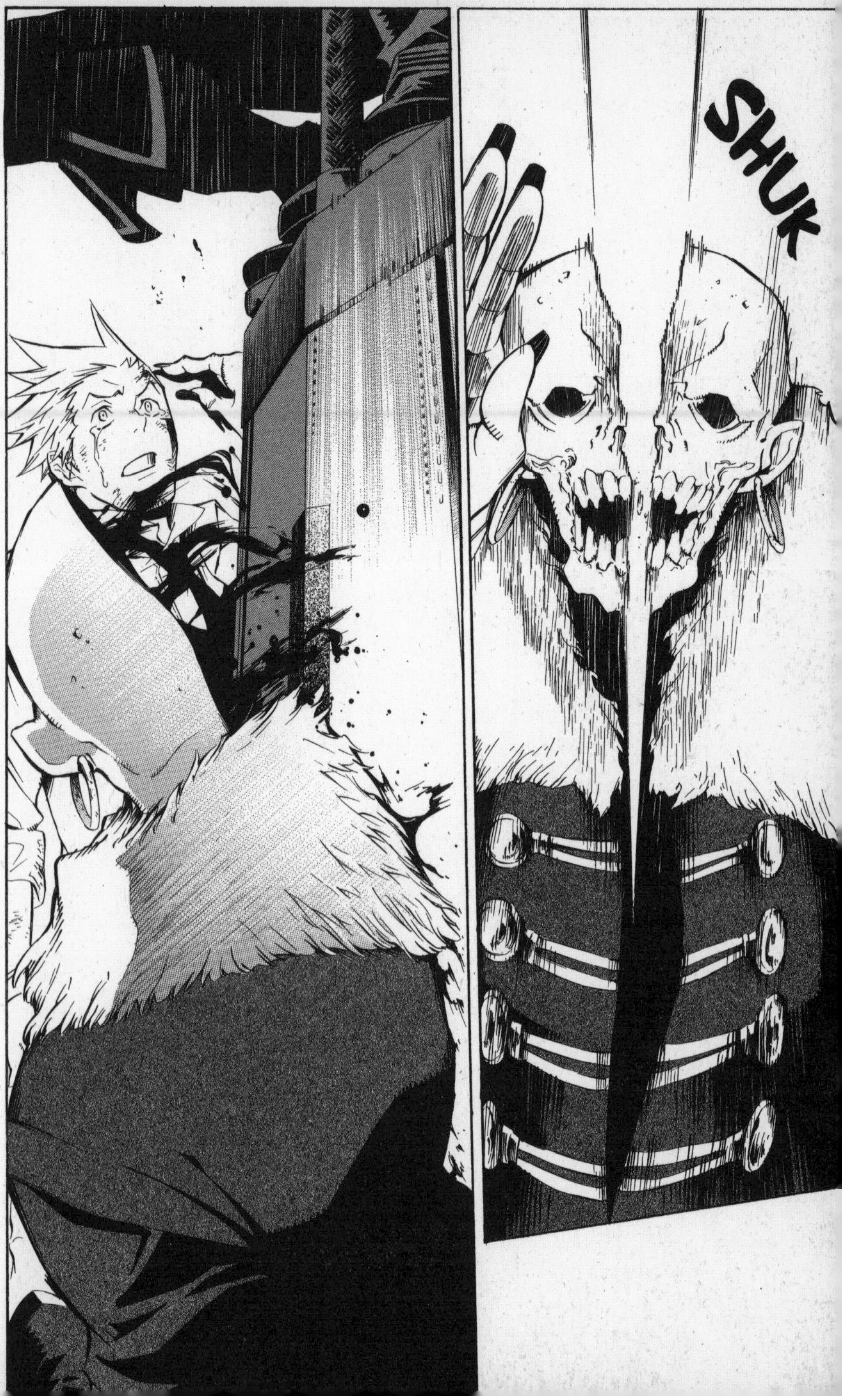
SHUK

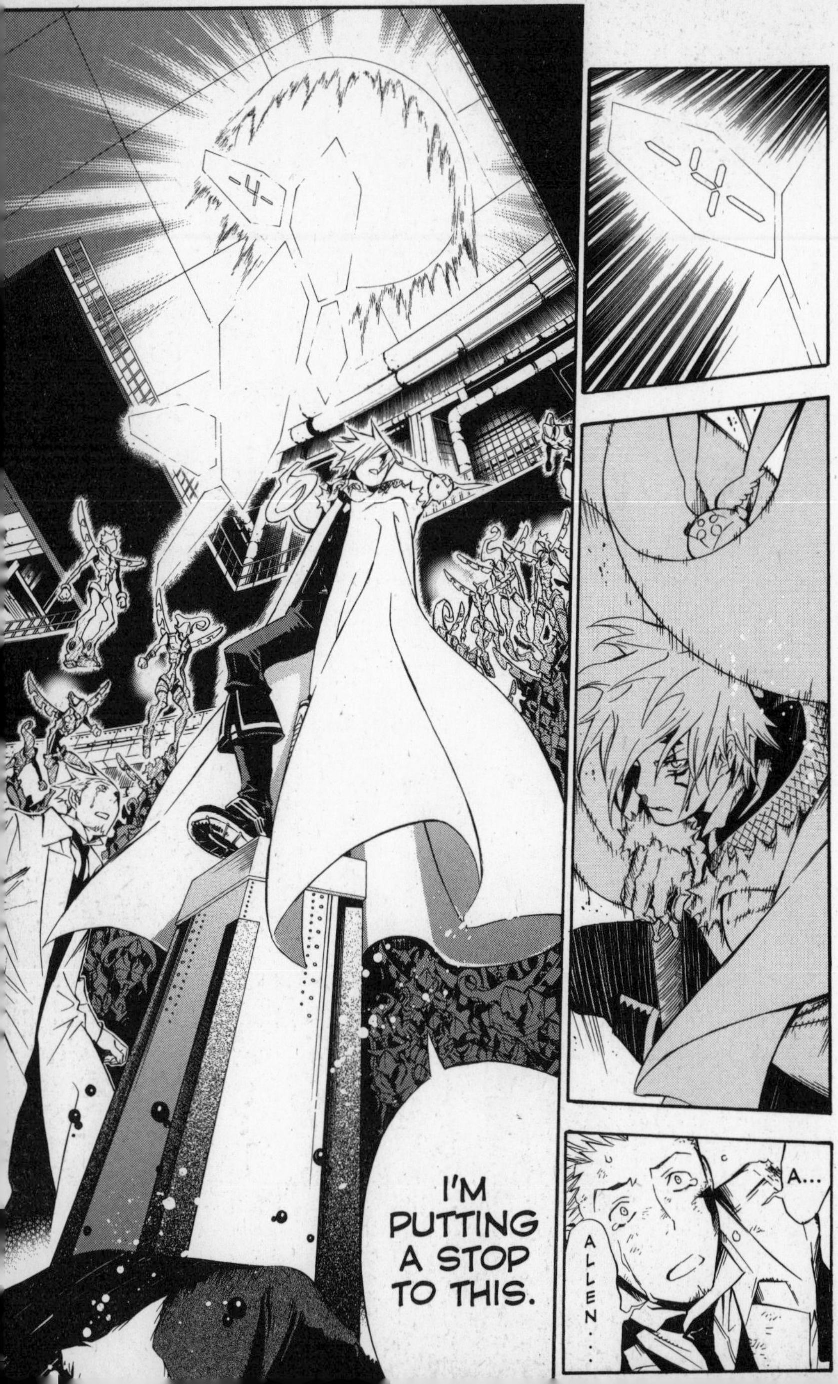
A...
ALLEN...
I'M PUTTING A STOP TO THIS.

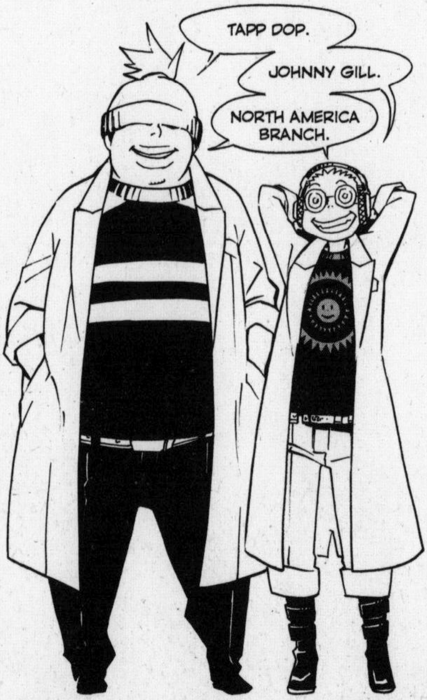
TAPP DOP.
JOHNNY GILL.
NORTH AMERICA BRANCH.

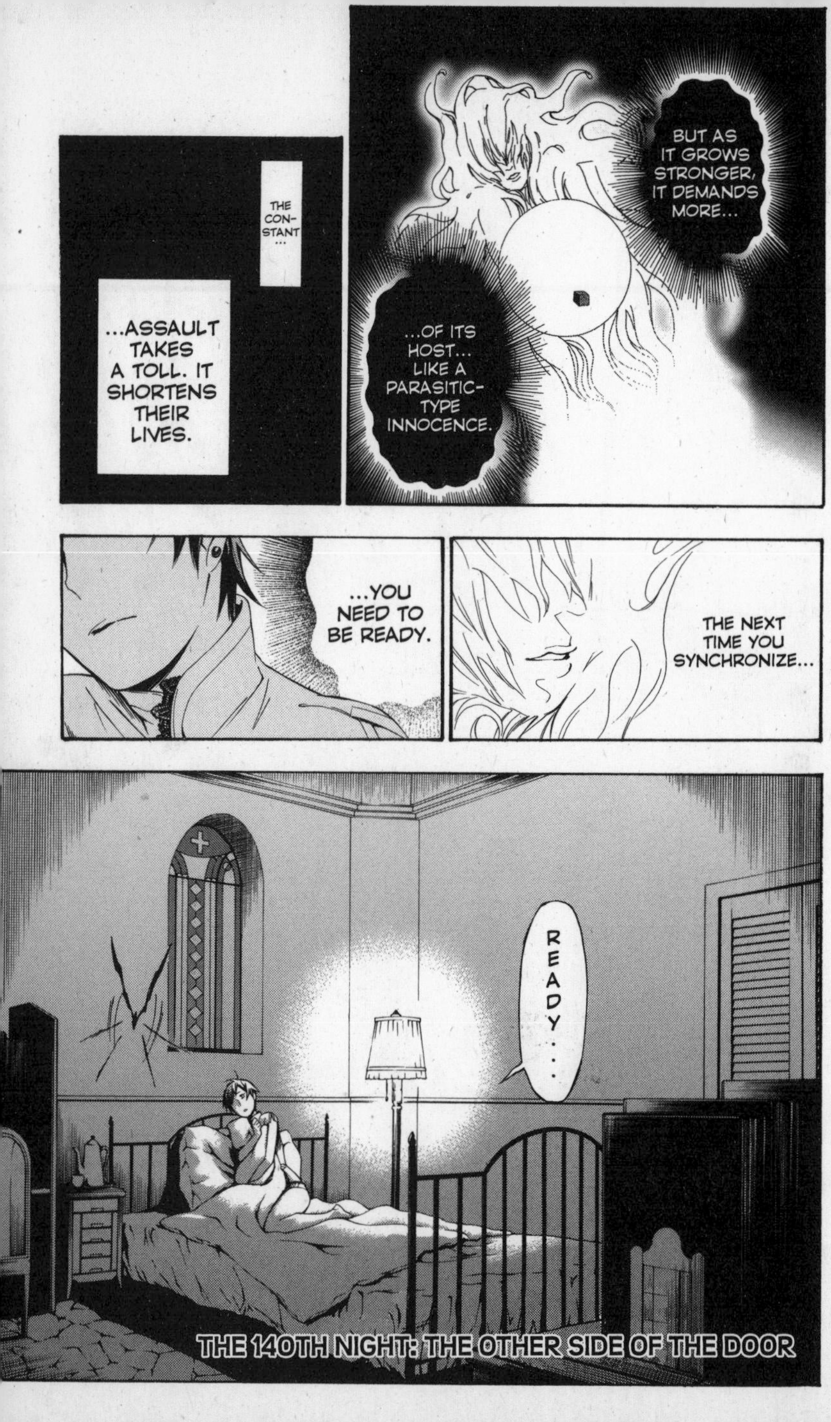
BUT AS IT GROWS STRONGER, IT DEMANDS MORE...
...OF ITS HOST... LIKE A PARASITIC-TYPE INNOCENCE.
THE CON-STANT...
...ASSAULT TAKES A TOLL. IT SHORTENS THEIR LIVES.
THE NEXT TIME YOU SYNCHRONIZE...
...YOU NEED TO BE READY.
READY...

THE 140TH NIGHT: THE OTHER SIDE OF THE DOOR

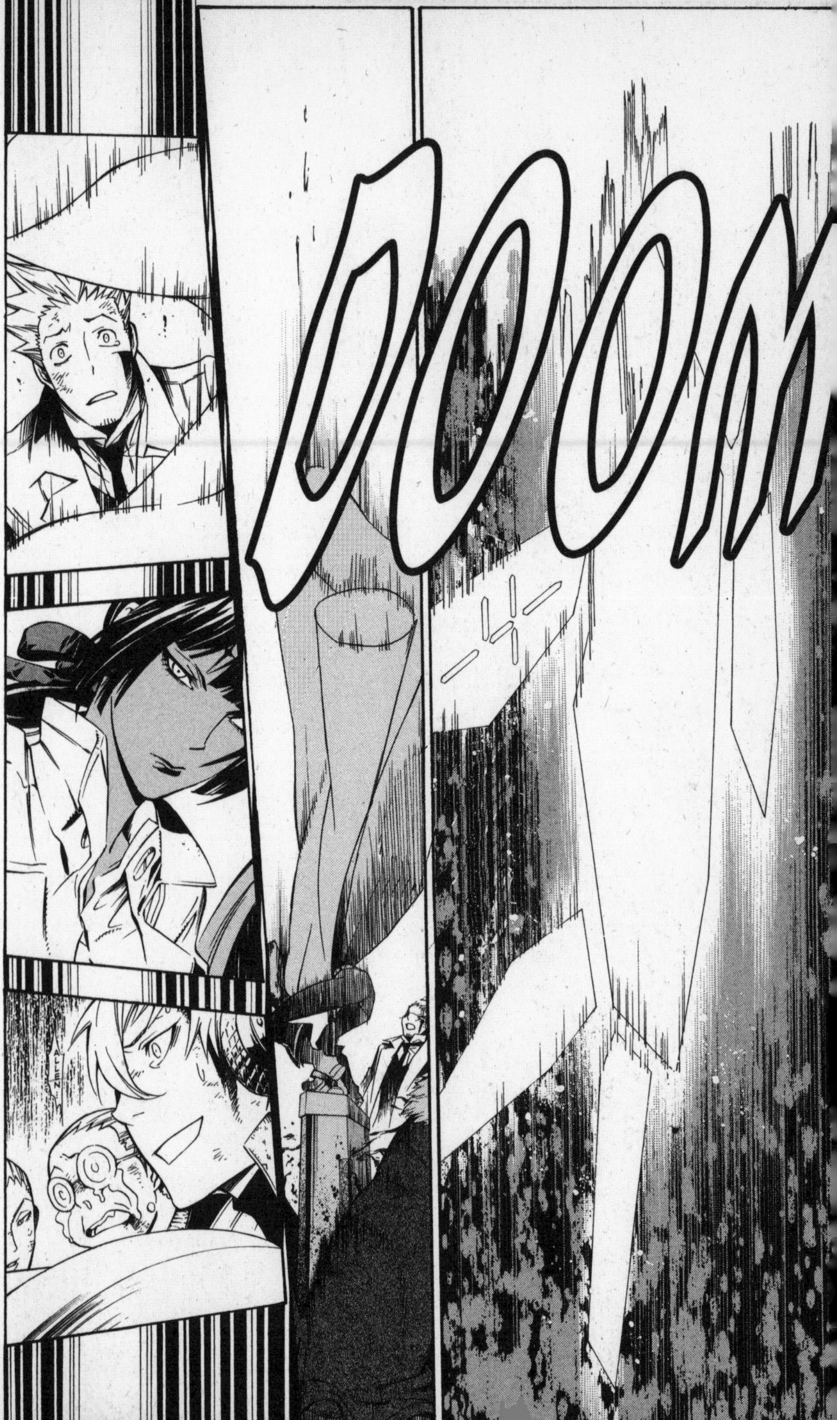
DOOM
ALLEN...

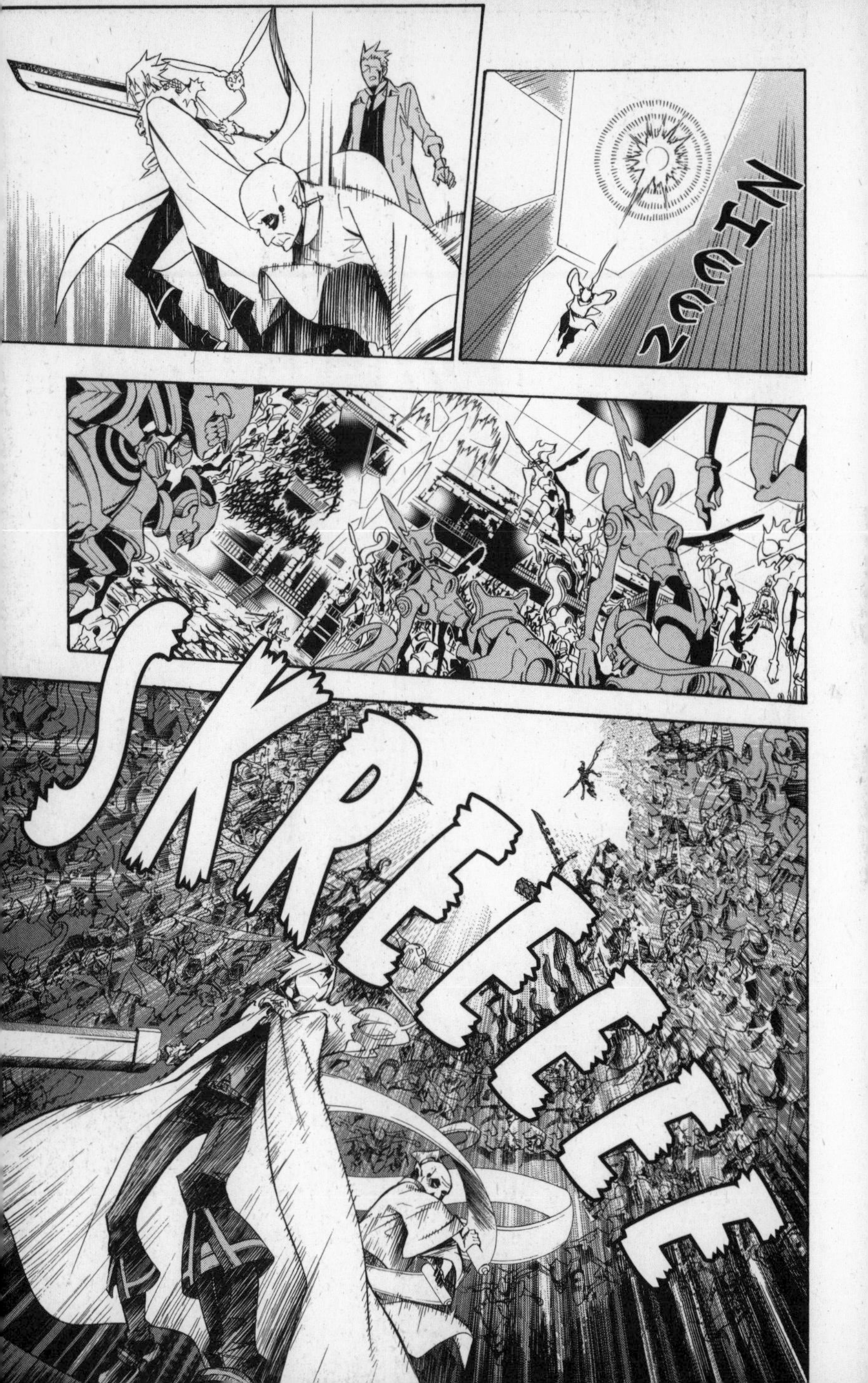
ZHEEN
SKREEEEEE

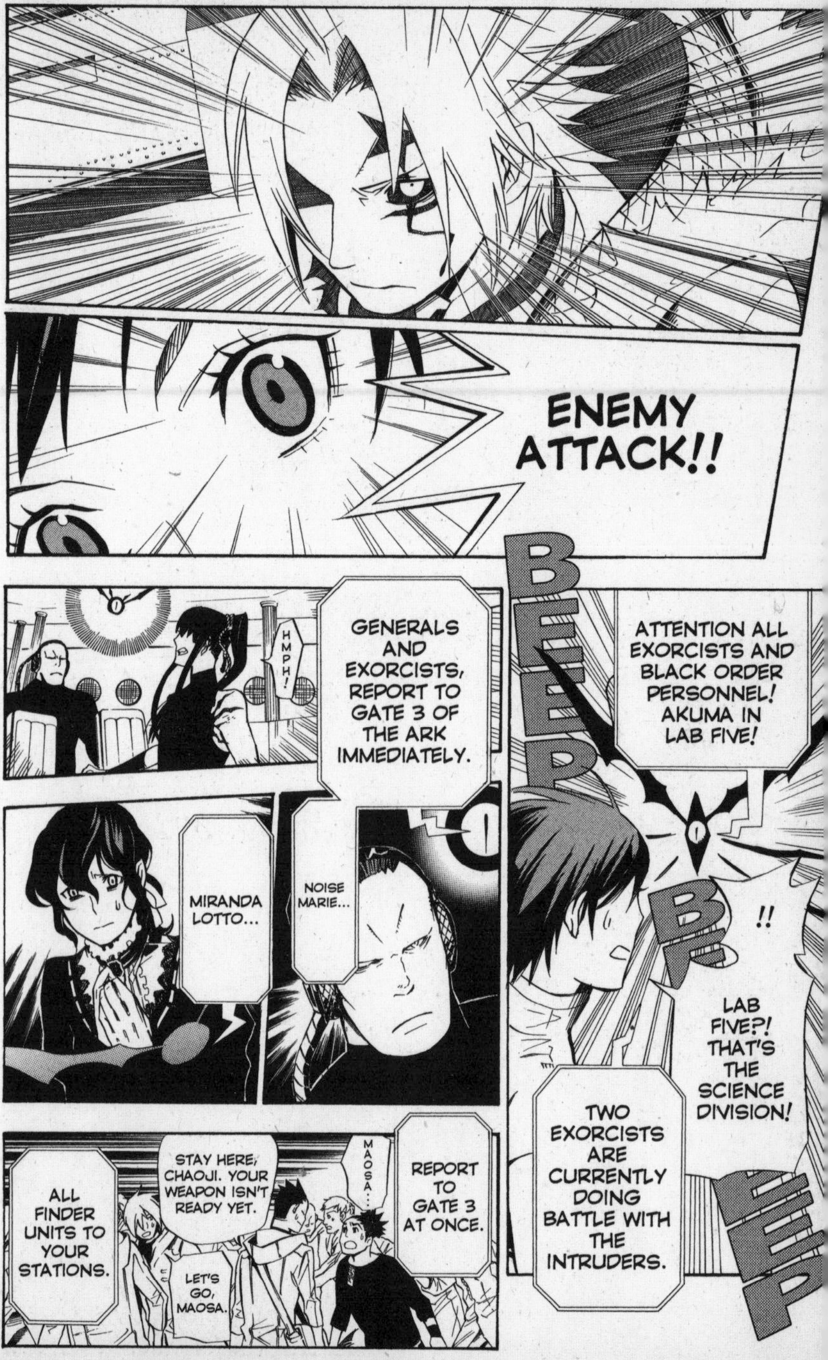
ENEMY ATTACK!!
BEEP
ATTENTION ALL EXORCISTS AND BLACK ORDER PERSONNEL! AKUMA IN LAB FIVE!
BEEP
!!
LAB FIVE?! THAT'S THE SCIENCE DIVISION!
TWO EXORCISTS ARE CURRENTLY DOING BATTLE WITH THE INTRUDERS.
BEEP
GENERALS AND EXORCISTS, REPORT TO GATE 3 OF THE ARK IMMEDIATELY.
HMPH!
NOISE MARIE...
MIRANDA LOTTO...
REPORT TO GATE 3 AT ONCE.
MAOSA...
STAY HERE, CHAOJI. YOUR WEAPON ISN'T READY YET.
LET'S GO, MAOSA.
ALL FINDER UNITS TO YOUR STATIONS.

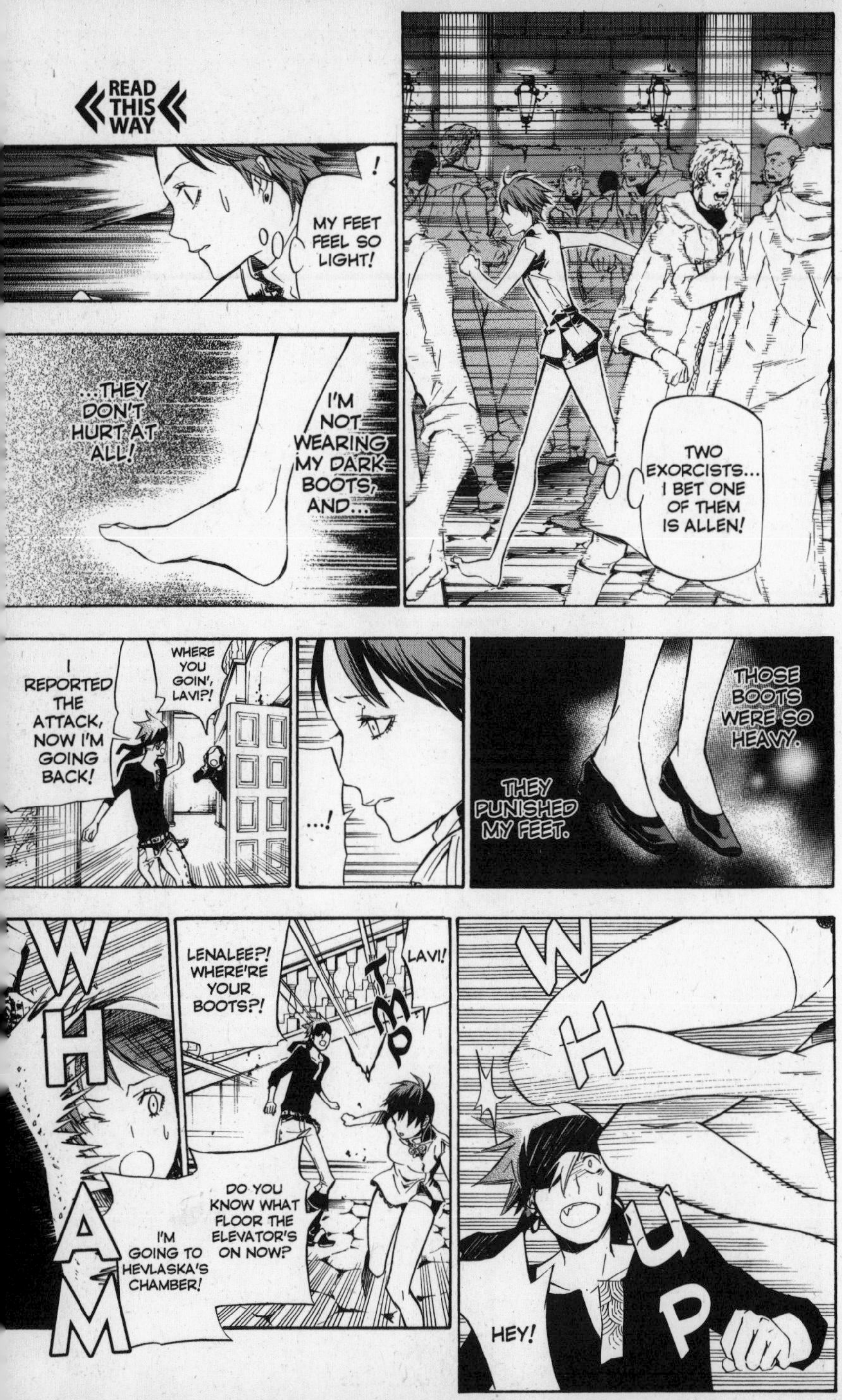

READ THIS WAY
TWO EXORCISTS... I BET ONE OF THEM IS ALLEN!
!
MY FEET FEEL SO LIGHT!
I'M NOT WEARING MY DARK BOOTS, AND...
...THEY DON'T HURT AT ALL!
THOSE BOOTS WERE SO HEAVY.
THEY PUNISHED MY FEET.
...!
WHERE YOU GOIN', LAVI?!
I REPORTED THE ATTACK, NOW I'M GOING BACK!
WHUP
HEY!
LAVI!
TMP
LENALEE?! WHERE'RE YOUR BOOTS?!
DO YOU KNOW WHAT FLOOR THE ELEVATOR'S ON NOW?
I'M GOING TO HEVLASKA'S CHAMBER!
WHAM

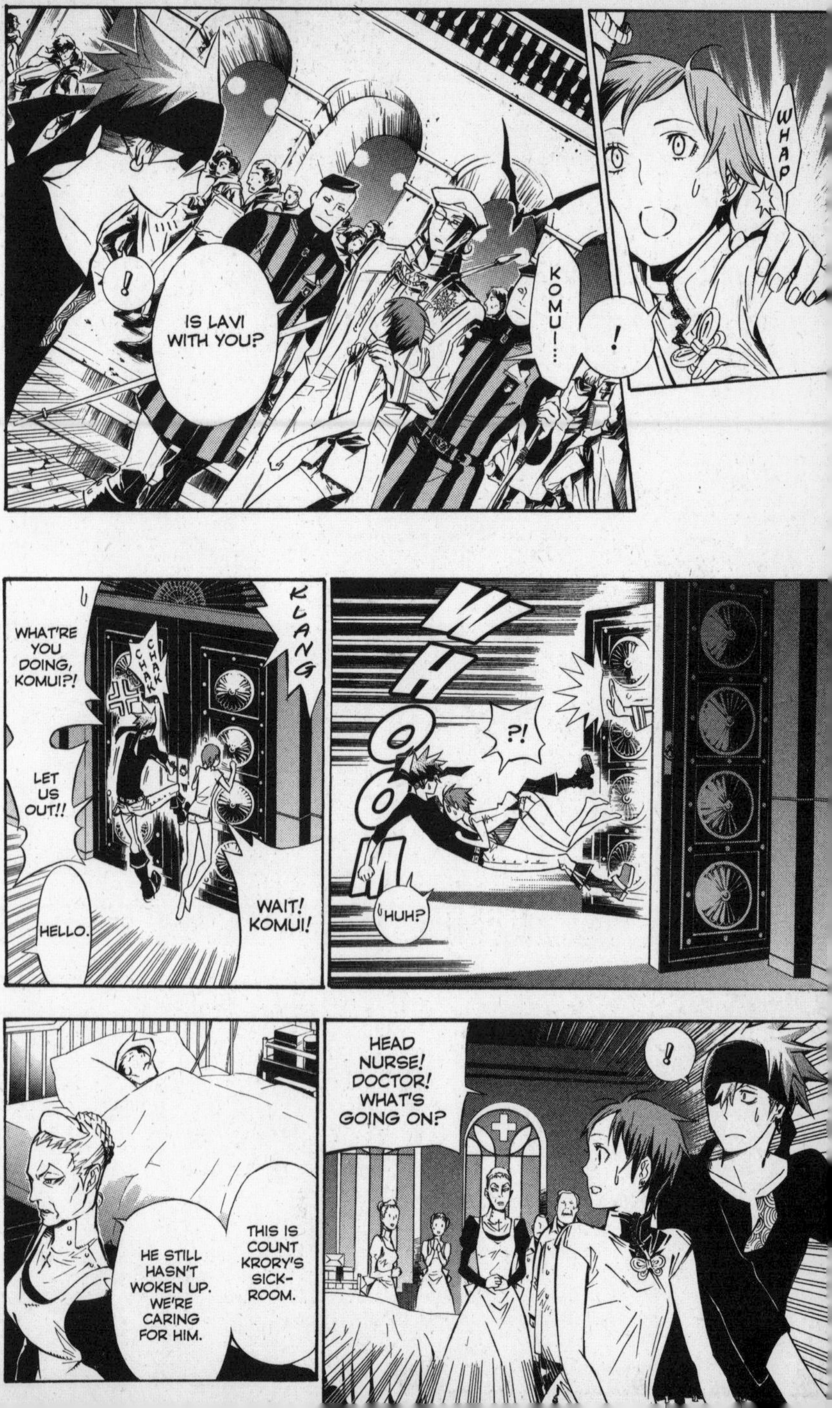
WHAP
!
KOMUI...
!
IS LAVI WITH YOU?
WHOOOM
?!
HUH?
KLANG
WHAT'RE YOU DOING, KOMUI?!
CHAK CHAK
LET US OUT!!
WAIT! KOMUI!
HELLO.
!
HEAD NURSE! DOCTOR! WHAT'S GOING ON?
THIS IS COUNT KRORY'S SICK-ROOM.
HE STILL HASN'T WOKEN UP. WE'RE CARING FOR HIM.

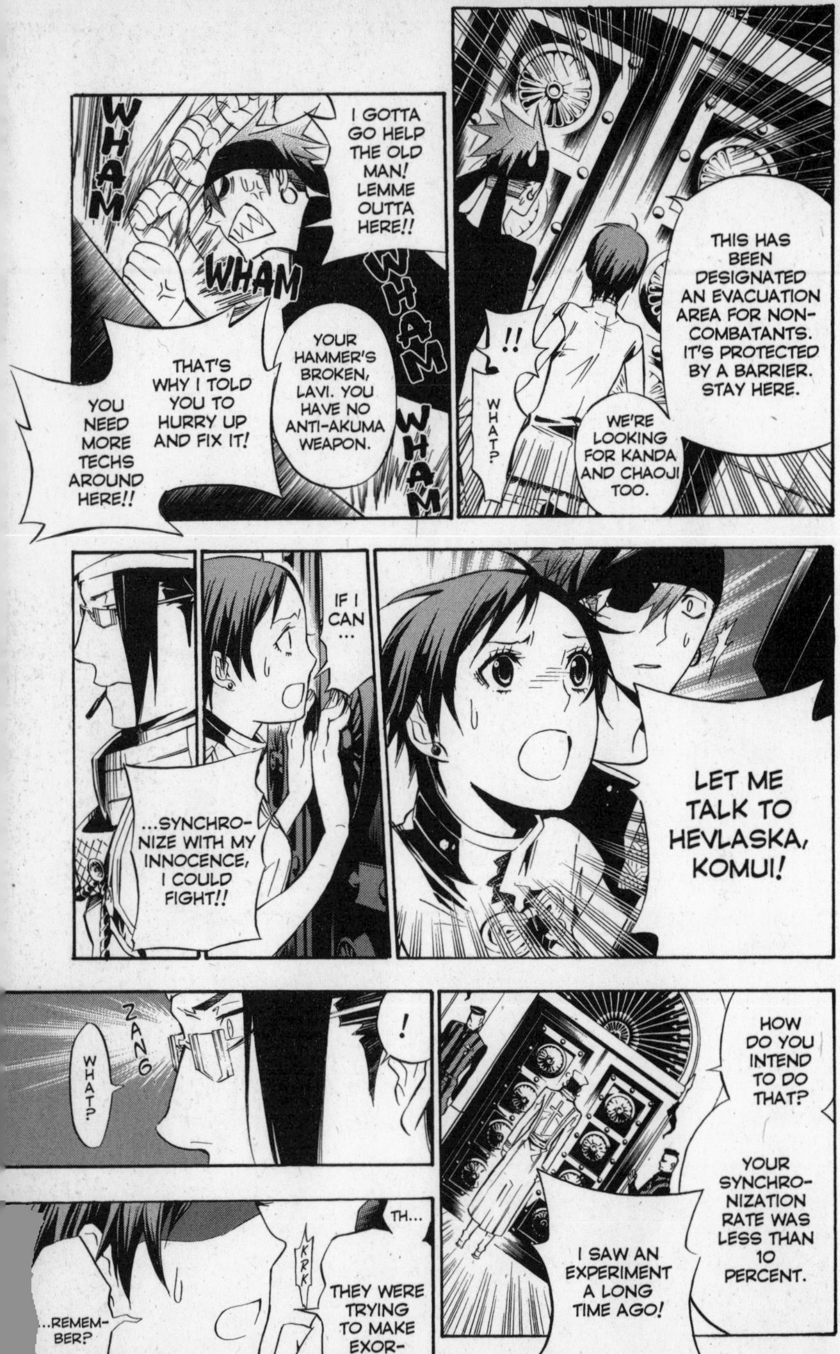
THIS HAS BEEN DESIGNATED AN EVACUATION AREA FOR NON-COMBATANTS. IT'S PROTECTED BY A BARRIER. STAY HERE.
WE'RE LOOKING FOR KANDA AND CHAOJI TOO.
!!
WHAT?
I GOTTA GO HELP THE OLD MAN! LEMME OUTTA HERE!!
WHAM
WHAM
WHAM
WHAM
YOUR HAMMER'S BROKEN, LAVI. YOU HAVE NO ANTI-AKUMA WEAPON.
THAT'S WHY I TOLD YOU TO HURRY UP AND FIX IT!
YOU NEED MORE TECHS AROUND HERE!!
LET ME TALK TO HEVLASKA, KOMUI!
IF I CAN...
...SYNCHRONIZE WITH MY INNOCENCE, I COULD FIGHT!!
HOW DO YOU INTEND TO DO THAT?
YOUR SYNCHRONIZATION RATE WAS LESS THAN 10 PERCENT.
I SAW AN EXPERIMENT A LONG TIME AGO!
!
ZANG
WHAT?
TH...
KRK
THEY WERE TRYING TO MAKE EXORCISTS...
...REMEMBER?

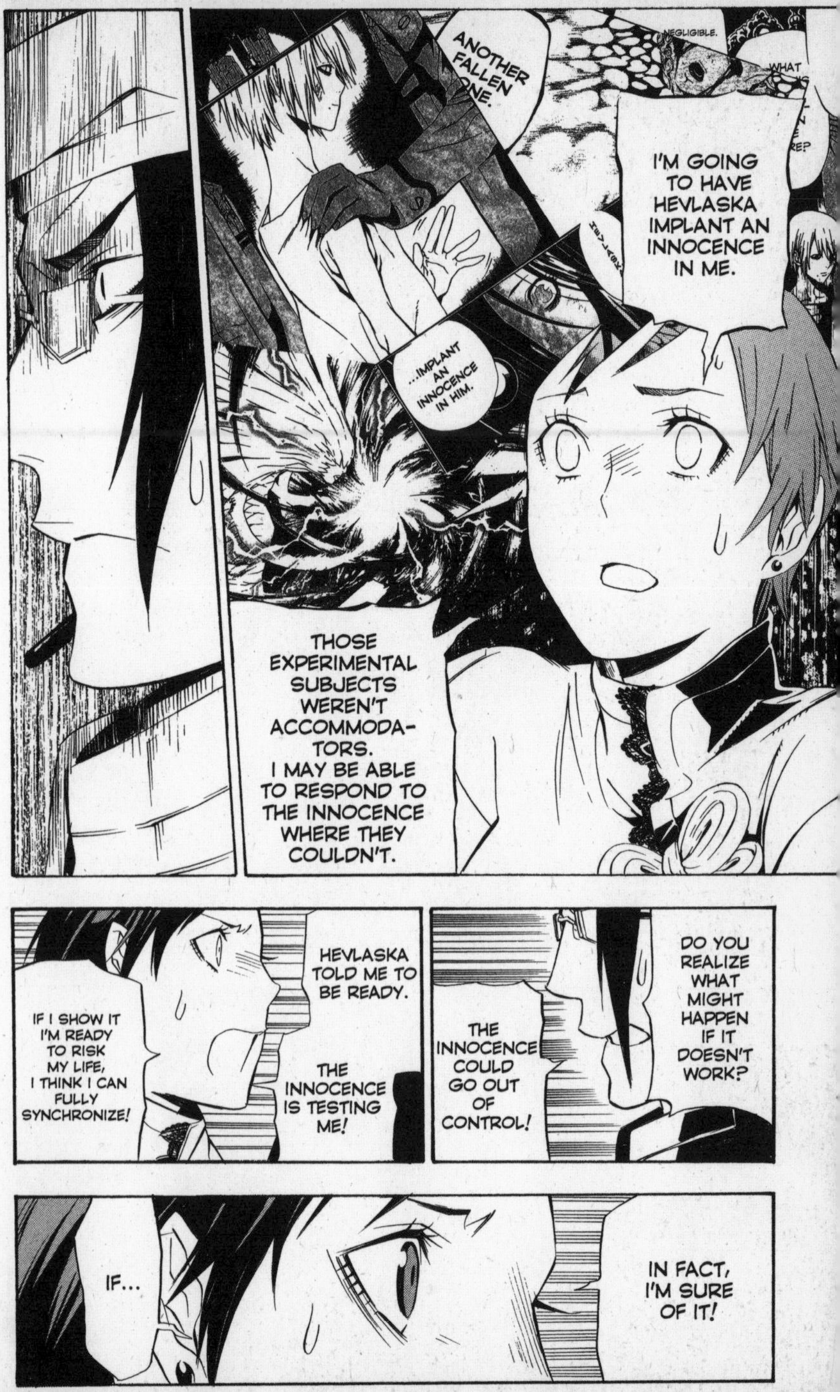
NEGLIGIBLE.
ANOTHER FALLEN ONE.
...IMPLANT AN INNOCENCE IN HIM.
I'M GOING TO HAVE HEVLASKA IMPLANT AN INNOCENCE IN ME.
THOSE EXPERIMENTAL SUBJECTS WEREN'T ACCOMMODA-TORS. I MAY BE ABLE TO RESPOND TO THE INNOCENCE WHERE THEY COULDN'T.
DO YOU REALIZE WHAT MIGHT HAPPEN IF IT DOESN'T WORK?
THE INNOCENCE COULD GO OUT OF CONTROL!
HEVLASKA TOLD ME TO BE READY.
THE INNOCENCE IS TESTING ME!
IF I SHOW IT I'M READY TO RISK MY LIFE, I THINK I CAN FULLY SYNCHRONIZE!
IN FACT, I'M SURE OF IT!
IF...

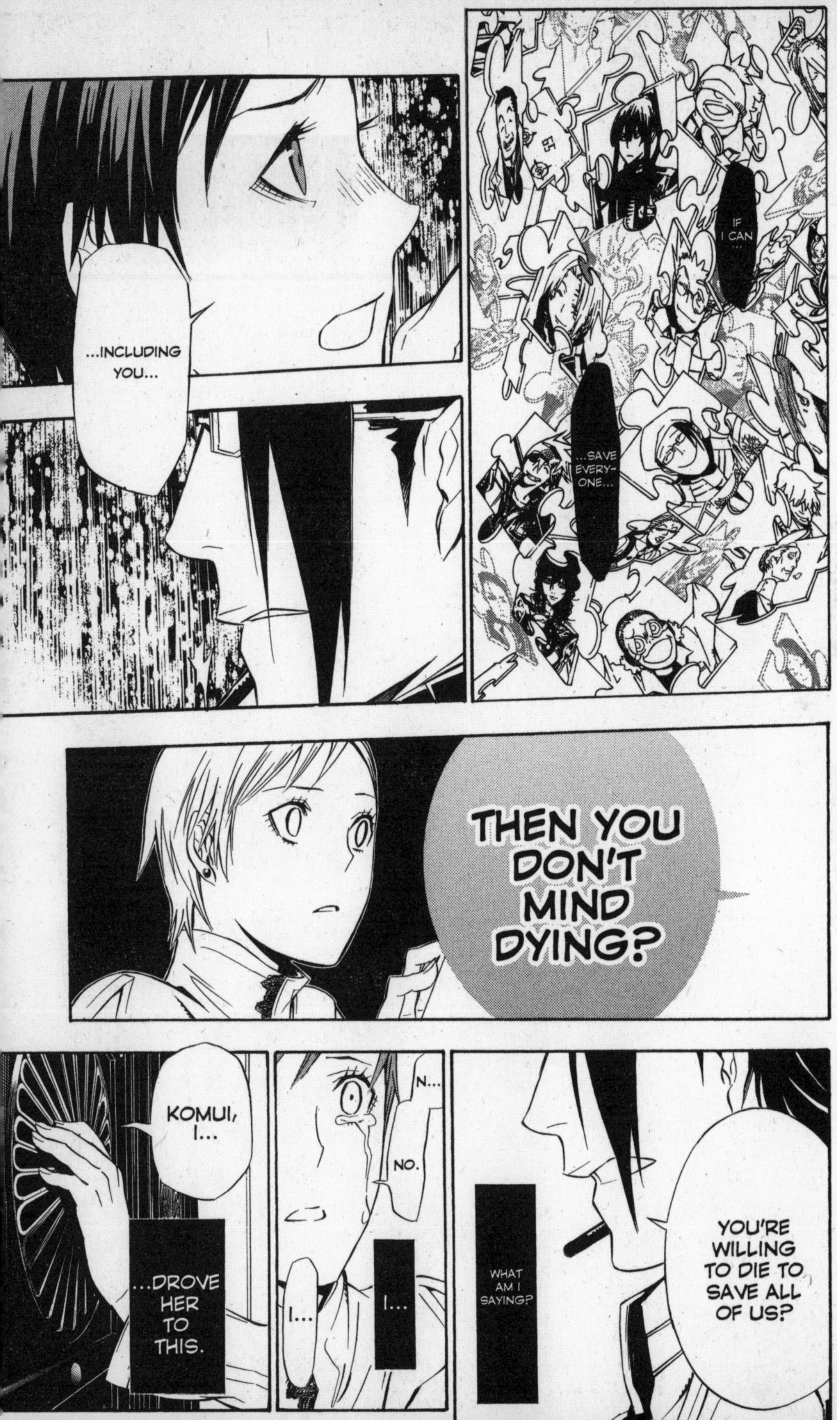
IF I CAN...
...SAVE EVERY-ONE...
...INCLUDING YOU...
THEN YOU DON'T MIND DYING?
YOU'RE WILLING TO DIE TO SAVE ALL OF US?
WHAT AM I SAYING?
N...
NO.
I...
I...
KOMUI, I...
...DROVE HER TO THIS.

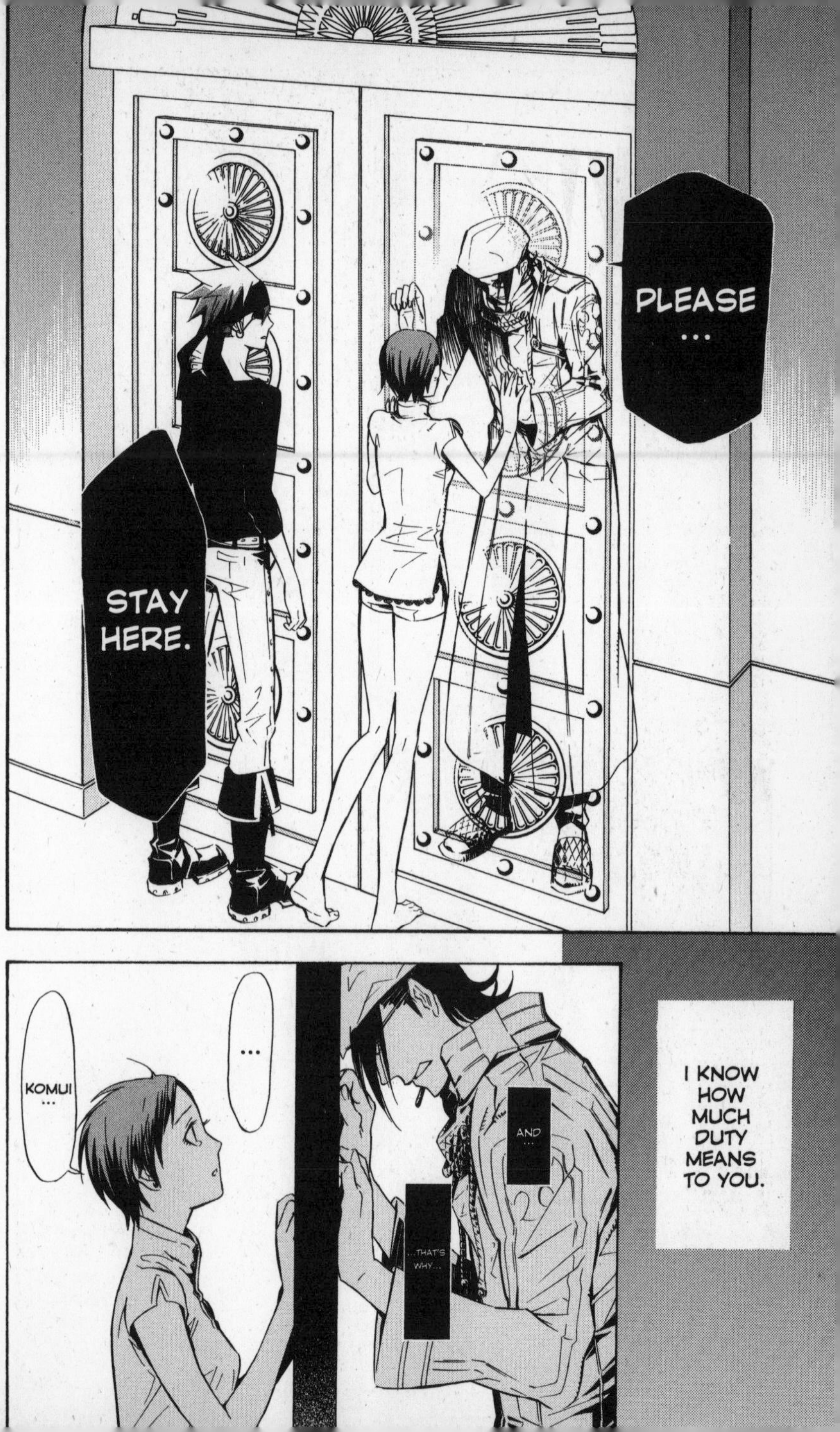
PLEASE . . .
STAY HERE.
I KNOW HOW MUCH DUTY MEANS TO YOU.
AND . . .
. . .THAT'S WHY. . .
. . .
KOMUI . . .

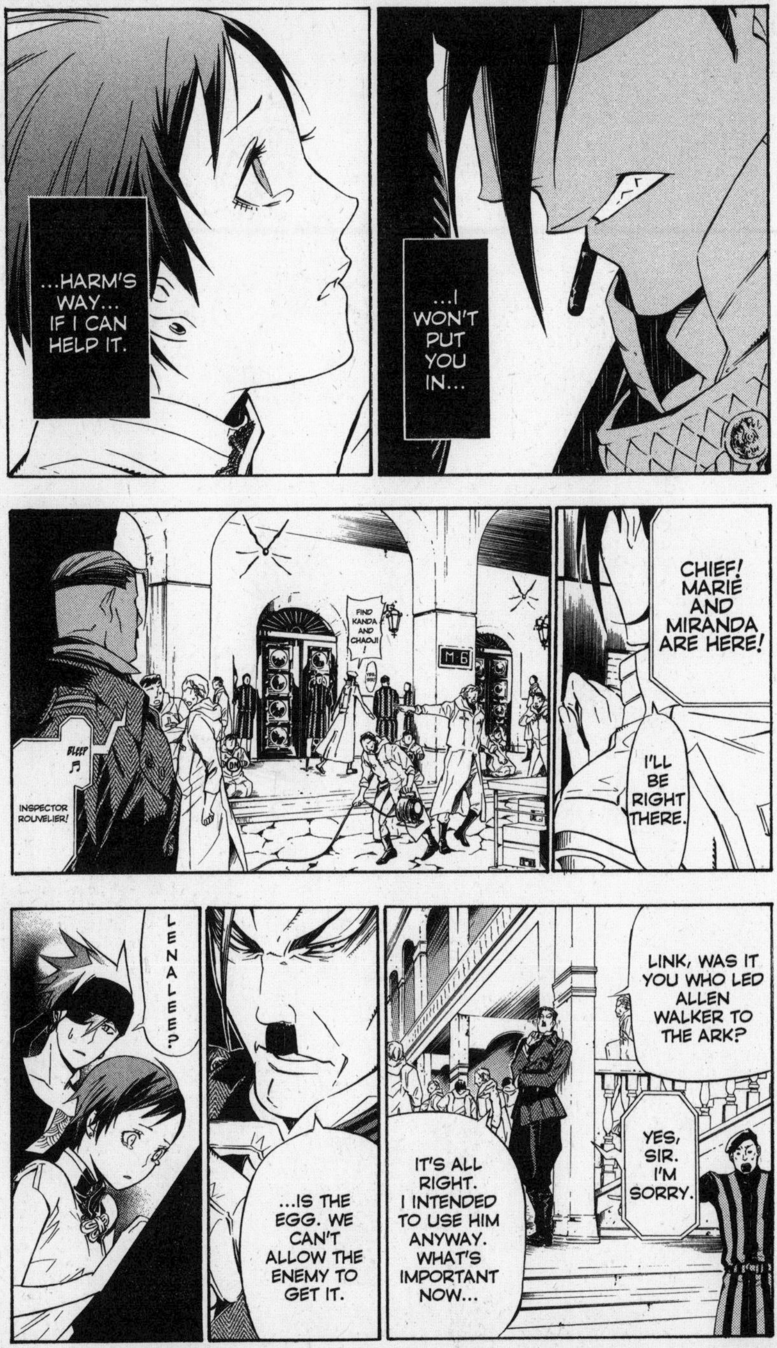
...I WON'T PUT YOU IN...
...HARM'S WAY... IF I CAN HELP IT.
CHIEF! MARIE AND MIRANDA ARE HERE!
I'LL BE RIGHT THERE.
FIND KANDA AND CHAOJI!
BLEEP ♪
INSPECTOR ROUVELIER!
LINK, WAS IT YOU WHO LED ALLEN WALKER TO THE ARK?
YES, SIR. I'M SORRY.
IT'S ALL RIGHT. I INTENDED TO USE HIM ANYWAY. WHAT'S IMPORTANT NOW...
...IS THE EGG. WE CAN'T ALLOW THE ENEMY TO GET IT.
LENALEE?

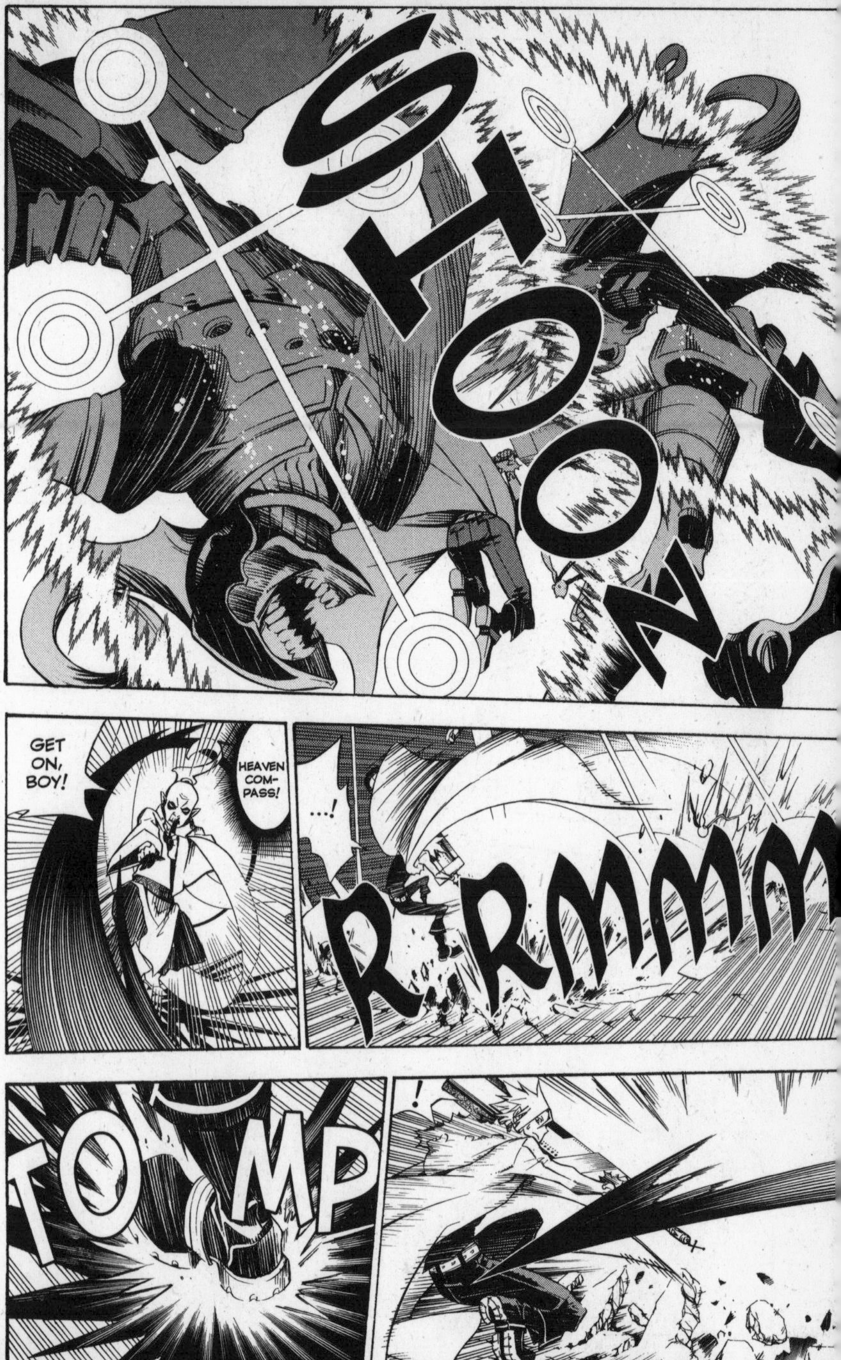
SHOOOM
...!
RRMMMM
HEAVEN COMPASS!
GET ON, BOY!
!
TOMP

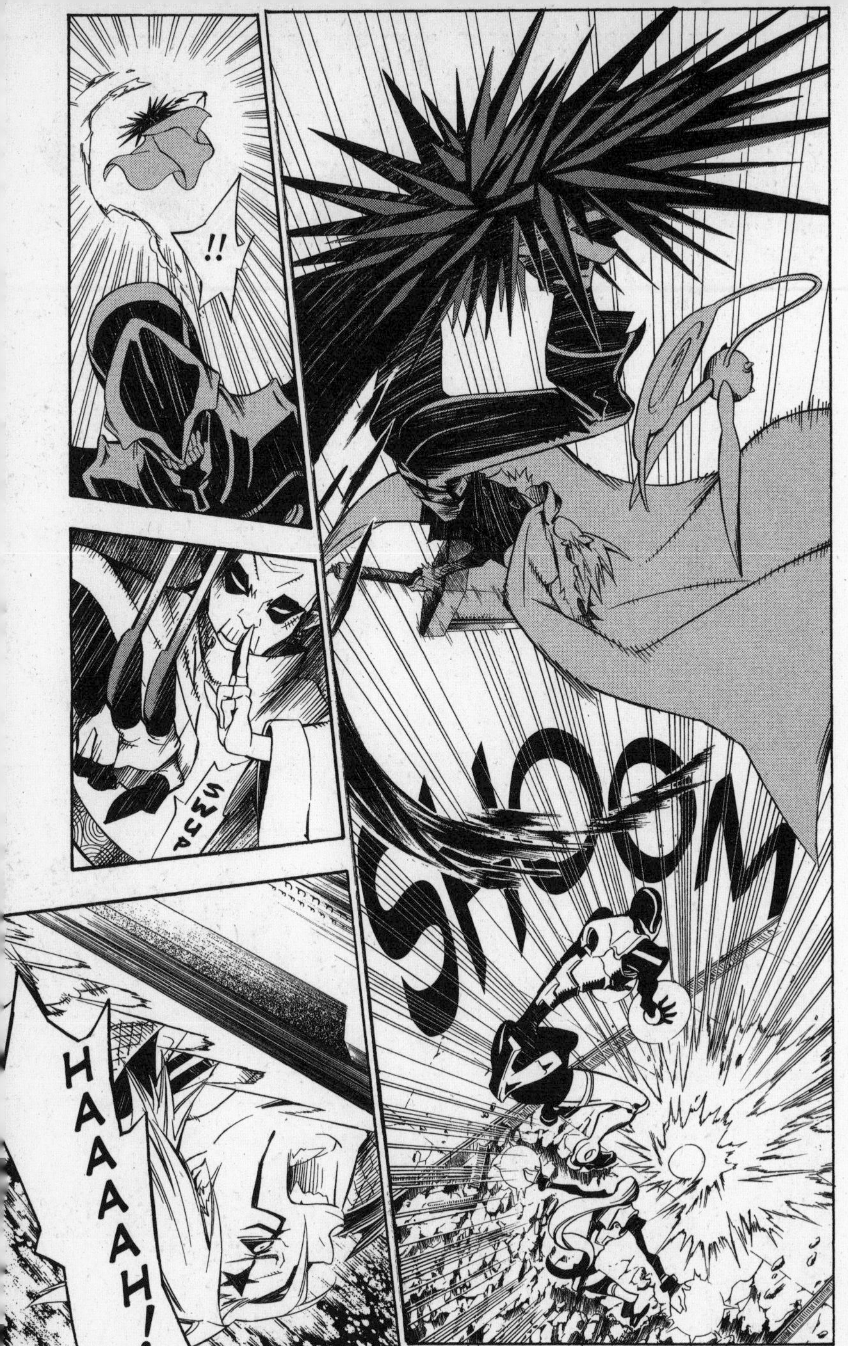
SHOOM
!!
SWUP
HAAAAH!

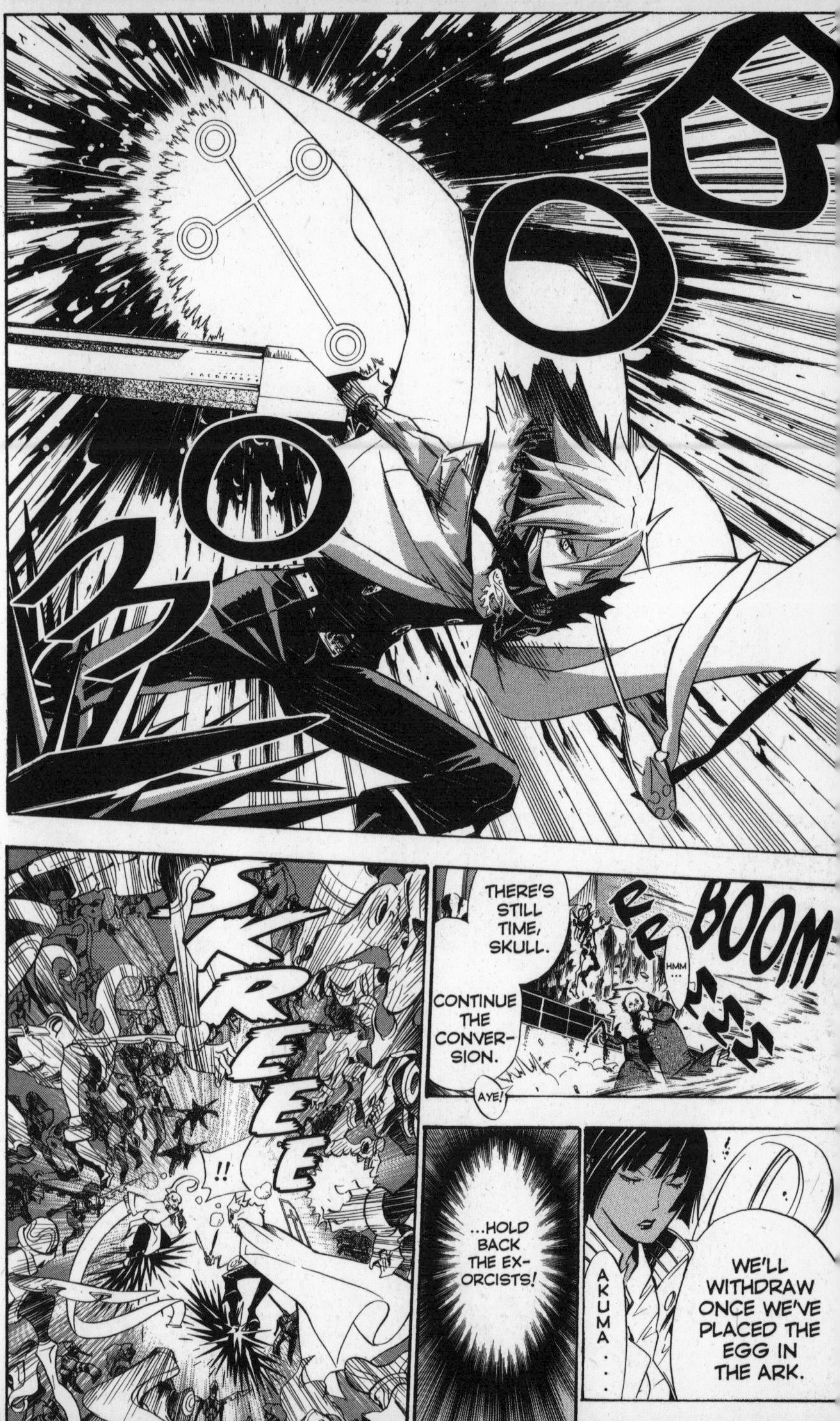
THERE'S STILL TIME, SKULL.
CONTINUE THE CONVERSION.
AYE!
HMM...
BOOM
WE'LL WITHDRAW ONCE WE'VE PLACED THE EGG IN THE ARK.
AKUMA...
...HOLD BACK THE EXORCISTS!
SKREEE
!!

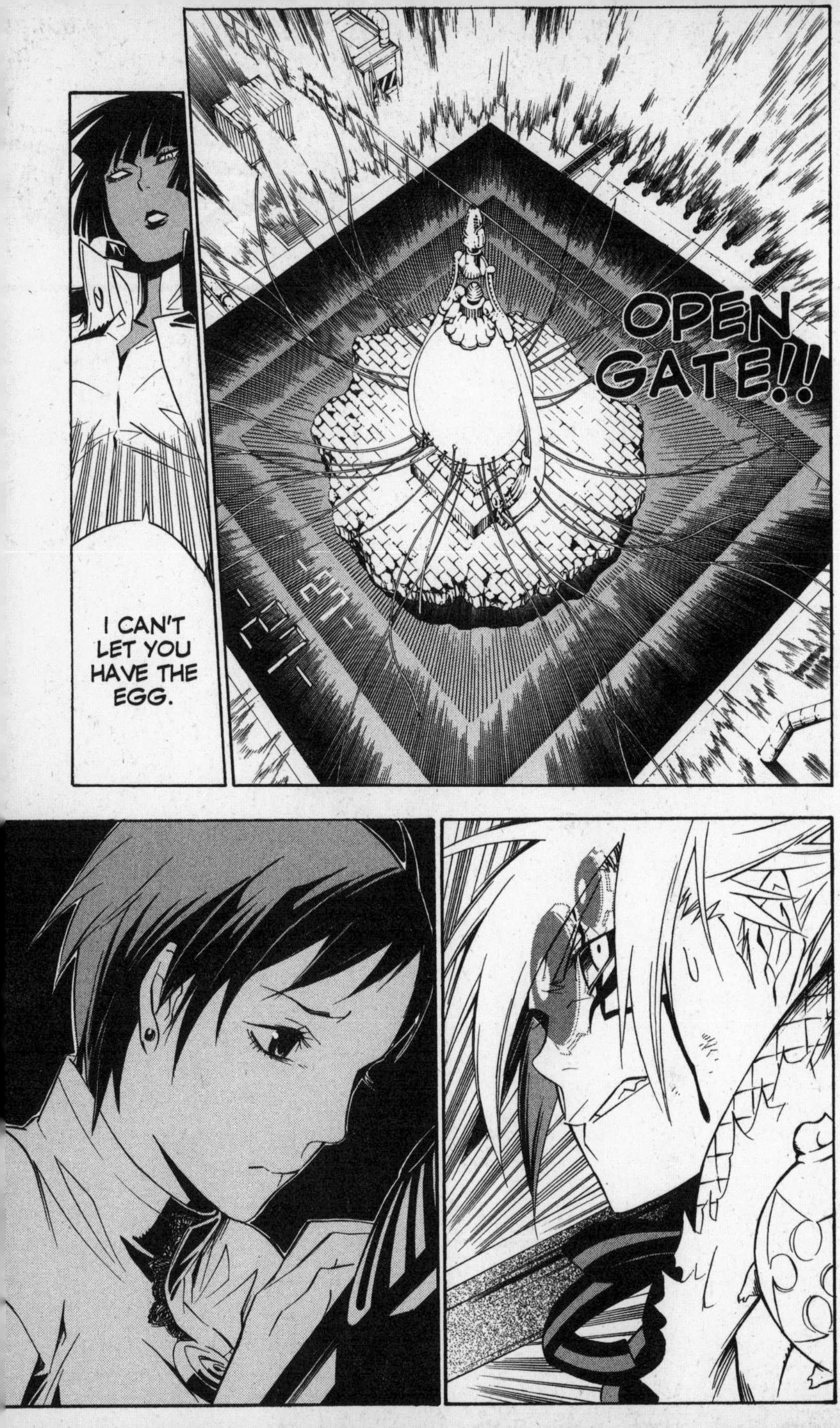
OPEN GATE!!
I CAN'T LET YOU HAVE THE EGG.

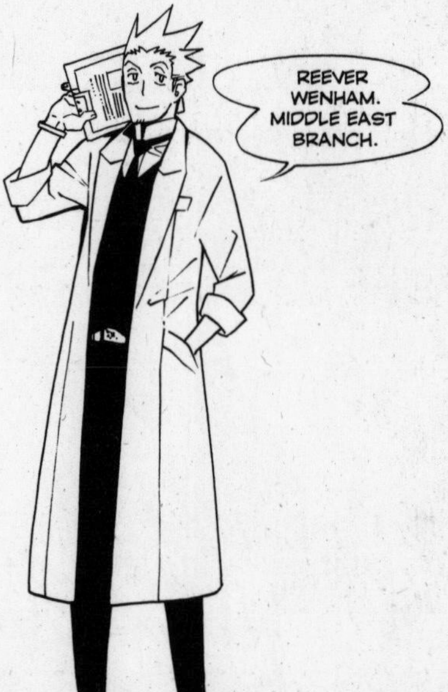
REEVER WENHAM. MIDDLE EAST BRANCH.

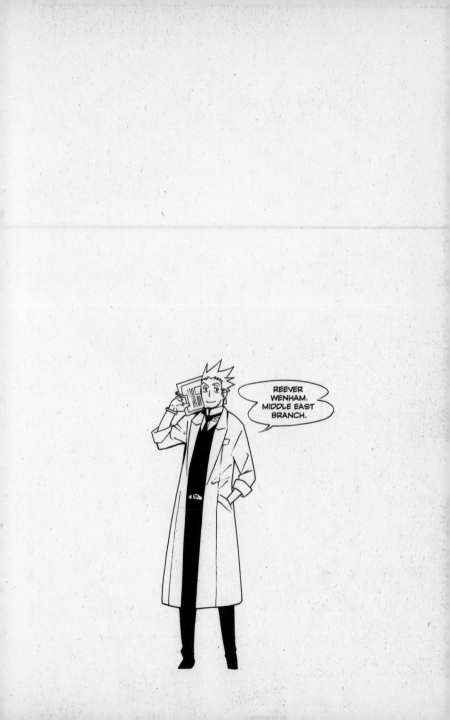

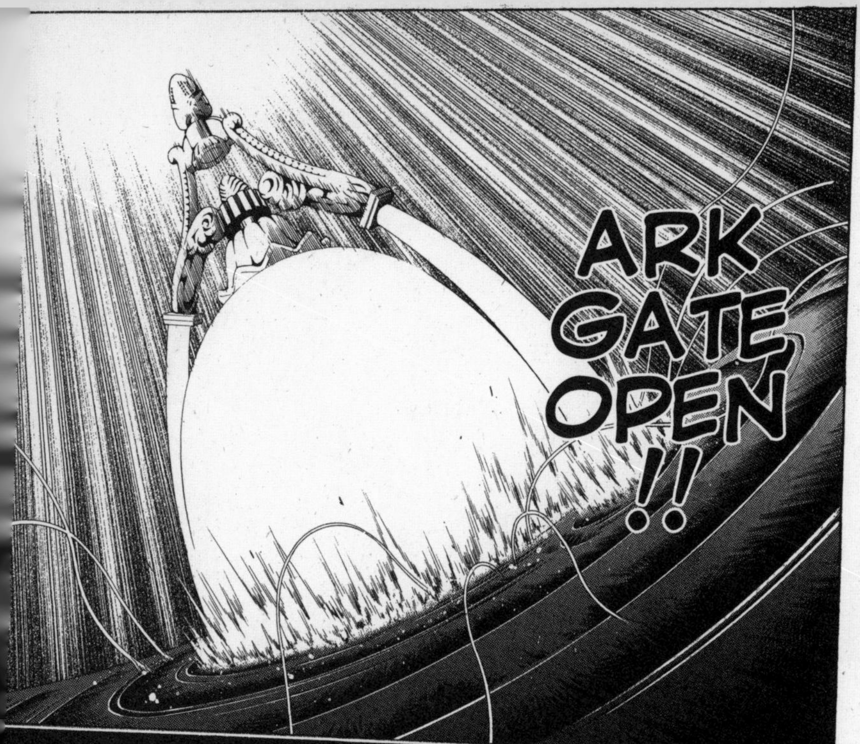
ARK GATE OPEN!!

THE 141ST NIGHT: ALLIES

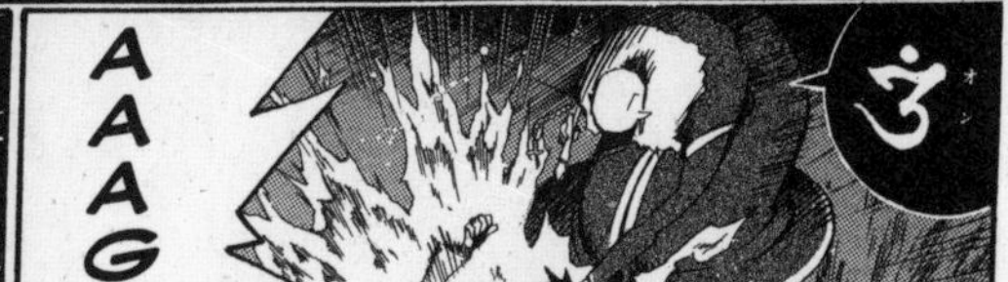
オン
AAAAGH!

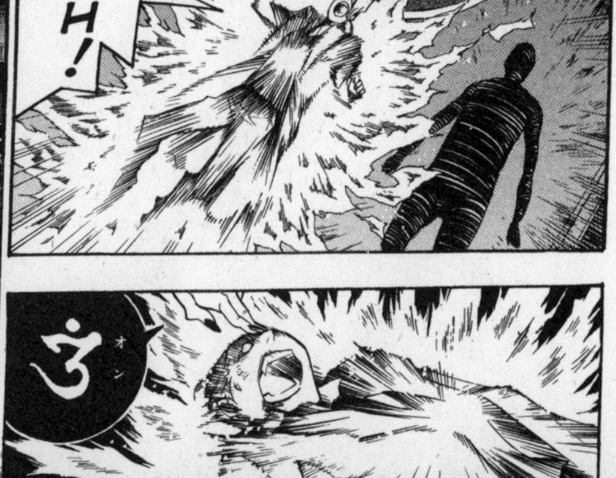
オン

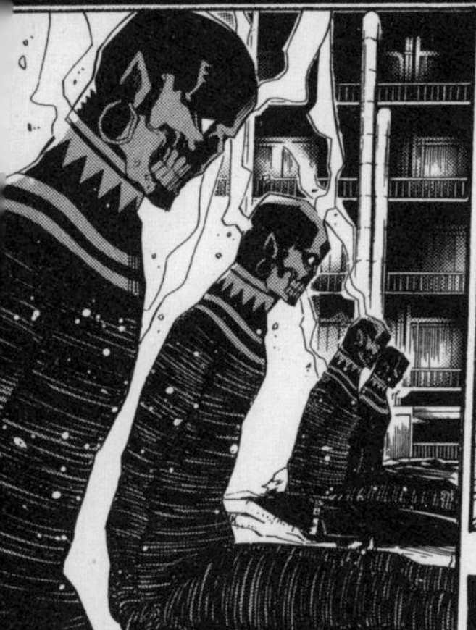

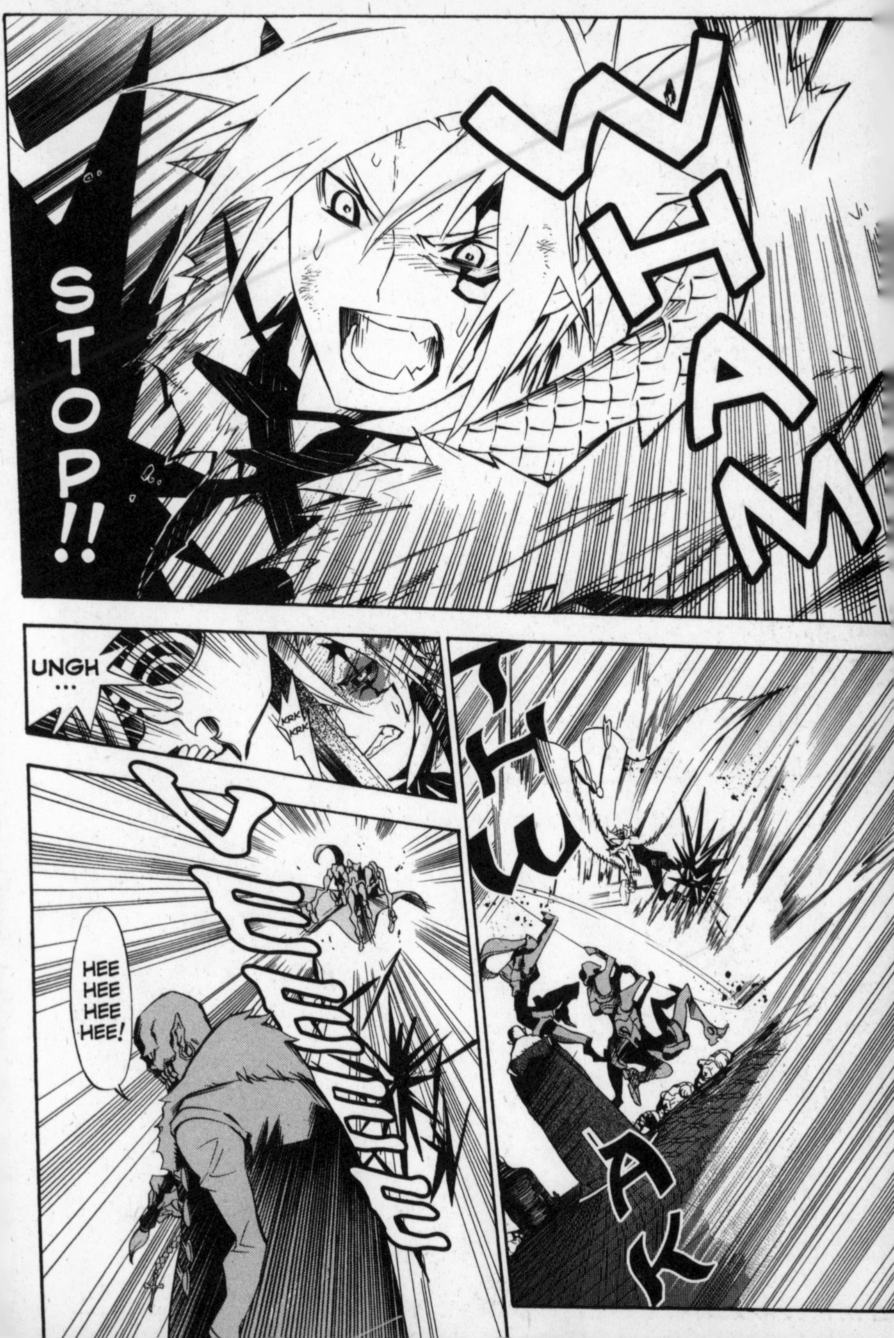
WHAM
STOP!!
THWAK
UNGH ...
KRK KRK
HEE HEE HEE HEE!

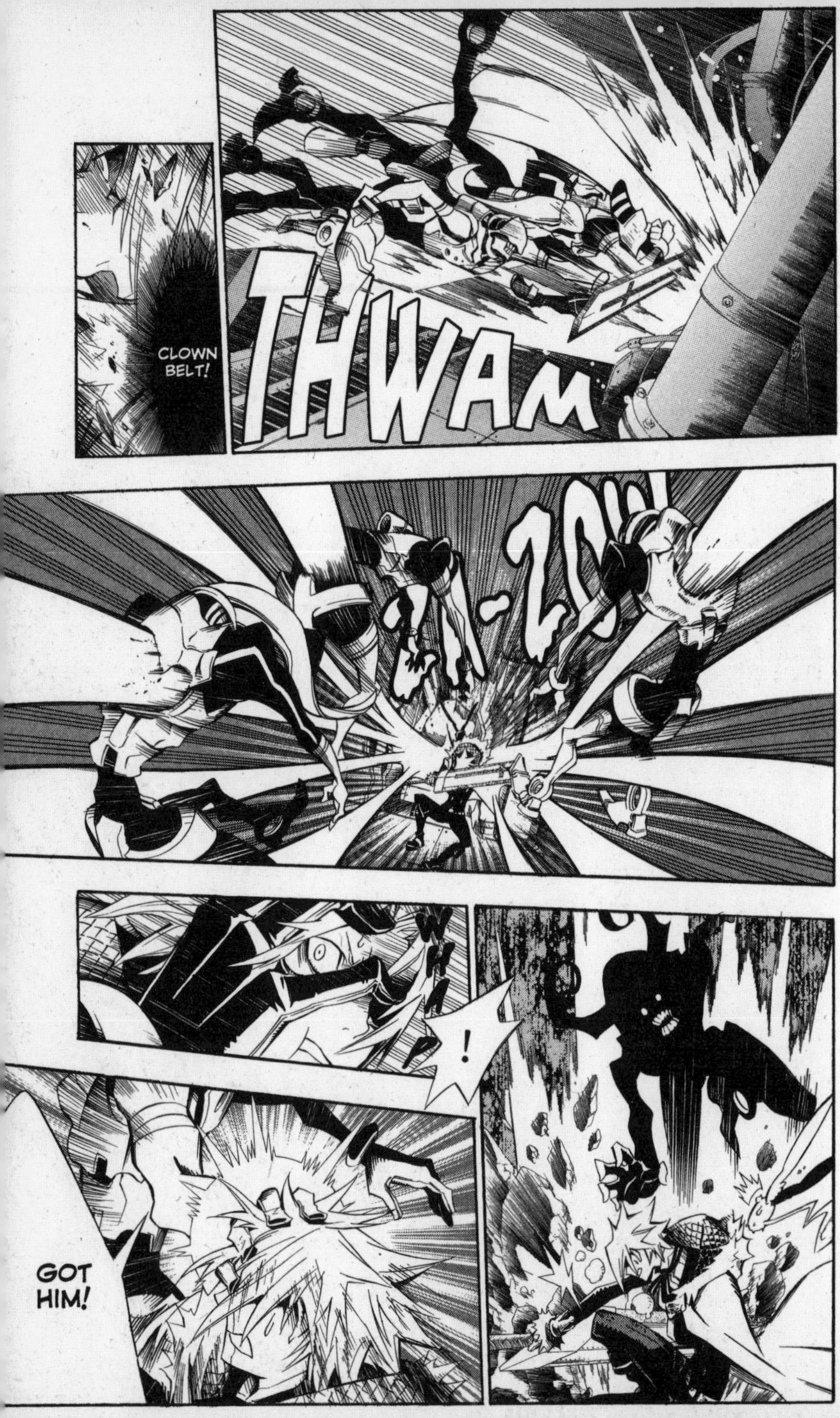
THWAM
CLOWN BELT!
!
GOT HIM!

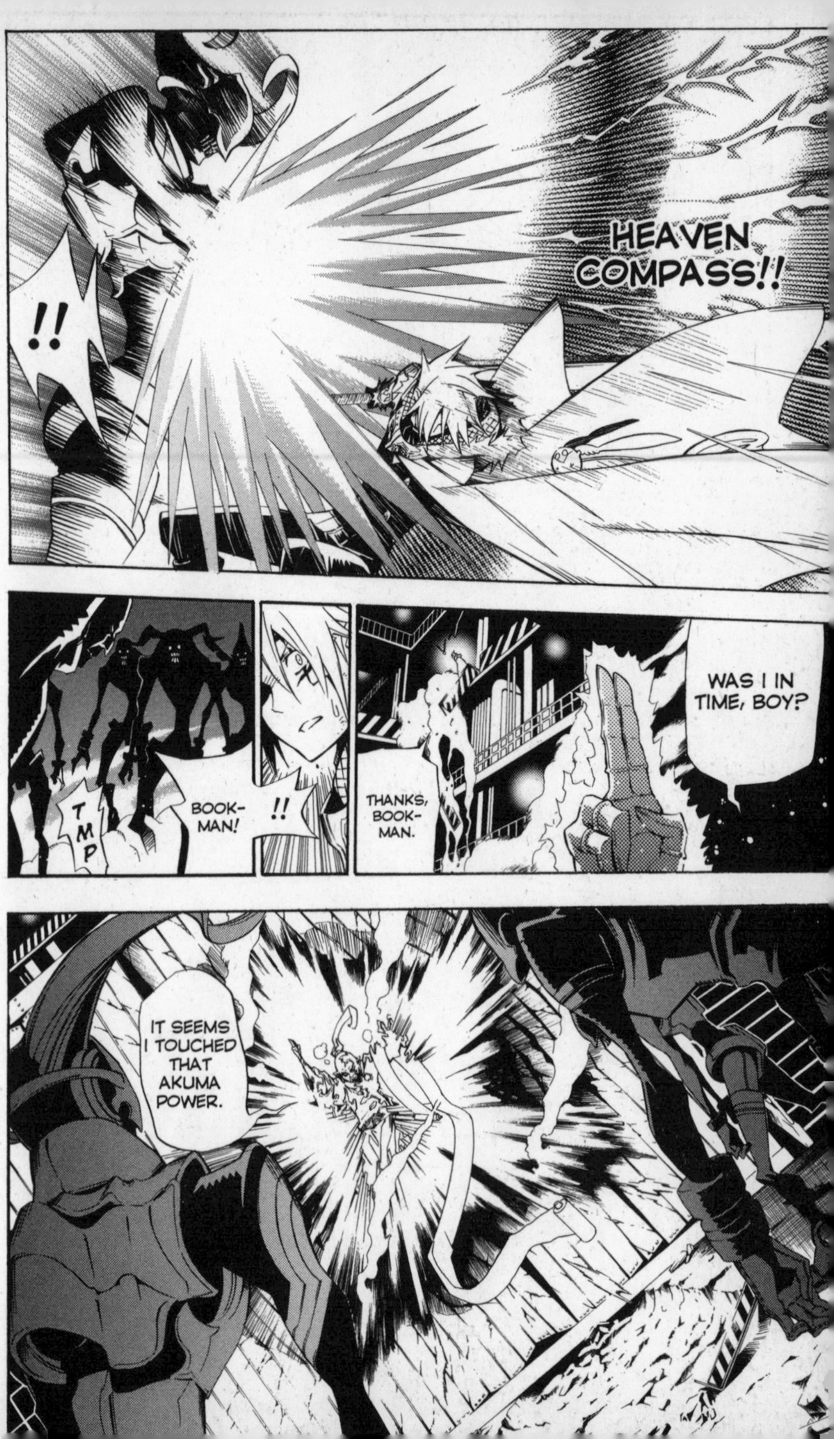
HEAVEN COMPASS!!
!!
WAS I IN TIME, BOY?
THANKS, BOOK-MAN.
!!
BOOK-MAN!
TMP
IT SEEMS I TOUCHED THAT AKUMA POWER.

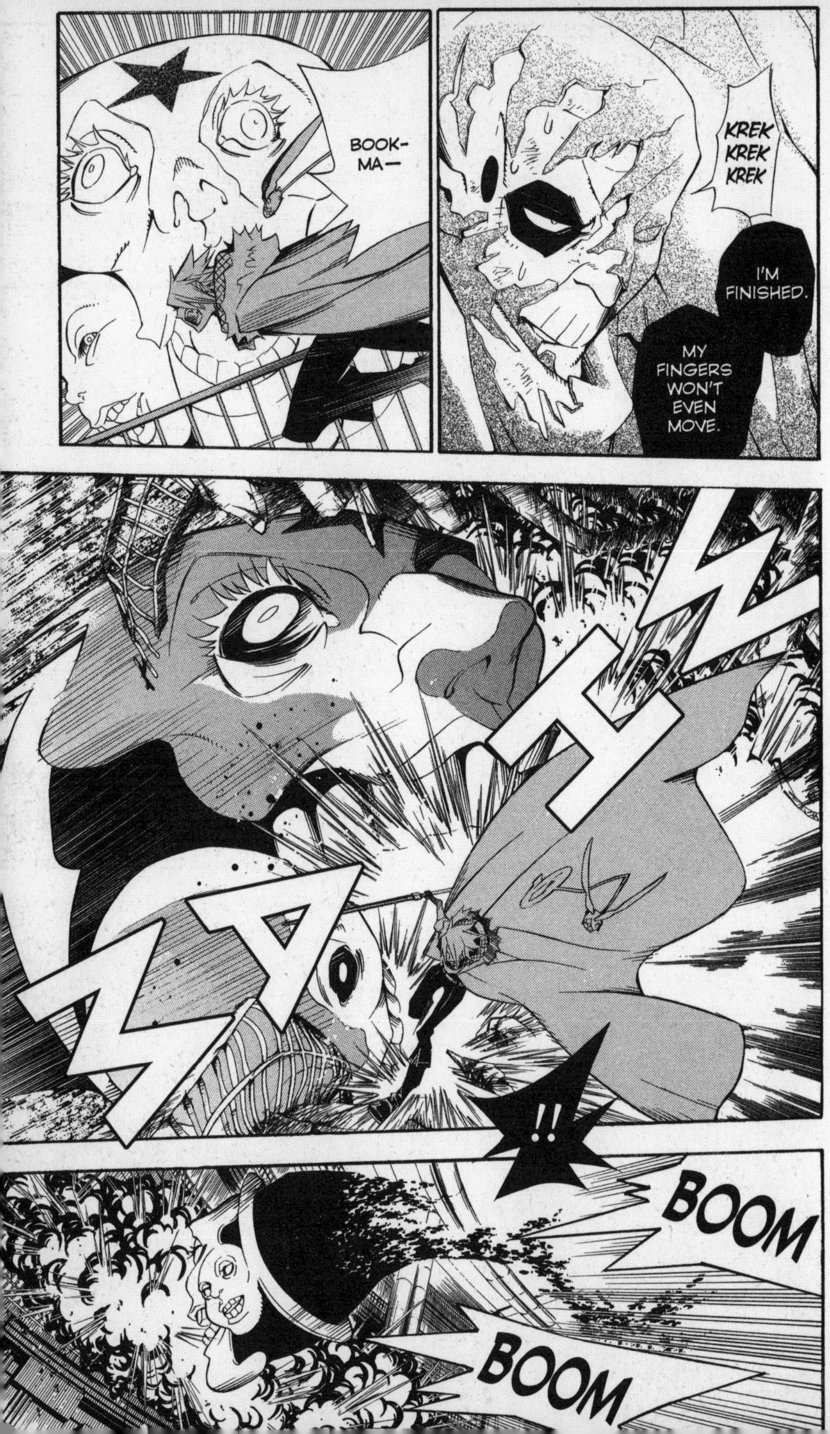
KREK KREK KREK
I'M FINISHED.
MY FINGERS WON'T EVEN MOVE.
BOOK-MA—
WHAM
!!
BOOM
BOOM

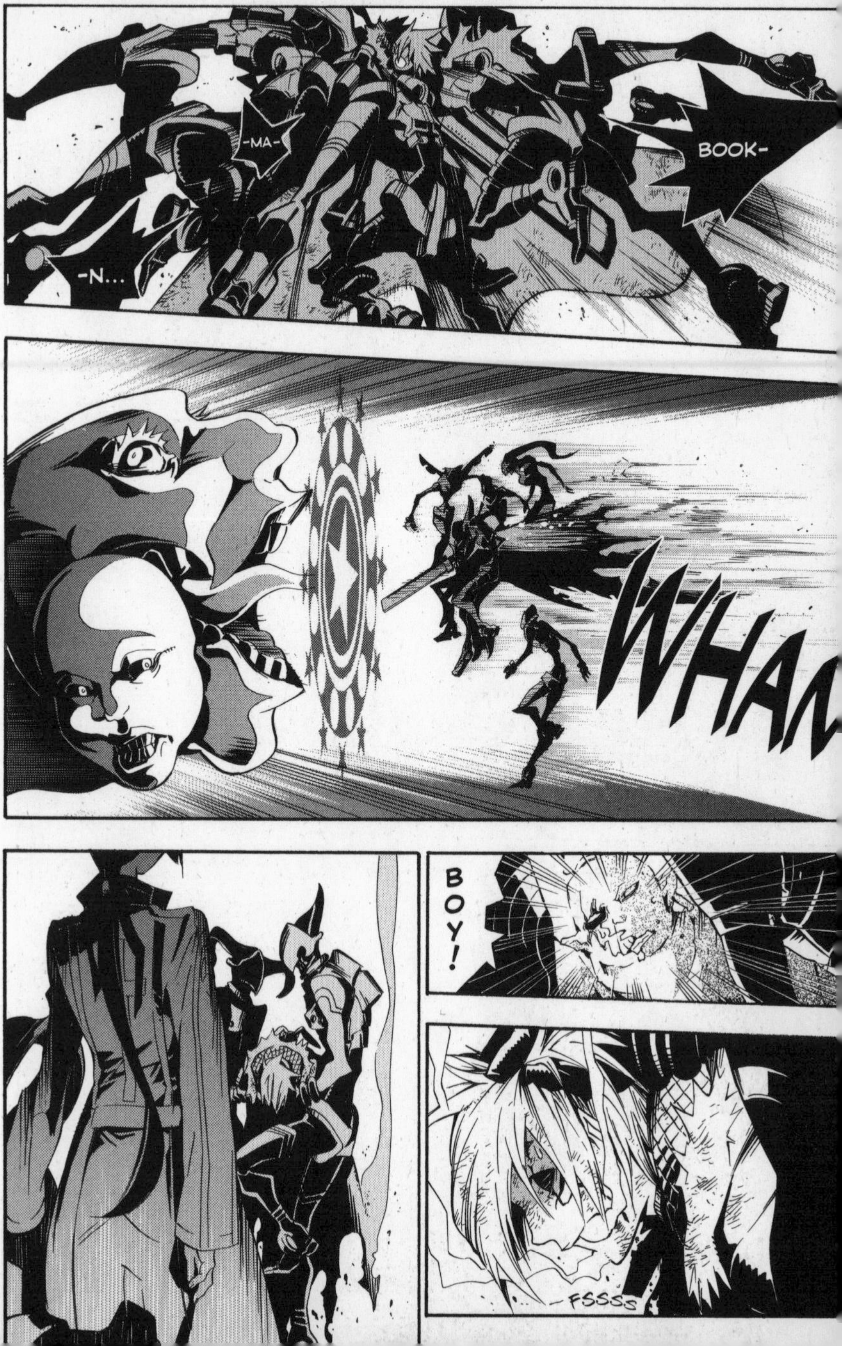
BOOK-
-MA-
-N...
WHAM
BOY!
FSSSS

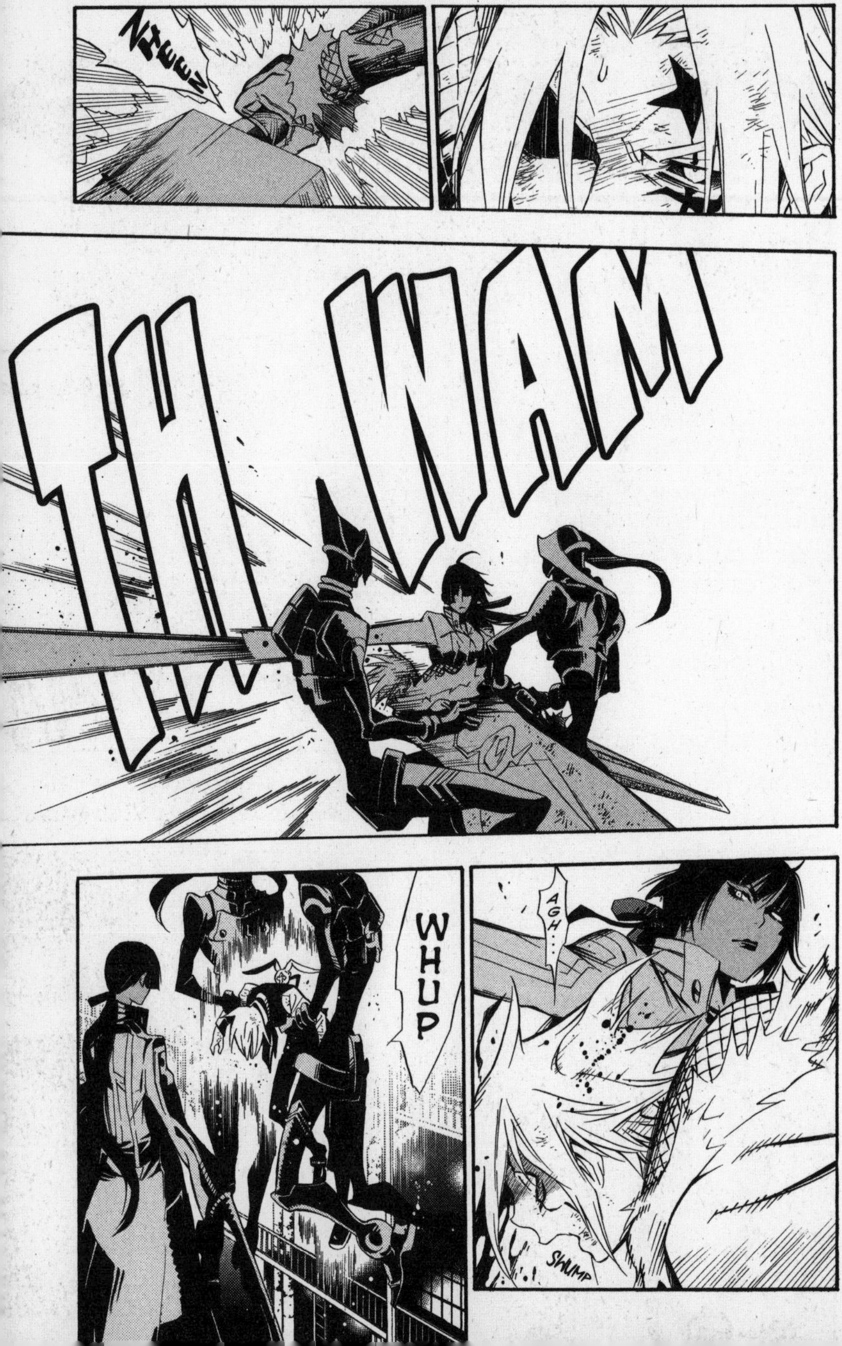
THWAM
AGH...
SHUMP
WHUP

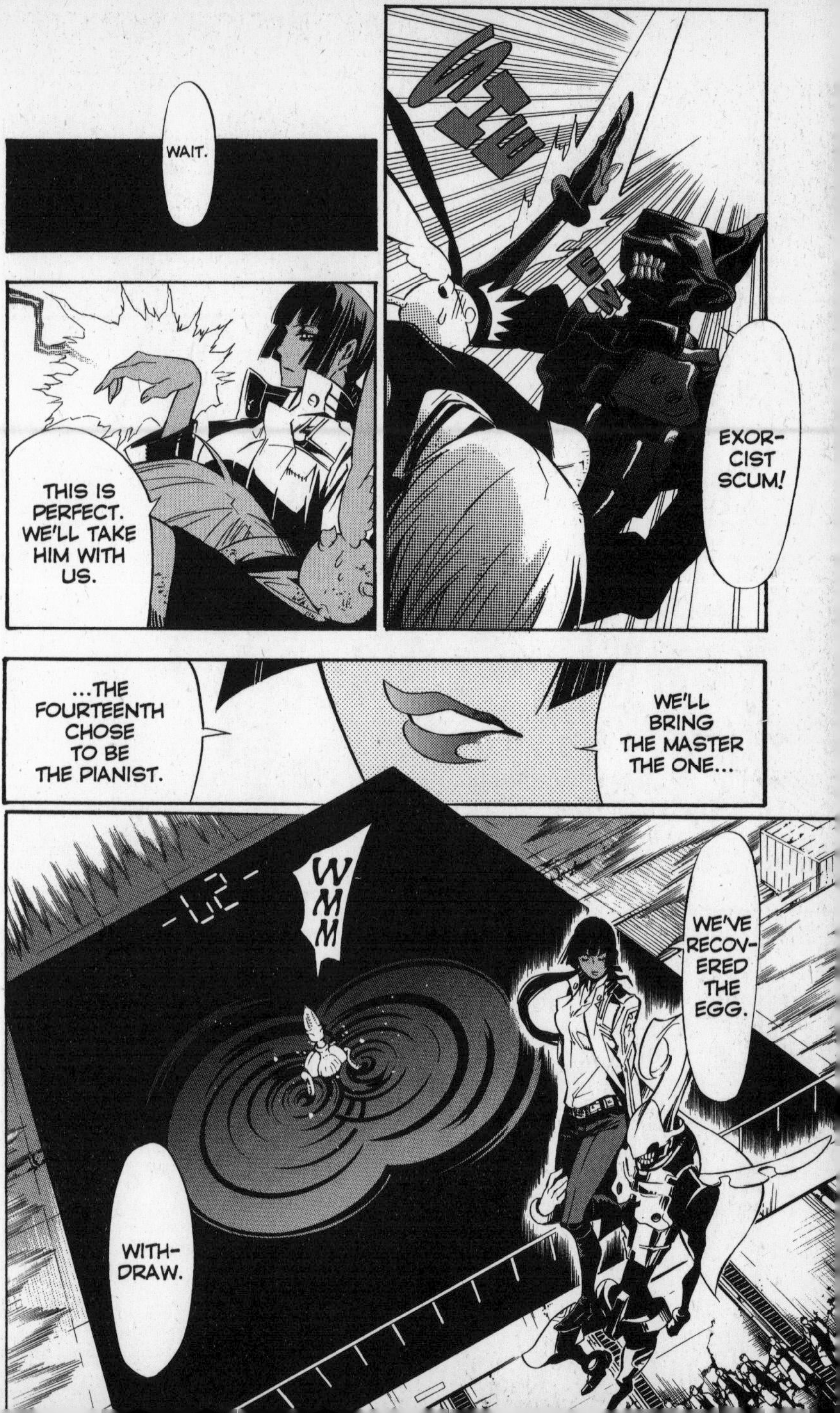
EXOR-
CIST
SCUM!
WAIT.
THIS IS PERFECT. WE'LL TAKE HIM WITH US.
WE'LL BRING THE MASTER THE ONE...
...THE FOURTEENTH CHOSE TO BE THE PIANIST.
WE'VE RECOV-
ERED THE EGG.
WMM
WITH-
DRAW.

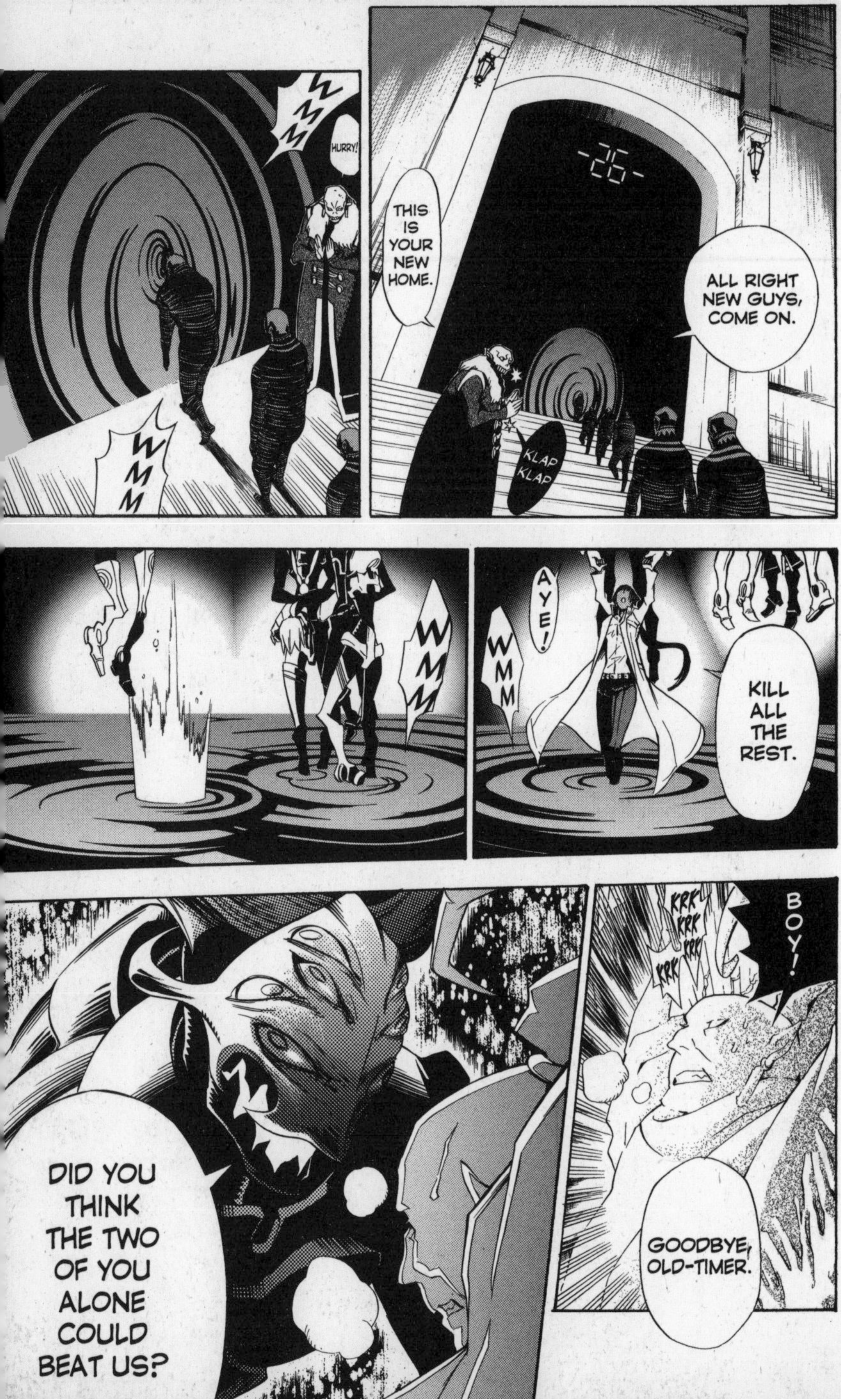
-26-
ALL RIGHT NEW GUYS, COME ON.
THIS IS YOUR NEW HOME.
KLAP KLAP
WMM
HURRY!
WMM
KILL ALL THE REST.
AYE!
WMM
WMM
BOY!
KRK KRK KRK KRK
GOODBYE, OLD-TIMER.
DID YOU THINK THE TWO OF YOU ALONE COULD BEAT US?

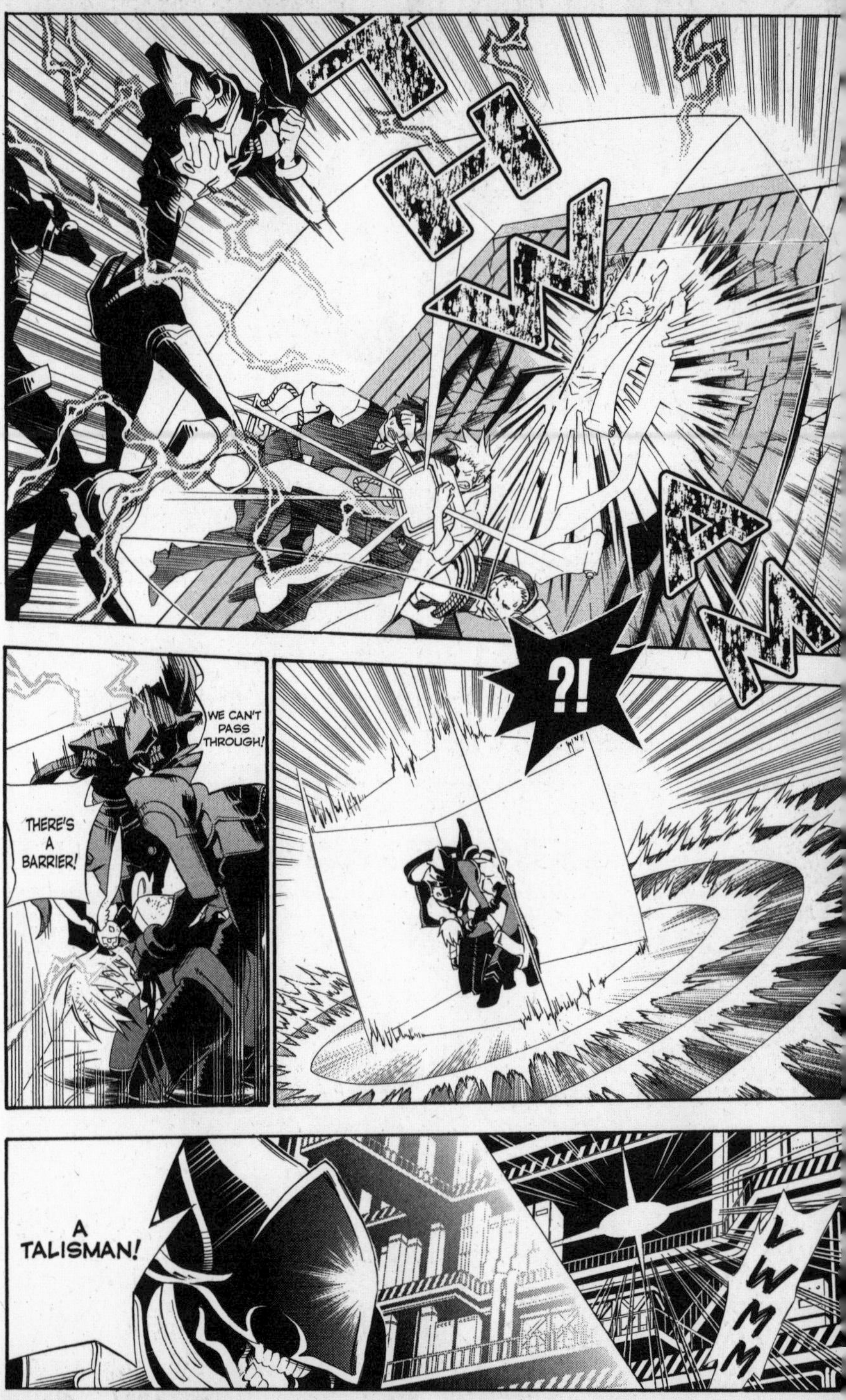
THWAM
?!
WE CAN'T PASS THROUGH!
THERE'S A BARRIER!
VWMM
A TALISMAN!

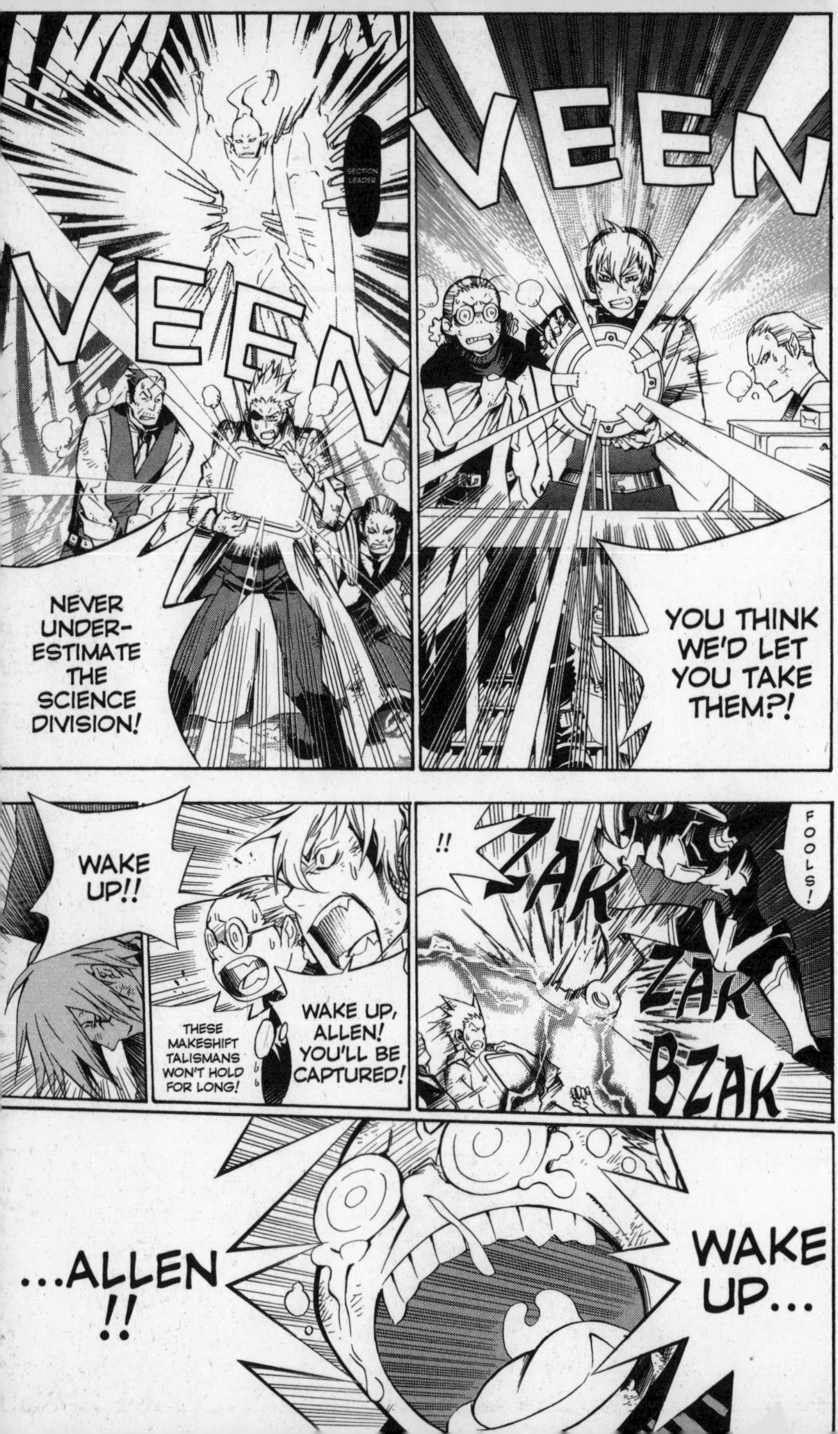
VEEN
YOU THINK WE'D LET YOU TAKE THEM?!
SECTION LEADER
VEEN
NEVER UNDER-ESTIMATE THE SCIENCE DIVISION!
FOOLS!
!!
ZAK
ZAK
BZAK
WAKE UP, ALLEN! YOU'LL BE CAPTURED!
THESE MAKESHIFT TALISMANS WON'T HOLD FOR LONG!
WAKE UP!!
WAKE UP...
...ALLEN !!

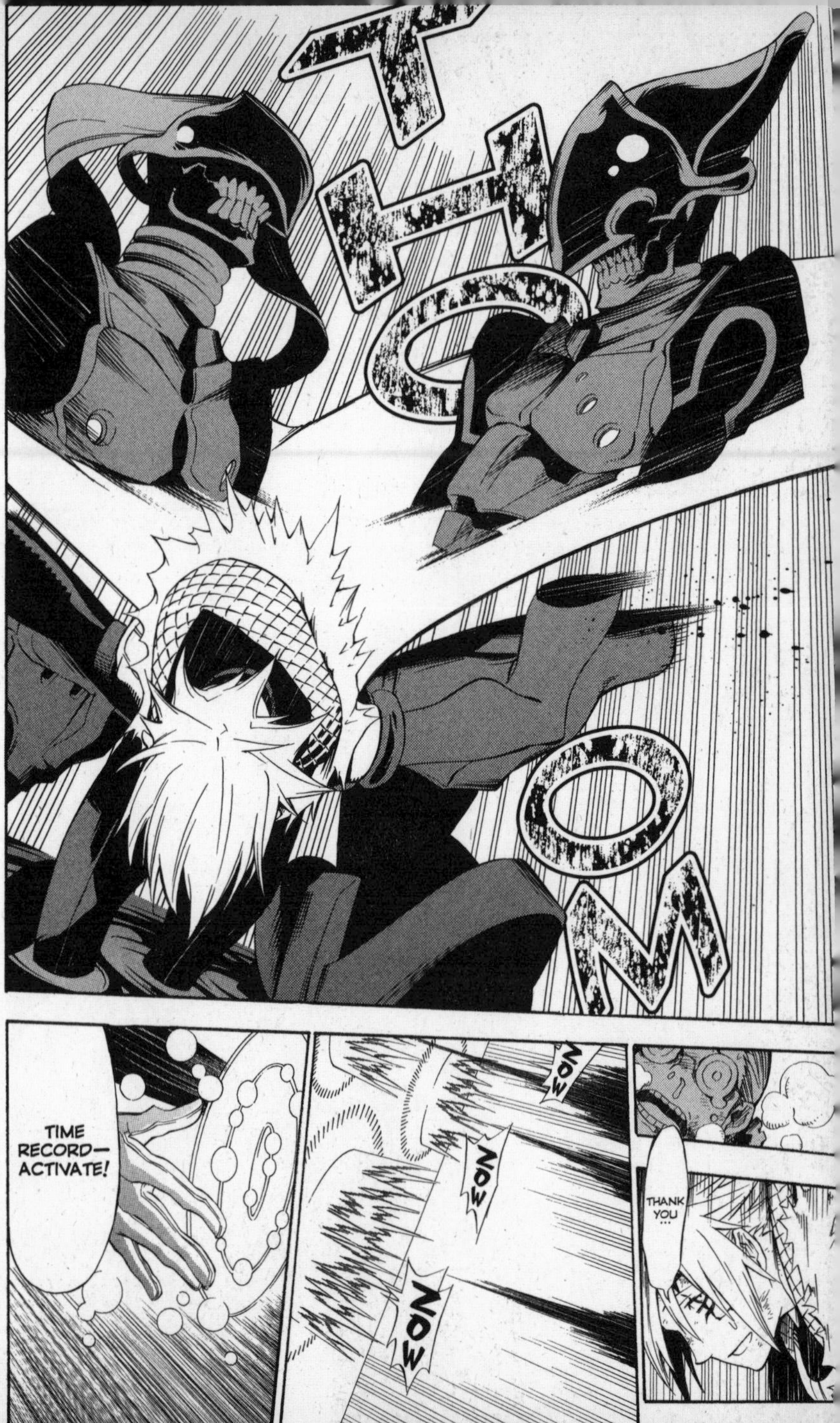
THOOM
THANK YOU...
ZOOM
ZOOM
ZOOM
TIME RECORD—ACTIVATE!

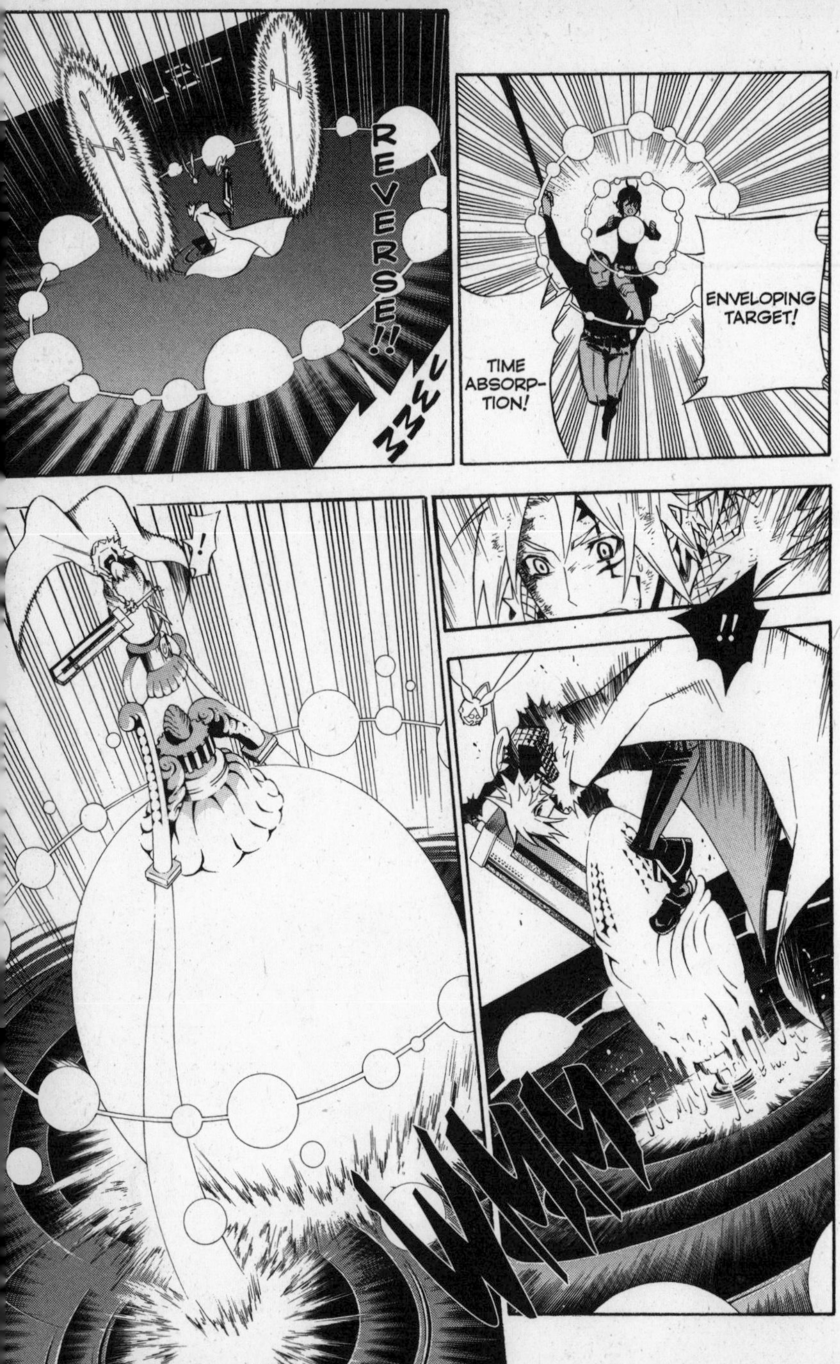
ENVELOPING TARGET!
TIME ABSORPTION!
REVERSE!!
VWMMM
!!
!
VWMM

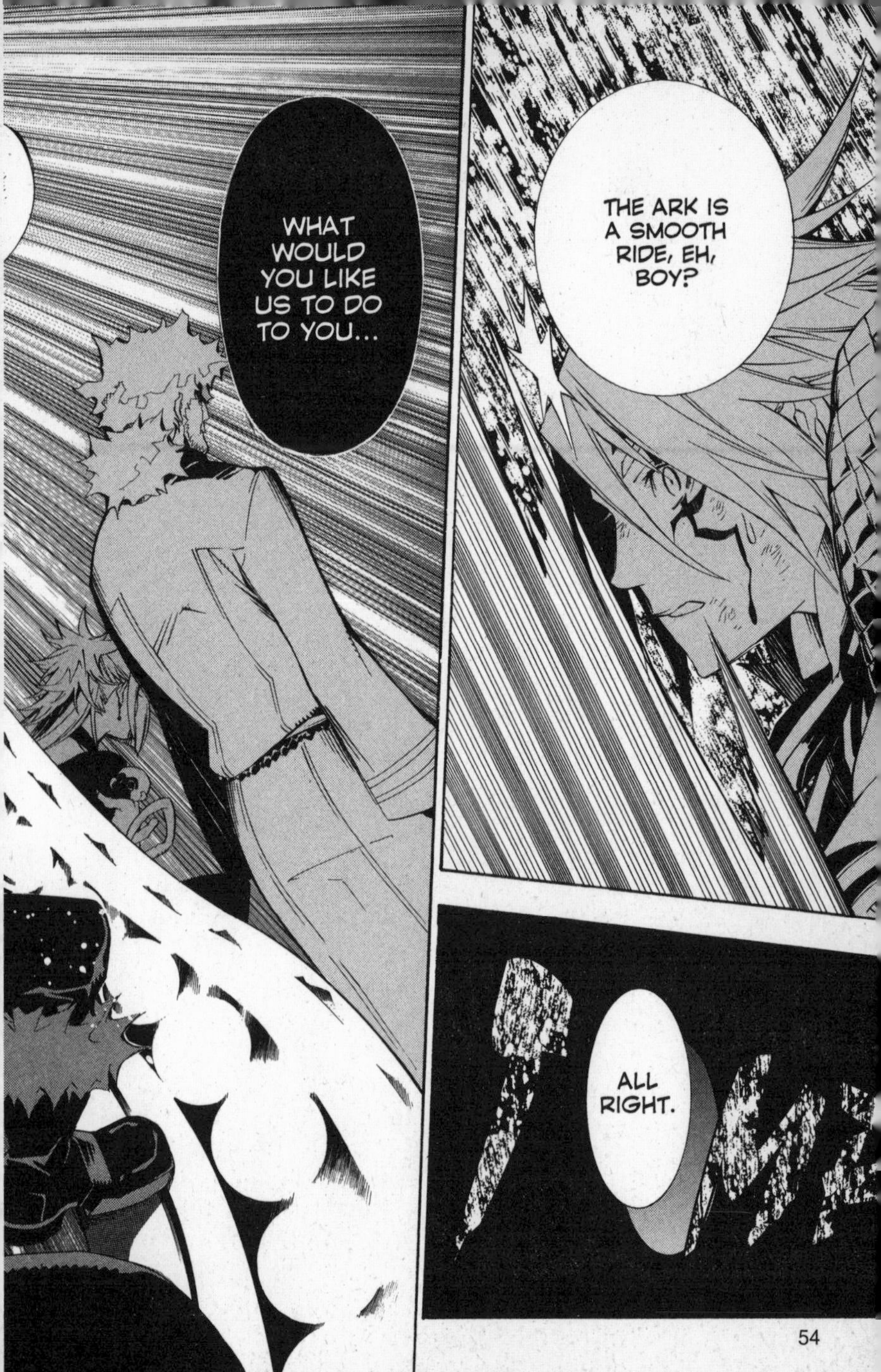
THE ARK IS A SMOOTH RIDE, EH, BOY?
ALL RIGHT.
WHAT WOULD YOU LIKE US TO DO TO YOU...

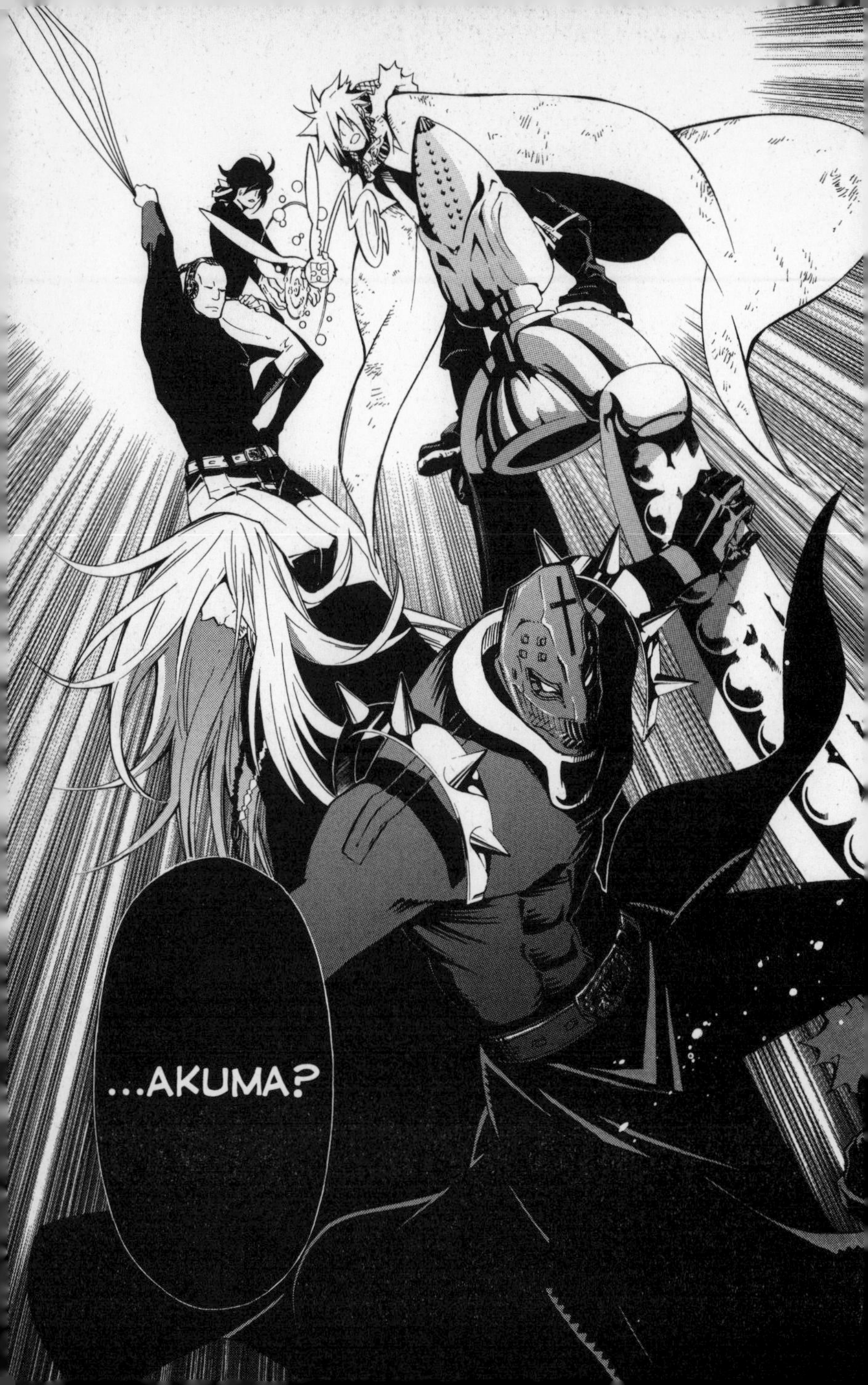
...AKUMA?

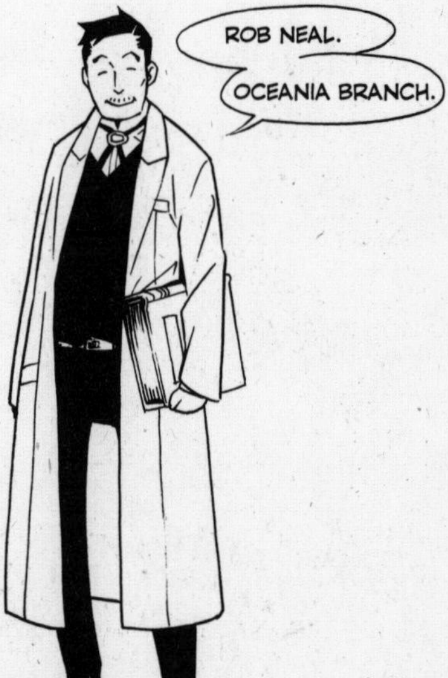
ROB NEAL.
OCEANIA BRANCH.

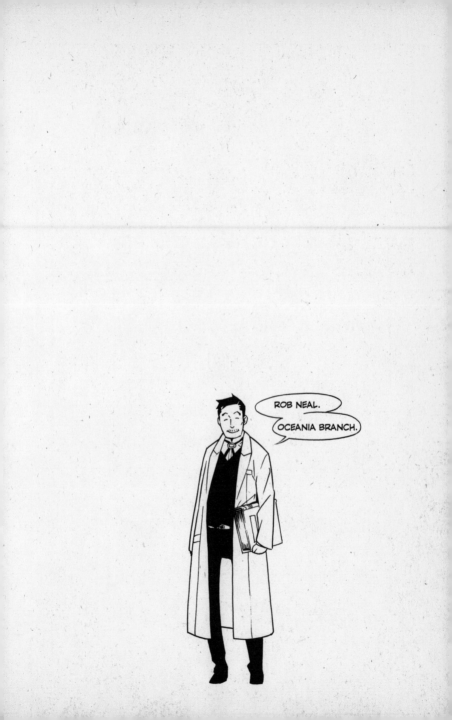

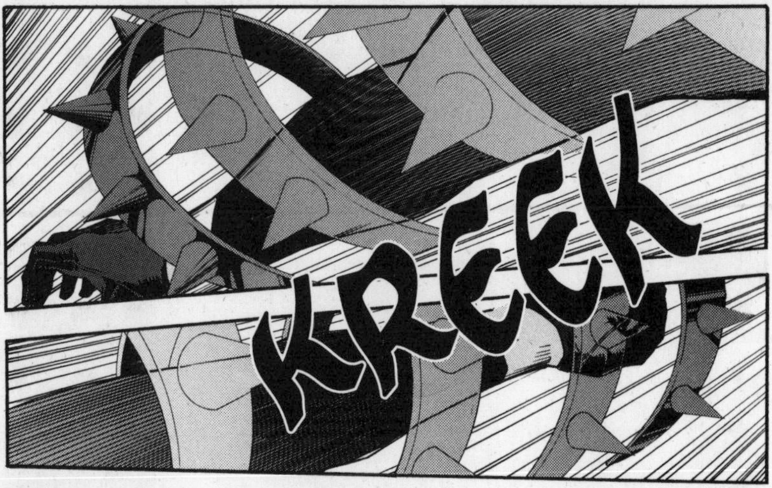
KREEK

THE 142ND NIGHT: COME ON NOW

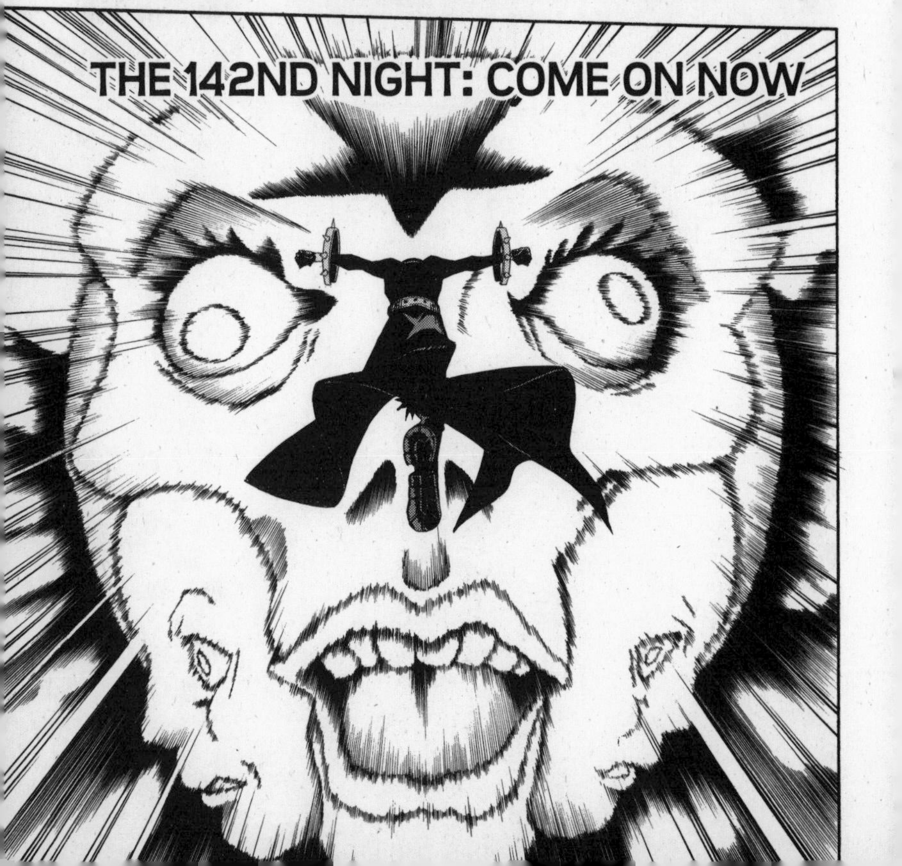

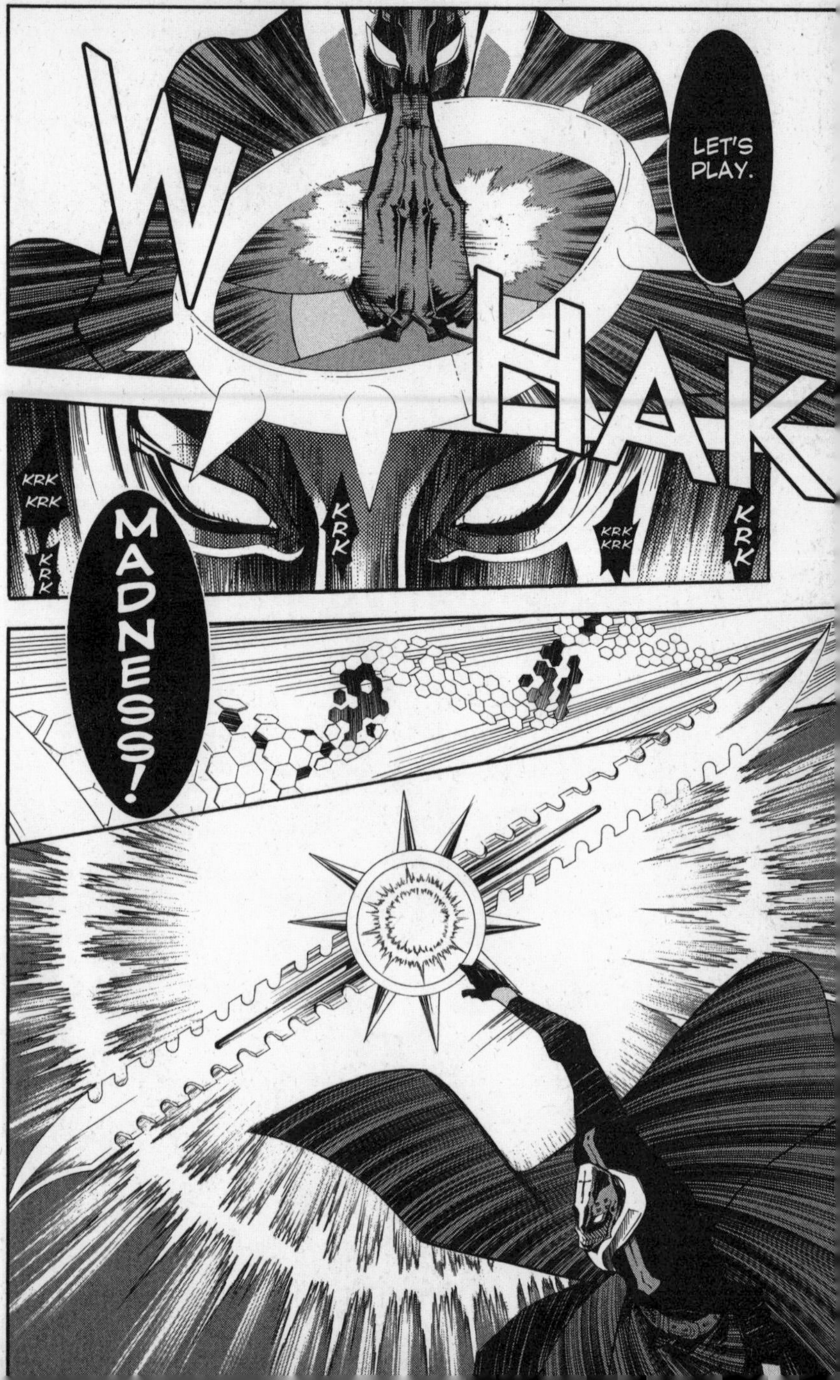
LET'S PLAY.
WHAK
KRK
KRK KRK
KRK
MADNESS!
KRK KRK
KRK

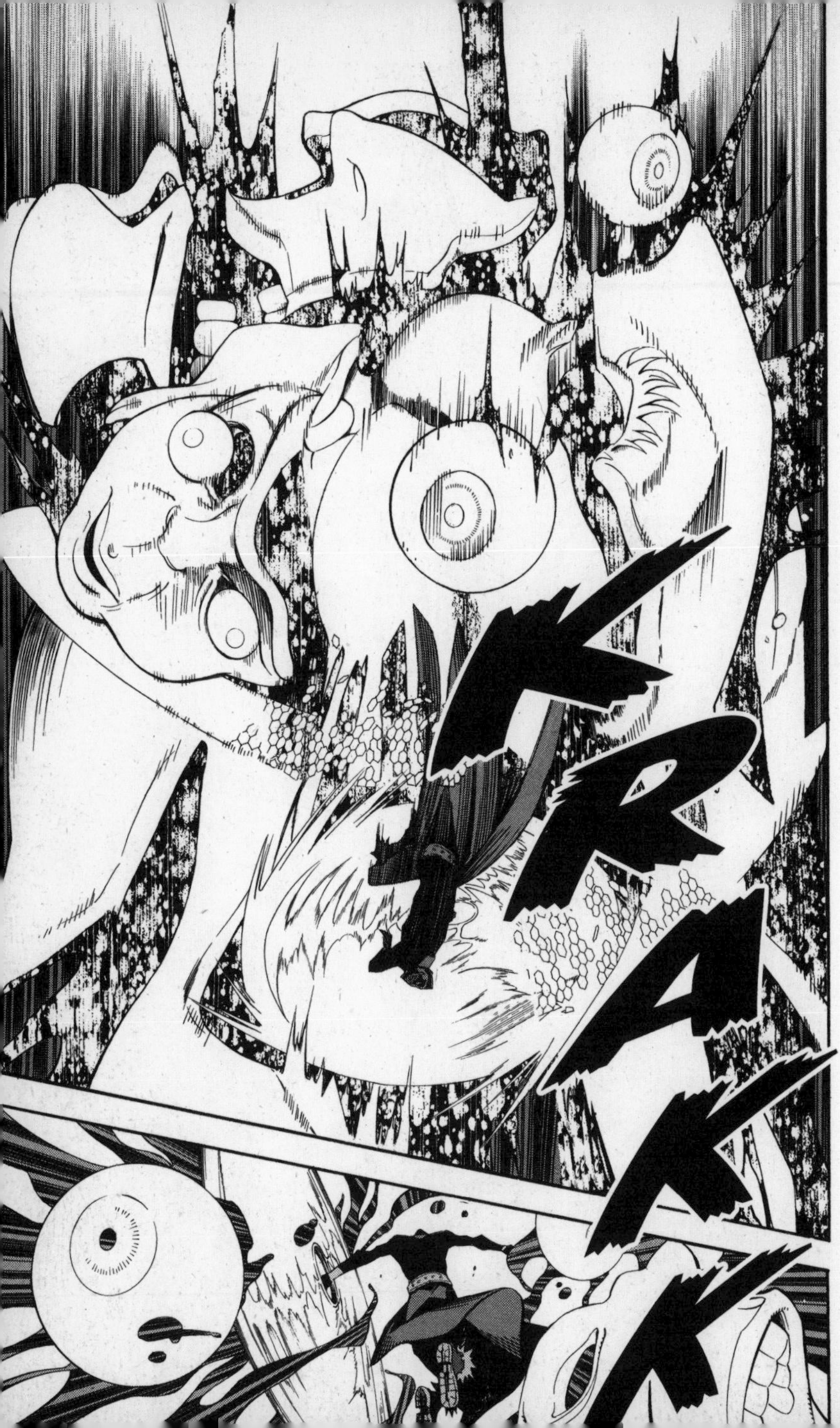
KRAKK

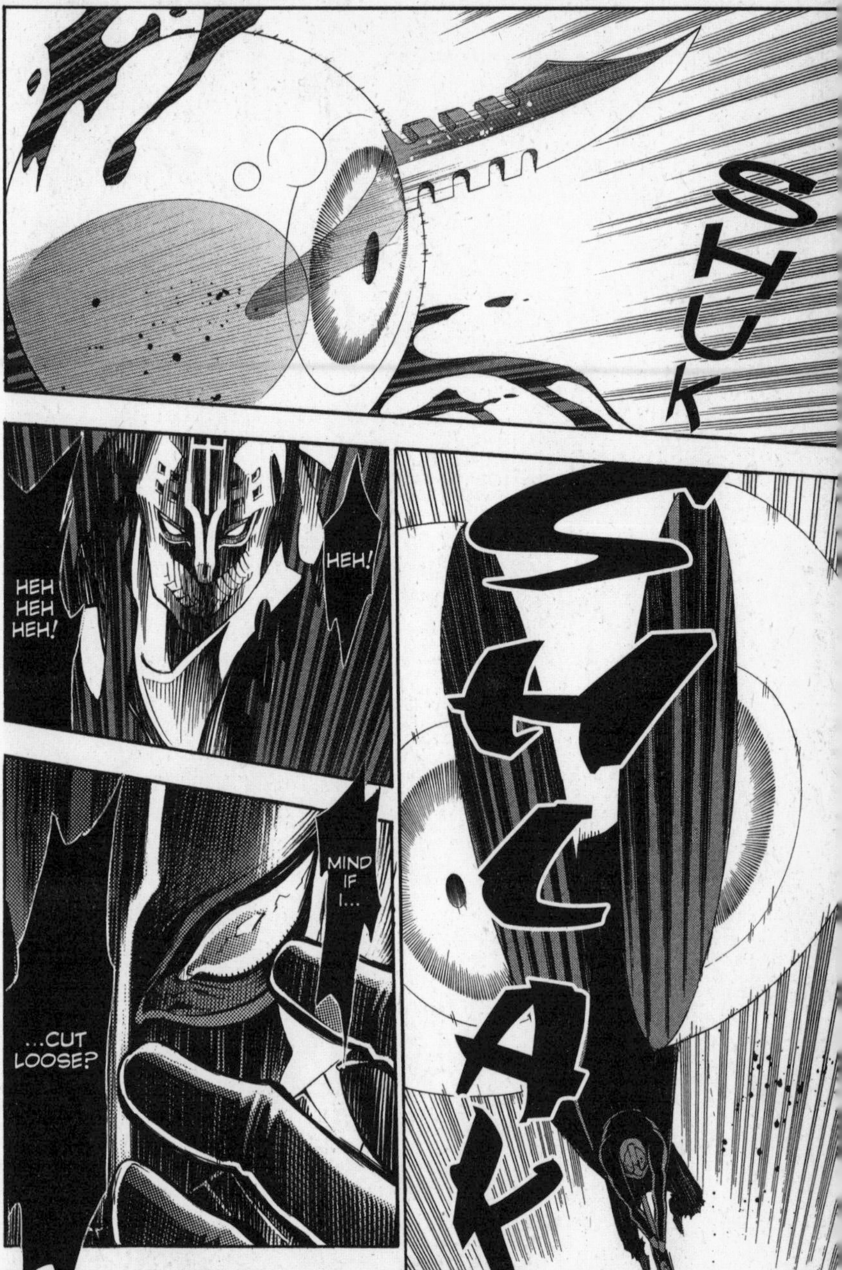
SHUK
HEH!
HEH HEH HEH!
MIND IF I...
...CUT LOOSE?

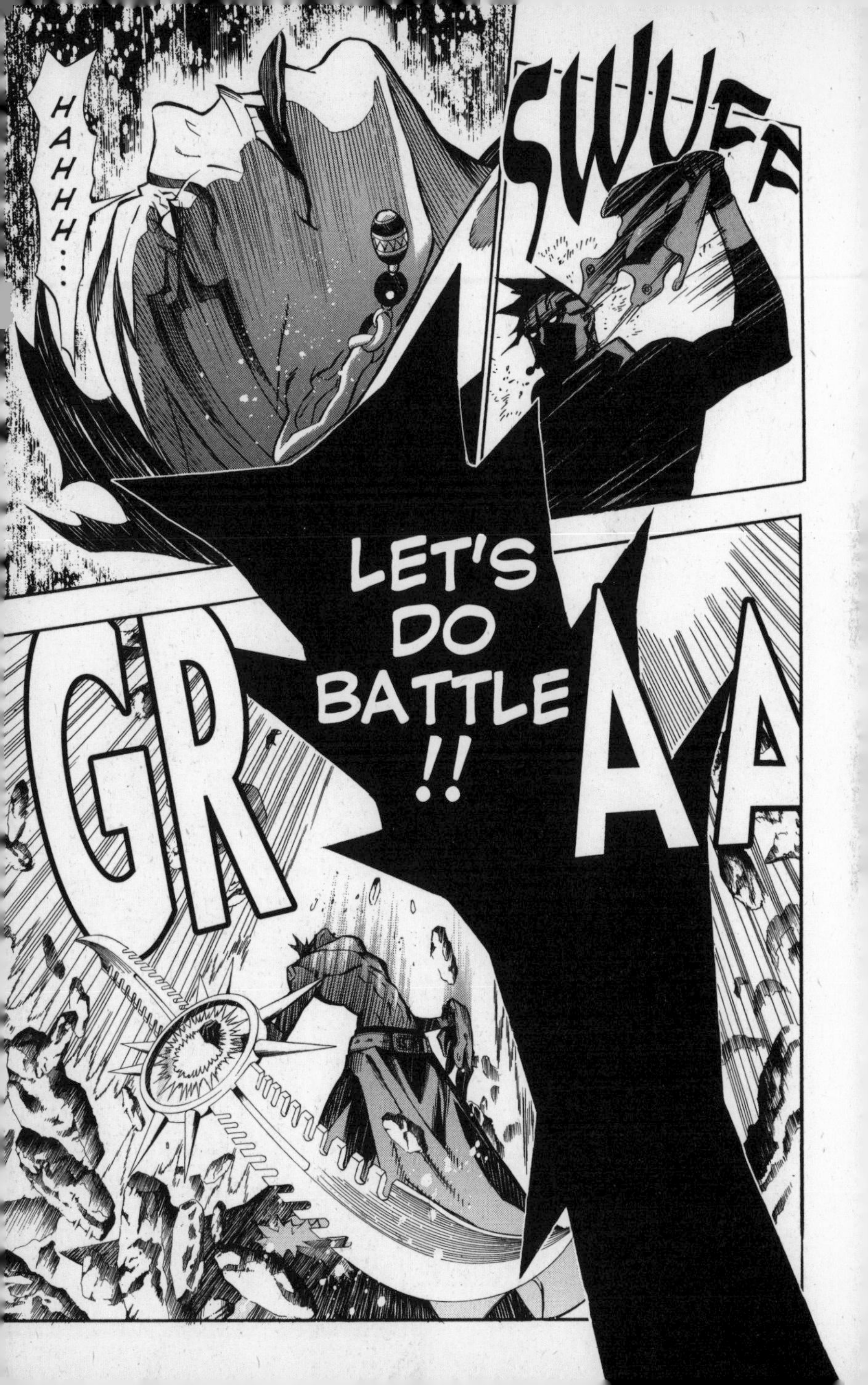
SWUFF
HAHHH...
LET'S DO BATTLE!!
GRAA

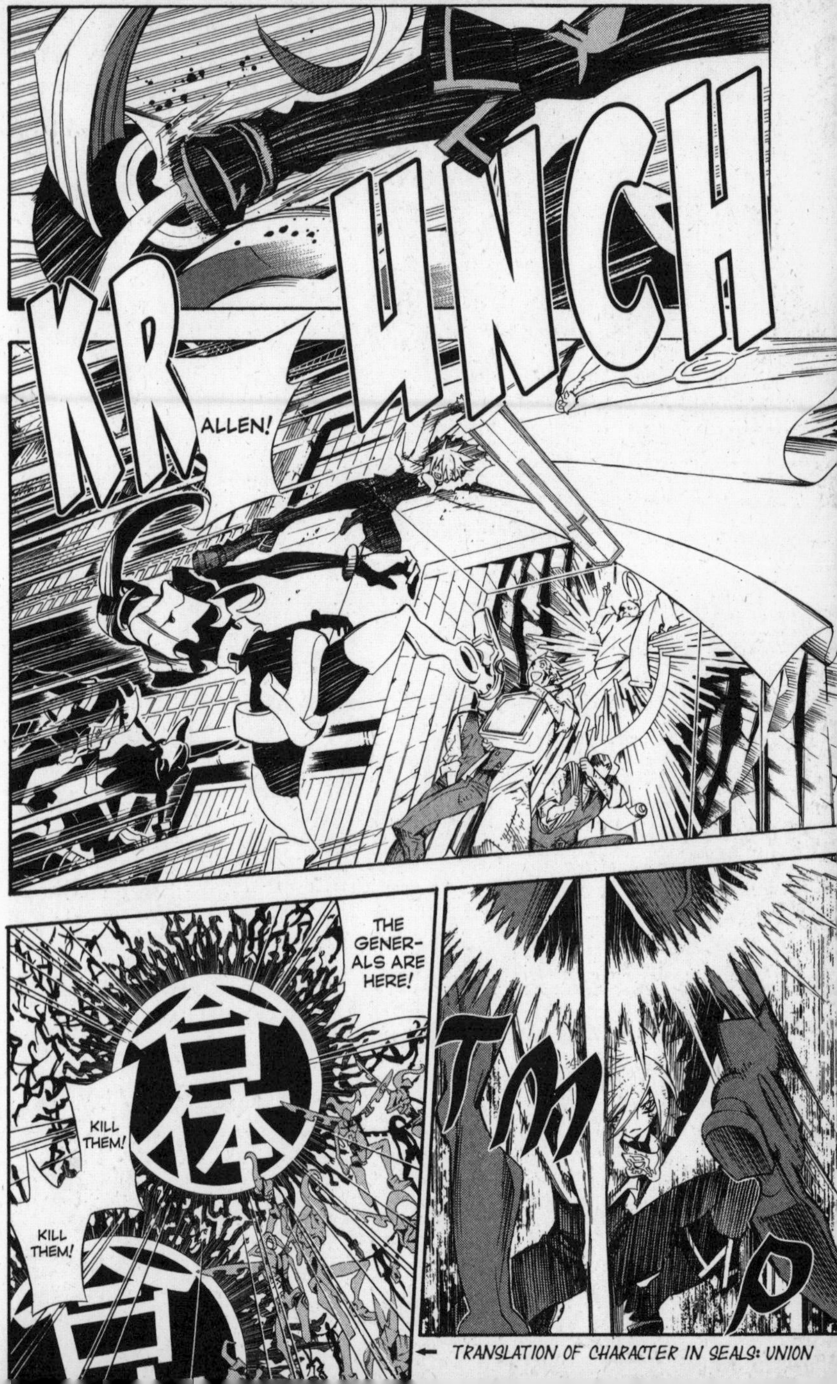
KR-UNCH
ALLEN!
THE GENER-ALS ARE HERE!
合体
KILL THEM!
KILL THEM!
← TRANSLATION OF CHARACTER IN SEALS: UNION

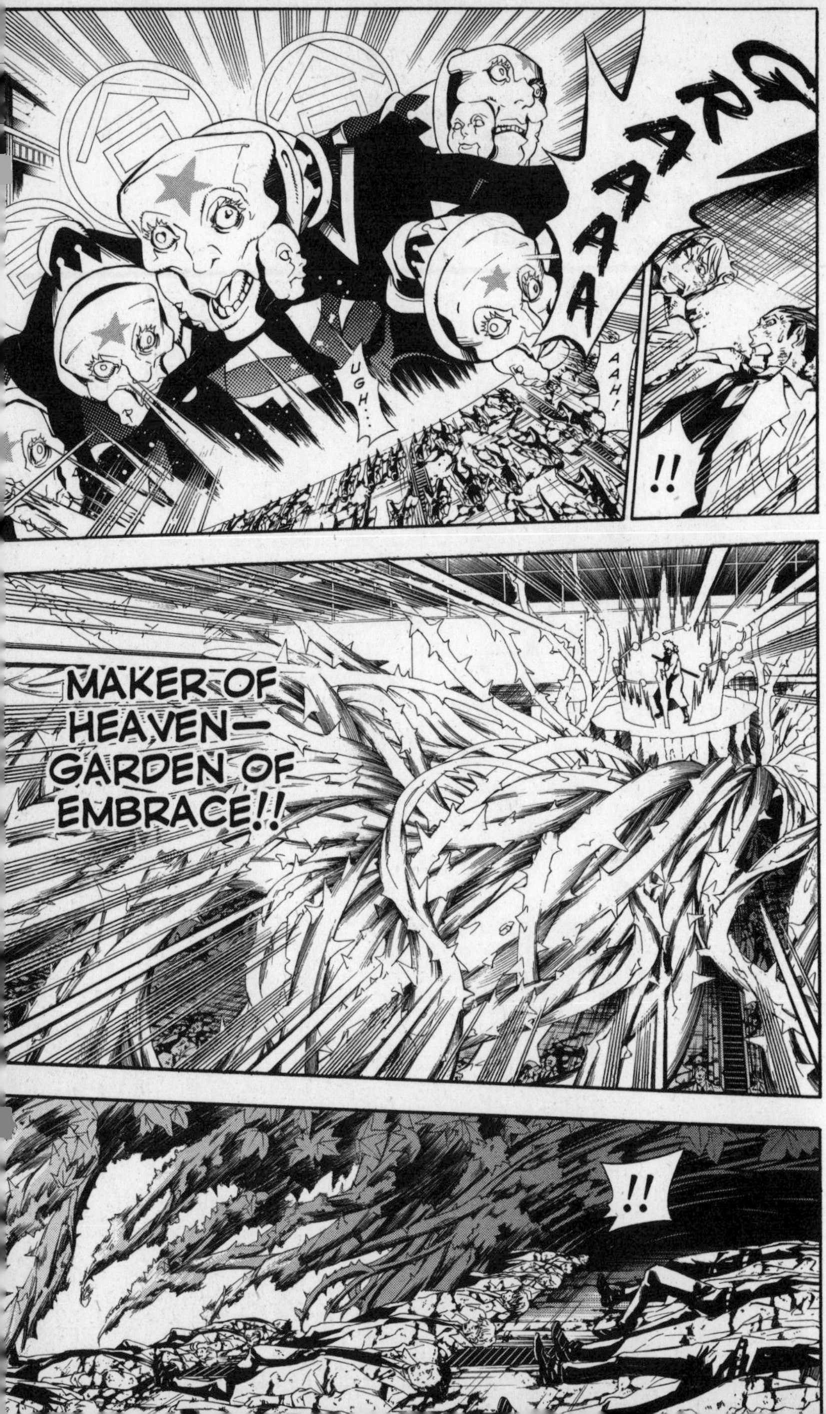
!!
GRAAAA
AAH!
UGH...
MAKER OF HEAVEN— GARDEN OF EMBRACE!!
!!

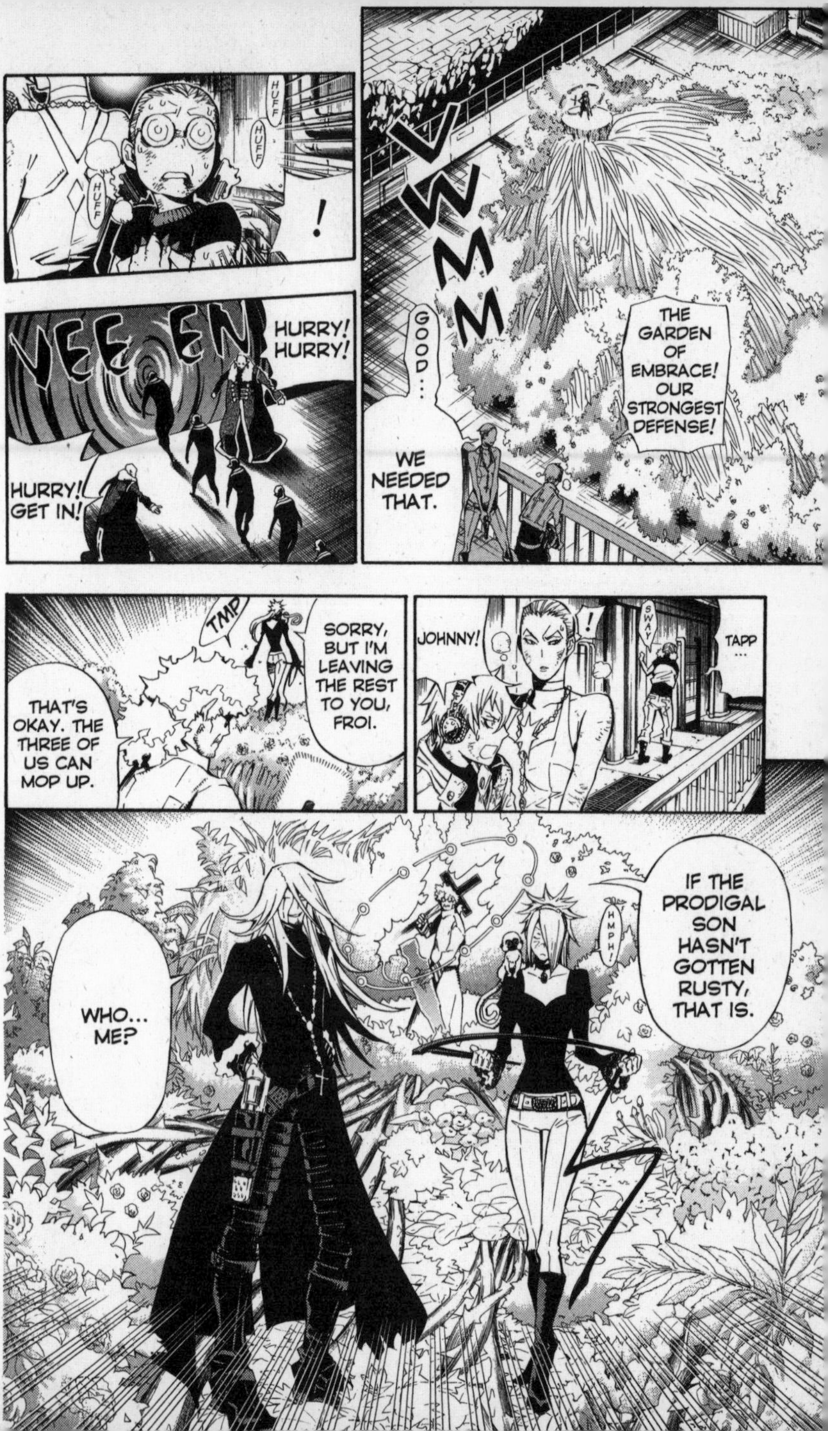
VWMM
THE GARDEN OF EMBRACE! OUR STRONGEST DEFENSE!
GOOD...
WE NEEDED THAT.
HUFF
HUFF
HUFF
!
VEE EN
HURRY! HURRY!
HURRY! GET IN!
TAPP...
SWAY
!
JOHNNY!
TMP
SORRY, BUT I'M LEAVING THE REST TO YOU, FROI.
THAT'S OKAY. THE THREE OF US CAN MOP UP.
IF THE PRODIGAL SON HASN'T GOTTEN RUSTY, THAT IS.
HMPH!
WHO... ME?

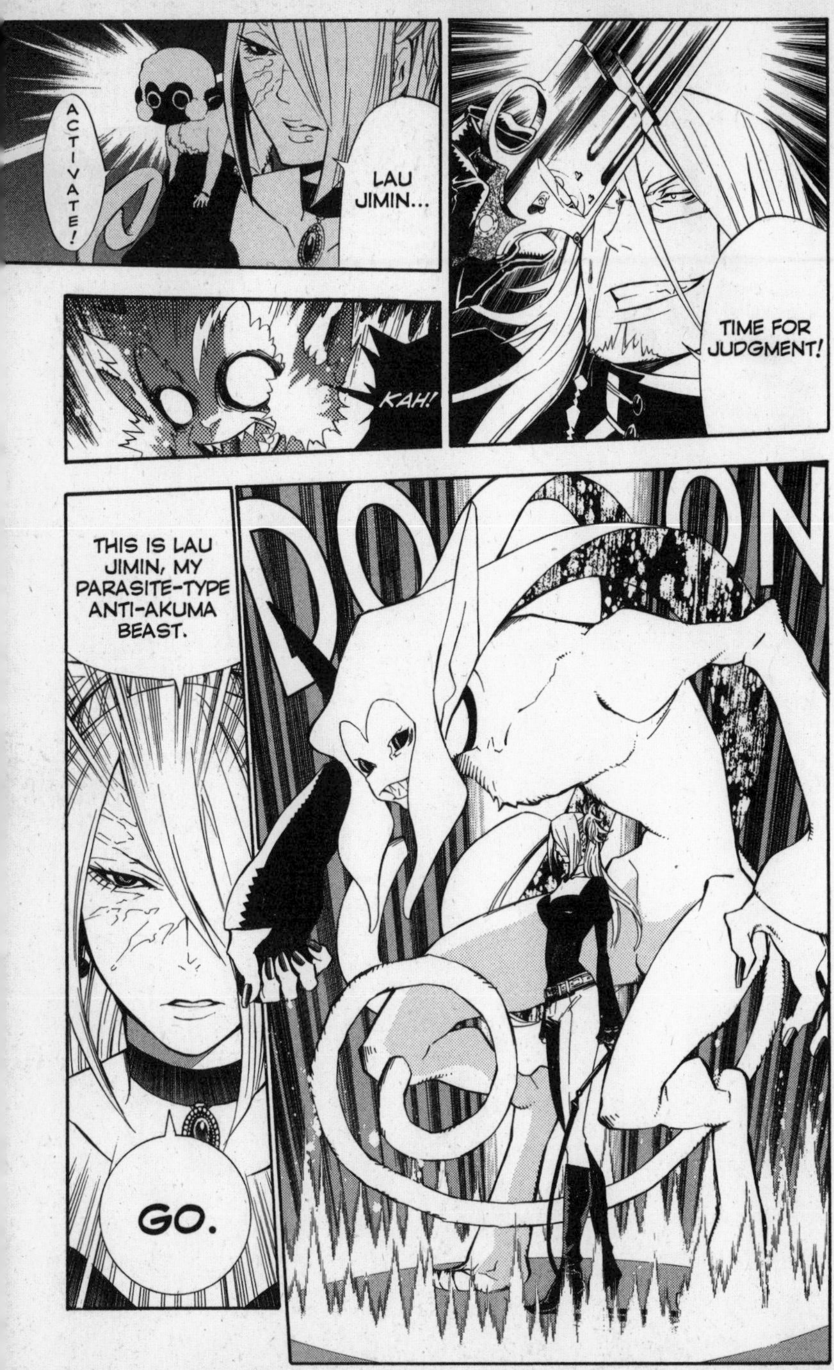
TIME FOR JUDGMENT!
LAU JIMIN...
ACTIVATE!
KAH!
DOOOON
THIS IS LAU JIMIN, MY PARASITE-TYPE ANTI-AKUMA BEAST.
GO.

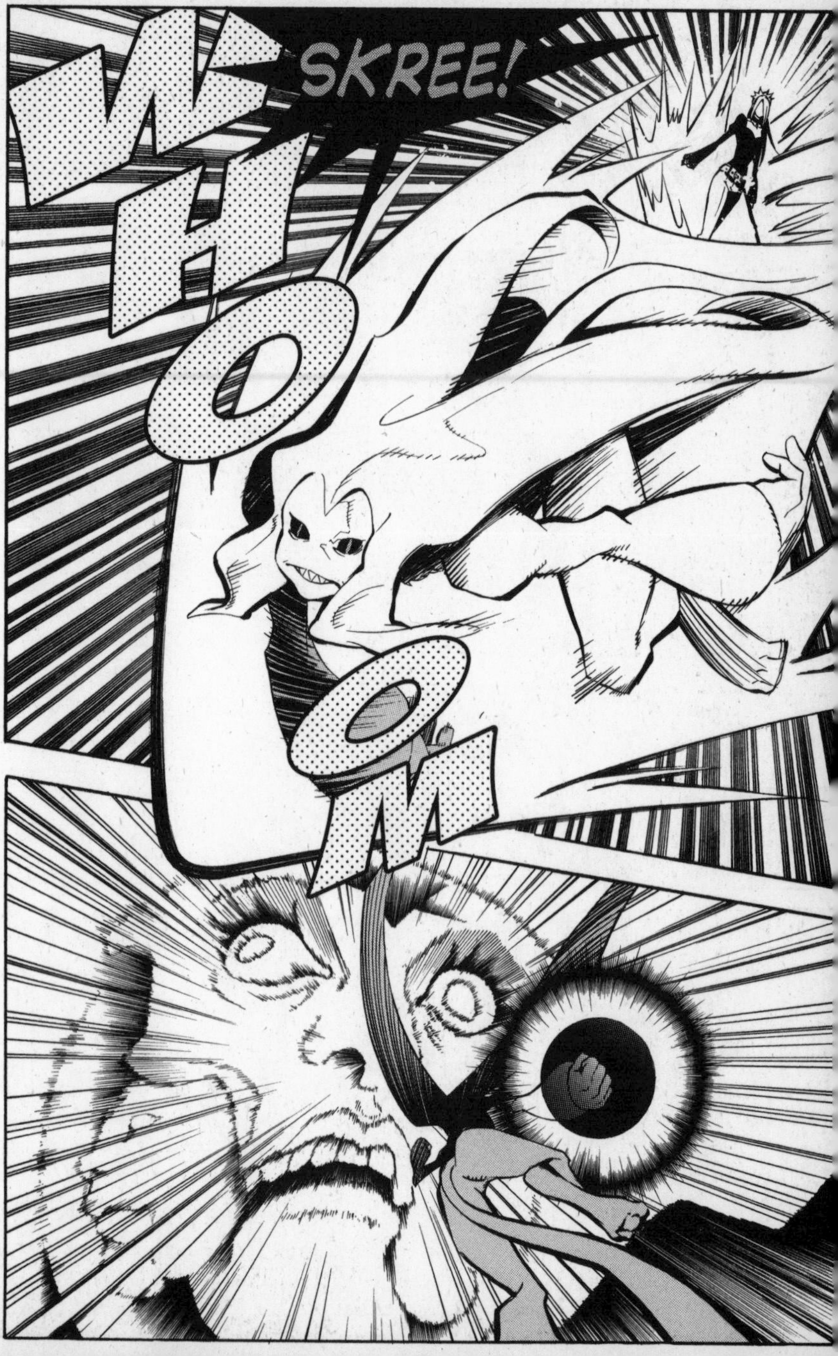
SKREE!
WHOOOM

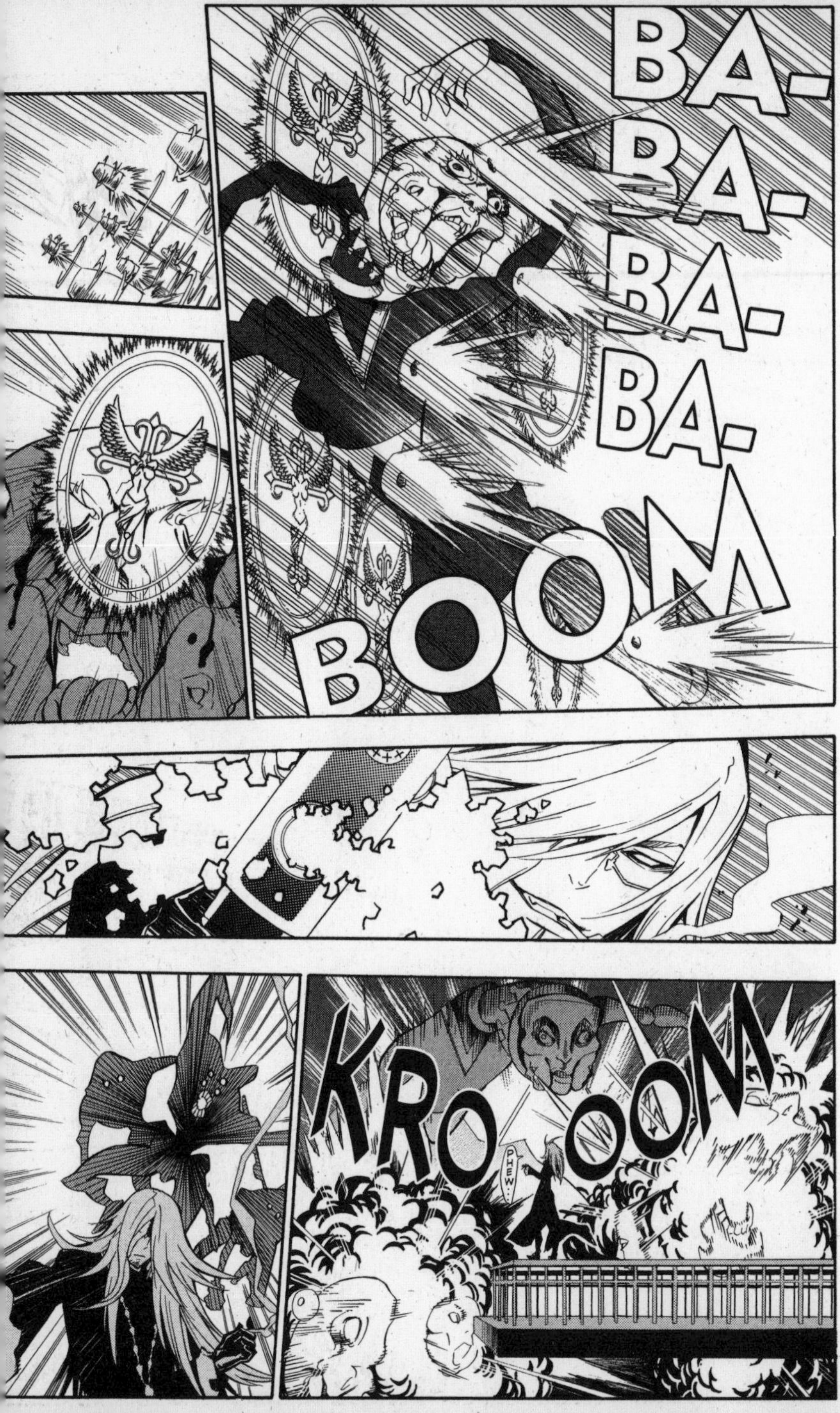
BA-BA-BA-BA-BOOM
KRO OOM
PHEW...

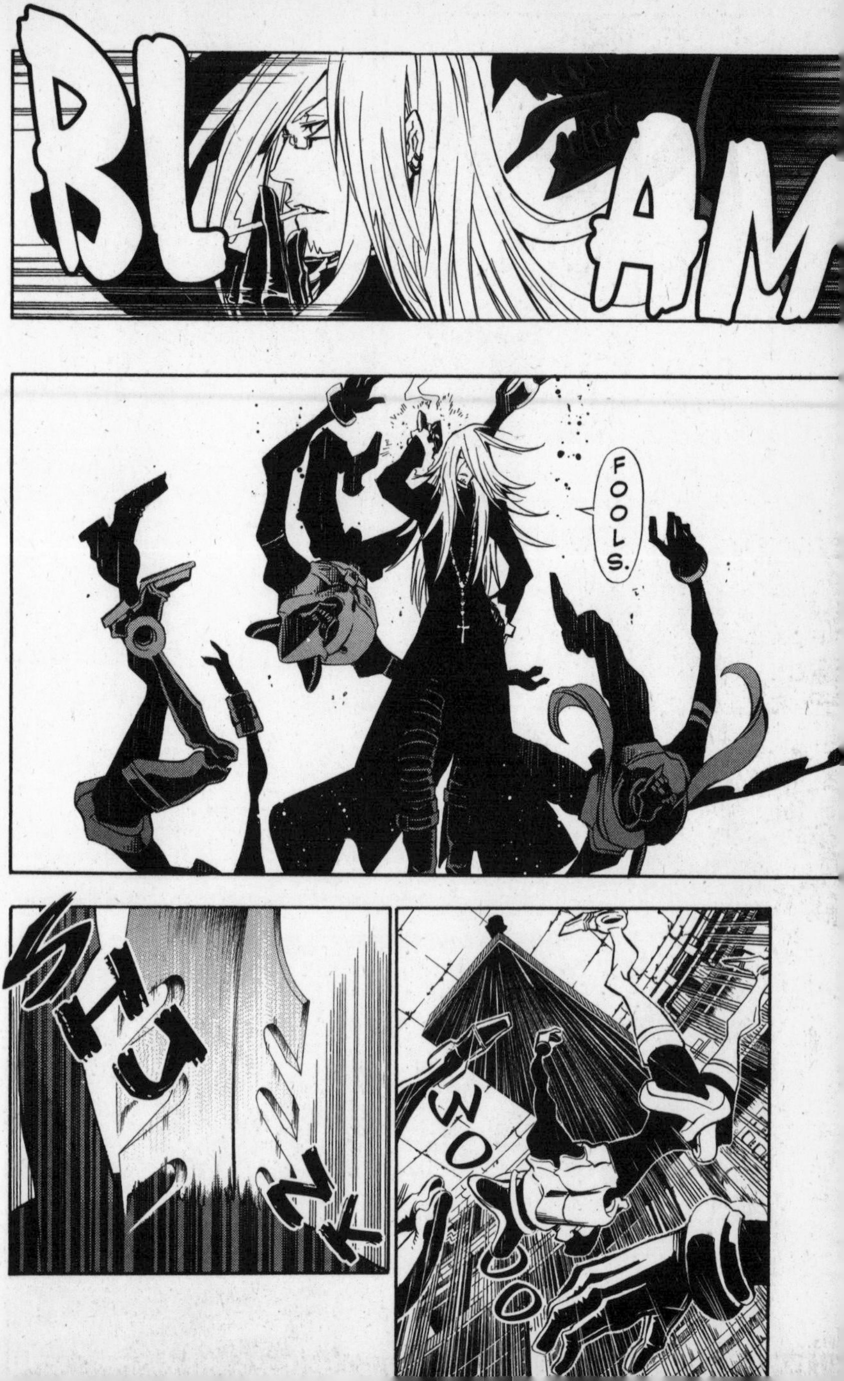
BLAM
FOOLS.
WO...
SHUNK

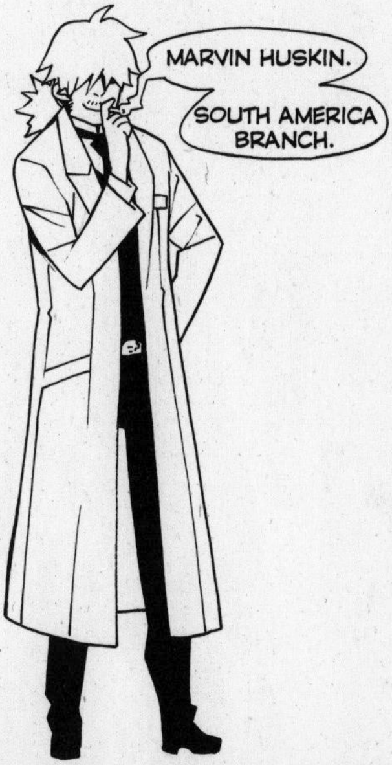
MARVIN HUSKIN.
SOUTH AMERICA BRANCH.

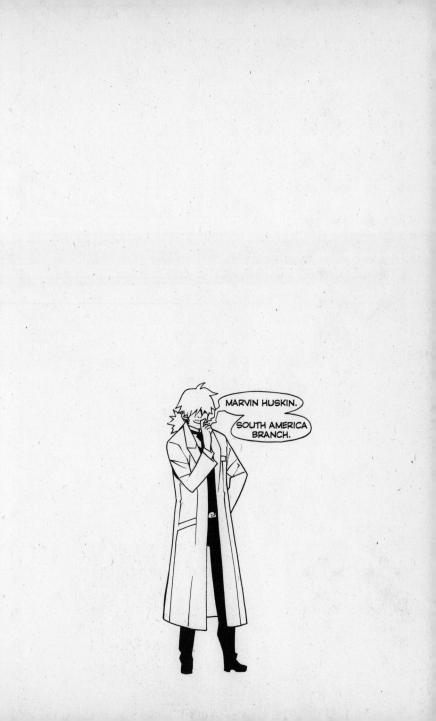

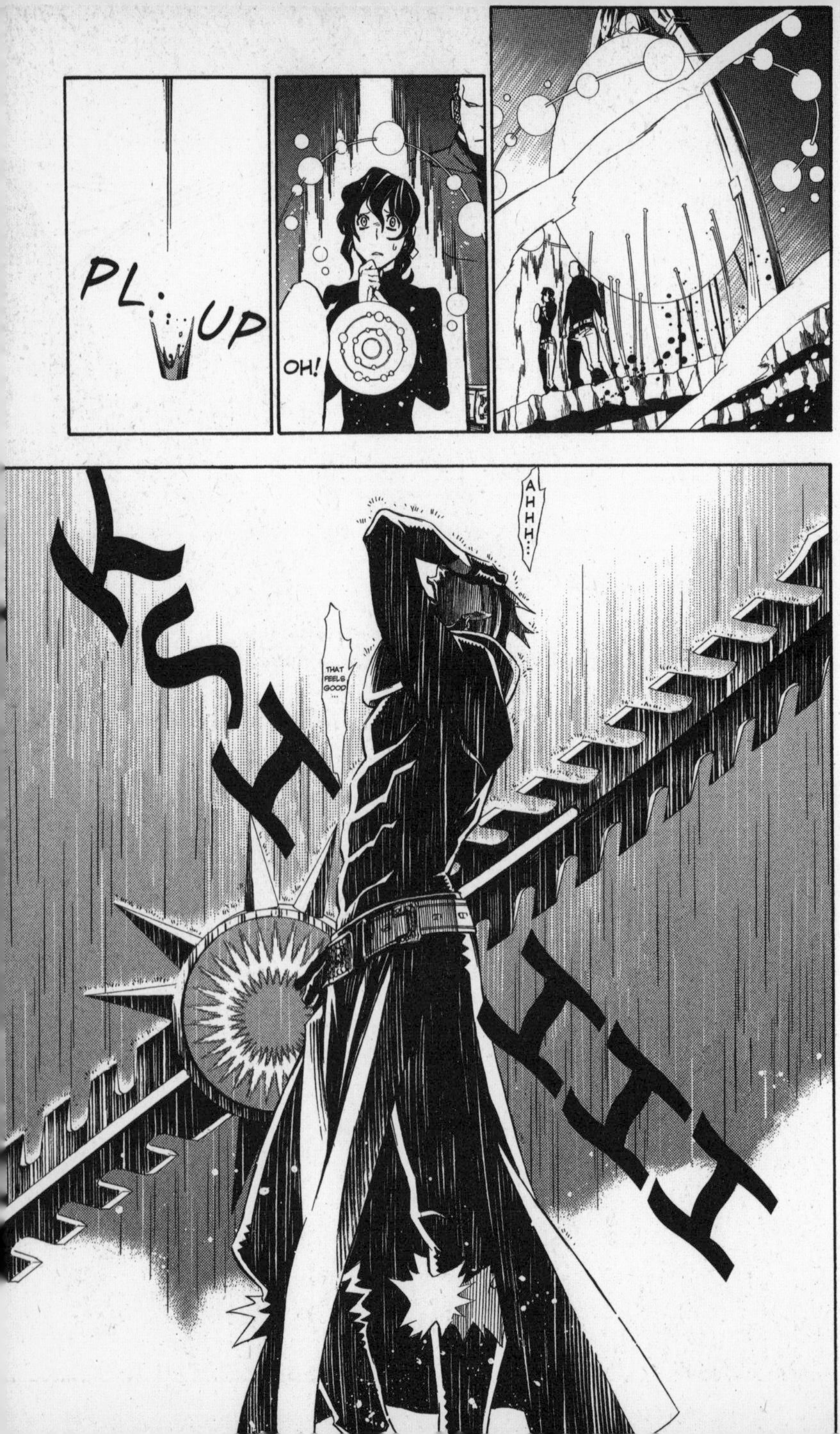
OH!
PL...UP
AHHH...
THAT FEELS GOOD...
KSHHHH

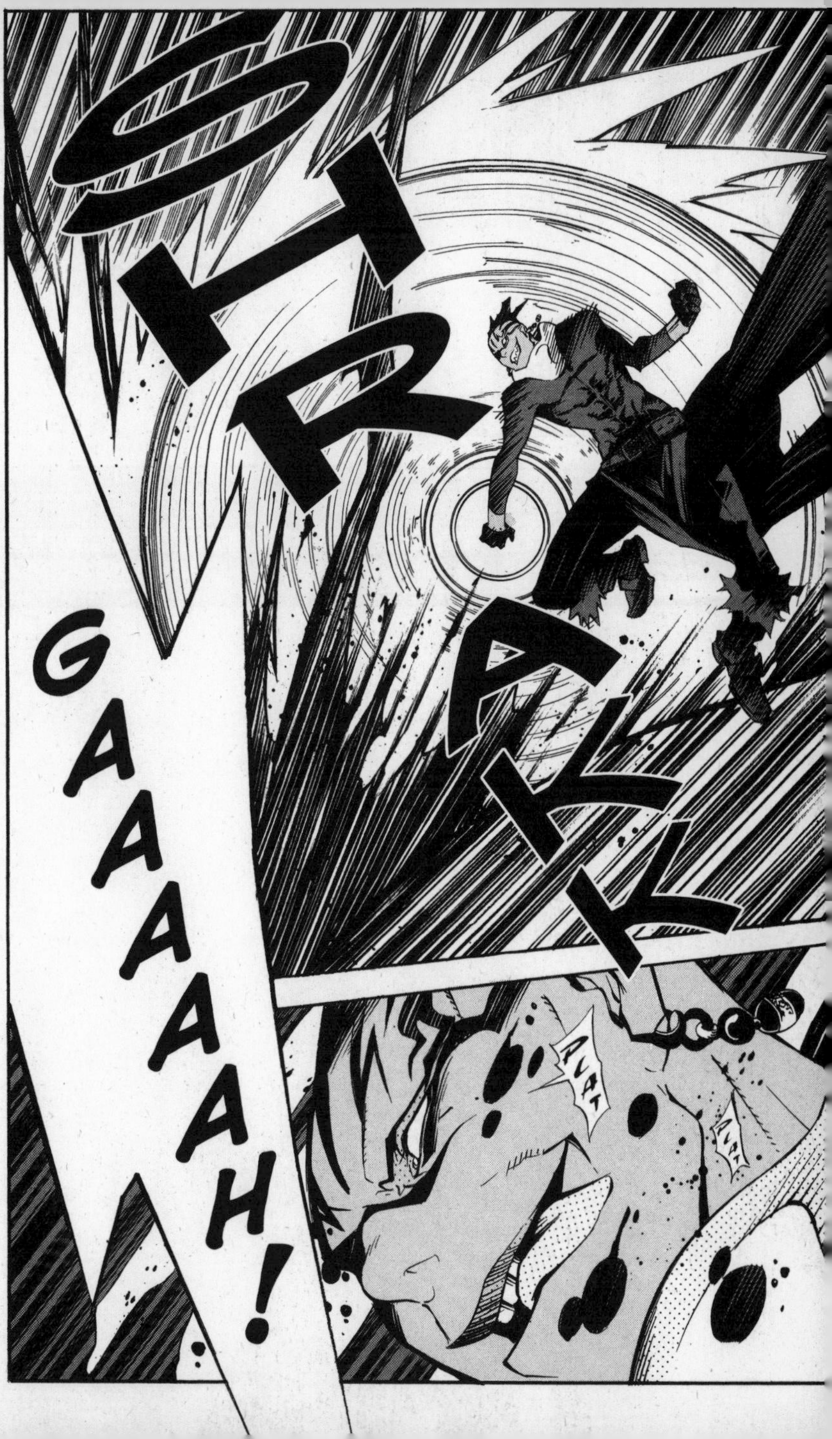
SHRAKK
GAAAAAH!

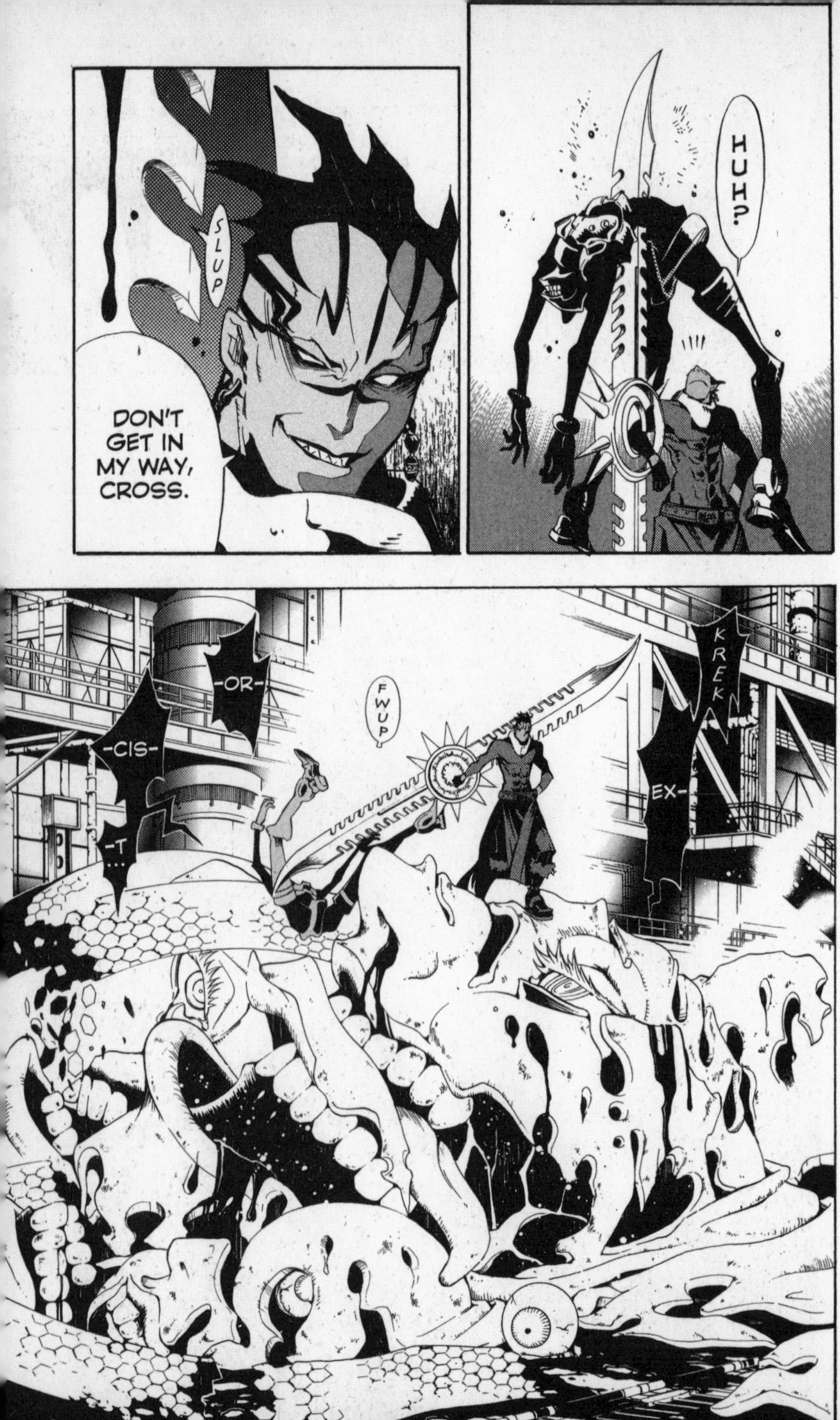
HUH?
SLUP
DON'T GET IN MY WAY, CROSS.
KREK
EX-
FWUP
-OR-
-CIS-
-T...

THE 143RD NIGHT: LINE OF SIGHT

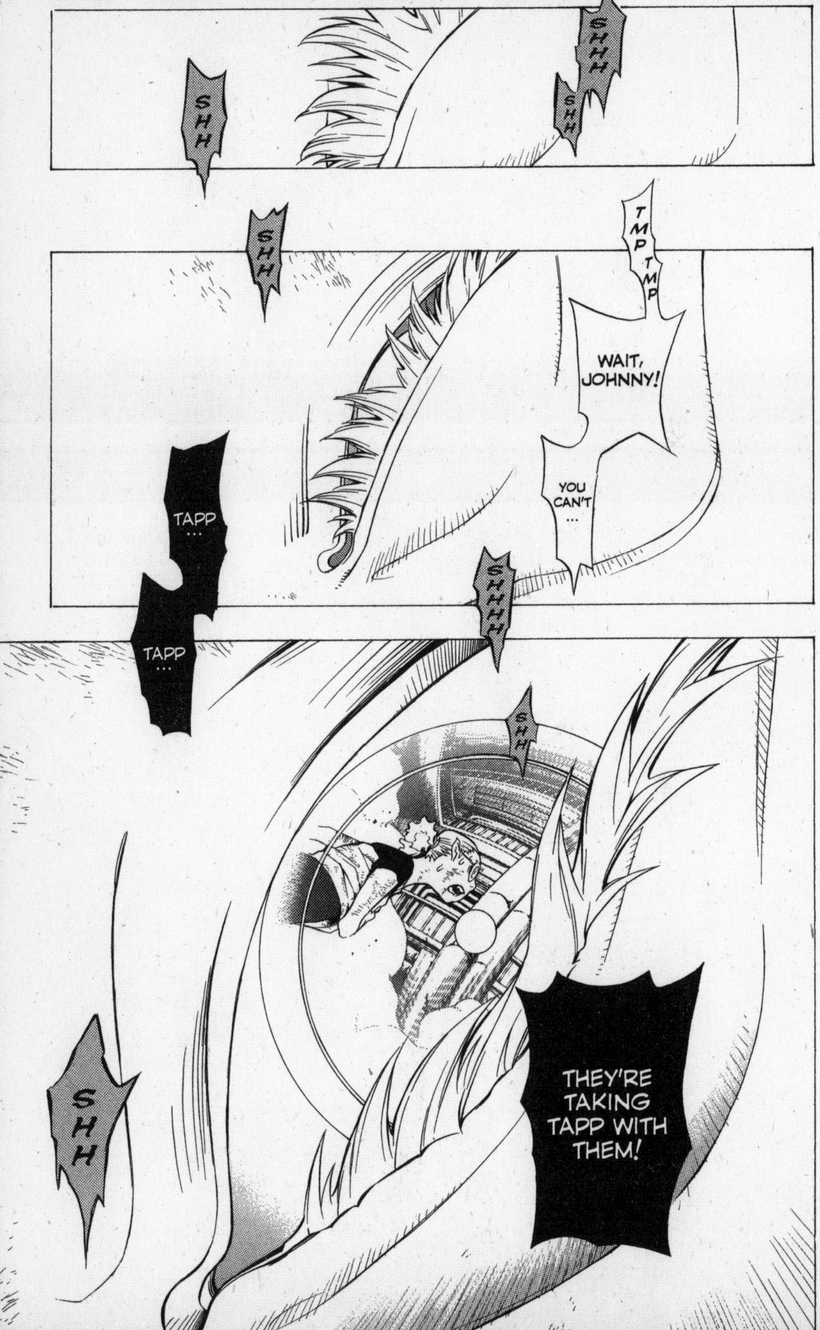
SHHH
SHH
SHH
SHH
TMP TMP
WAIT, JOHNNY!
YOU CAN'T ...
TAPP ...
TAPP ...
SHHHH
SHH
THEY'RE TAKING TAPP WITH THEM!
SHH

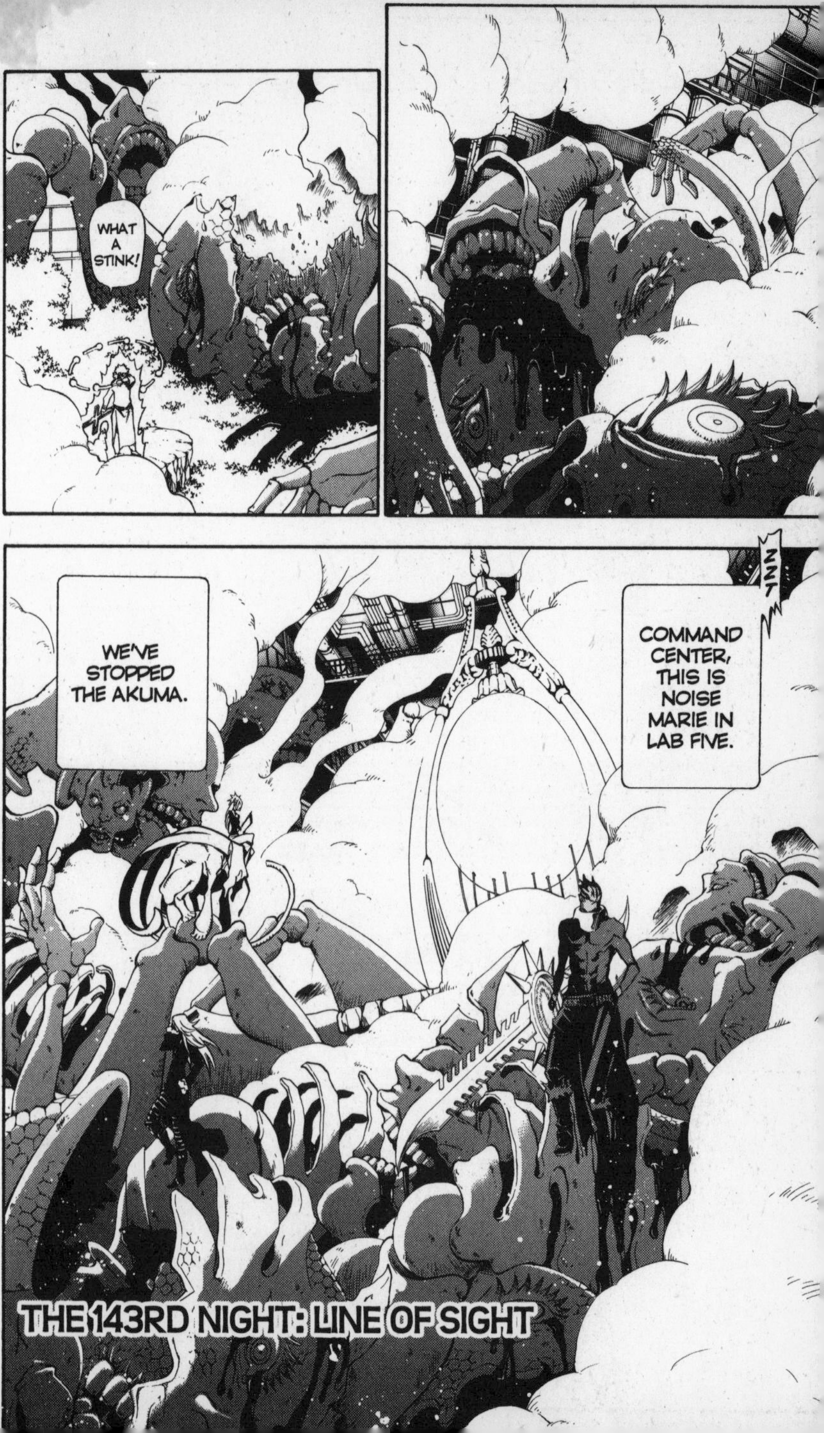
WHAT A STINK!
ZZT
COMMAND CENTER, THIS IS NOISE MARIE IN LAB FIVE.
WE'VE STOPPED THE AKUMA.
THE 143RD NIGHT: LINE OF SIGHT

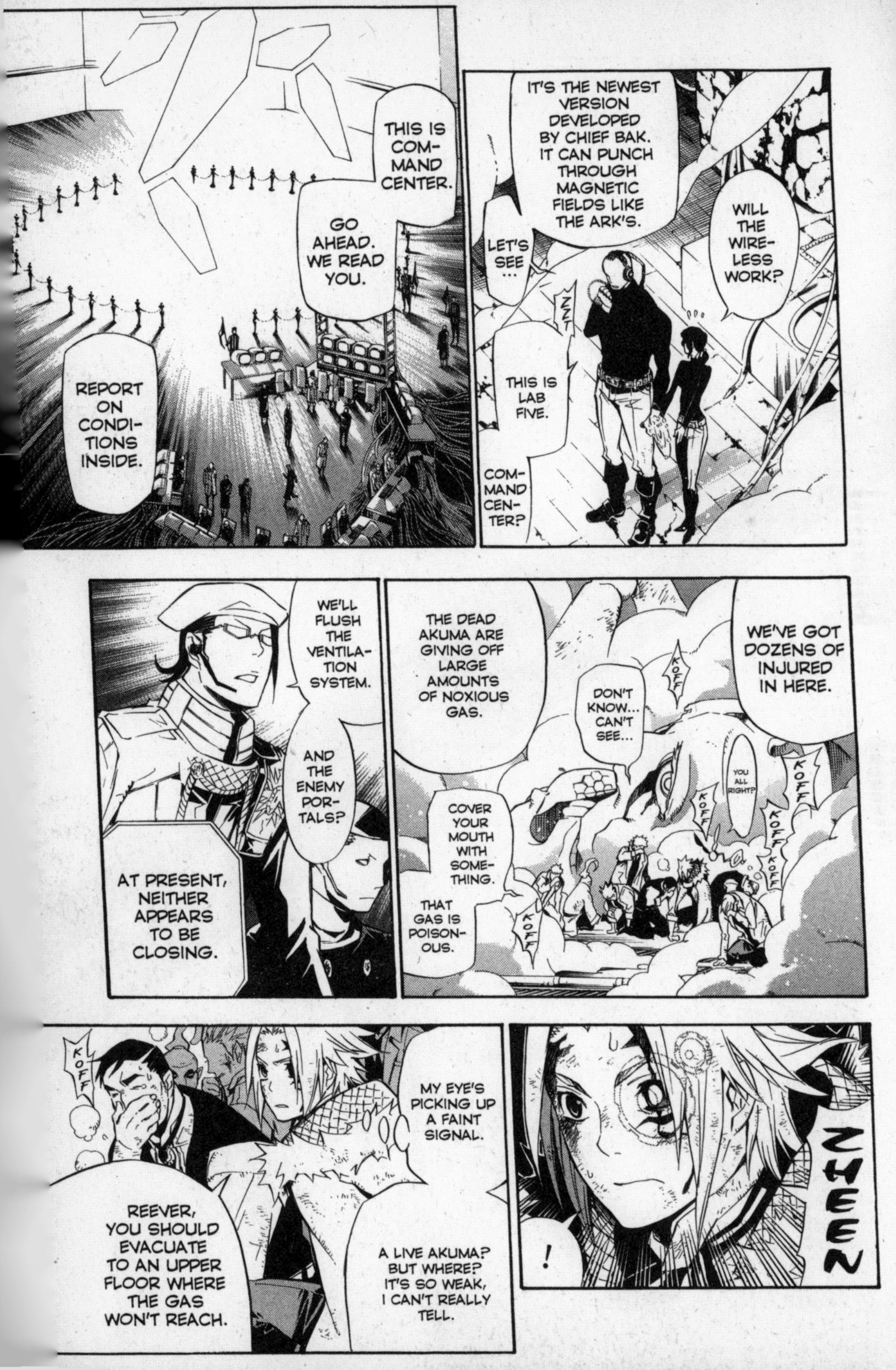
WILL THE WIRELESS WORK?
IT'S THE NEWEST VERSION DEVELOPED BY CHIEF BAK. IT CAN PUNCH THROUGH MAGNETIC FIELDS LIKE THE ARK'S.
LET'S SEE...
ZZT
THIS IS LAB FIVE.
COMMAND CENTER?
THIS IS COMMAND CENTER.
GO AHEAD. WE READ YOU.
REPORT ON CONDITIONS INSIDE.
WE'VE GOT DOZENS OF INJURED IN HERE.
KOFF
DON'T KNOW... CAN'T SEE...
THE DEAD AKUMA ARE GIVING OFF LARGE AMOUNTS OF NOXIOUS GAS.
KOFF
KOFF
YOU ALL RIGHT?
KOFF
KOFF
COVER YOUR MOUTH WITH SOMETHING.
THAT GAS IS POISONOUS.
KOFF
WE'LL FLUSH THE VENTILATION SYSTEM.
AND THE ENEMY PORTALS?
AT PRESENT, NEITHER APPEARS TO BE CLOSING.
ZHEEN
!
MY EYE'S PICKING UP A FAINT SIGNAL.
KOFF
A LIVE AKUMA? BUT WHERE? IT'S SO WEAK, I CAN'T REALLY TELL.
REEVER, YOU SHOULD EVACUATE TO AN UPPER FLOOR WHERE THE GAS WON'T REACH.

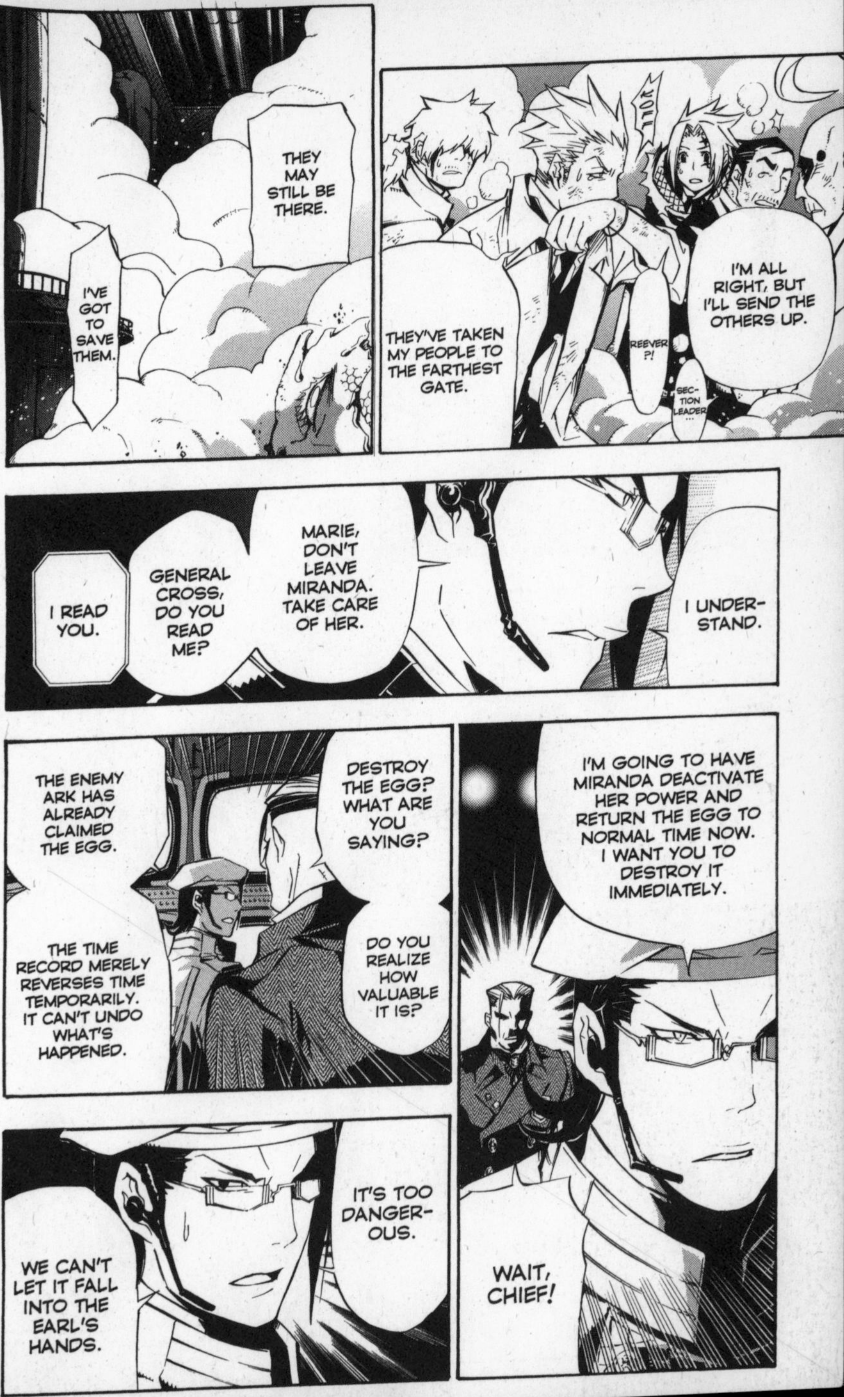
KOFF!
I'M ALL RIGHT, BUT I'LL SEND THE OTHERS UP.
REEVER ?!
SECTION LEADER ...
THEY'VE TAKEN MY PEOPLE TO THE FARTHEST GATE.
THEY MAY STILL BE THERE.
I'VE GOT TO SAVE THEM.
I UNDERSTAND.
MARIE, DON'T LEAVE MIRANDA. TAKE CARE OF HER.
GENERAL CROSS, DO YOU READ ME?
I READ YOU.
I'M GOING TO HAVE MIRANDA DEACTIVATE HER POWER AND RETURN THE EGG TO NORMAL TIME NOW. I WANT YOU TO DESTROY IT IMMEDIATELY.
WAIT, CHIEF!
DESTROY THE EGG? WHAT ARE YOU SAYING?
DO YOU REALIZE HOW VALUABLE IT IS?
THE ENEMY ARK HAS ALREADY CLAIMED THE EGG.
THE TIME RECORD MERELY REVERSES TIME TEMPORARILY. IT CAN'T UNDO WHAT'S HAPPENED.
IT'S TOO DANGEROUS.
WE CAN'T LET IT FALL INTO THE EARL'S HANDS.

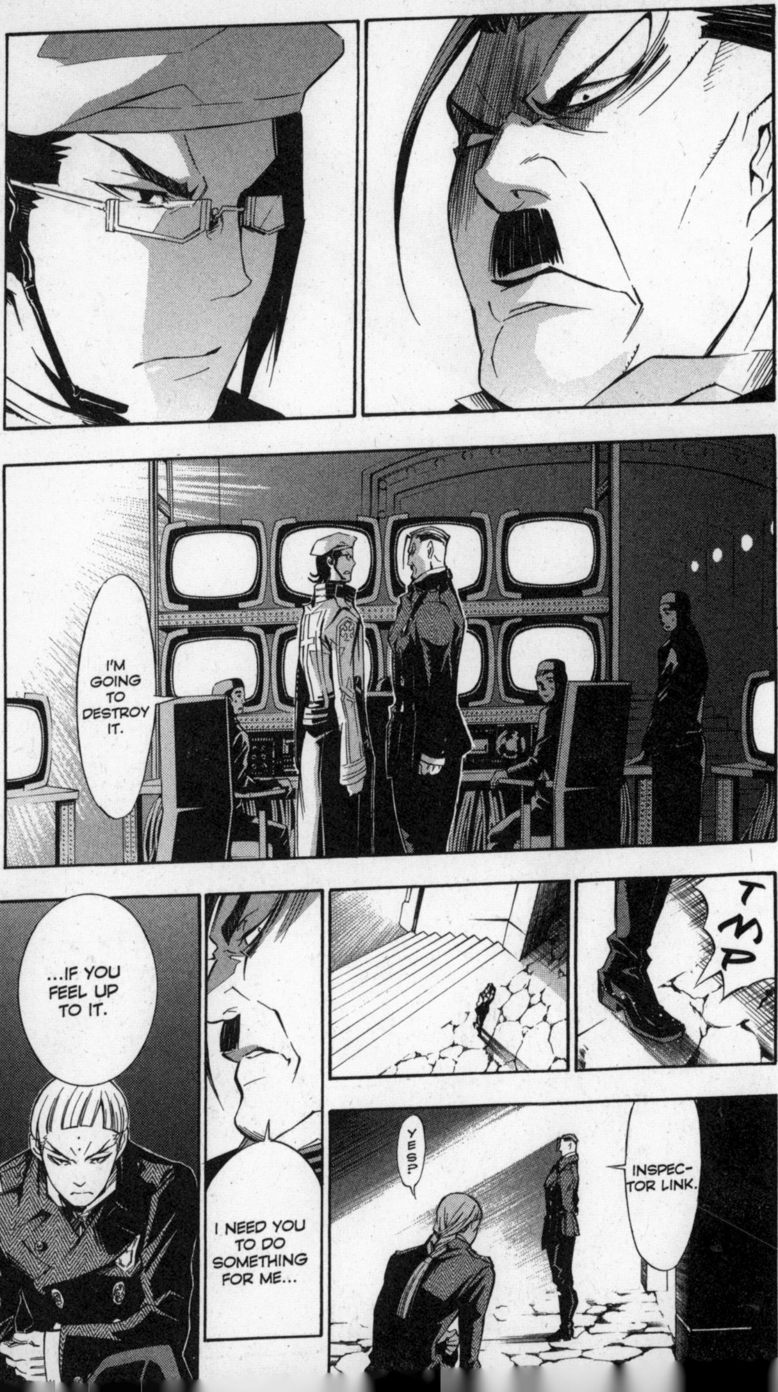
I'M GOING TO DESTROY IT.
TMP
INSPECTOR LINK.
YES?
I NEED YOU TO DO SOMETHING FOR ME...
...IF YOU FEEL UP TO IT.

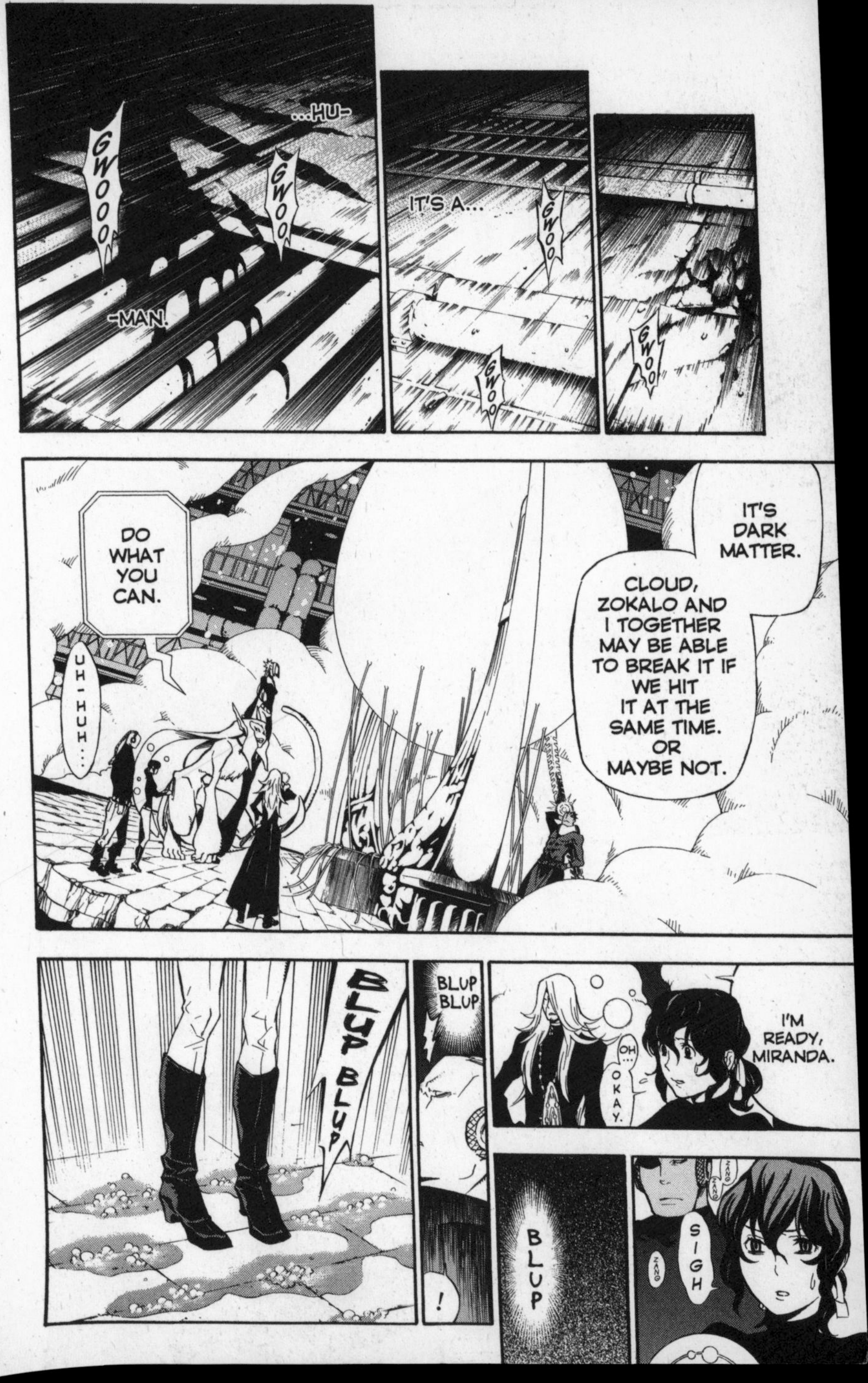
GWOO
GWOO
IT'S A...
GWOO
GWOO
...HU-
GWOOO
GWOO
-MAN.
IT'S DARK MATTER.
CLOUD, ZOKALO AND I TOGETHER MAY BE ABLE TO BREAK IT IF WE HIT IT AT THE SAME TIME. OR MAYBE NOT.
DO WHAT YOU CAN.
UH-HUH...
I'M READY, MIRANDA.
OH... OKAY.
BLUP BLUP
ZANG
ZANG
SIGH
BLUP
!
BLUP BLUP BLUP

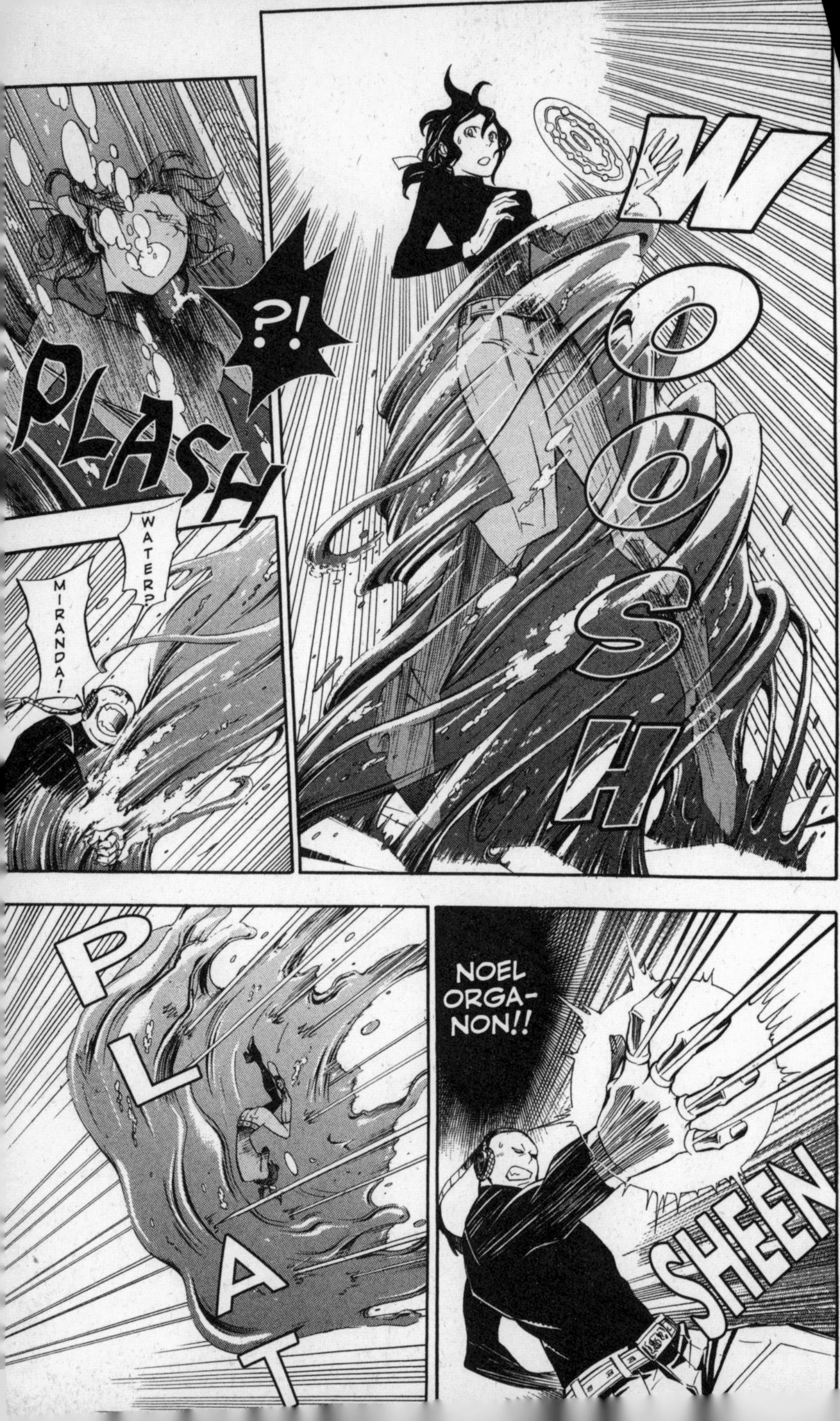
WOOOSH
?!
PLASH
WATER?
MIRANDA!
NOEL ORGA-NON!!
SHEEN
PLAT

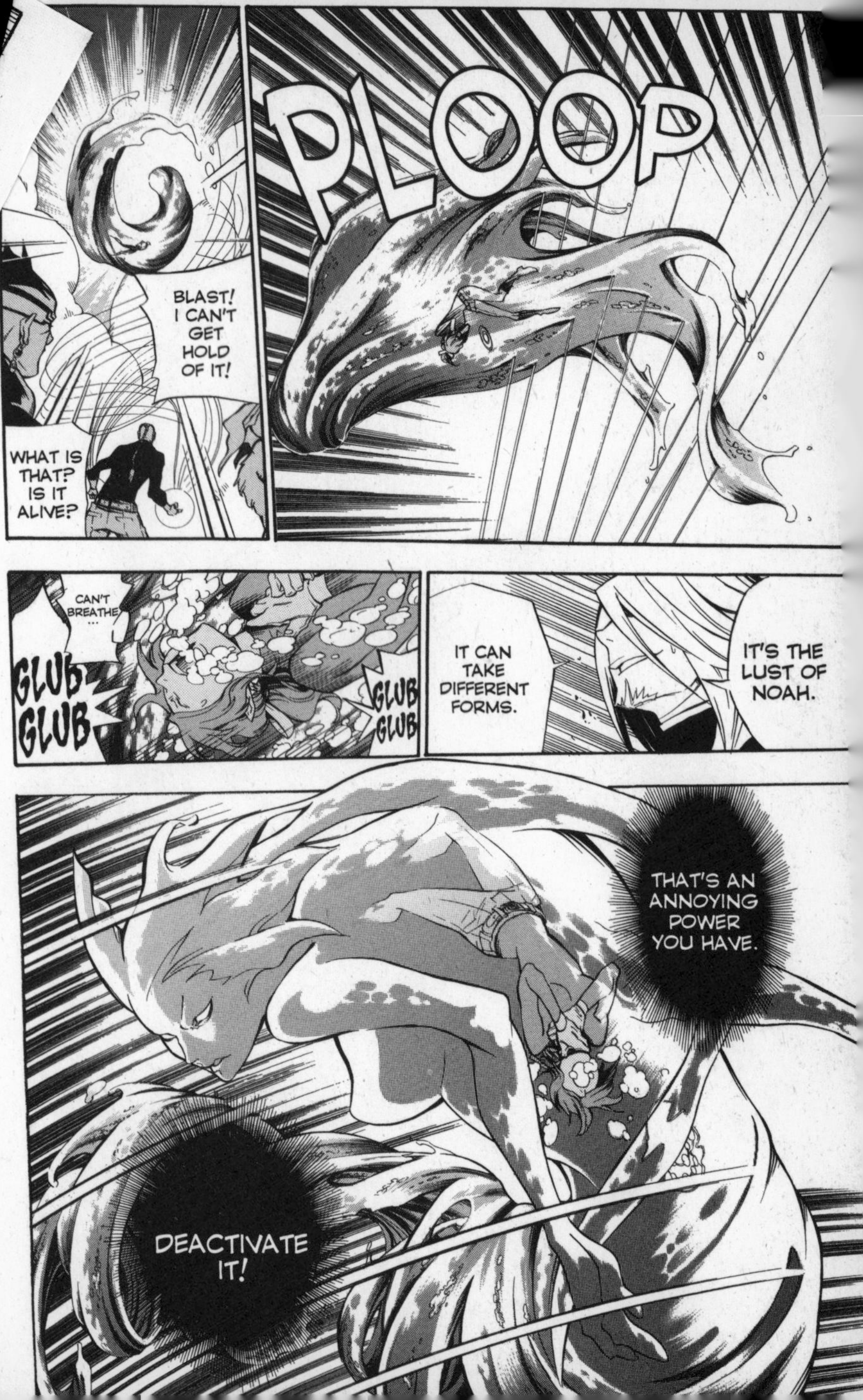
PLOOP
BLAST! I CAN'T GET HOLD OF IT!
WHAT IS THAT? IS IT ALIVE?
IT'S THE LUST OF NOAH.
IT CAN TAKE DIFFERENT FORMS.
CAN'T BREATHE...
GLUB GLUB
GLUB GLUB
THAT'S AN ANNOYING POWER YOU HAVE.
DEACTIVATE IT!

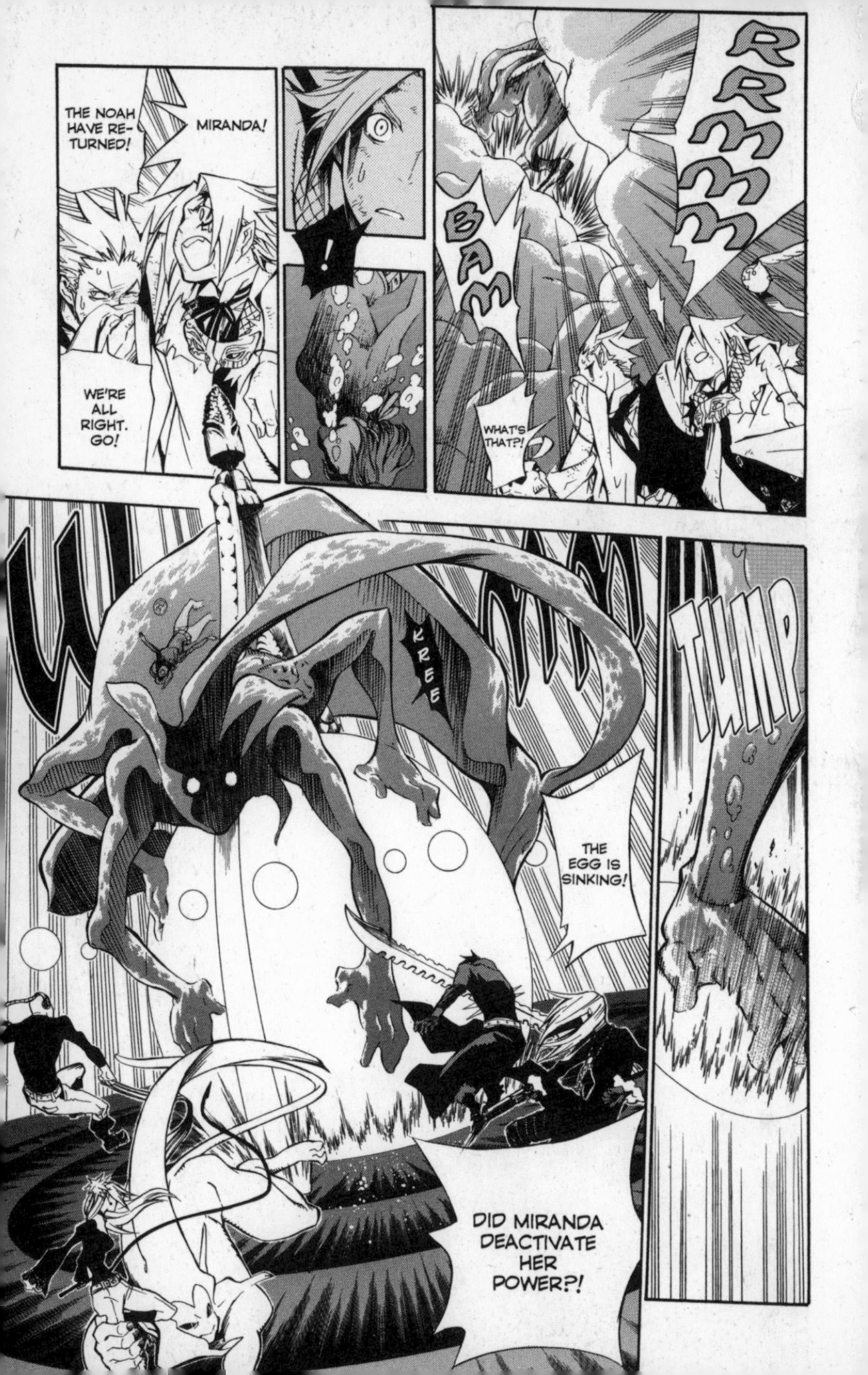
RRMMMM
BAM
WHAT'S THAT?!
!
MIRANDA!
THE NOAH HAVE RE-TURNED!
WE'RE ALL RIGHT. GO!
THUMP
KREE
THE EGG IS SINKING!
DID MIRANDA DEACTIVATE HER POWER?!

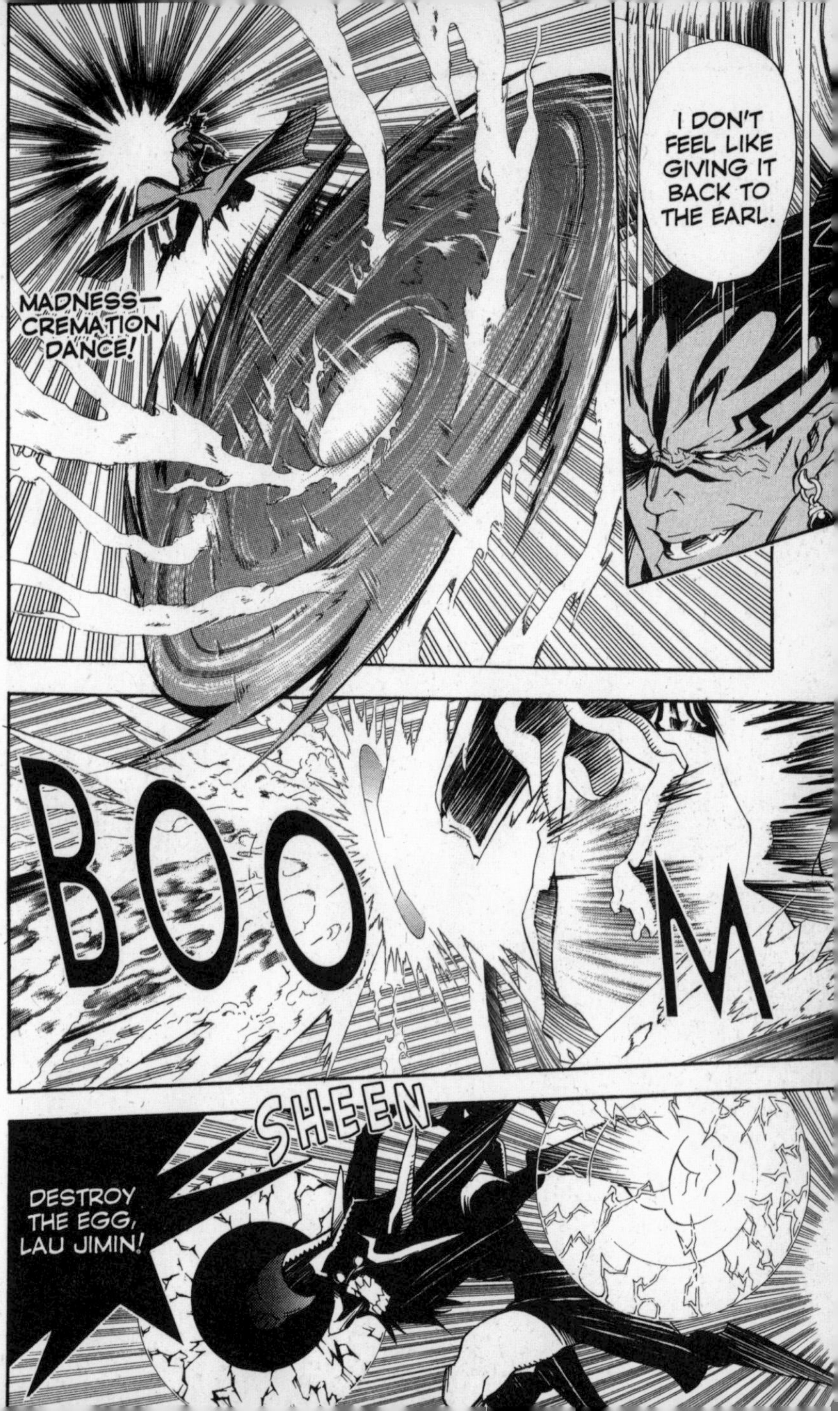
I DON'T FEEL LIKE GIVING IT BACK TO THE EARL.
MADNESS— CREMATION DANCE!
BOOOM
SHEEN
DESTROY THE EGG, LAU JIMIN!

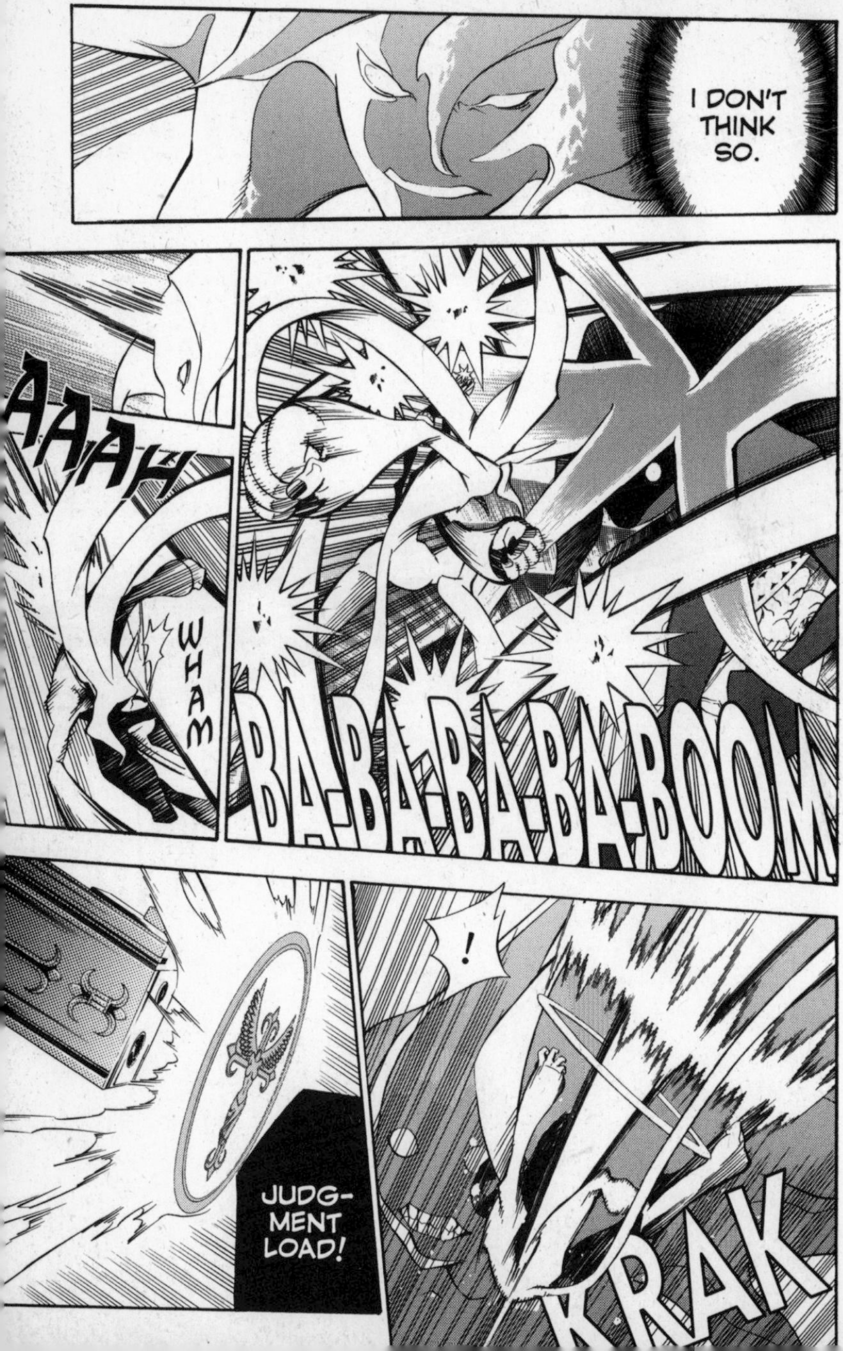
I DON'T THINK SO.
BA-BA-BA-BA-BOOM
AAAAH
WHAM
!
KRAK
JUDG-MENT LOAD!

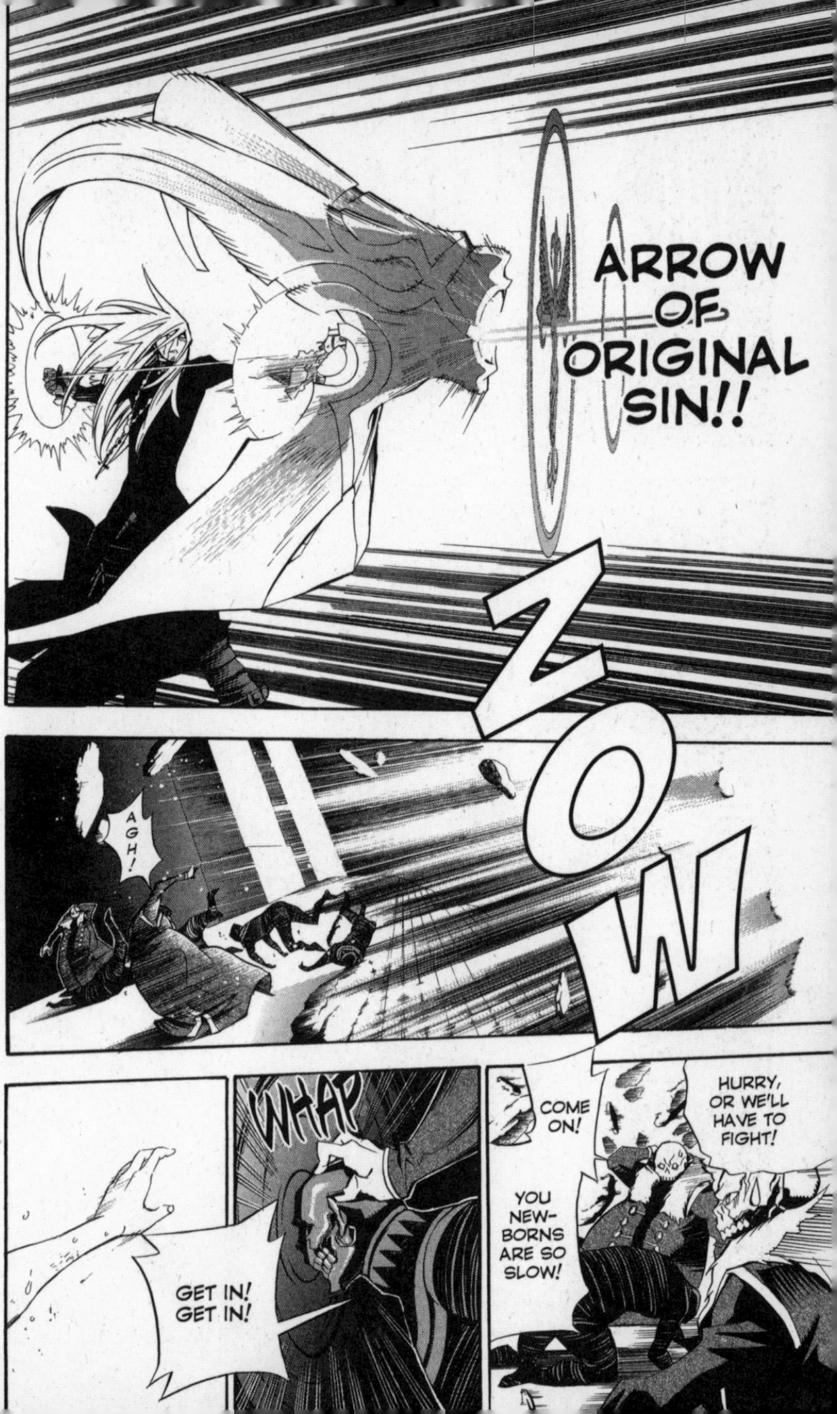
ARROW OF ORIGINAL SIN!!
ZOW
AGH!
HURRY, OR WE'LL HAVE TO FIGHT!
COME ON!
YOU NEW-BORNS ARE SO SLOW!
WHAP
GET IN! GET IN!

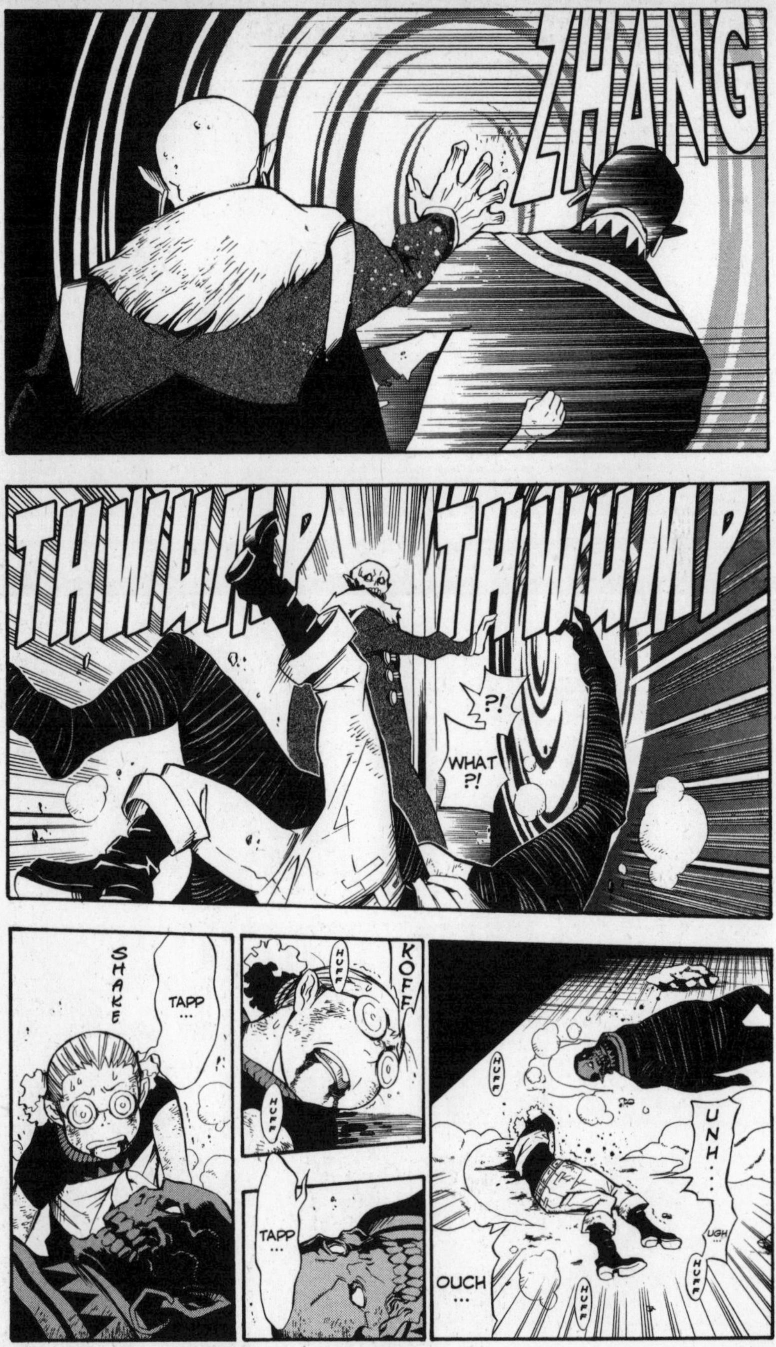
ZHANG
THWUMP
THWUMP
?!
WHAT ?!
UNH...
HUFF
UGH...
HUFF
HUFF
OUCH...
KOFF
HUFF
HUFF
TAPP...
SHAKE
TAPP...

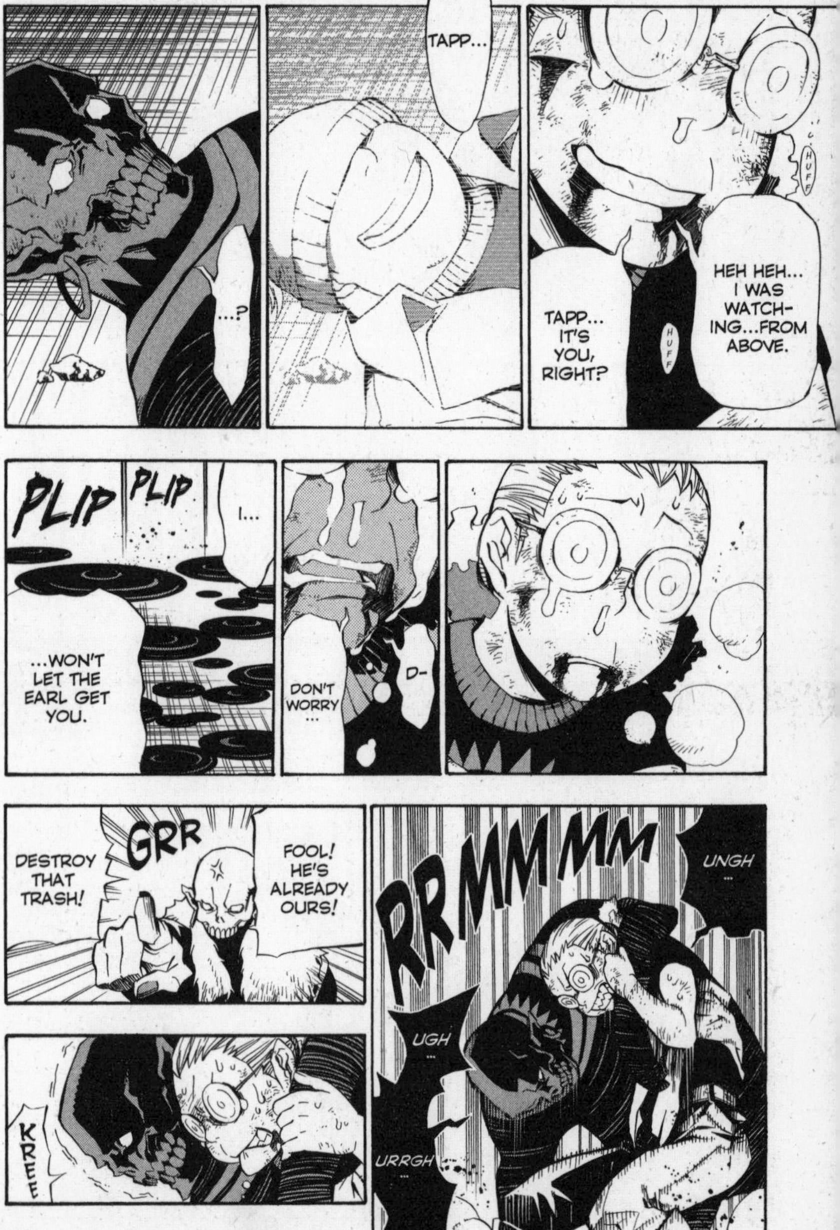
HUFF
HEH HEH... I WAS WATCHING...FROM ABOVE.
HUFF
TAPP... IT'S YOU, RIGHT?
TAPP...
...?
D-
DON'T WORRY...
I...
PLIP
PLIP
...WON'T LET THE EARL GET YOU.
RRMMMM
UNGH...
UGH...
URRGH...
FOOL! HE'S ALREADY OURS!
GRR
DESTROY THAT TRASH!
KREE

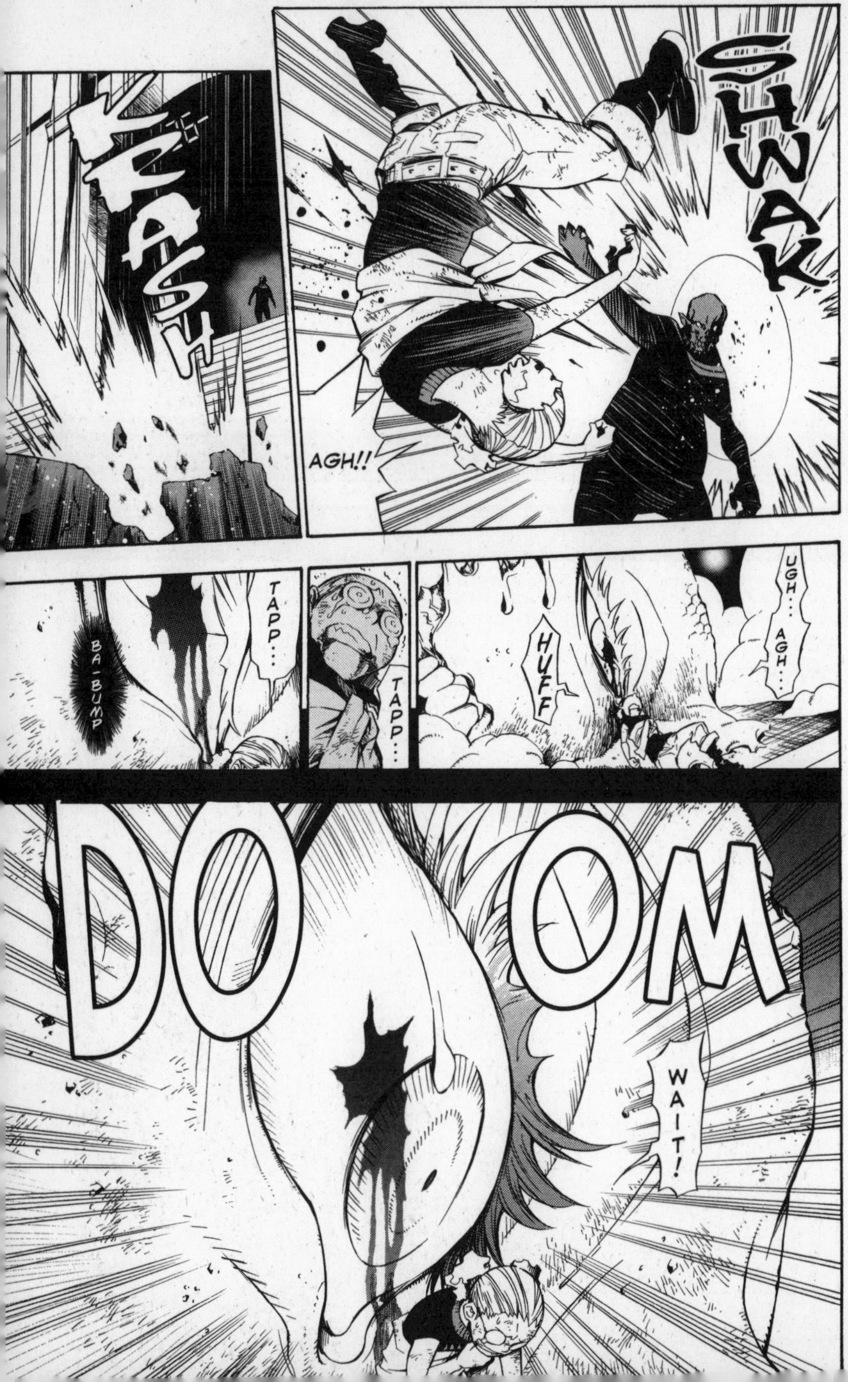
SHWAK
AGH!!
KRASH
UGH... AGH...
HUFF
TAPP... TAPP...
BA-BUMP
DOOM
WAIT!

SKULL.

HUMAN TRANSFORMED
BY MAGIC.
LIFESPAN: ABOUT 200
YEARS.
STRONG.
IMMUNE TO BULLETS.

WORK RESPONSIBILITIES:

* HELP CREATE AKUMA
* CLEAN ARKS
* MEND THE EARL'S
  CLOTHES
* ODD JOBS

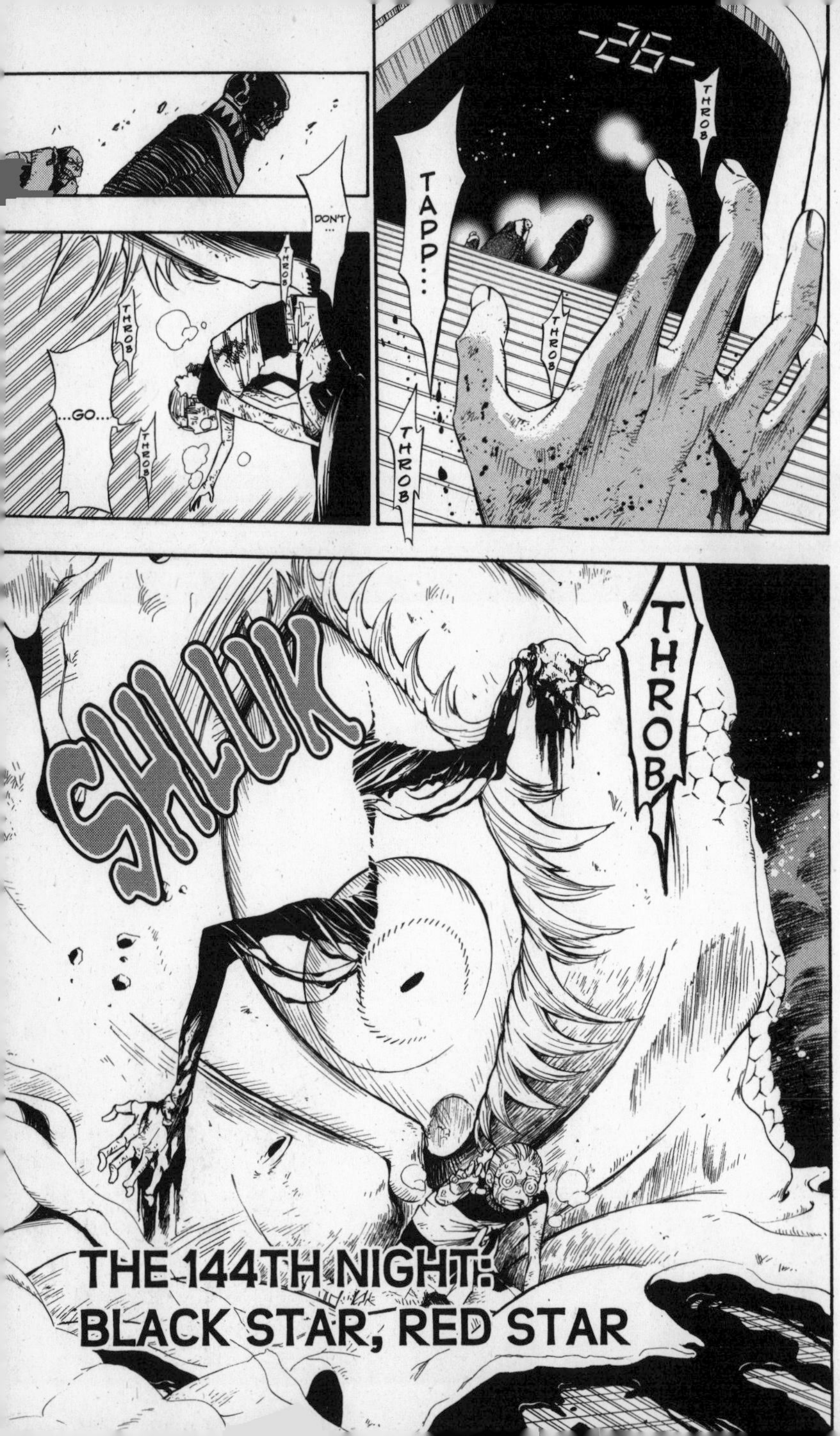
-26-
THROB
TAPP...
THROB
THROB
DON'T ...
THROB
THROB
...GO...
THROB
THROB
SHLUK
THE 144TH NIGHT: BLACK STAR, RED STAR

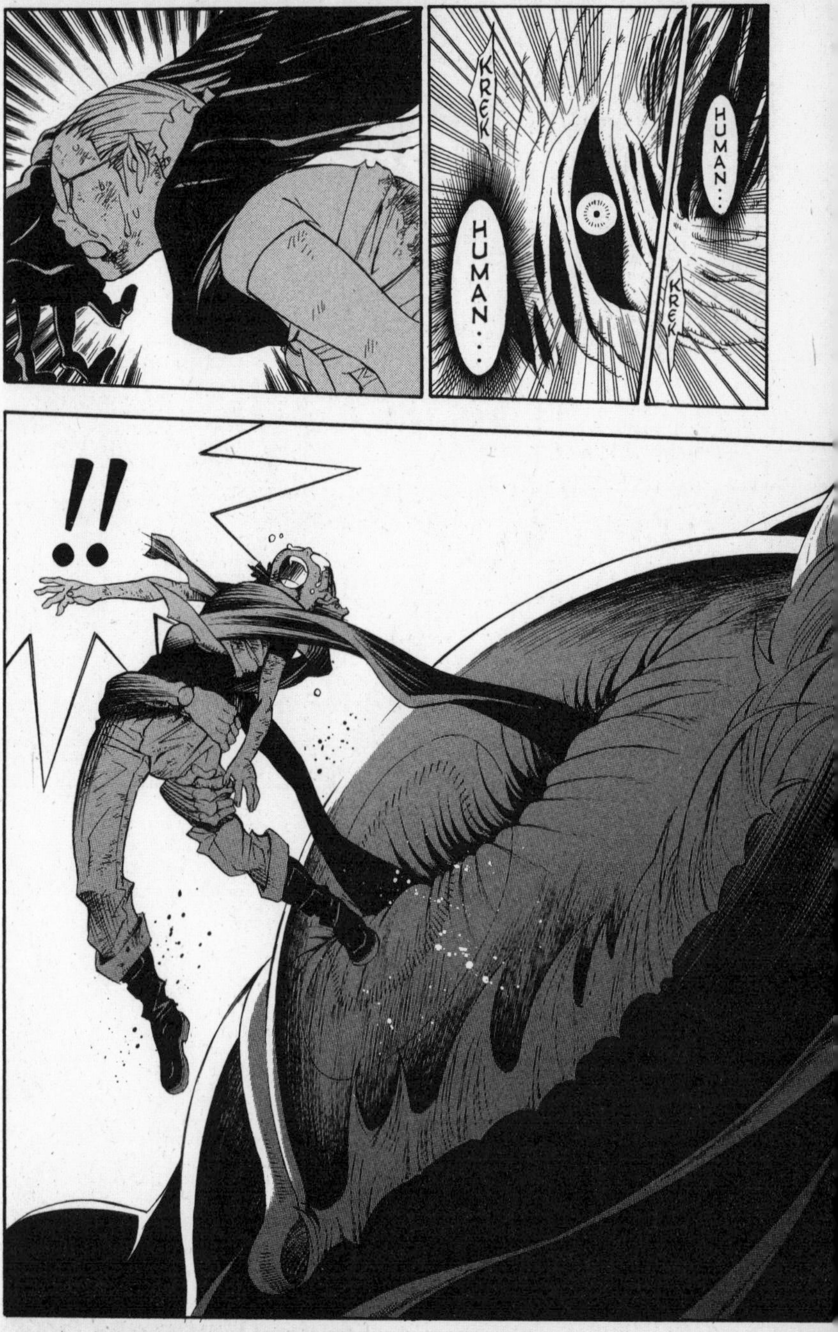
HUMAN...
KREK
KREK
HUMAN...
!!

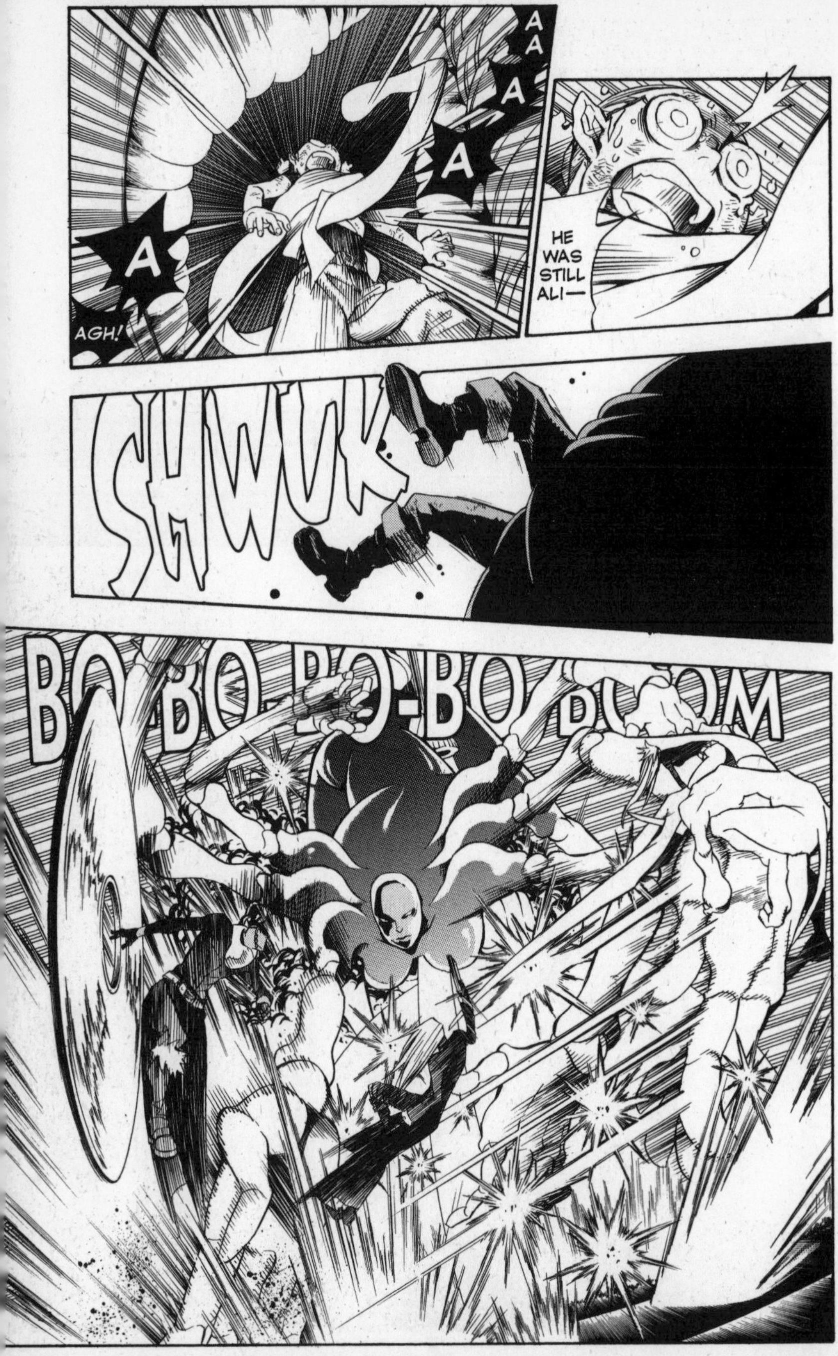
HE WAS STILL ALI—
AAAAA
AGH!
SHWUK
BO-BO-BO-BO-BOOM

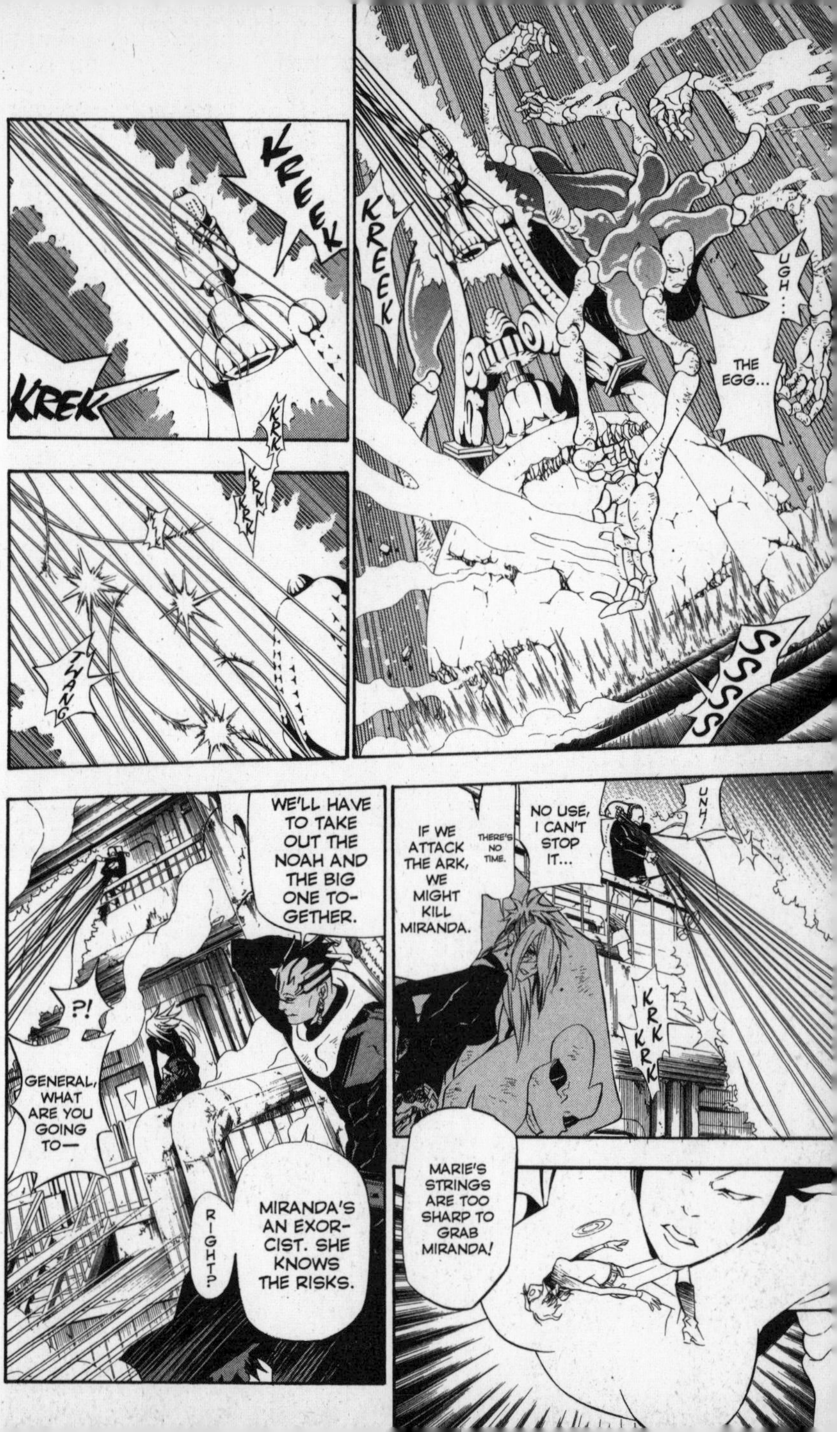
UGH...
THE EGG...
KREEK
SSSSS
KREEK
KREK
KRK
KRK KRK
TWANG
UNH!
NO USE, I CAN'T STOP IT...
THERE'S NO TIME.
IF WE ATTACK THE ARK, WE MIGHT KILL MIRANDA.
KRK KRK
MARIE'S STRINGS ARE TOO SHARP TO GRAB MIRANDA!
WE'LL HAVE TO TAKE OUT THE NOAH AND THE BIG ONE TO-GETHER.
?!
GENERAL, WHAT ARE YOU GOING TO—
MIRANDA'S AN EXOR-CIST. SHE KNOWS THE RISKS.
RIGHT?

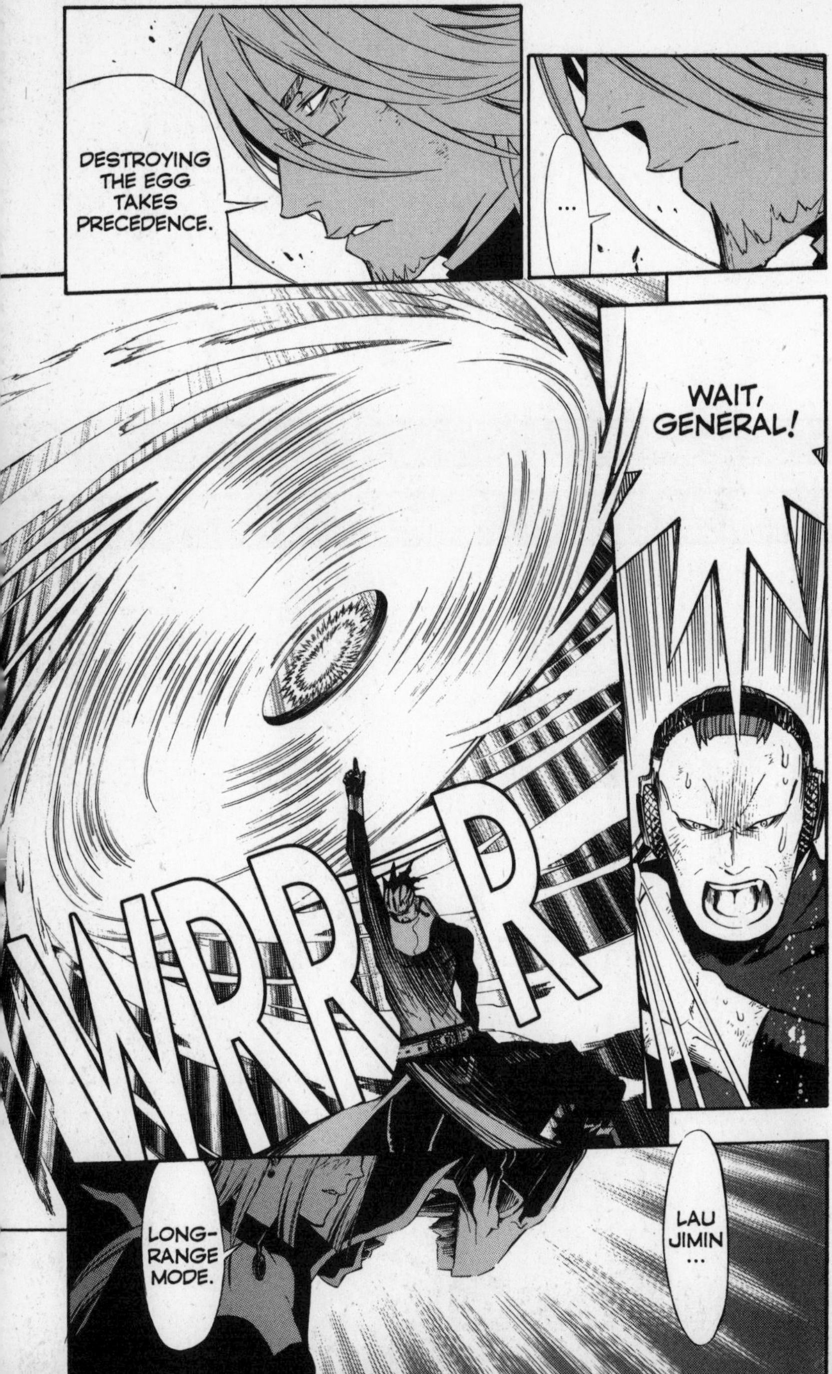
...
DESTROYING THE EGG TAKES PRECEDENCE.
WAIT, GENERAL!
WRRR
LAU JIMIN ...
LONG-RANGE MODE.

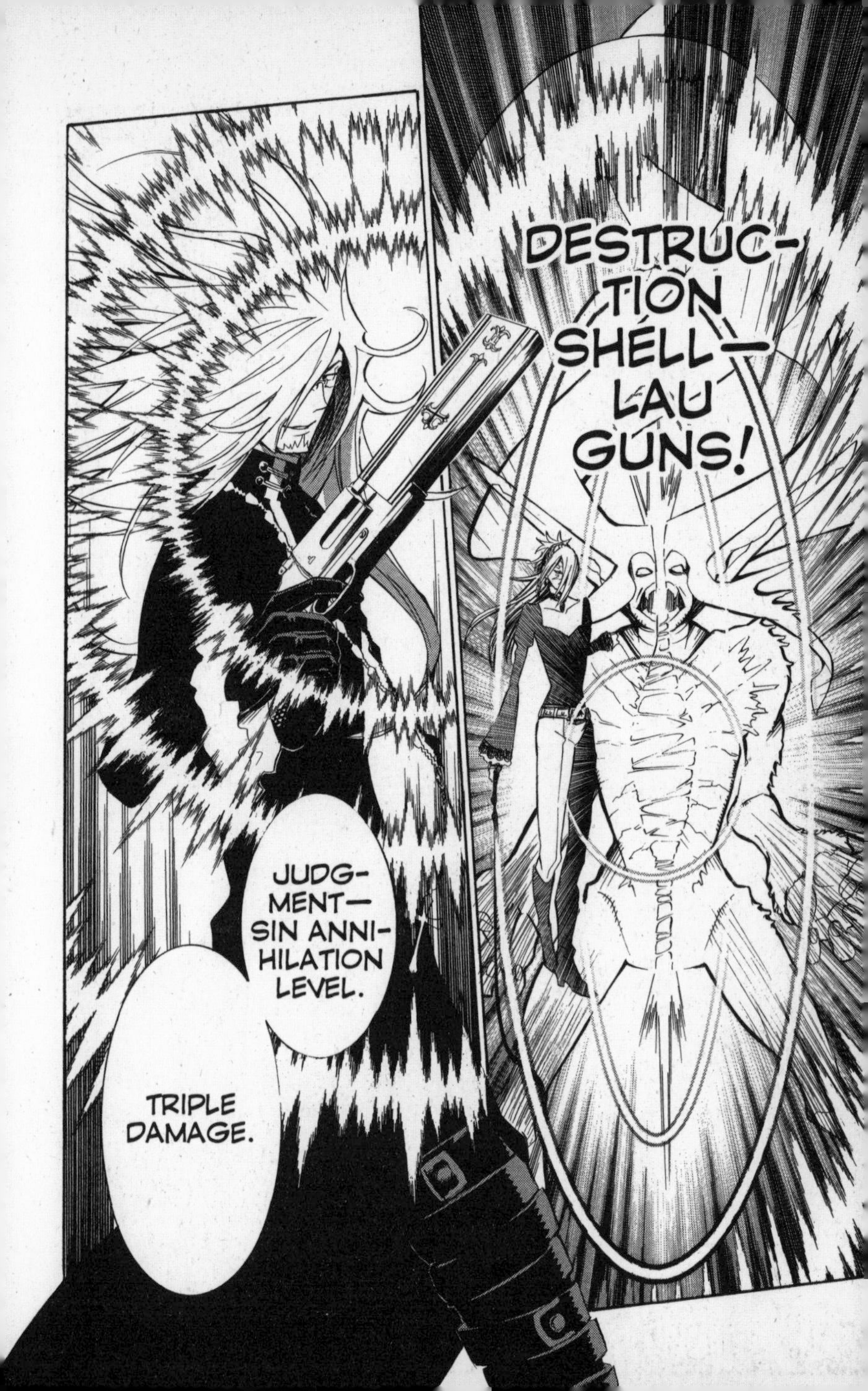
DESTRUCTION SHELL—LAU GUNS!
JUDGMENT—SIN ANNIHILATION LEVEL.
TRIPLE DAMAGE.

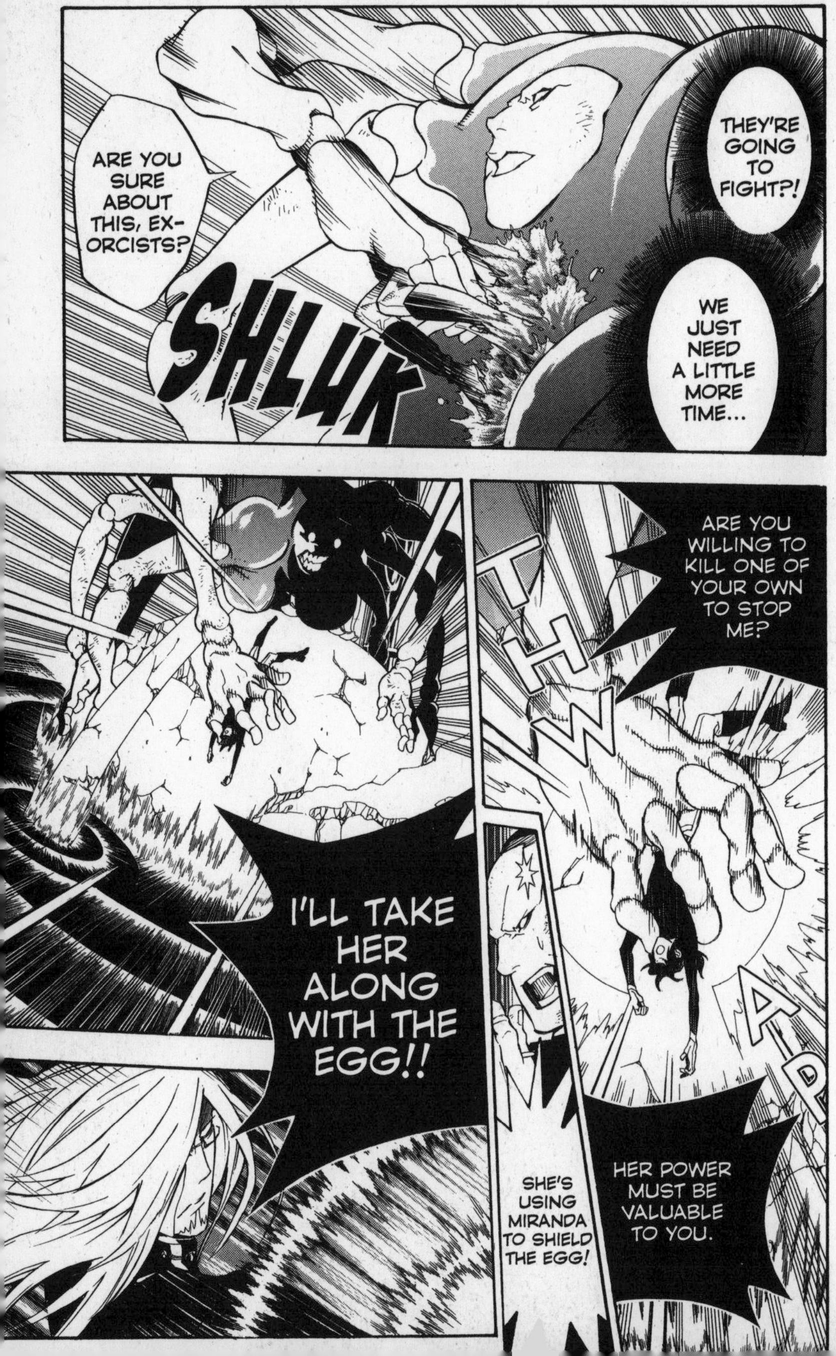
THEY'RE GOING TO FIGHT?!
WE JUST NEED A LITTLE MORE TIME...
ARE YOU SURE ABOUT THIS, EX-ORCISTS?
SHLUK
ARE YOU WILLING TO KILL ONE OF YOUR OWN TO STOP ME?
THWAP
HER POWER MUST BE VALUABLE TO YOU.
SHE'S USING MIRANDA TO SHIELD THE EGG!
I'LL TAKE HER ALONG WITH THE EGG!!

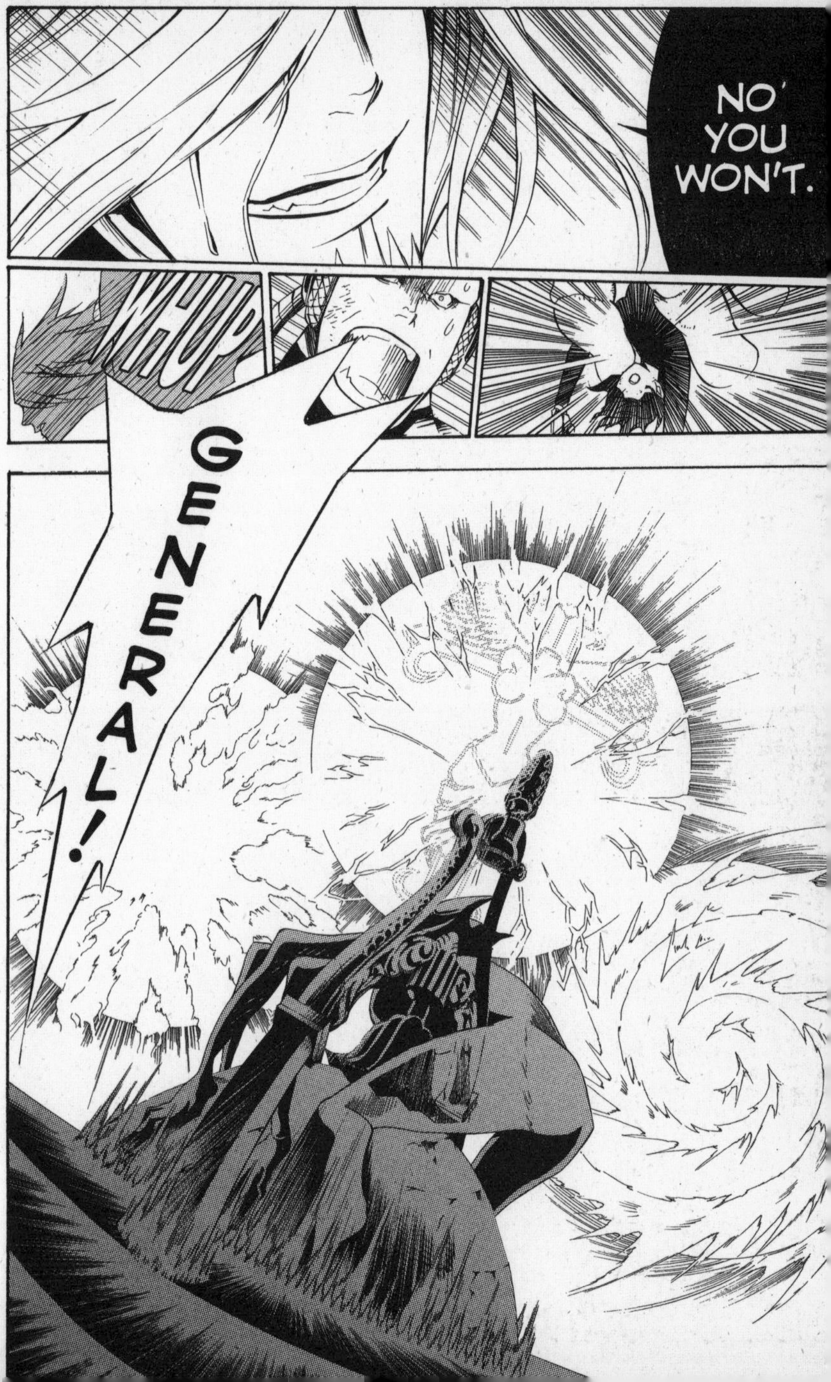
NO YOU WON'T.
WHUP
GENERAL!

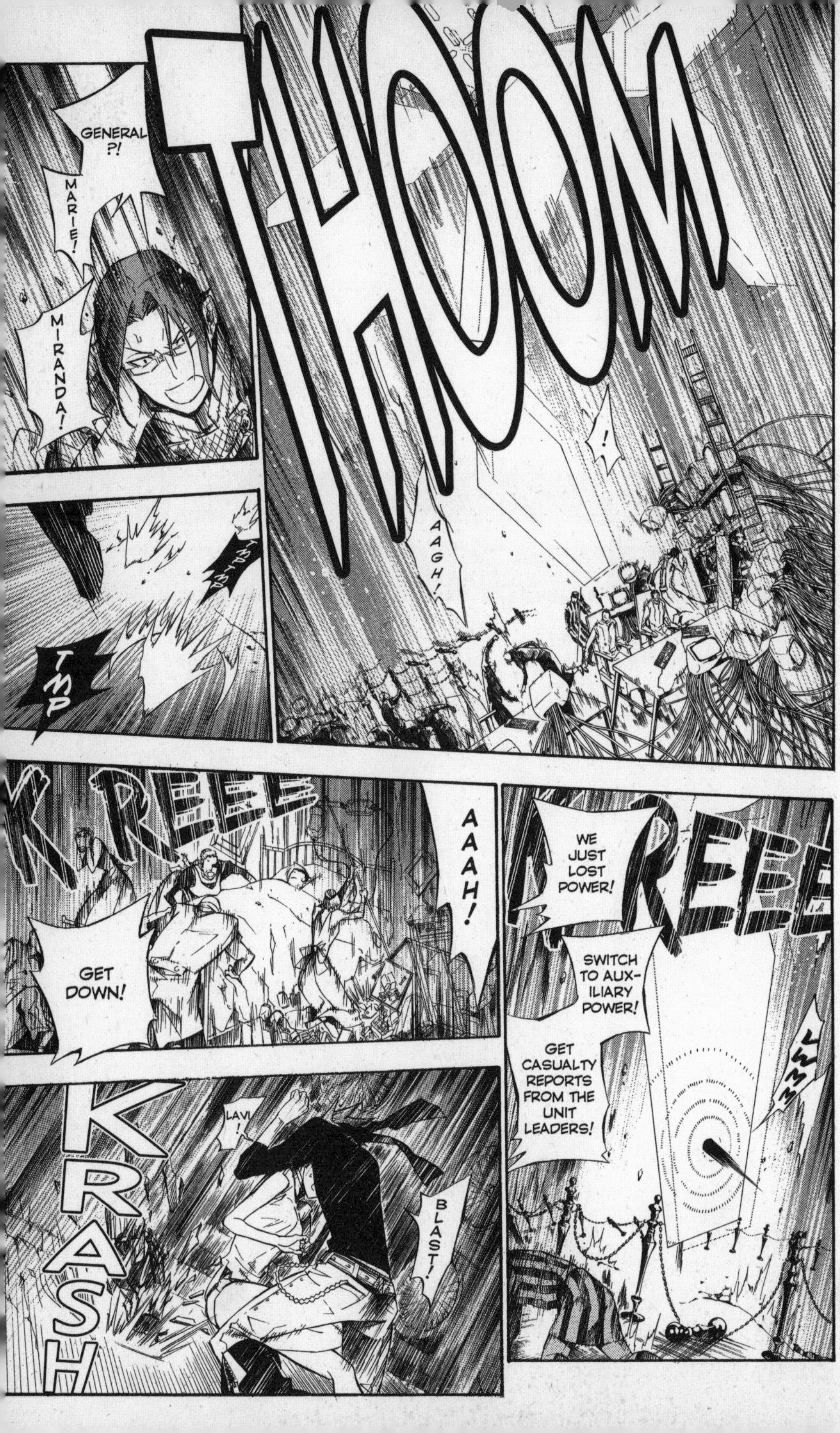
THOOM
!
AAGH!
GENERAL?!
MARIE!
MIRANDA!
TMPTMP
TMP
WE JUST LOST POWER!
REEE
SWITCH TO AUXILIARY POWER!
GET CASUALTY REPORTS FROM THE UNIT LEADERS!
VWMM
KREEE
AAAH!
GET DOWN!
KRASH
LAVI!
BLAST!

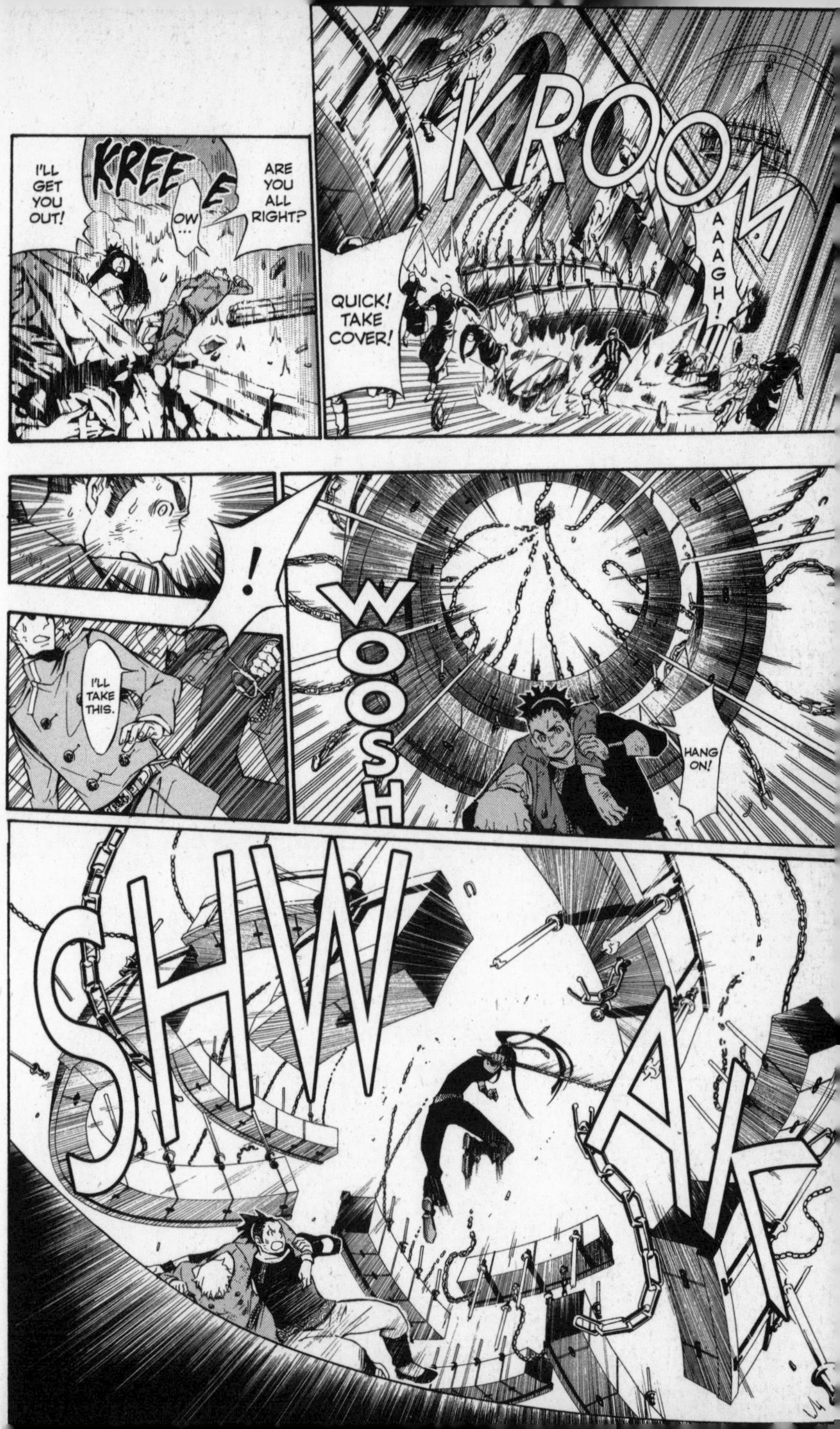
KROOM
AAAGH!
QUICK! TAKE COVER!
ARE YOU ALL RIGHT?
OW...
I'LL GET YOU OUT!
KREEE
WOOSH
HANG ON!
!
I'LL TAKE THIS.
SHWAK

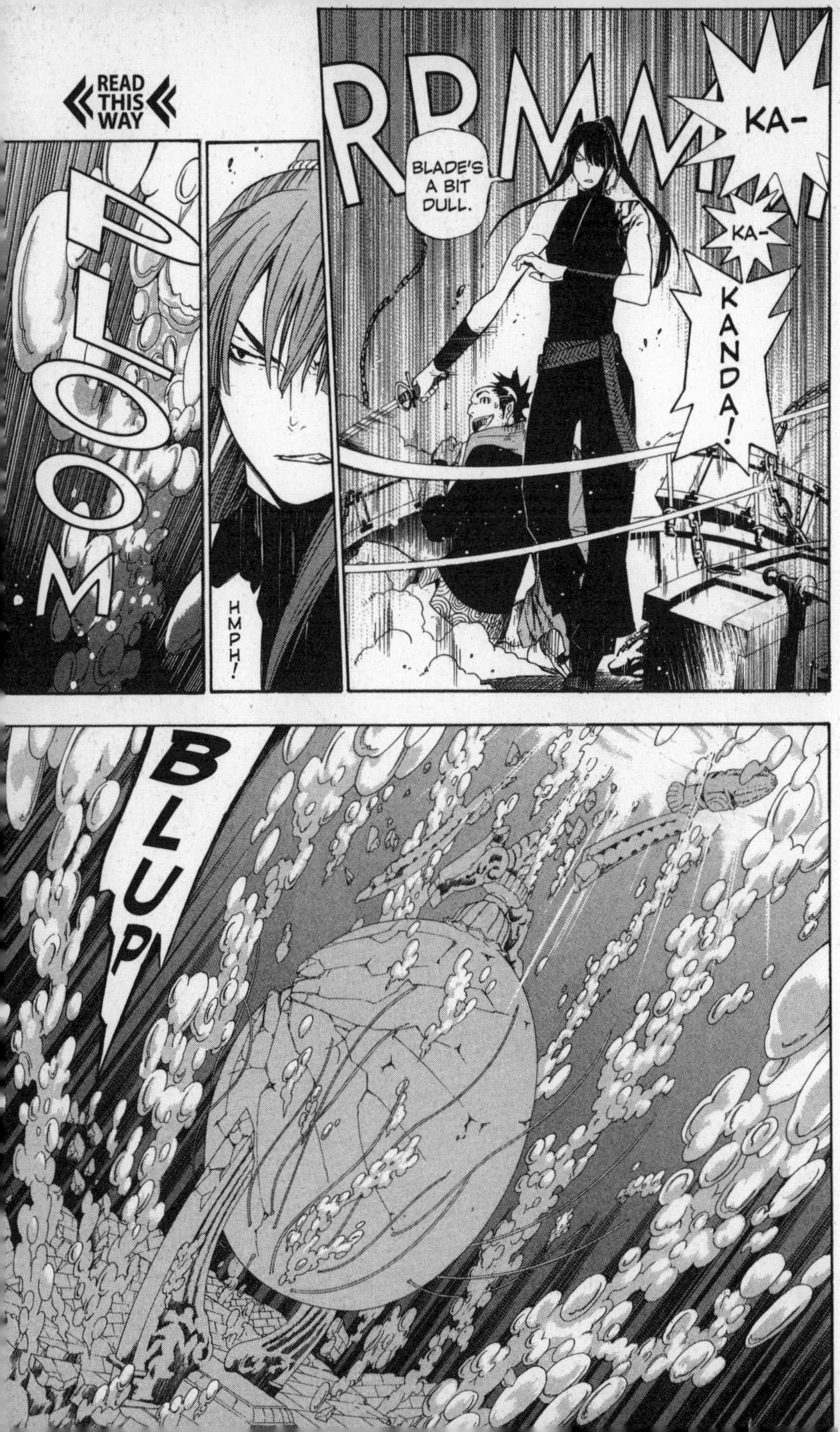

READ THIS WAY
KA-
KA-
KANDA!
RRMM
BLADE'S A BIT DULL.
HMPH!
FLOOM
BLUP

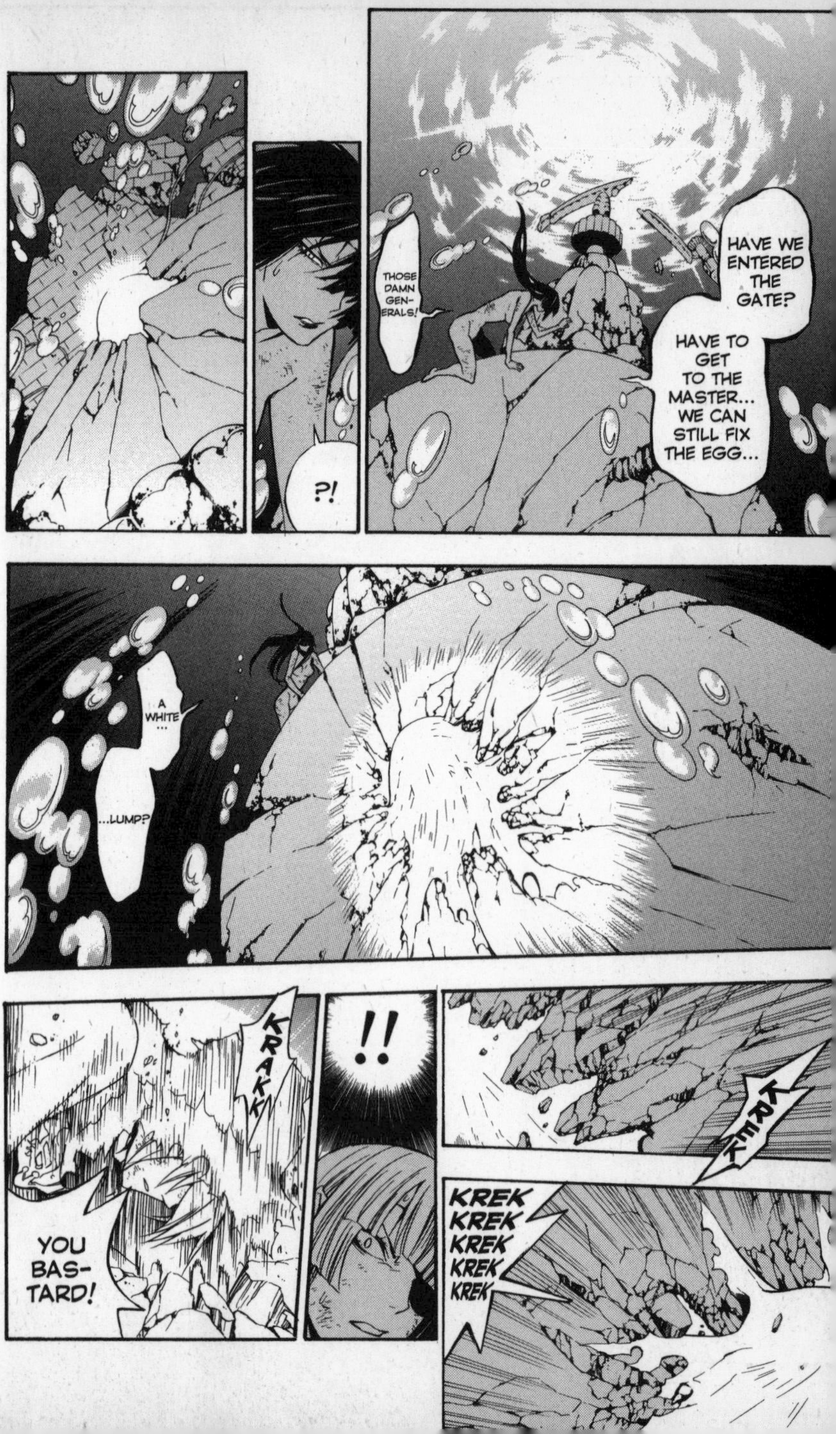

HAVE WE ENTERED THE GATE?
HAVE TO GET TO THE MASTER... WE CAN STILL FIX THE EGG...
THOSE DAMN GEN-ERALS!
?!
A WHITE...
...LUMP?
KREK
KREK KREK KREK KREK KREK
!!
KRAKK
YOU BAS-TARD!

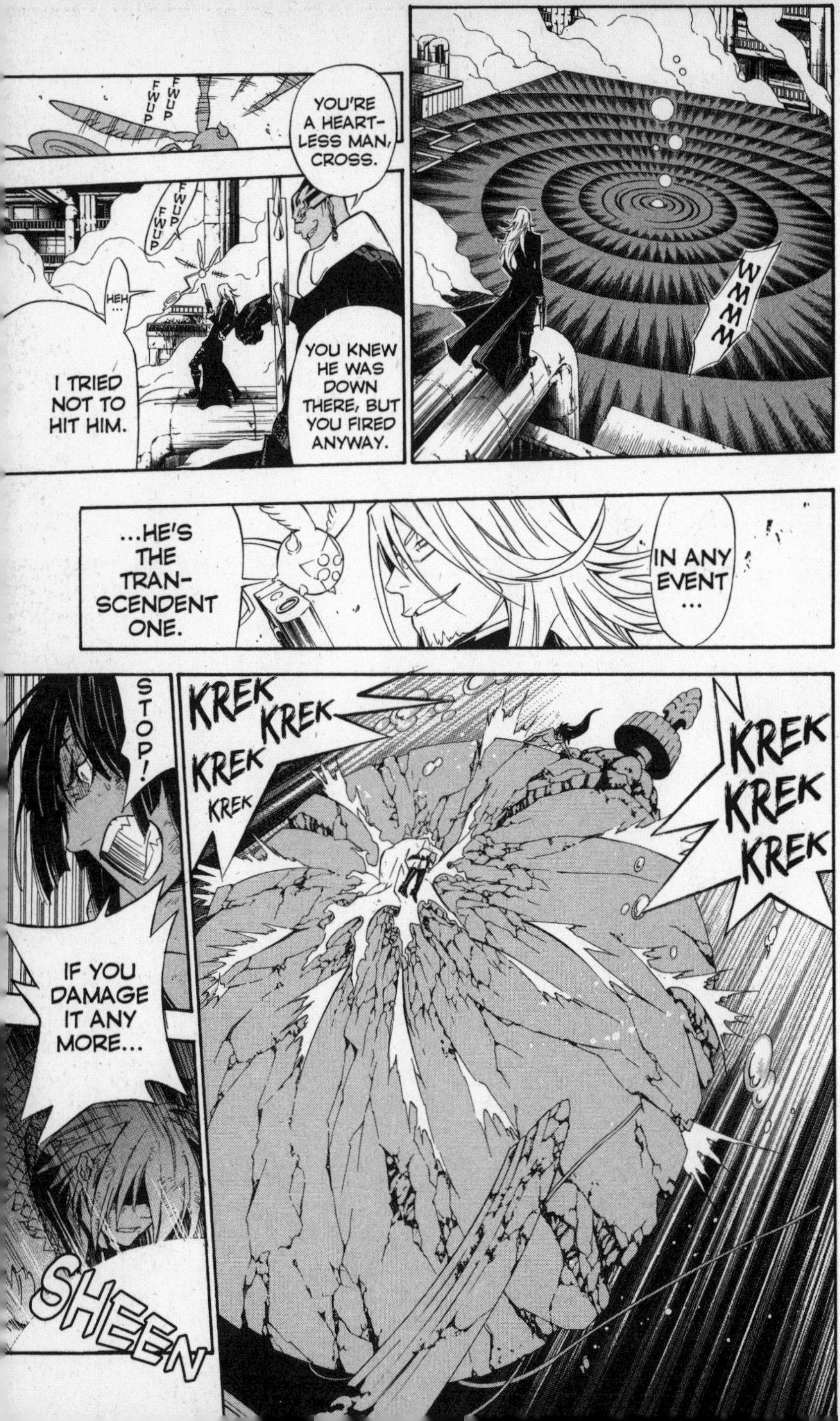
WMMM
FWUP FWUP
YOU'RE A HEART-LESS MAN, CROSS.
FWUP FWUP
YOU KNEW HE WAS DOWN THERE, BUT YOU FIRED ANYWAY.
HEH...
I TRIED NOT TO HIT HIM.
IN ANY EVENT...
...HE'S THE TRAN-SCENDENT ONE.
KREK KREK KREK
KREK KREK KREK KREK
STOP!
IF YOU DAMAGE IT ANY MORE...
SHEEN

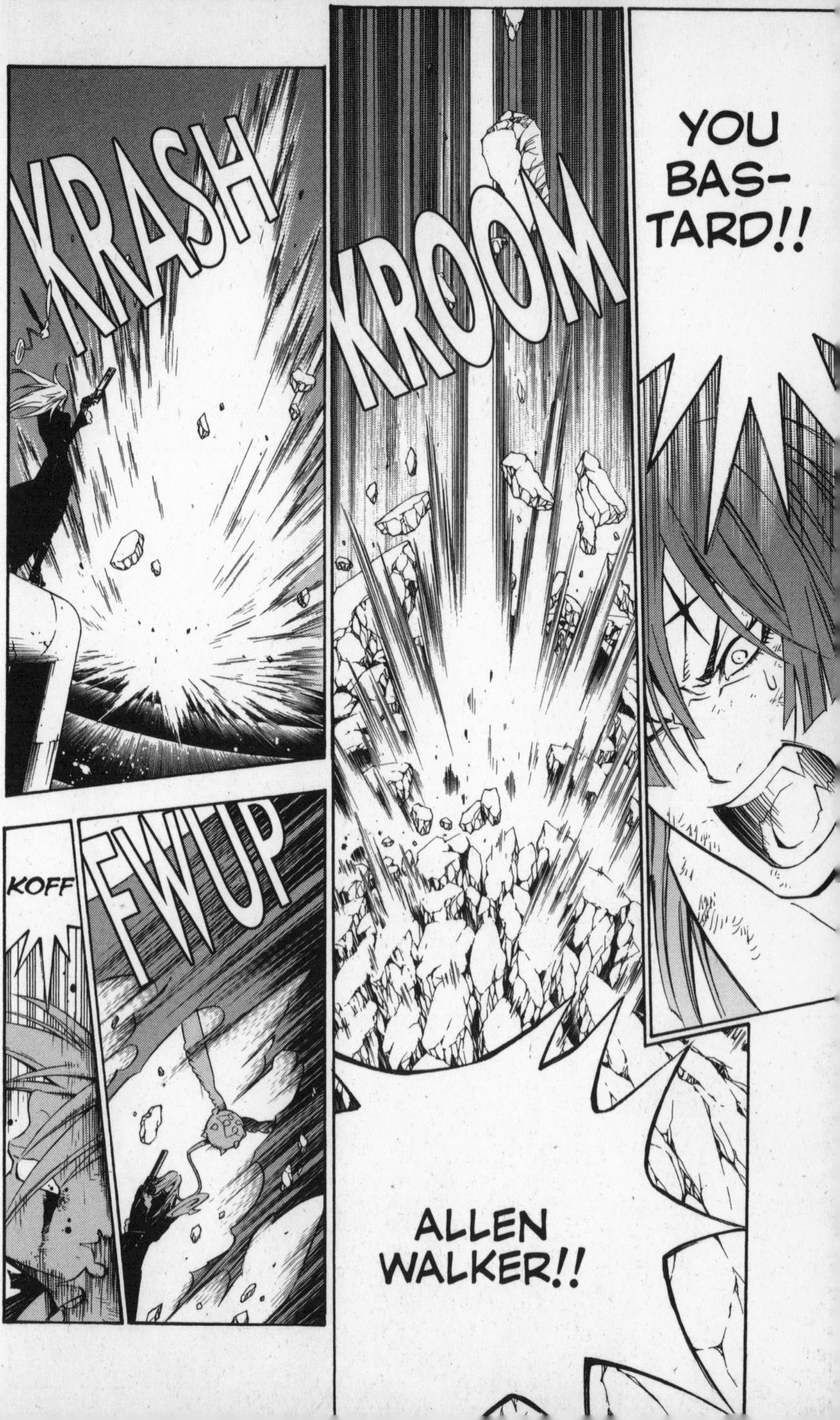
YOU BAS-TARD!!
KROOM
ALLEN WALKER!!
KRASH
FWUP
KOFF

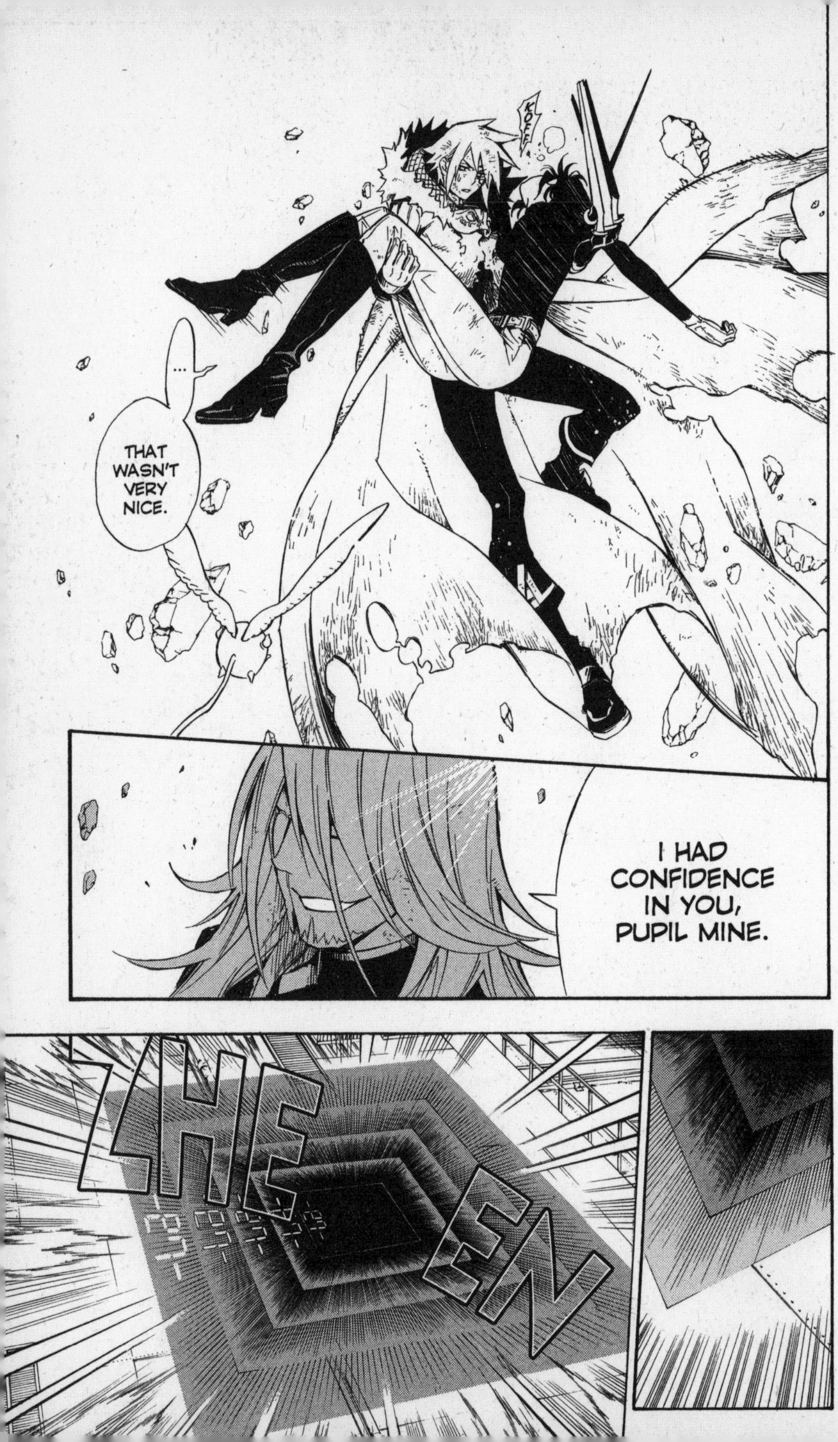
KOFF
...
THAT WASN'T VERY NICE.
I HAD CONFIDENCE IN YOU, PUPIL MINE.
ZHEEN

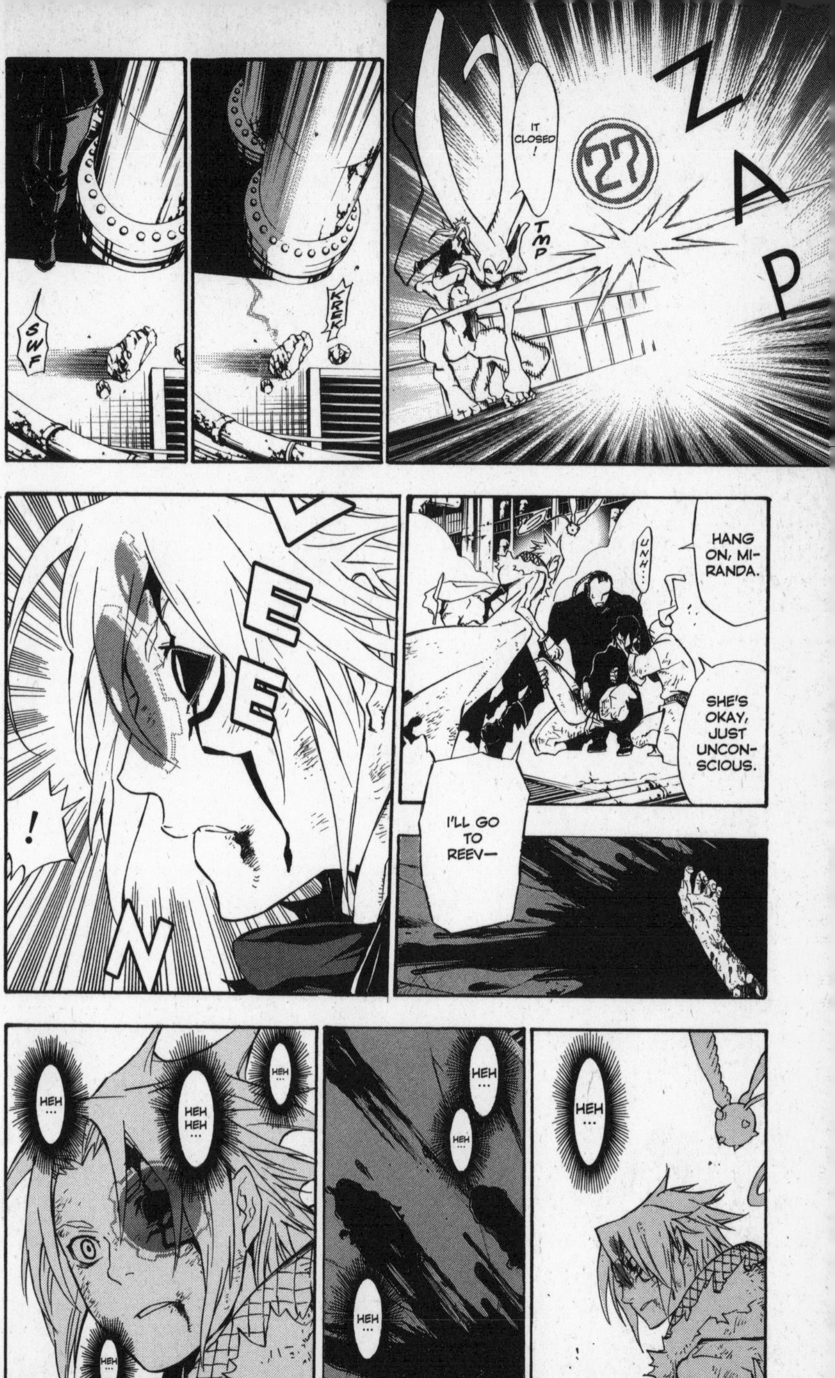
ZAP
27
IT CLOSED!
TMP
KREK
SWF
UNH...
HANG ON, MI-RANDA.
SHE'S OKAY, JUST UNCON-SCIOUS.
I'LL GO TO REEV—
DEEN
!
HEH...
HEH...
HEH...
HEH...
HEH...
HEH HEH...
HEH...
HEH...

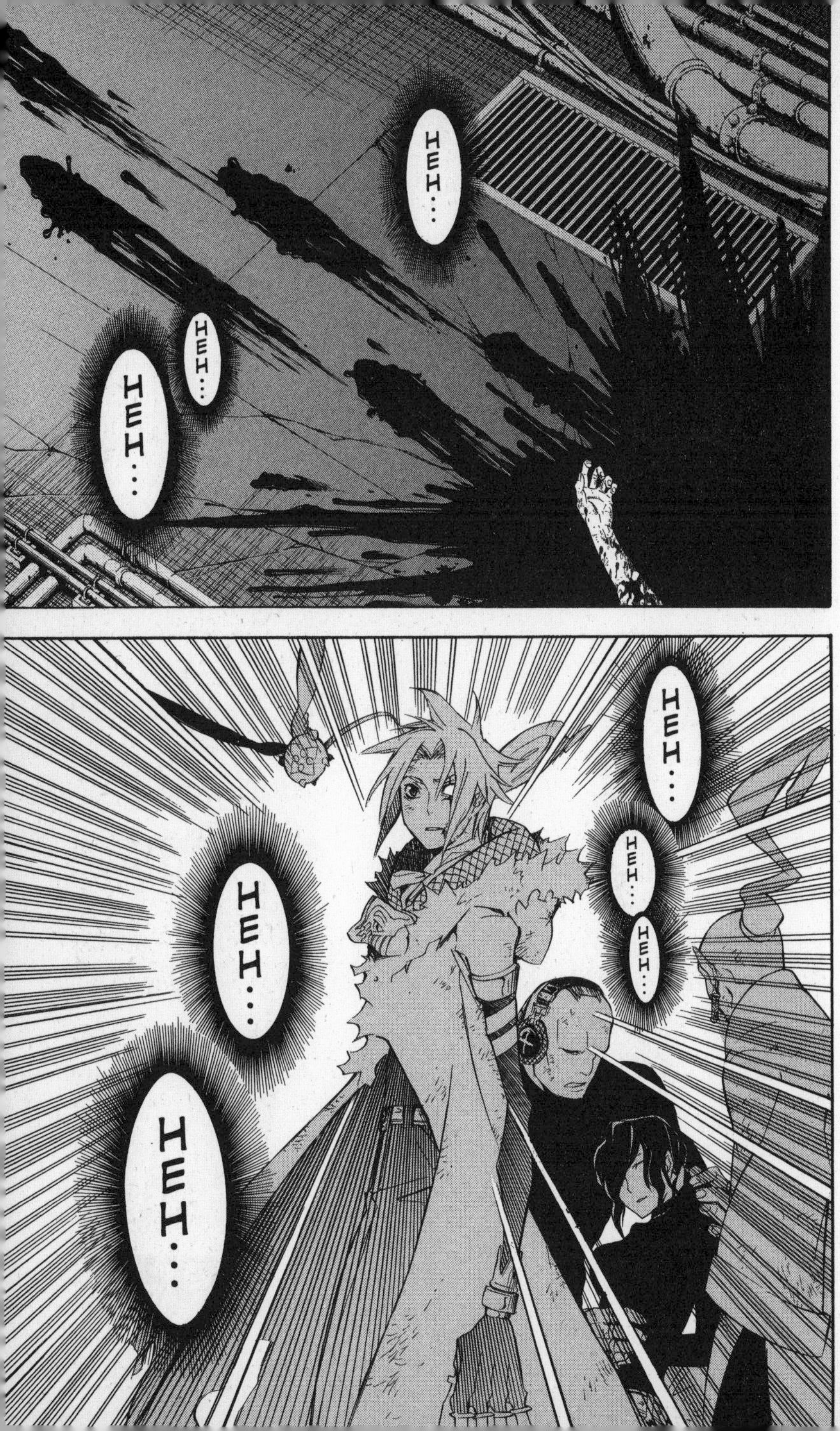
HEH...
HEH...
HEH...
HEH...
HEH...
HEH...
HEH...
HEH...

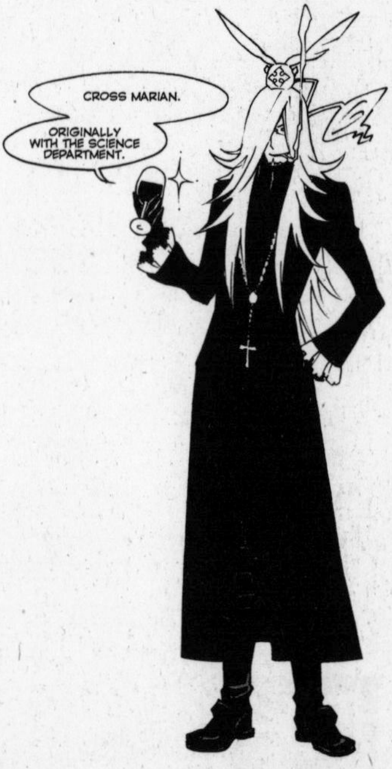
CROSS MARIAN.
ORIGINALLY WITH THE SCIENCE DEPARTMENT.

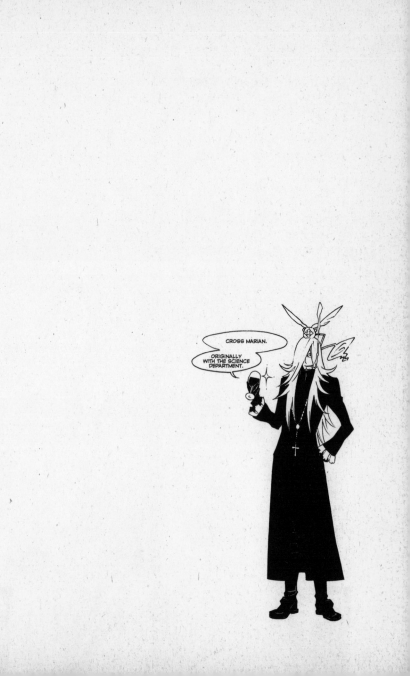

Darkness 4

THE 145TH NIGHT: DARKNESS 4

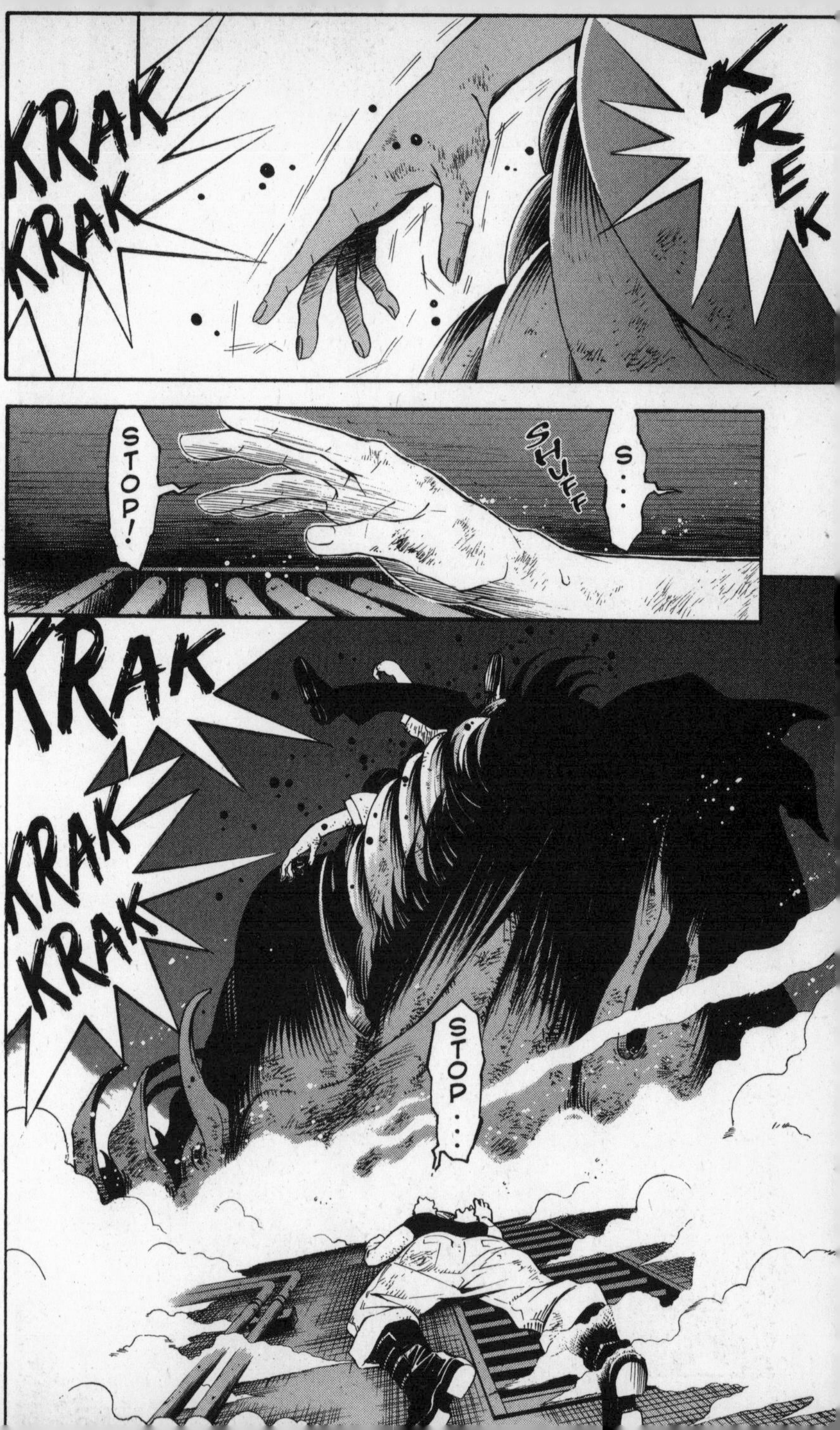
KREK
KRAK KRAK
S...
SHUFF
STOP!
KRAK
KRAK KRAK
STOP...

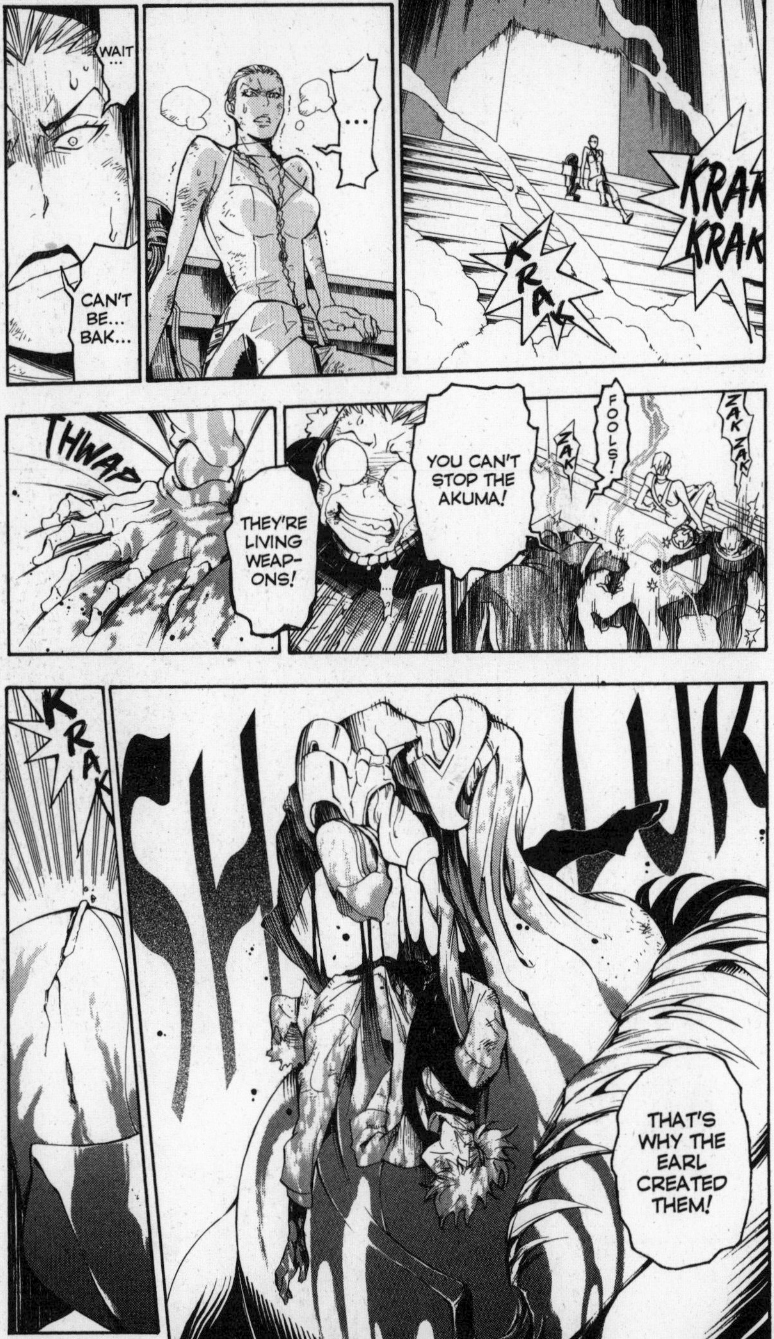
KRAK
KRAK
KRAK
...
WAIT...
CAN'T BE... BAK...
FOOLS!
ZAK ZAK
ZAK
YOU CAN'T STOP THE AKUMA!
THEY'RE LIVING WEAPONS!
THWAP
SHUK
THAT'S WHY THE EARL CREATED THEM!
KRAK

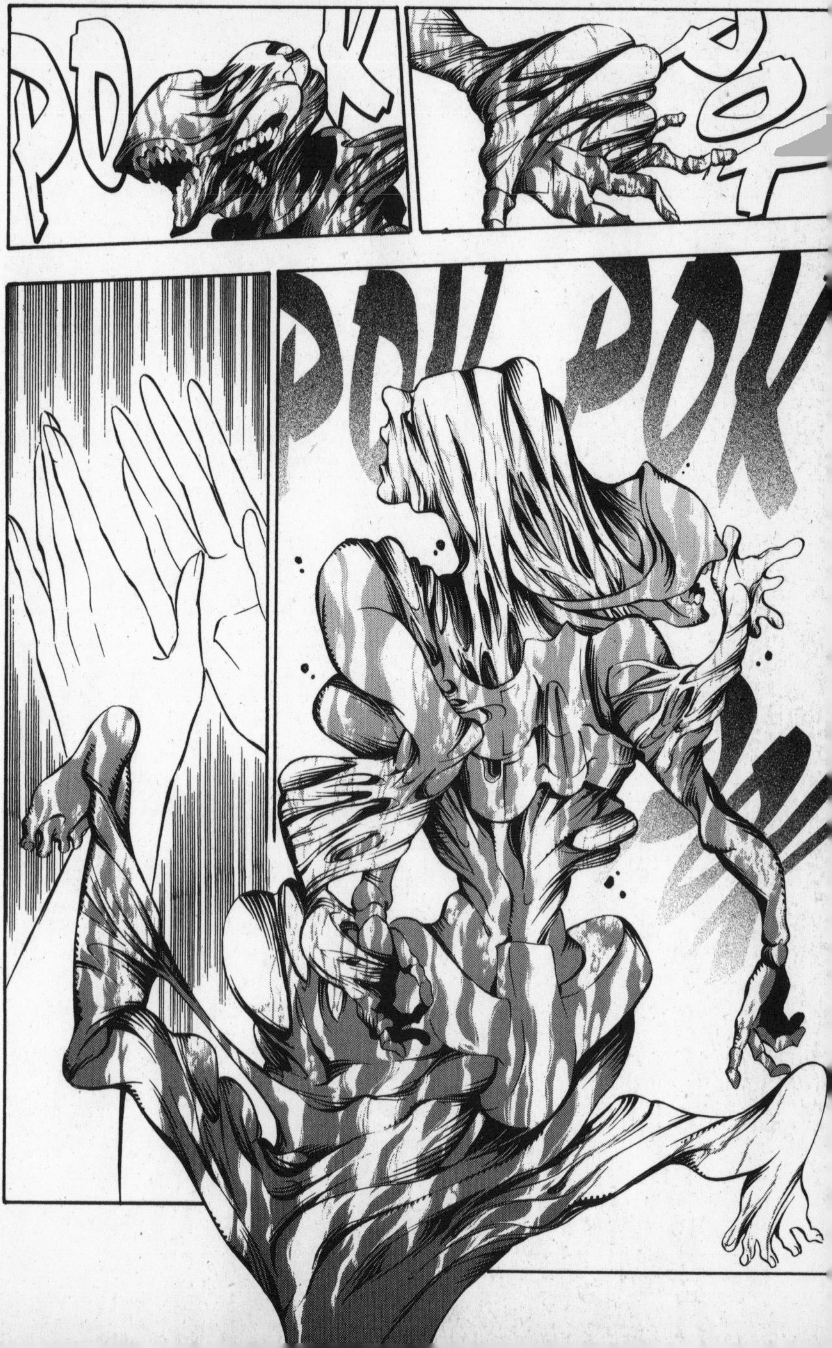

PO
POK
POK POK

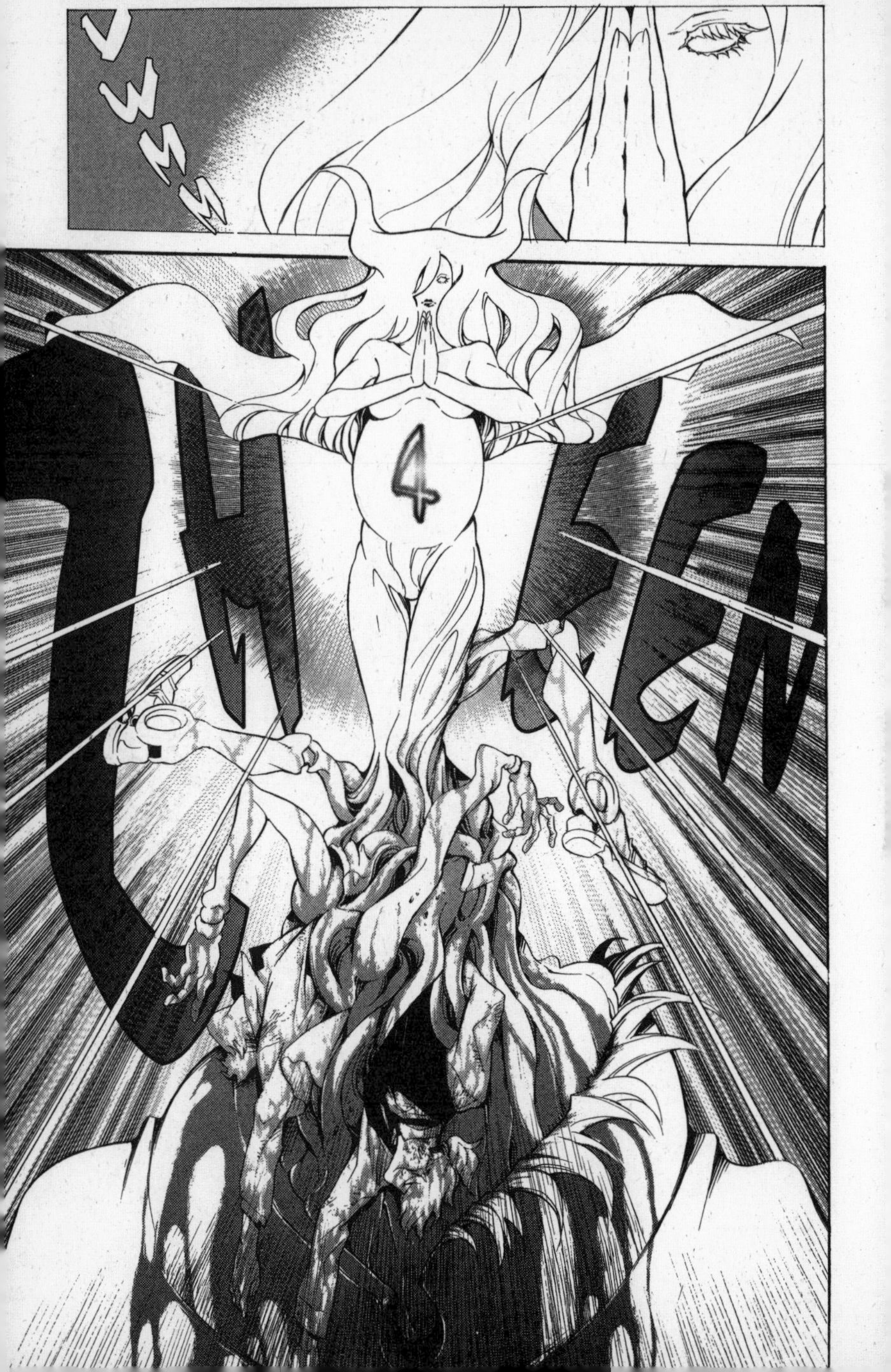

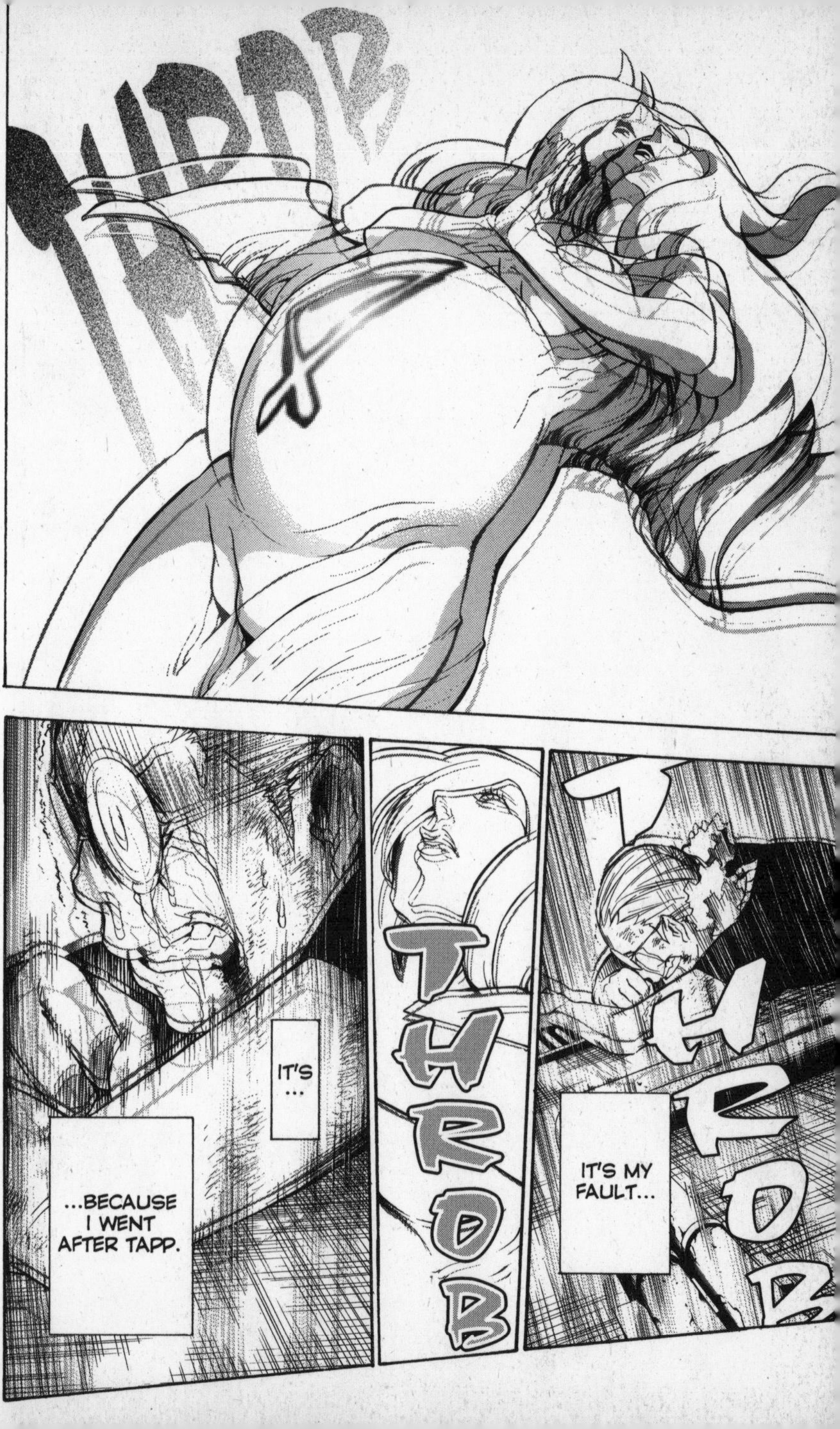
THROB
THROB
IT'S MY FAULT...
THROB
IT'S...
...BECAUSE I WENT AFTER TAPP.

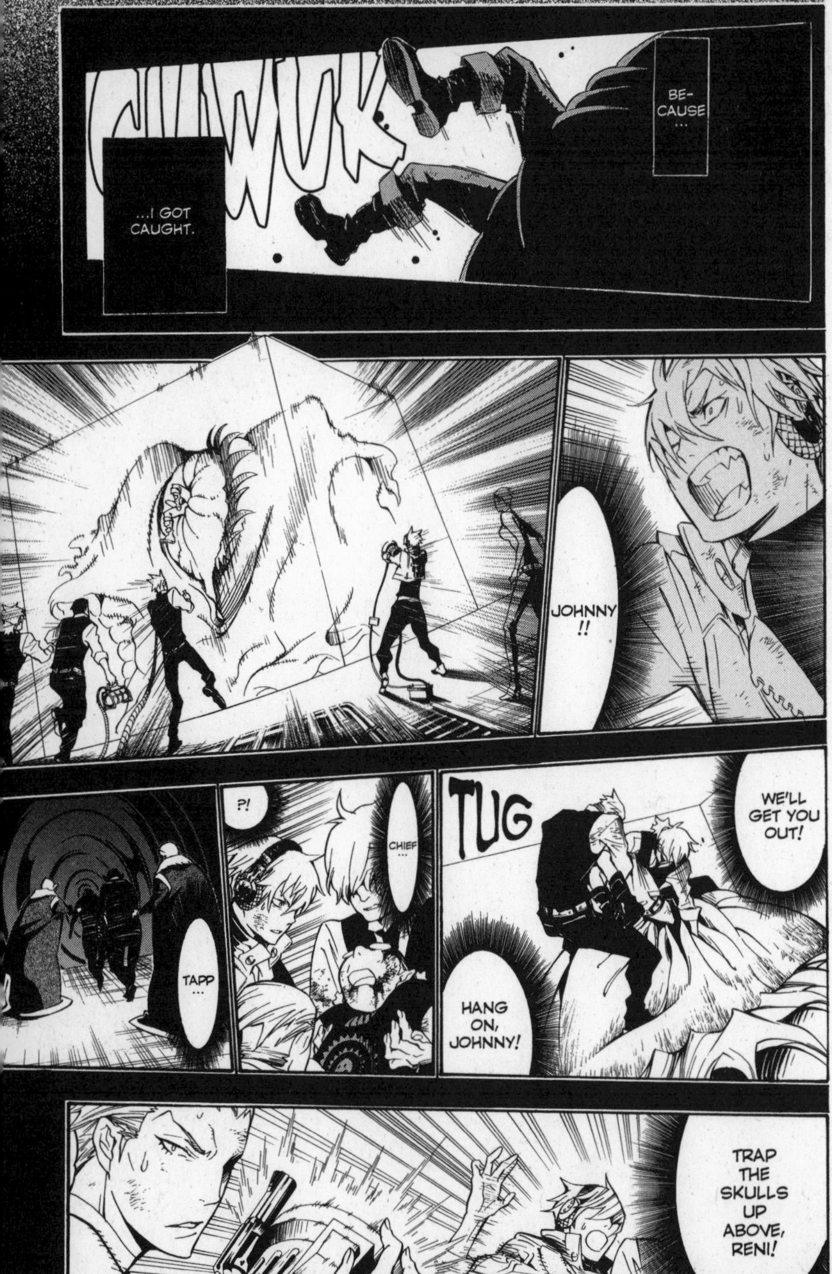
BE-CAUSE...
...I GOT CAUGHT.
JOHNNY!!
WE'LL GET YOU OUT!
TUG
HANG ON, JOHNNY!
CHIEF...
?!
TAPP...
TRAP THE SKULLS UP ABOVE, RENI!

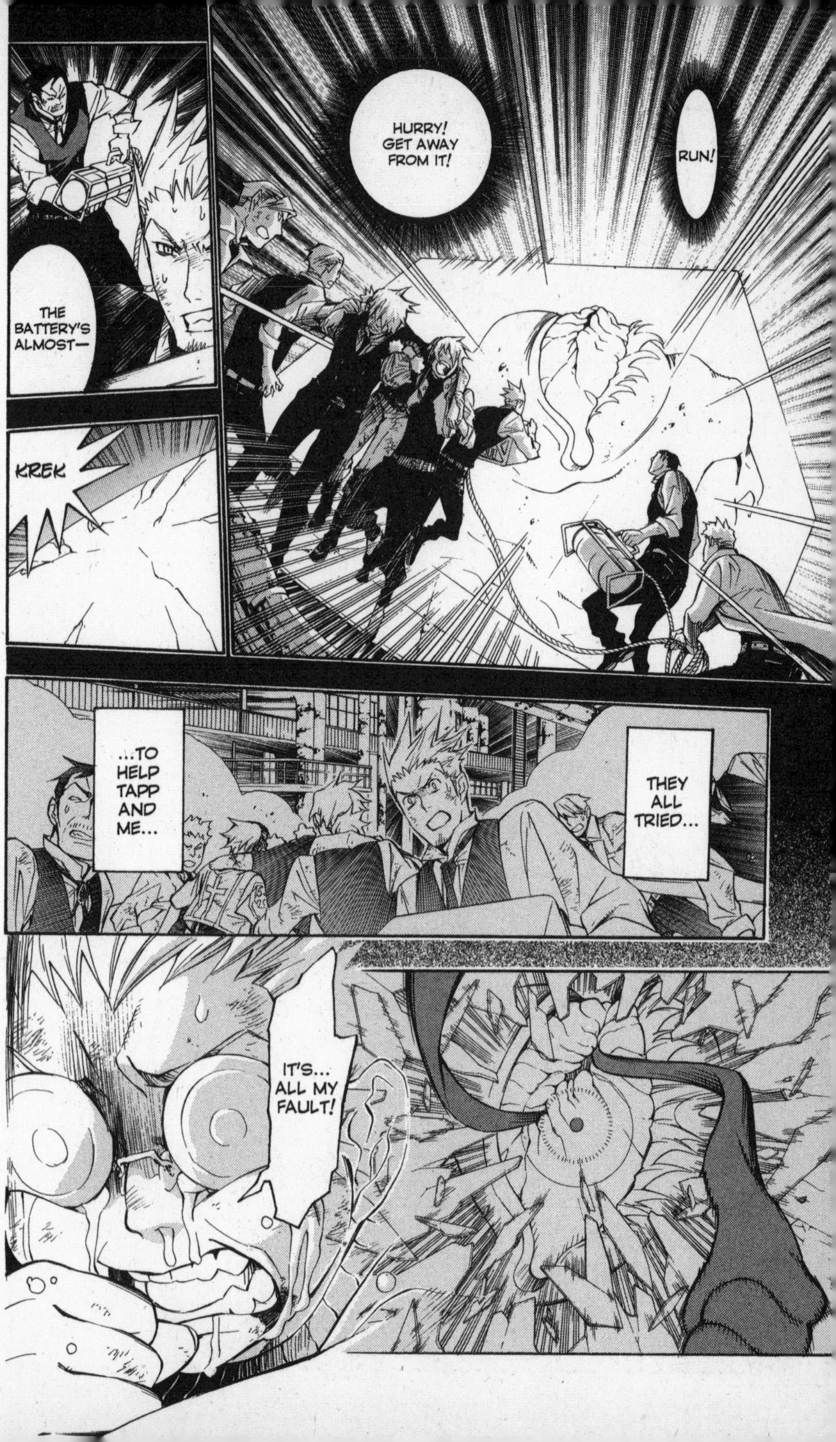
RUN!
HURRY! GET AWAY FROM IT!
THE BATTERY'S ALMOST—
KREK
THEY ALL TRIED...
...TO HELP TAPP AND ME...
IT'S... ALL MY FAULT!

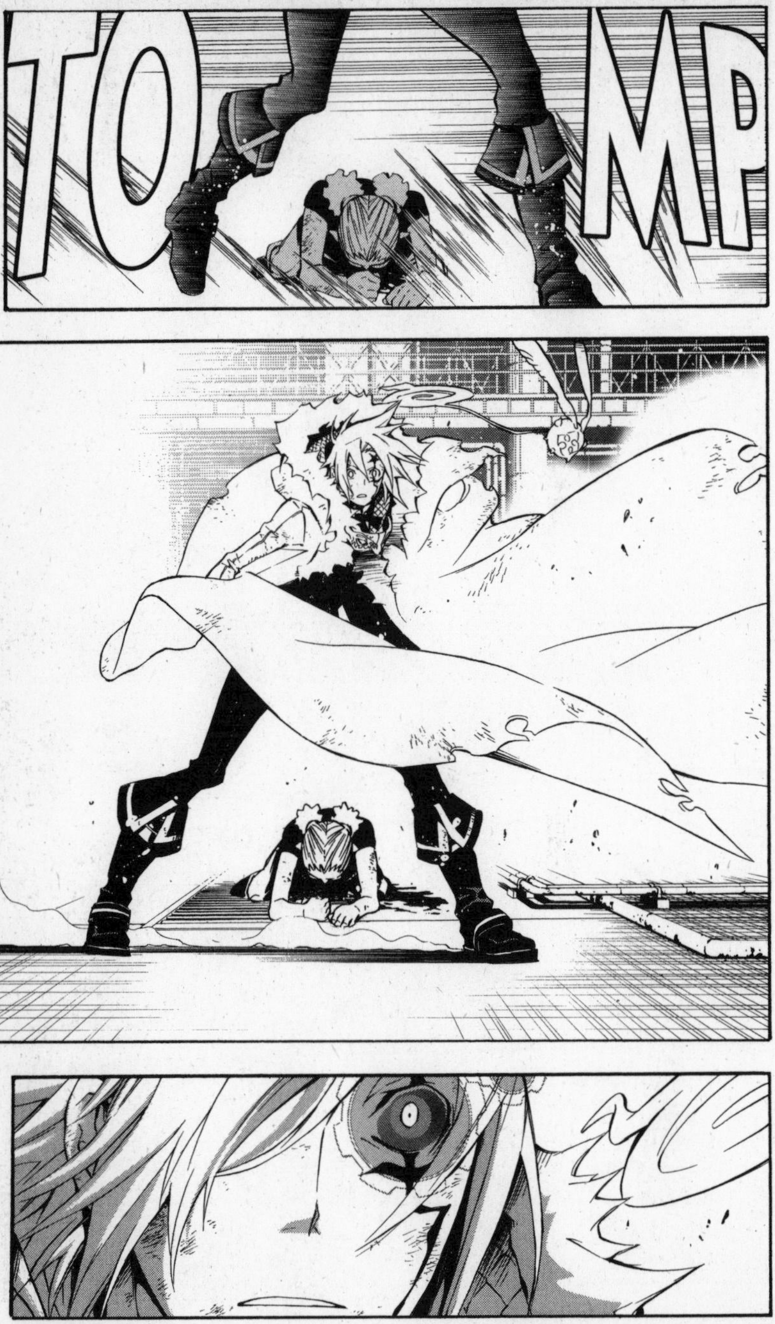
TOMP

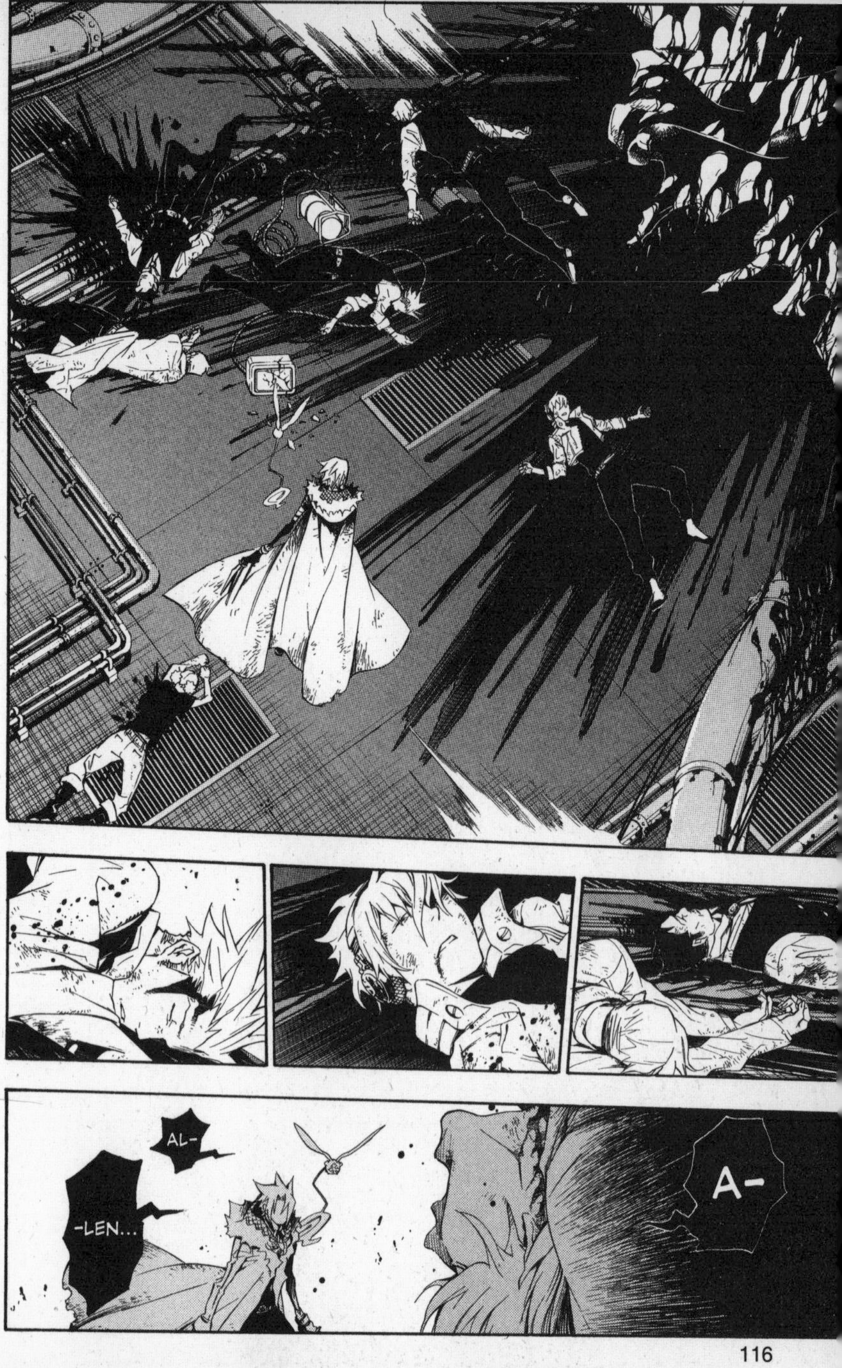
A-
AL-
-LEN...

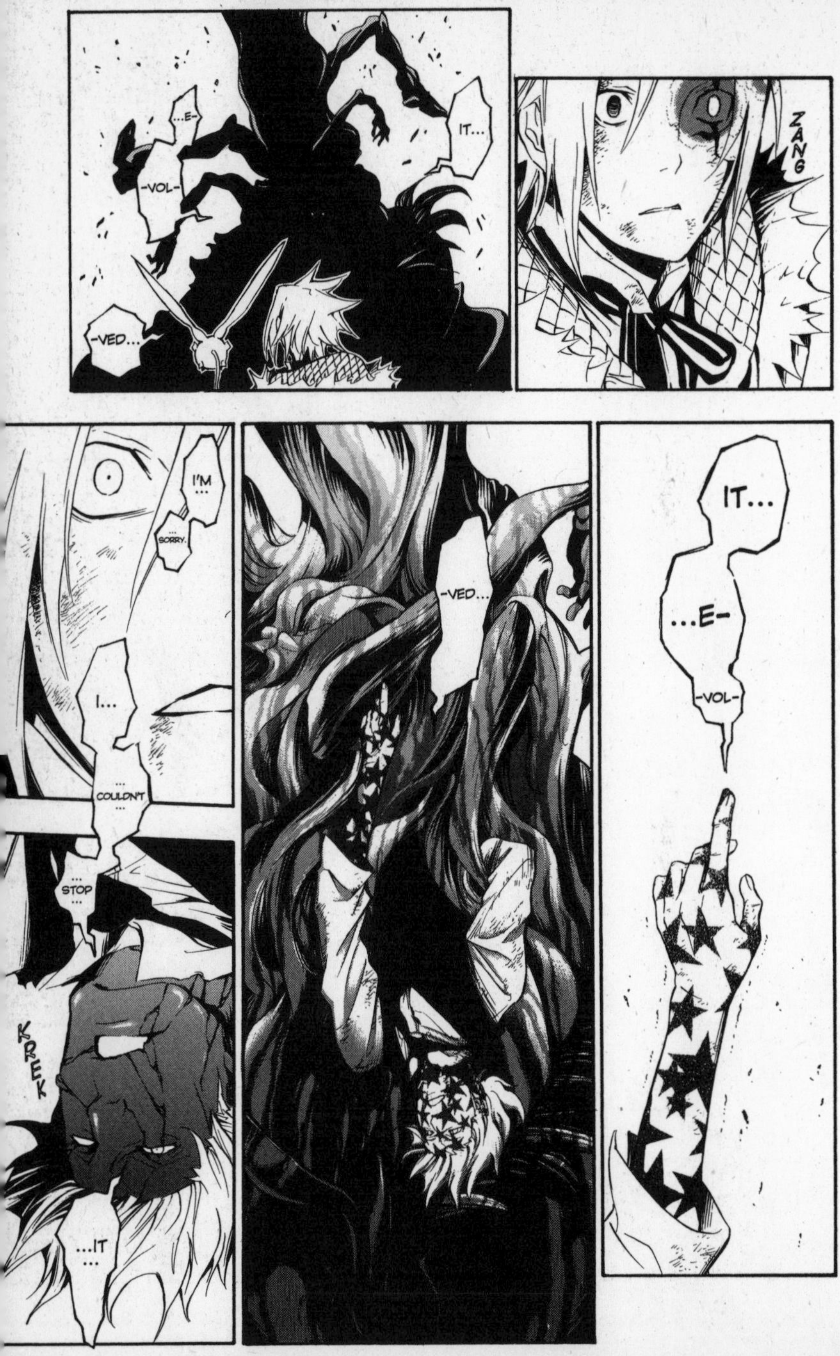
ZANG
IT...
...E-
-VOL-
-VED...
IT...
...E-
-VOL-
-VED...
I'M...
...SORRY.
I...
...COULDN'T...
...STOP...
KREK
...IT...

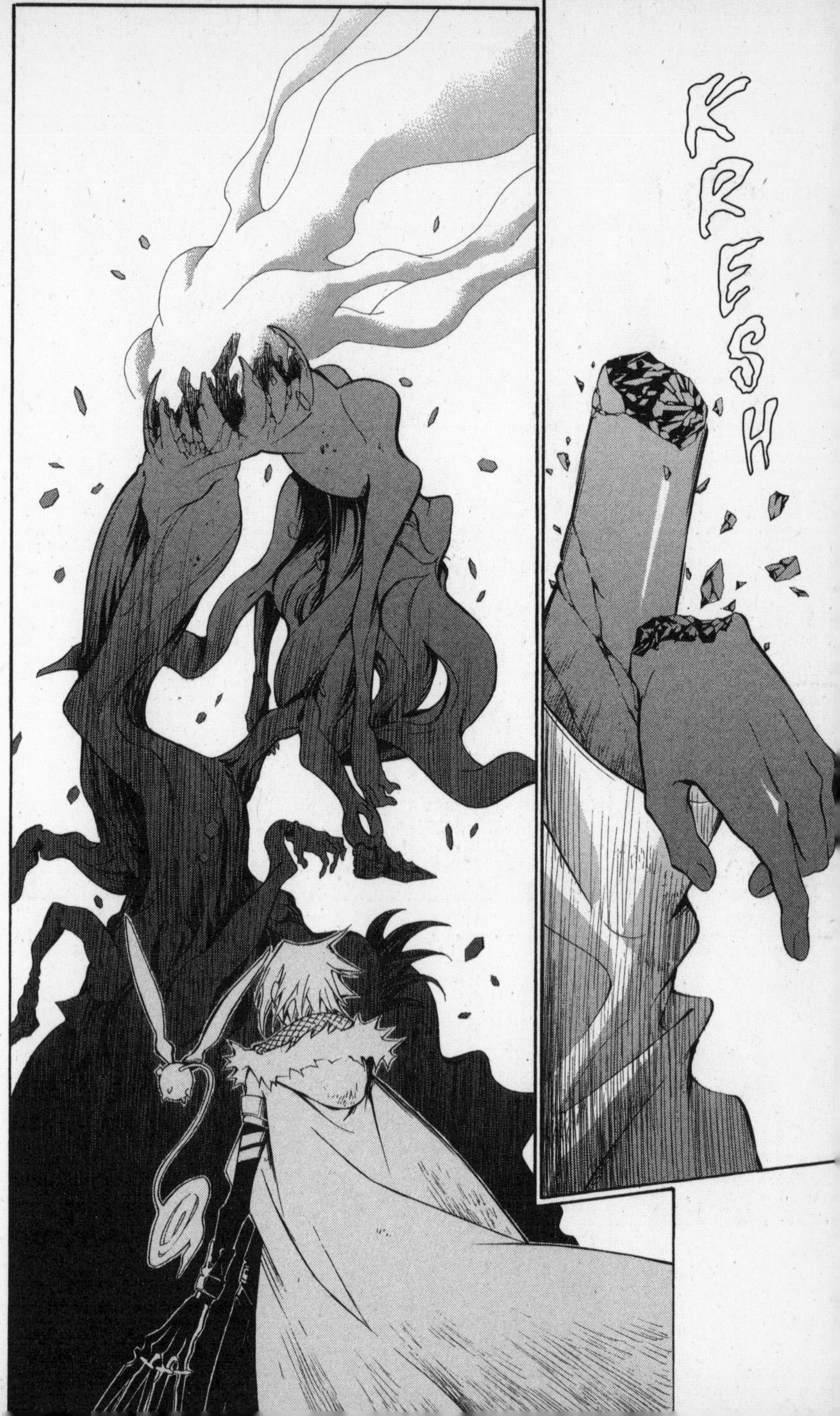
KRESH

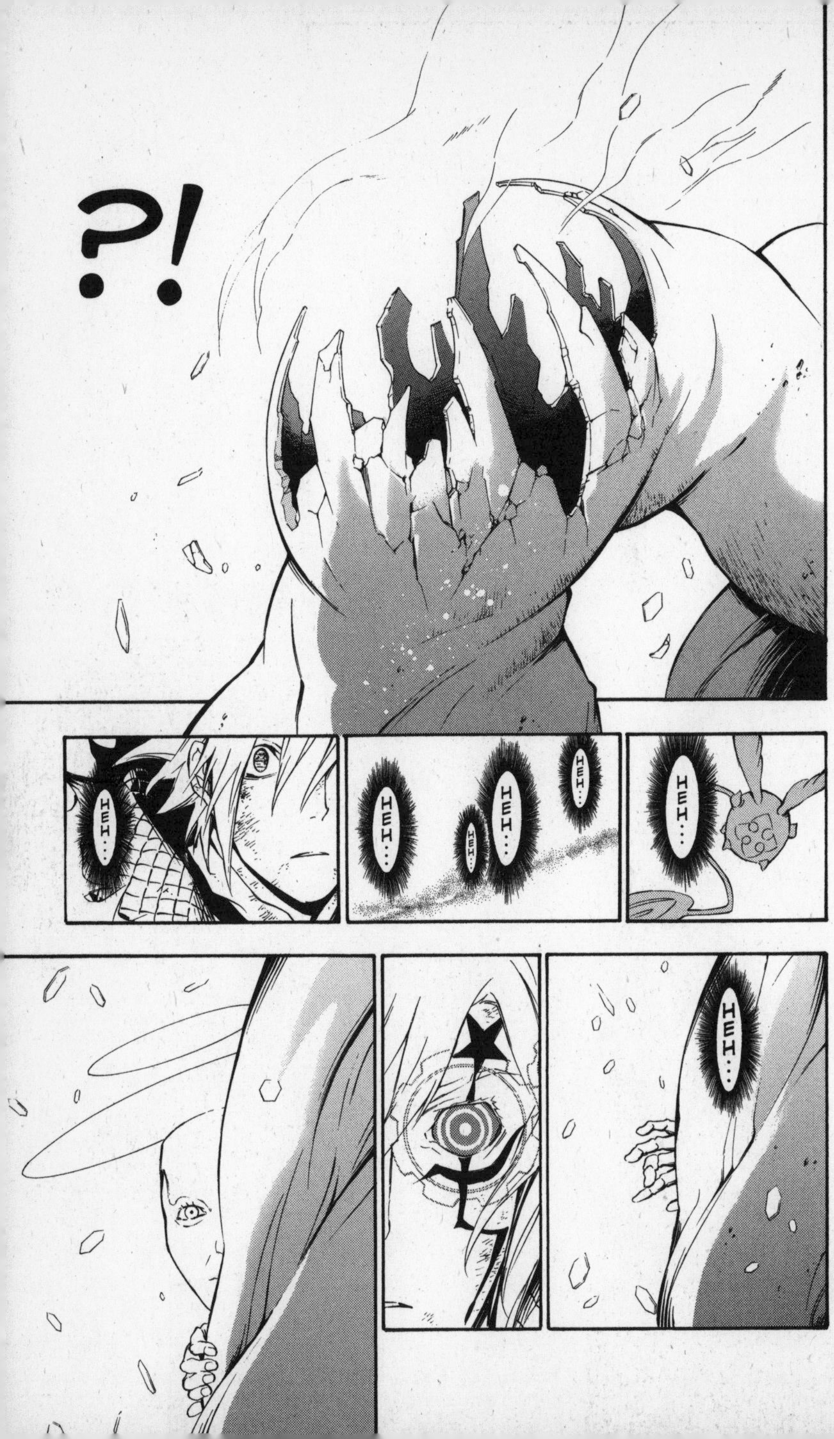
?!
HEH...
HEH...
HEH...
HEH...
HEH...
HEH...
HEH...

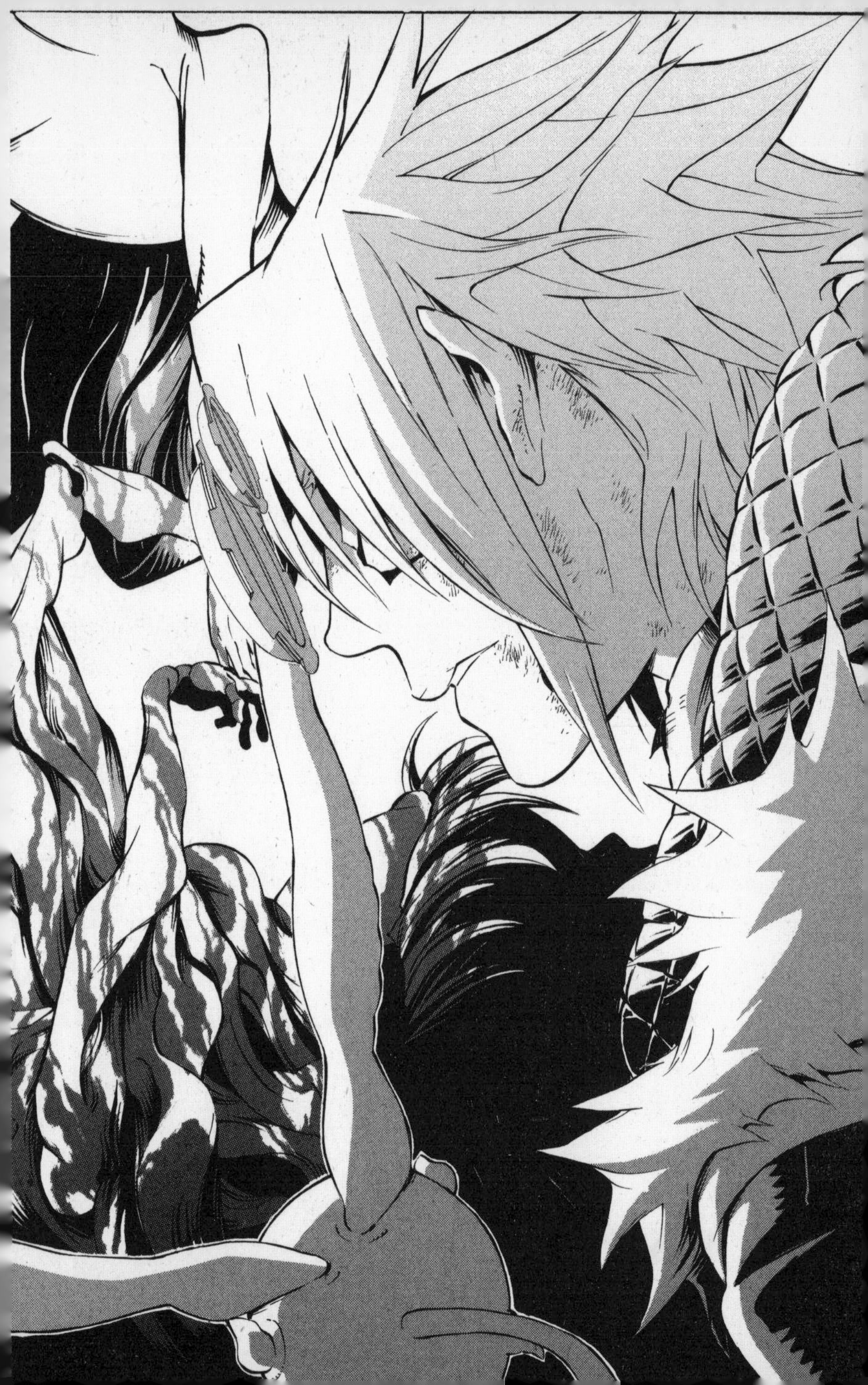

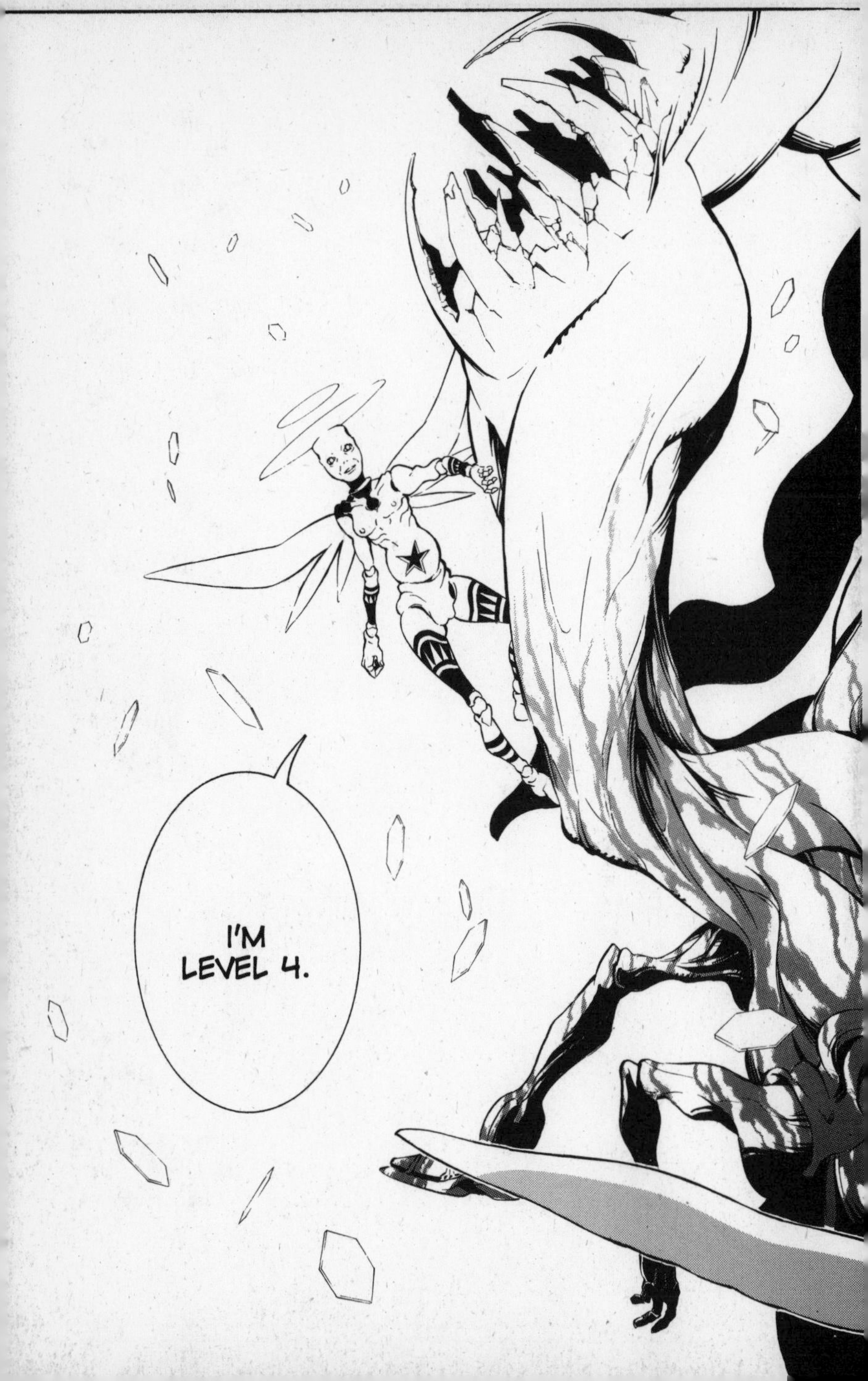
I'M LEVEL 4.

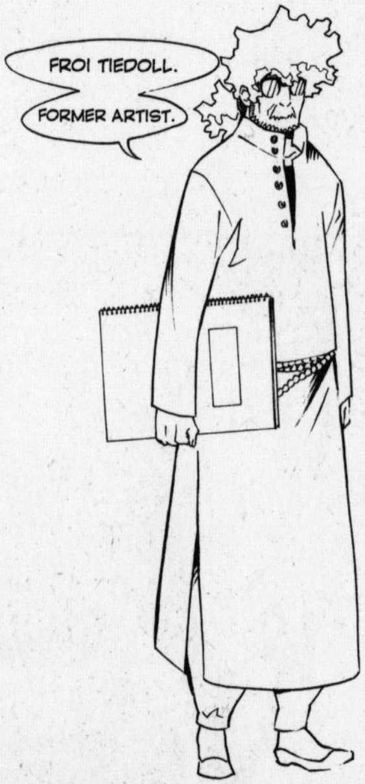
FROI TIEDOLL.
FORMER ARTIST.

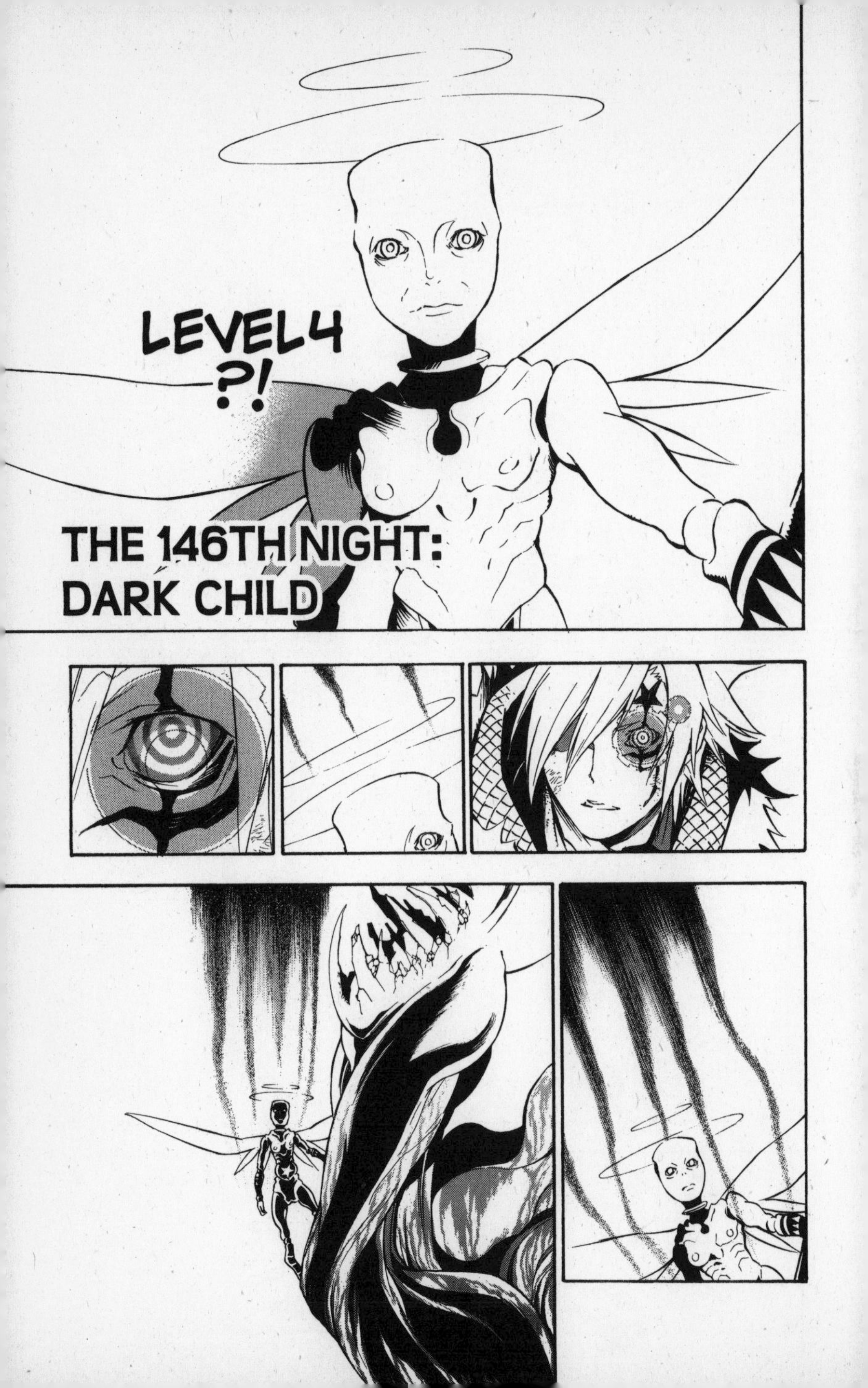
LEVEL 4 ?!
THE 146TH NIGHT:
DARK CHILD

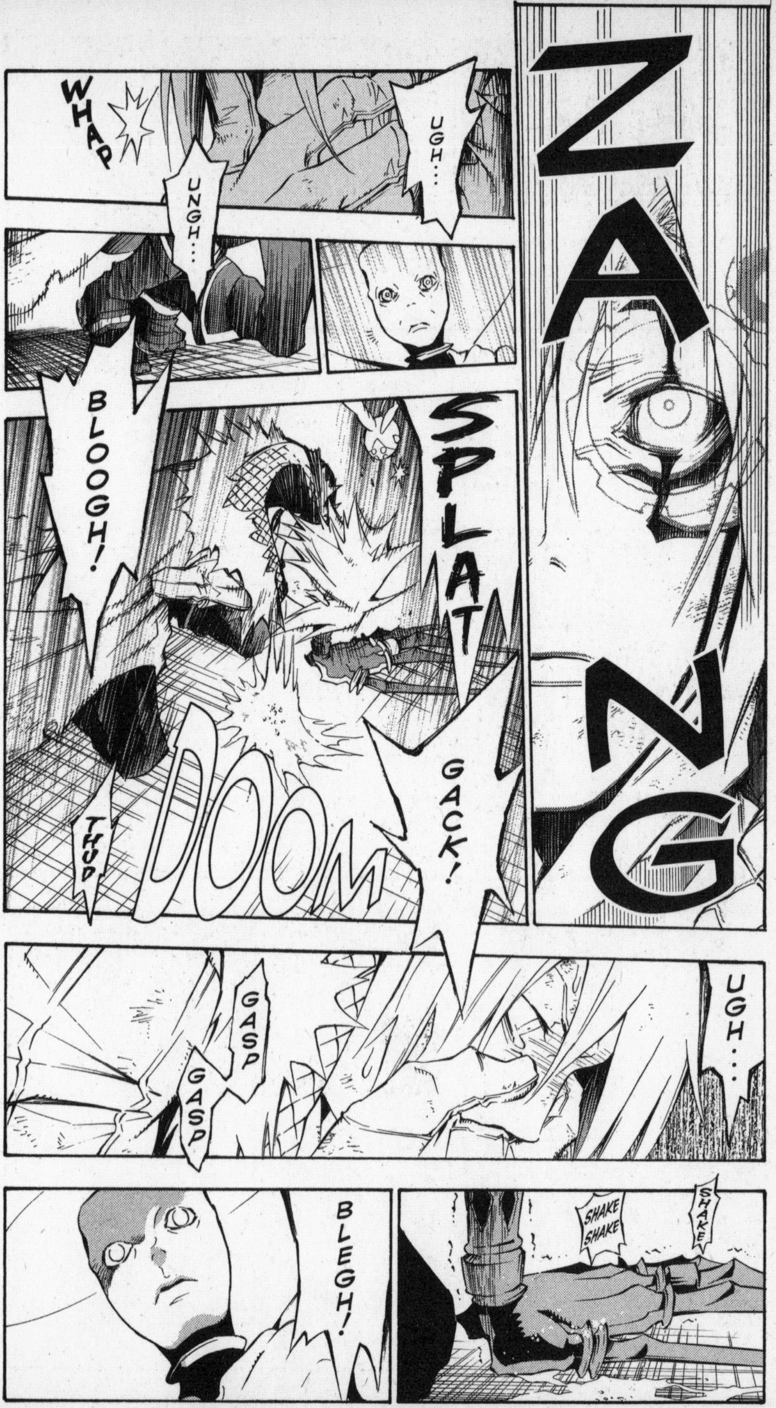
ZANG
UGH...
WHAP
UNGH...
SPLAT
GACK!
BLOOGH!
DOOM
THUD
UGH...
GASP
GASP
SHAKE
SHAKE SHAKE
BLEGH!

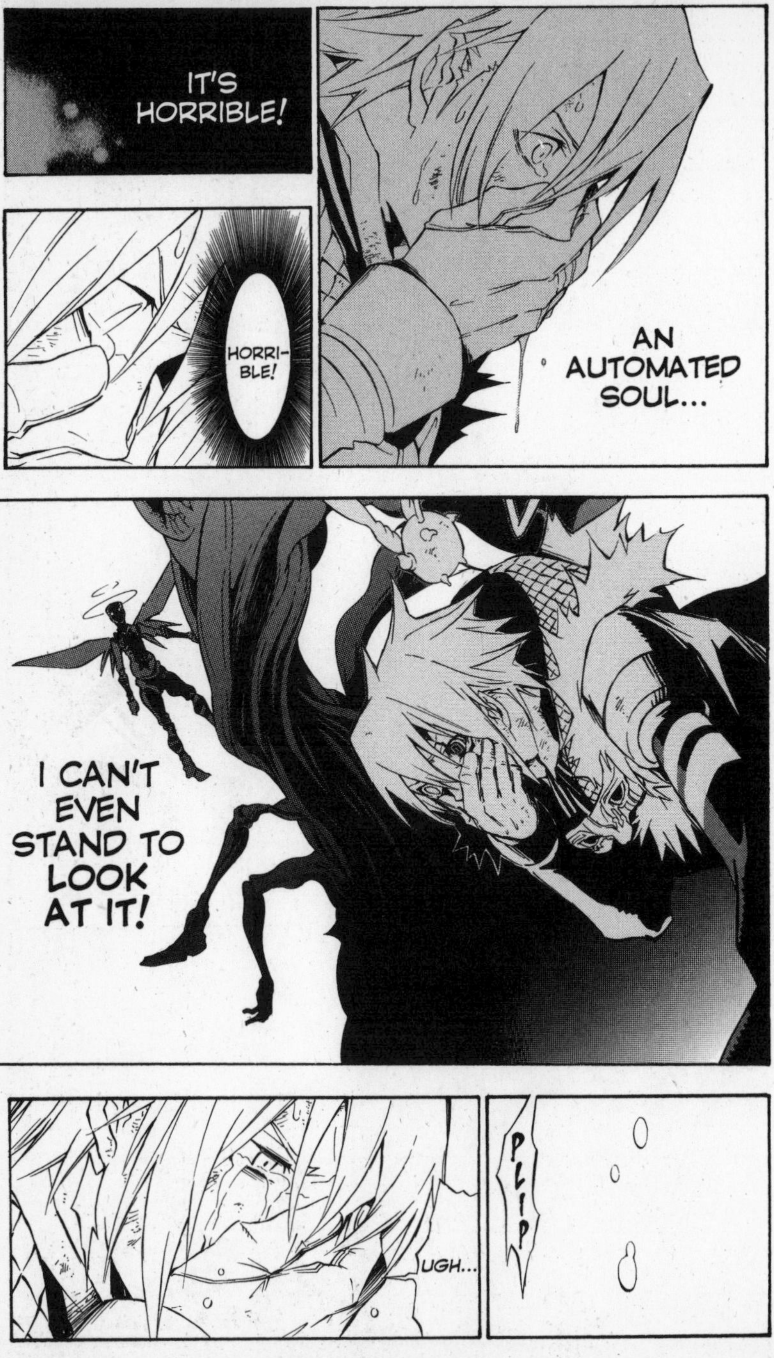
AN AUTOMATED SOUL...
IT'S HORRIBLE!
HORRI-BLE!
I CAN'T EVEN STAND TO LOOK AT IT!
PLIP
UGH...

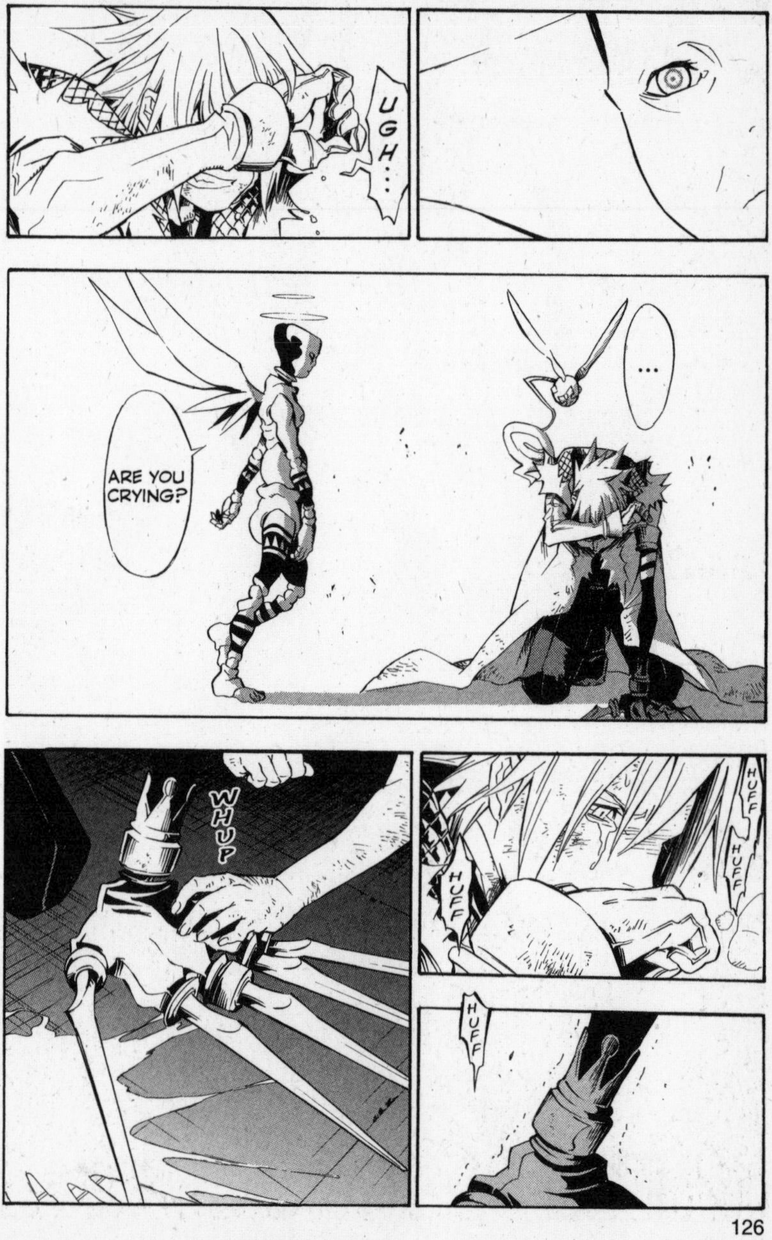
UGH...
...
ARE YOU CRYING?
HUFF HUFF
HUFF
WHUP
HUFF

READ THIS WAY

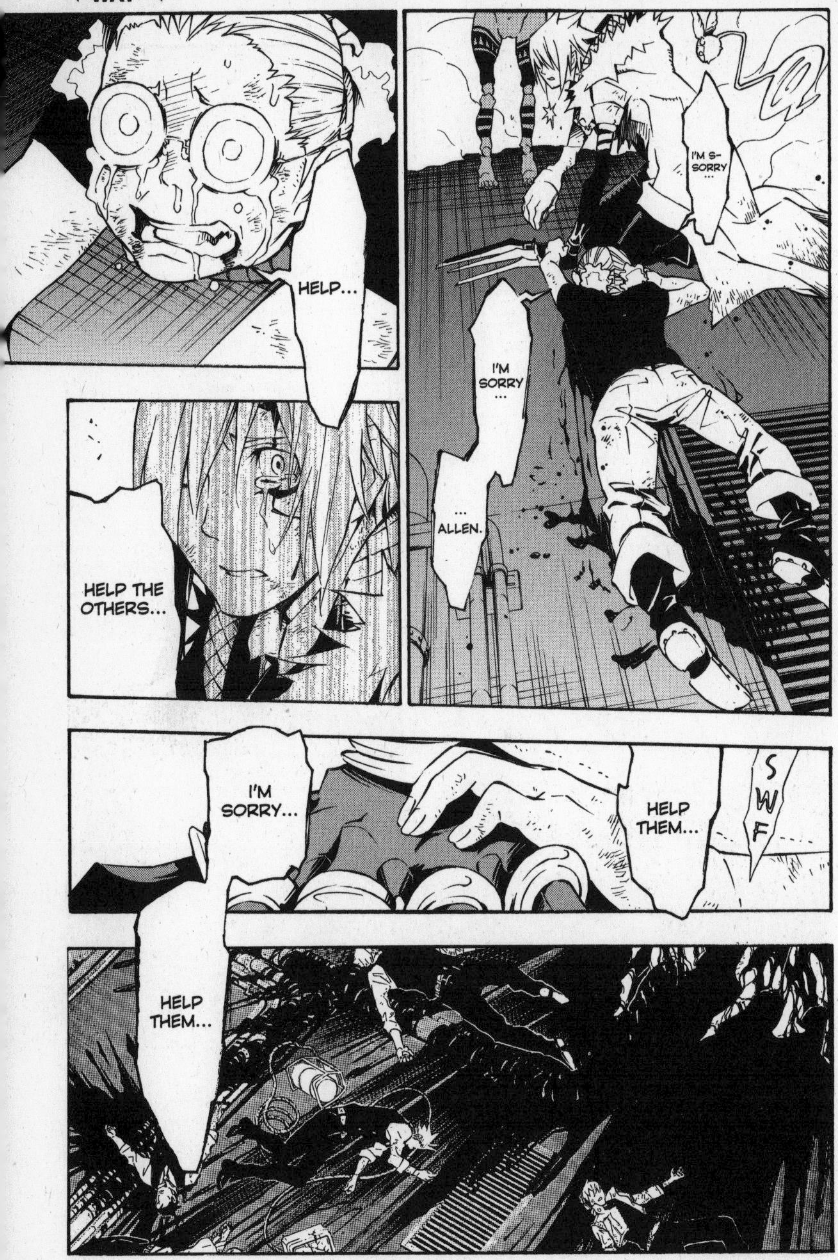
I'M S-SORRY...
I'M SORRY...
... ALLEN.
HELP...
HELP THE OTHERS...
SWF
HELP THEM...
I'M SORRY...
HELP THEM...

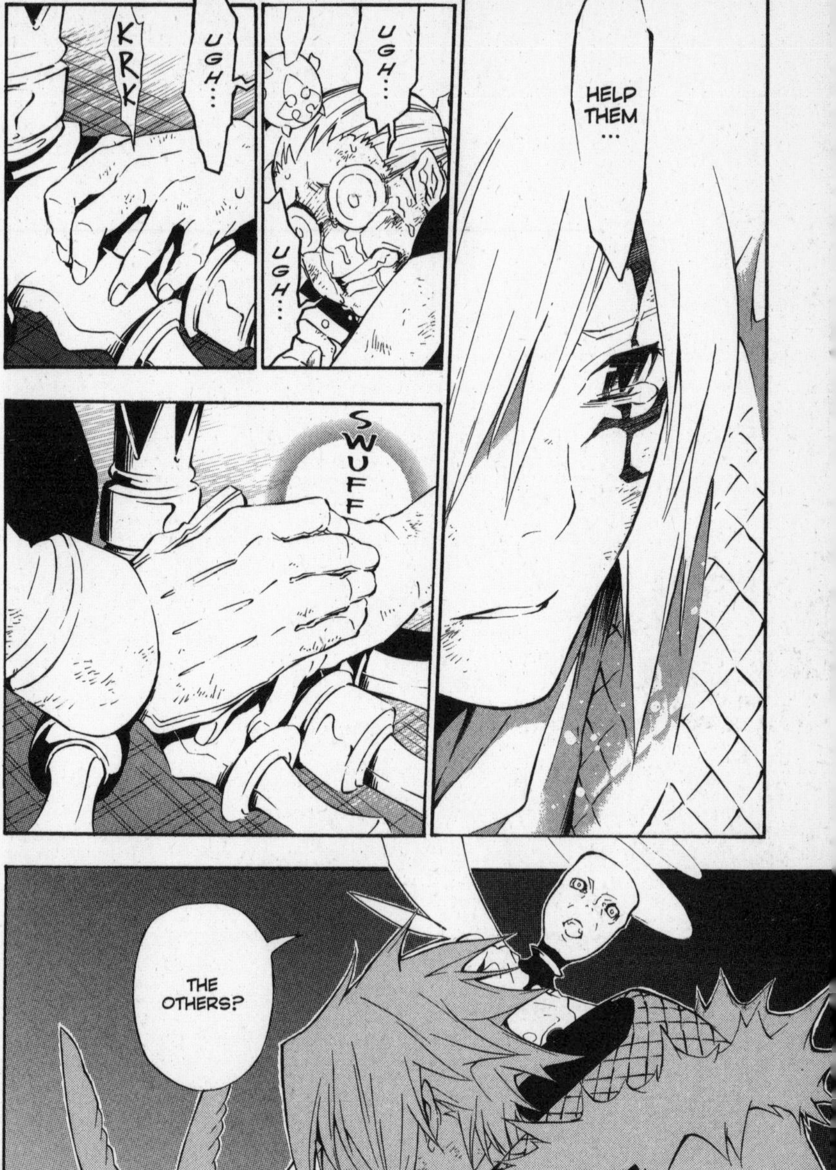
HELP THEM ...
UGH...
UGH...
UGH...
KRK
SWUFF
THE OTHERS?

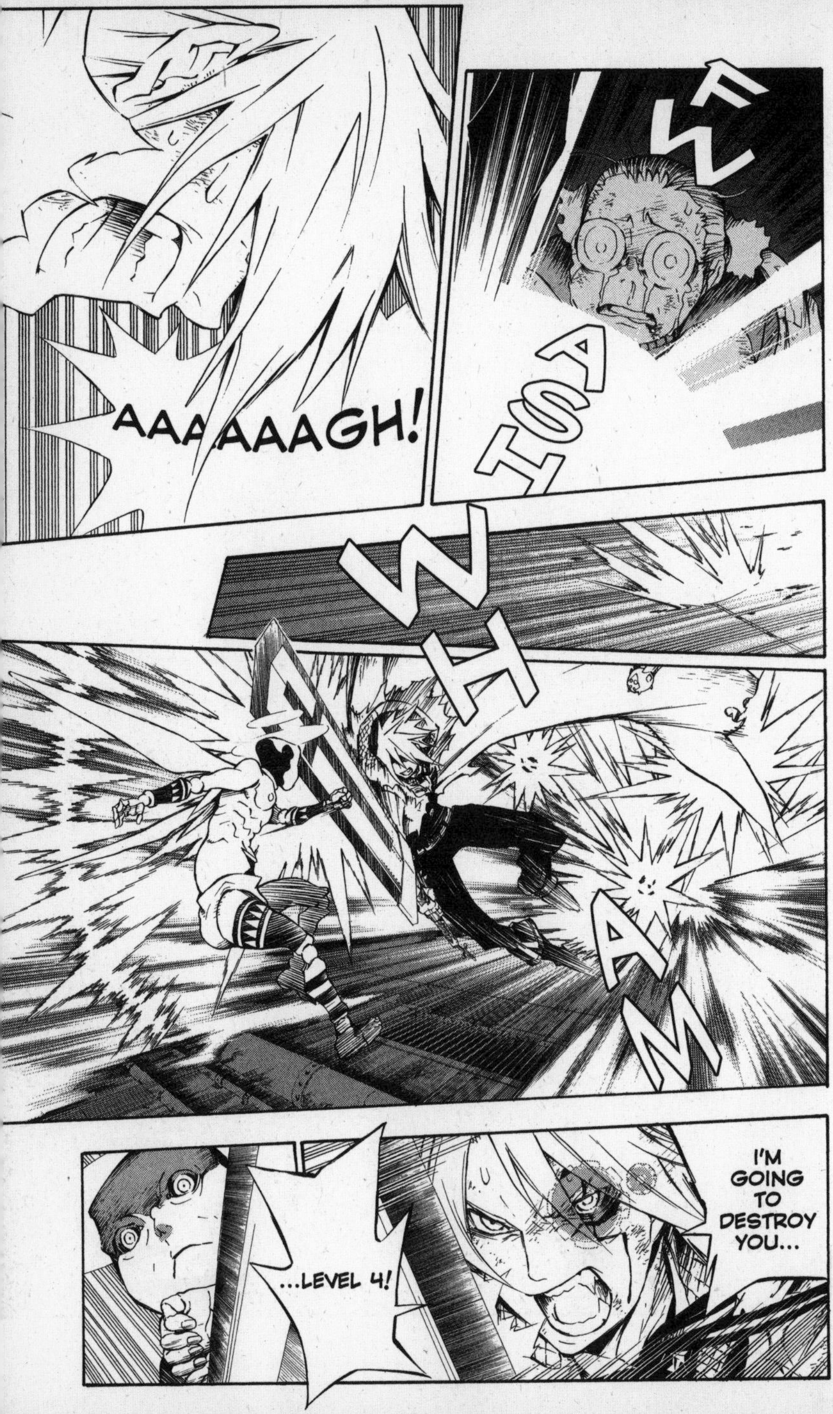
FWASH
AAAAAAAGH!
WHAM
I'M GOING TO DESTROY YOU...
...LEVEL 4!

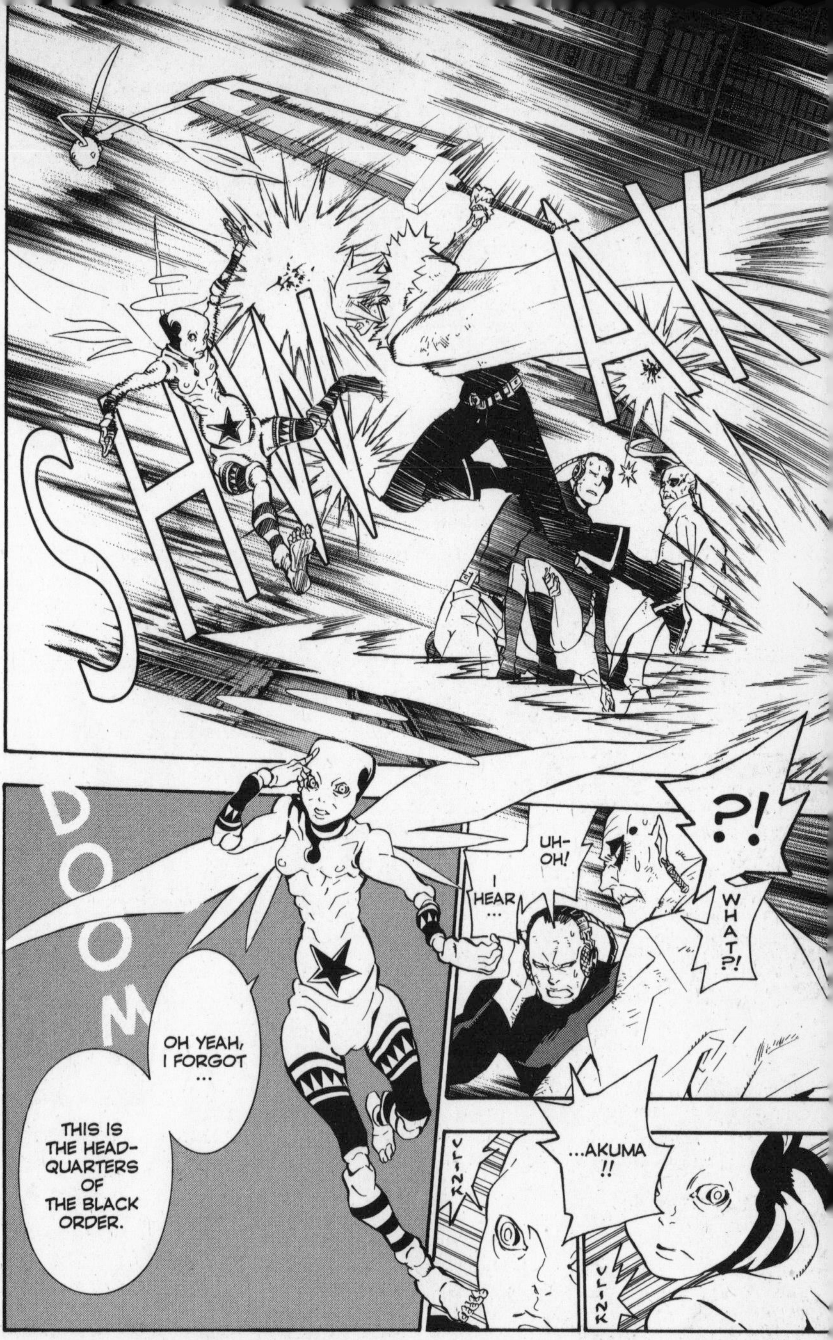
SHWAK
?!
WHAT?!
UH-OH! I HEAR...
...AKUMA!!
VLINK
VLINK
DOOM
OH YEAH, I FORGOT...
THIS IS THE HEAD-QUARTERS OF THE BLACK ORDER.

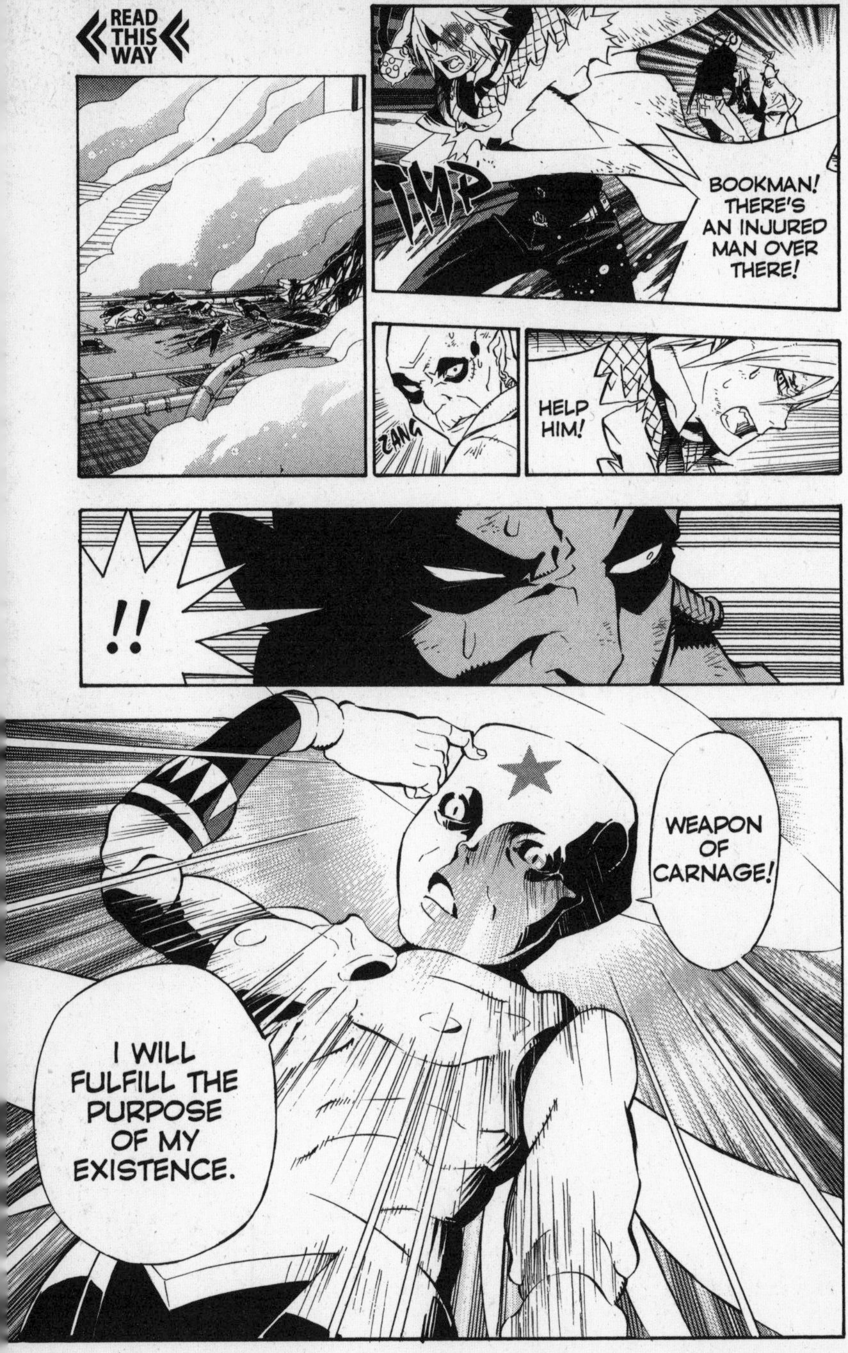
READ THIS WAY
TMP
BOOKMAN! THERE'S AN INJURED MAN OVER THERE!
HELP HIM!
ZANG
!!
WEAPON OF CARNAGE!
I WILL FULFILL THE PURPOSE OF MY EXISTENCE.

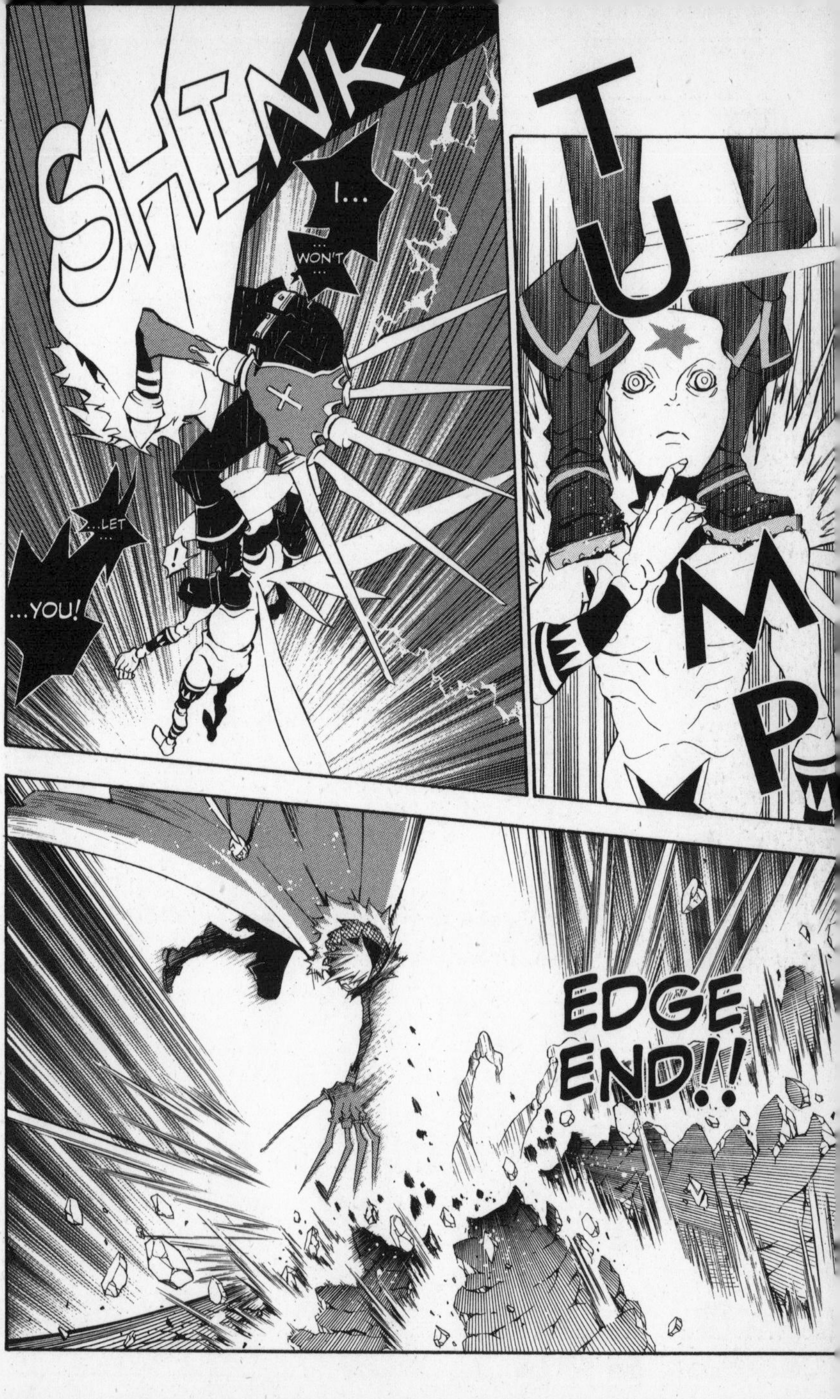
TUMP
SHINK
I...
...WON'T...
...LET...
!
...YOU!
EDGE END!!

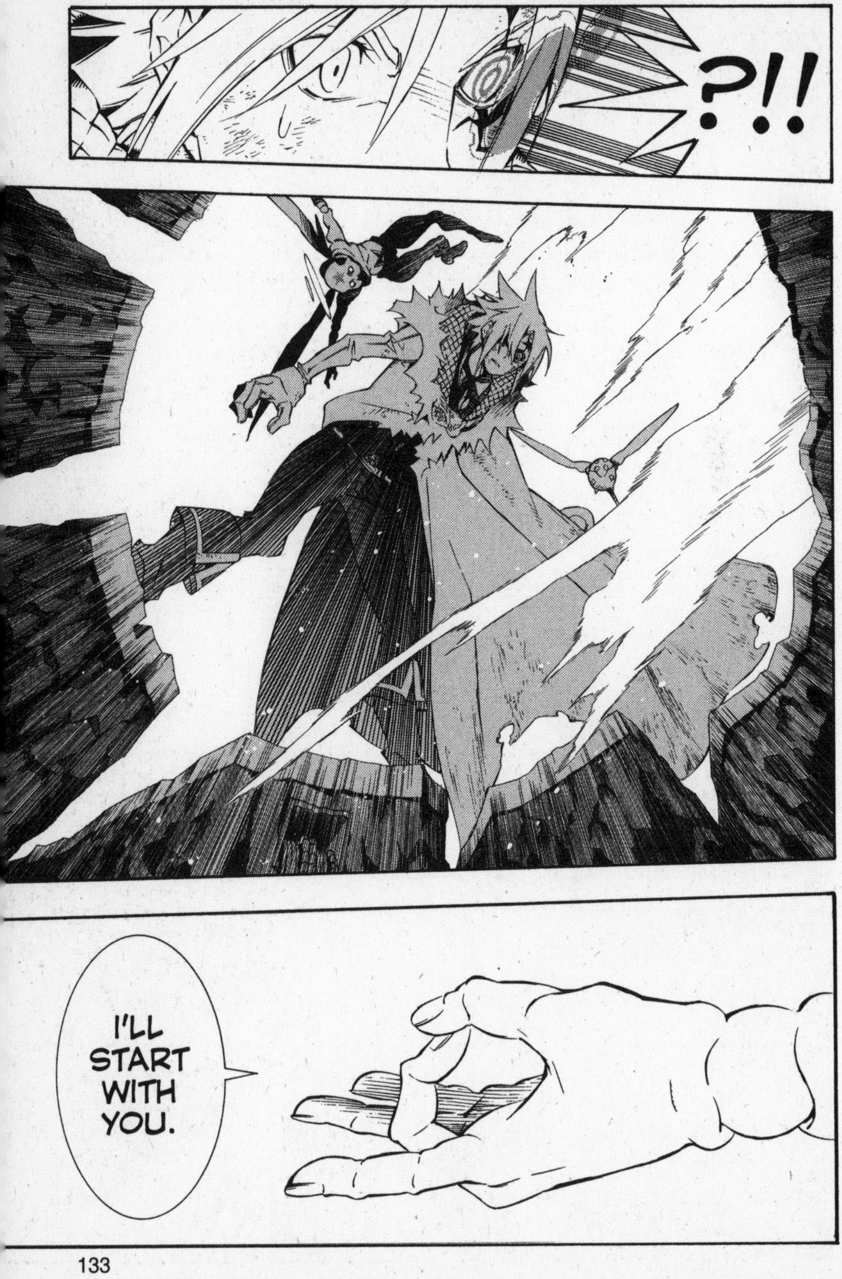
?!!
I'LL START WITH YOU.

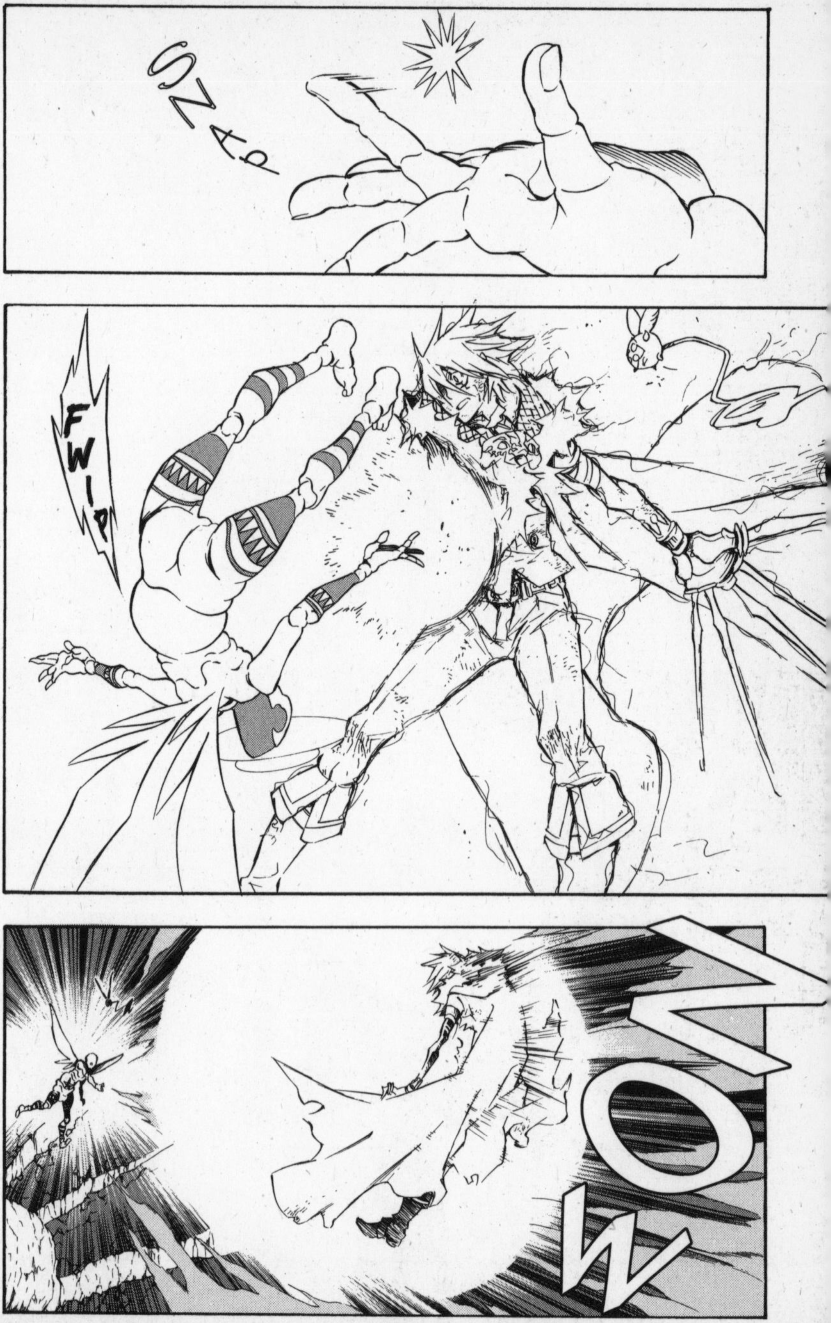
SNAP
FWIP

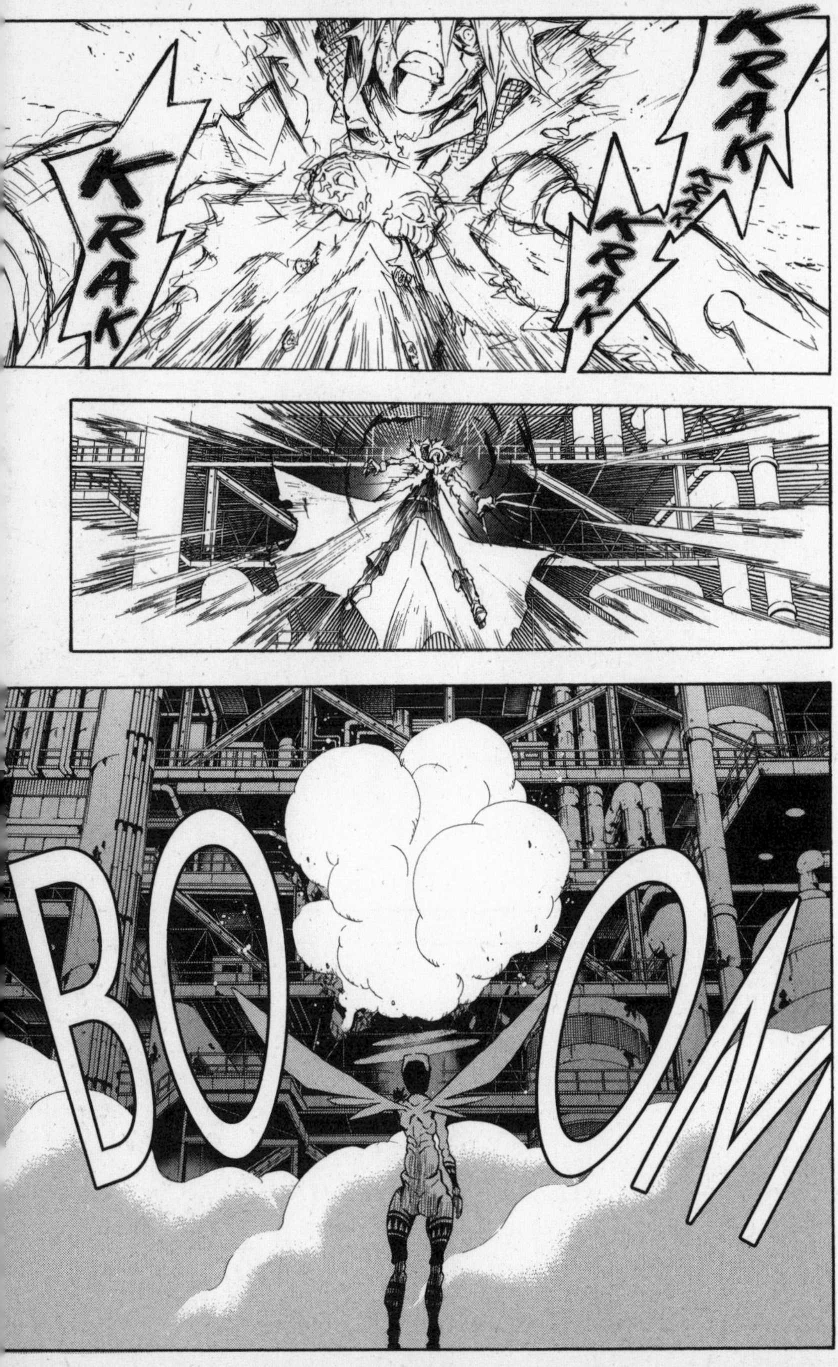
KRAK
KRAK
KRAK
KRAK
BOOM

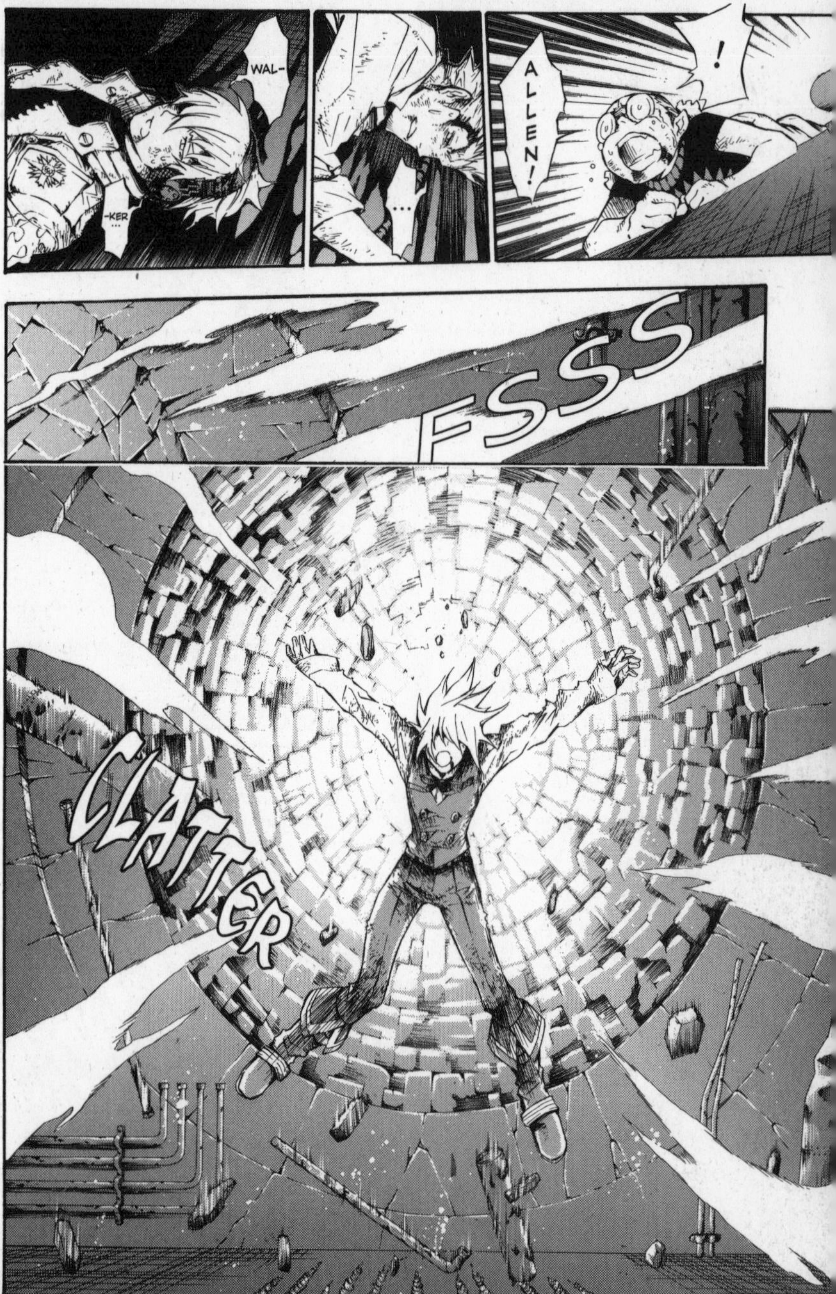
!
ALLEN!
...
WAL-
-KER
...
FSSS
CLATTER

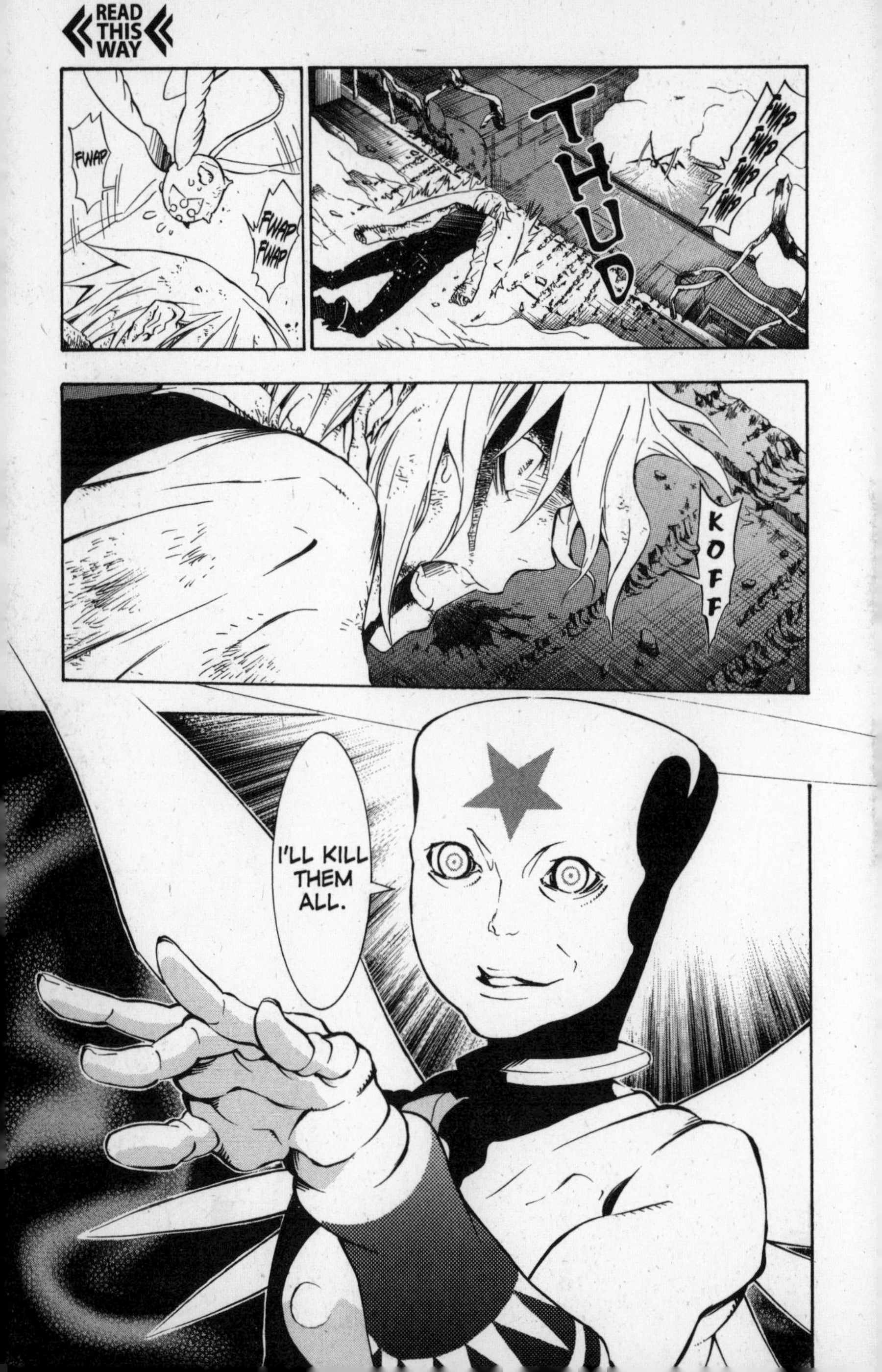
READ THIS WAY
FWIP FWIP FWIP FWIP
THUD
FWAP
FWAP FWAP
KOFF
I'LL KILL THEM ALL.

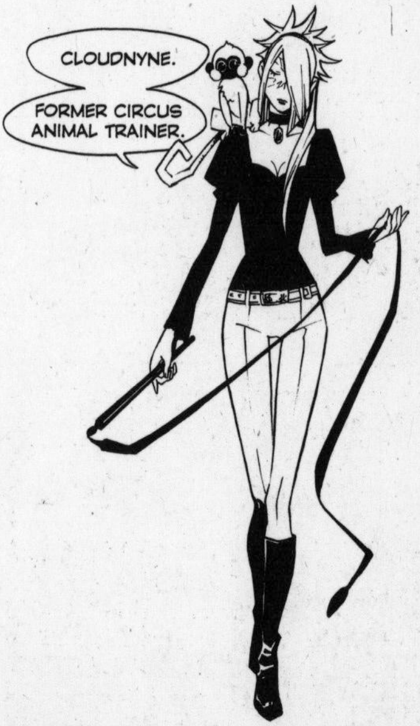
CLOUDNYNE.
FORMER CIRCUS ANIMAL TRAINER.

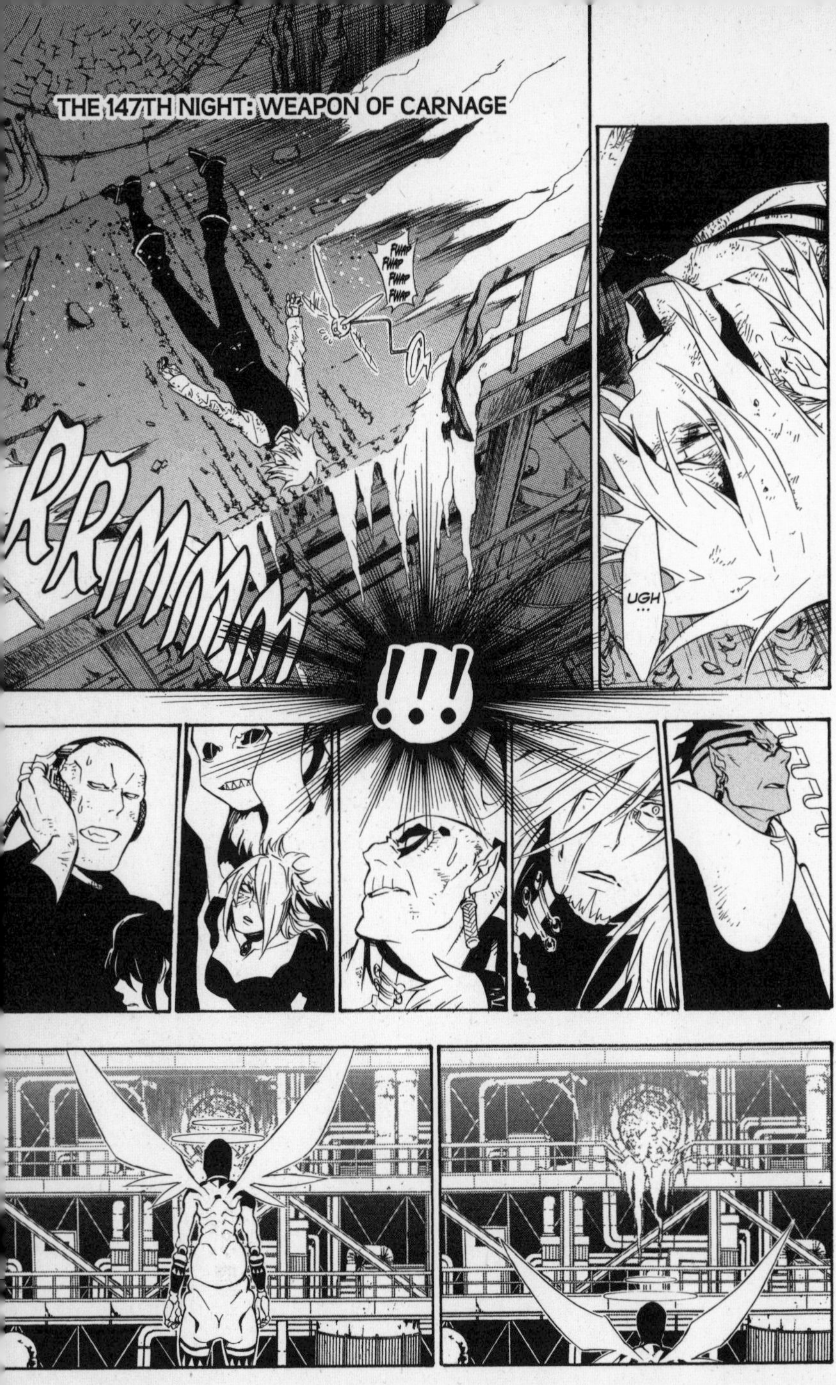
THE 147TH NIGHT: WEAPON OF CARNAGE
UGH...
FWAP FWAP FWAP FWAP
RRMMMM
!!!

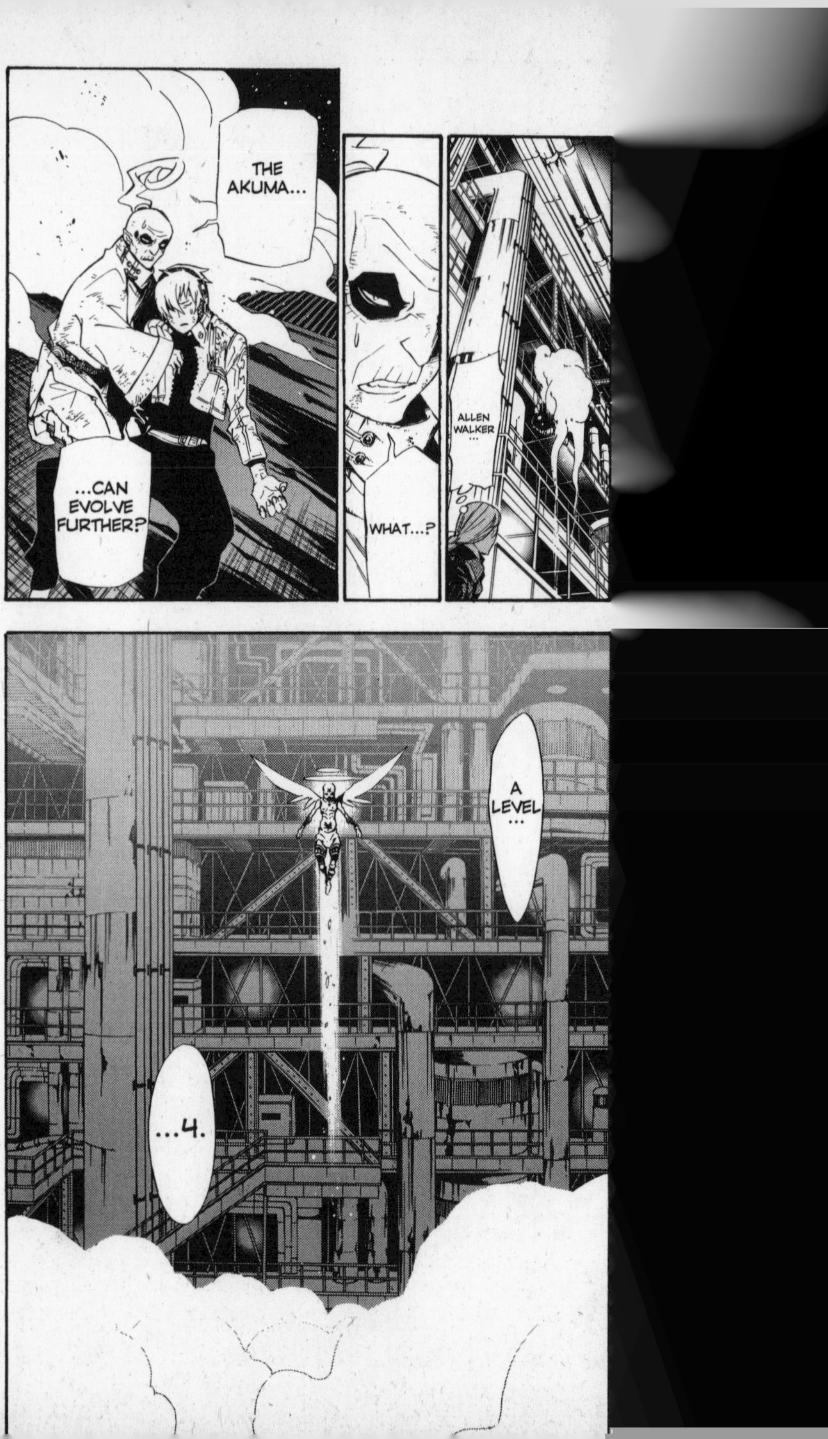
ALLEN WALKER ...
WHAT...?
THE AKUMA...
...CAN EVOLVE FURTHER?
A LEVEL ...
...4.

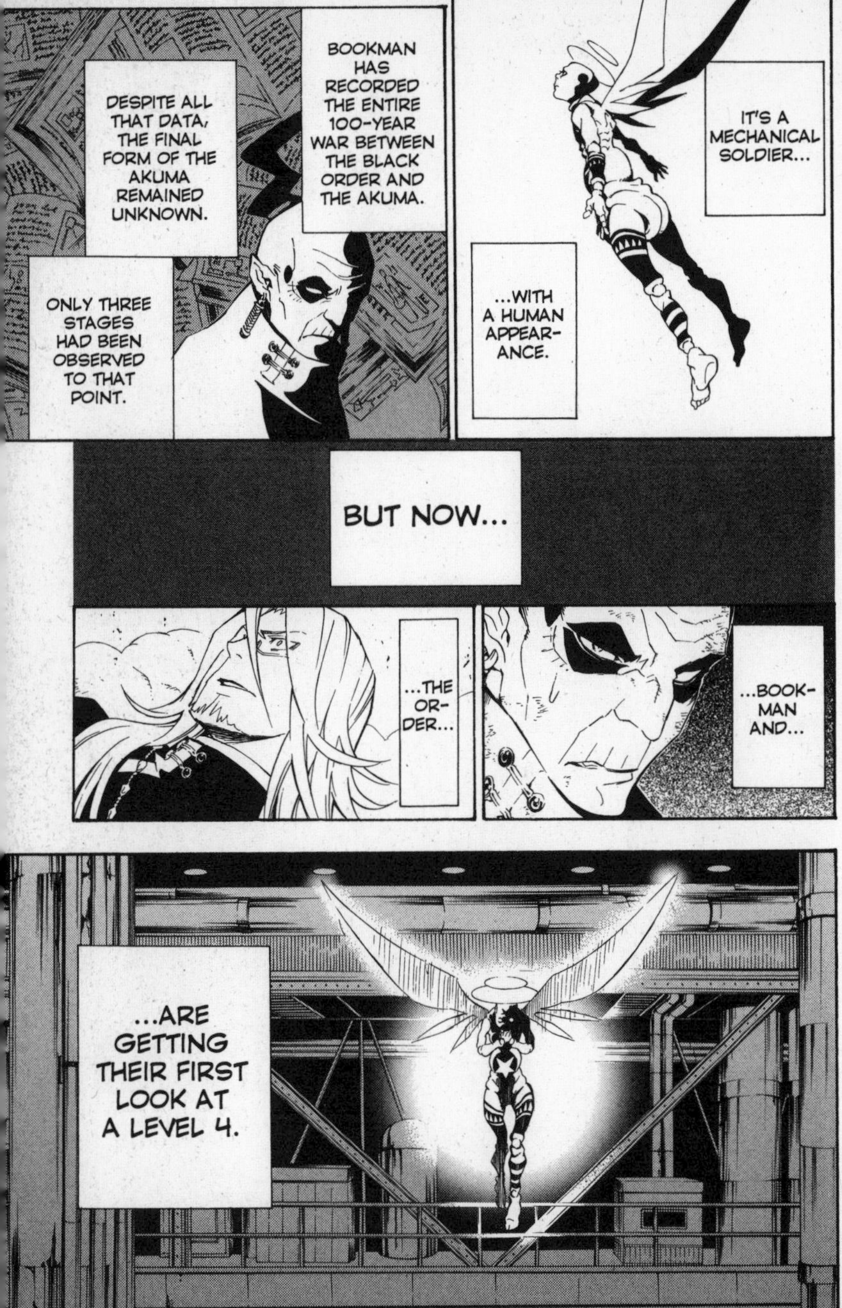
IT'S A MECHANICAL SOLDIER...
...WITH A HUMAN APPEARANCE.
BOOKMAN HAS RECORDED THE ENTIRE 100-YEAR WAR BETWEEN THE BLACK ORDER AND THE AKUMA.
DESPITE ALL THAT DATA, THE FINAL FORM OF THE AKUMA REMAINED UNKNOWN.
ONLY THREE STAGES HAD BEEN OBSERVED TO THAT POINT.
BUT NOW...
...BOOKMAN AND...
...THE ORDER...
...ARE GETTING THEIR FIRST LOOK AT A LEVEL 4.

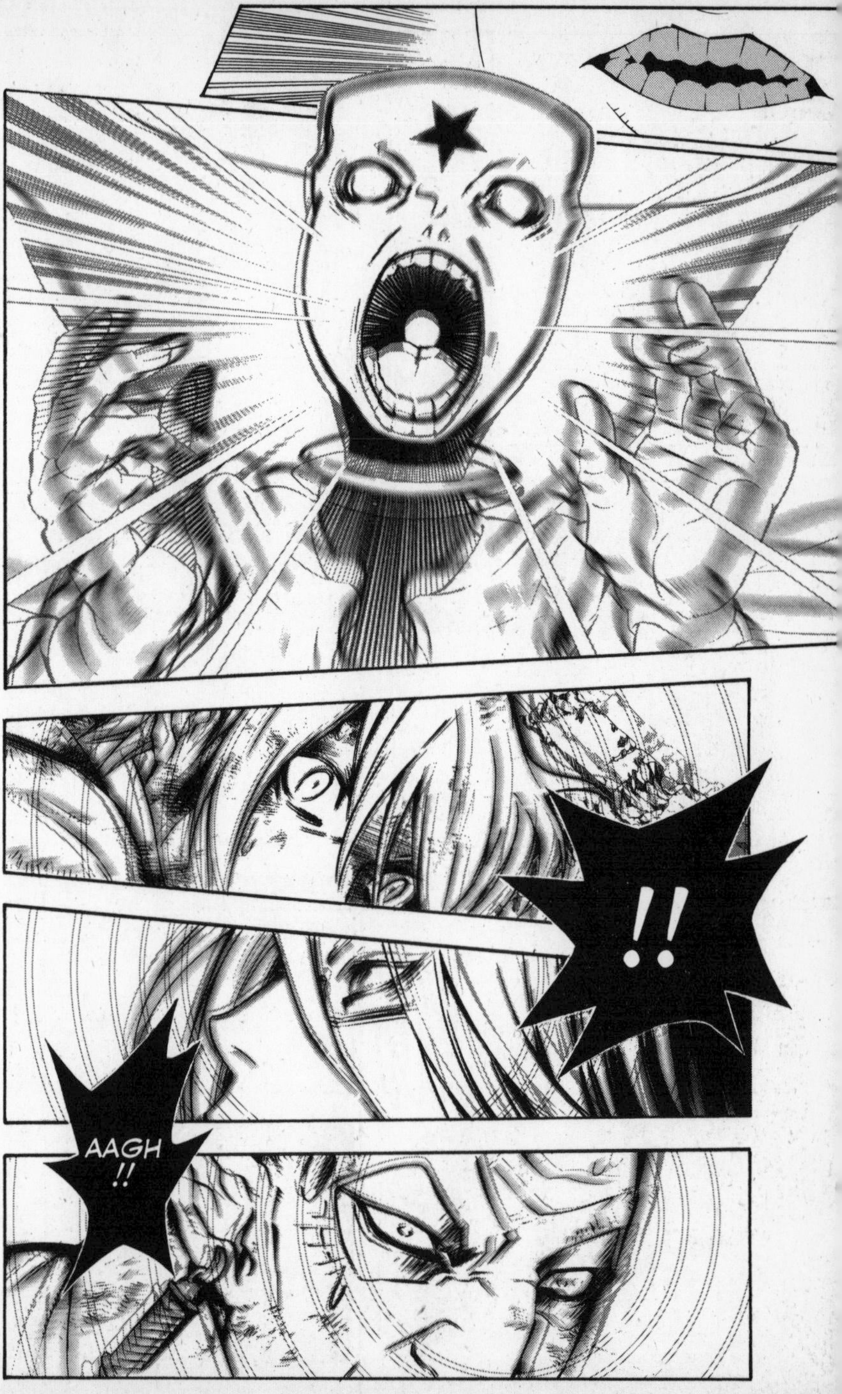
!!
AAGH !!

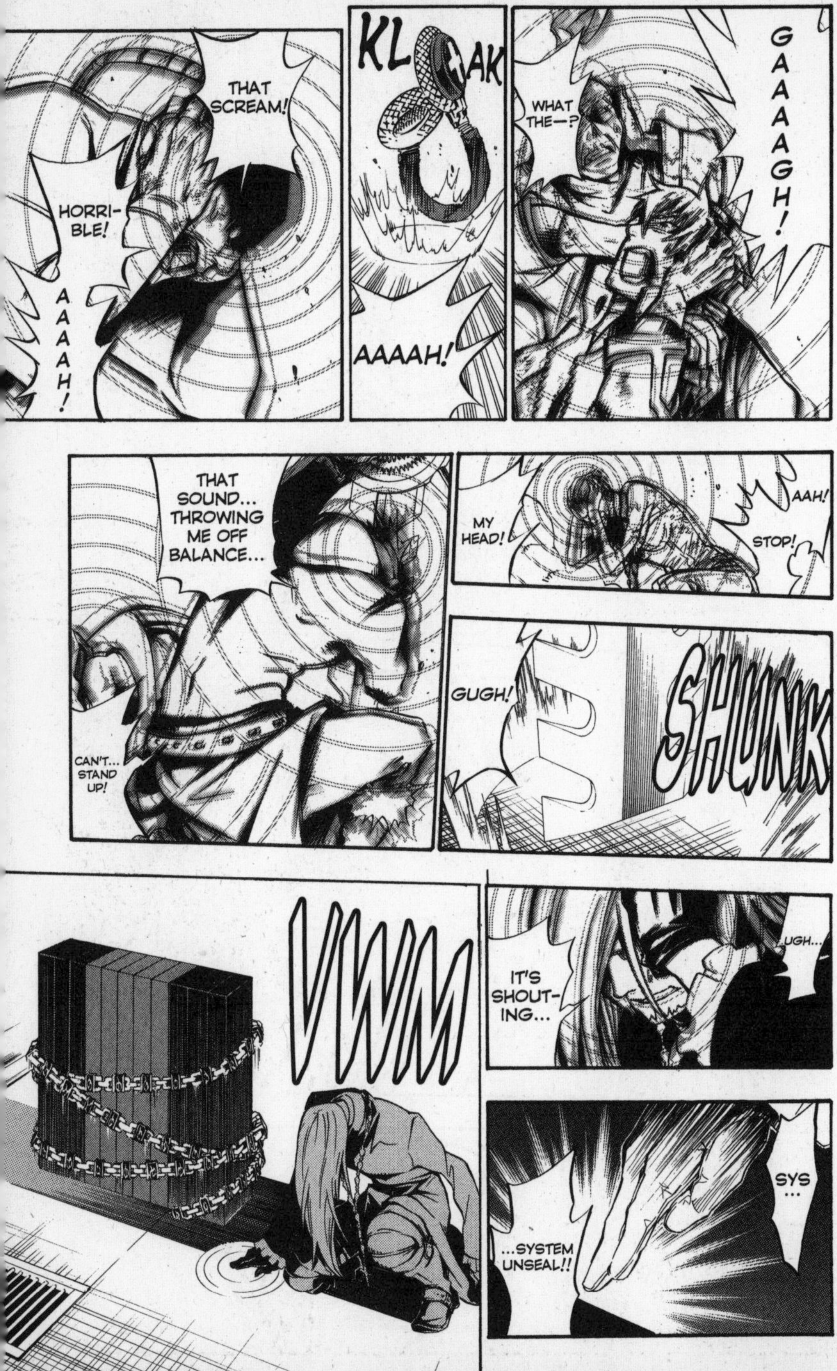

GAAAAGH!
WHAT THE—?
KL
AK
AAAAH!
THAT SCREAM!
HORRIBLE!
AAAAH!
AAH!
STOP!
MY HEAD!
SHUNK
GUGH!
THAT SOUND... THROWING ME OFF BALANCE...
CAN'T... STAND UP!
UGH...
IT'S SHOUTING...
SYS...
...SYSTEM UNSEAL!!
VWM

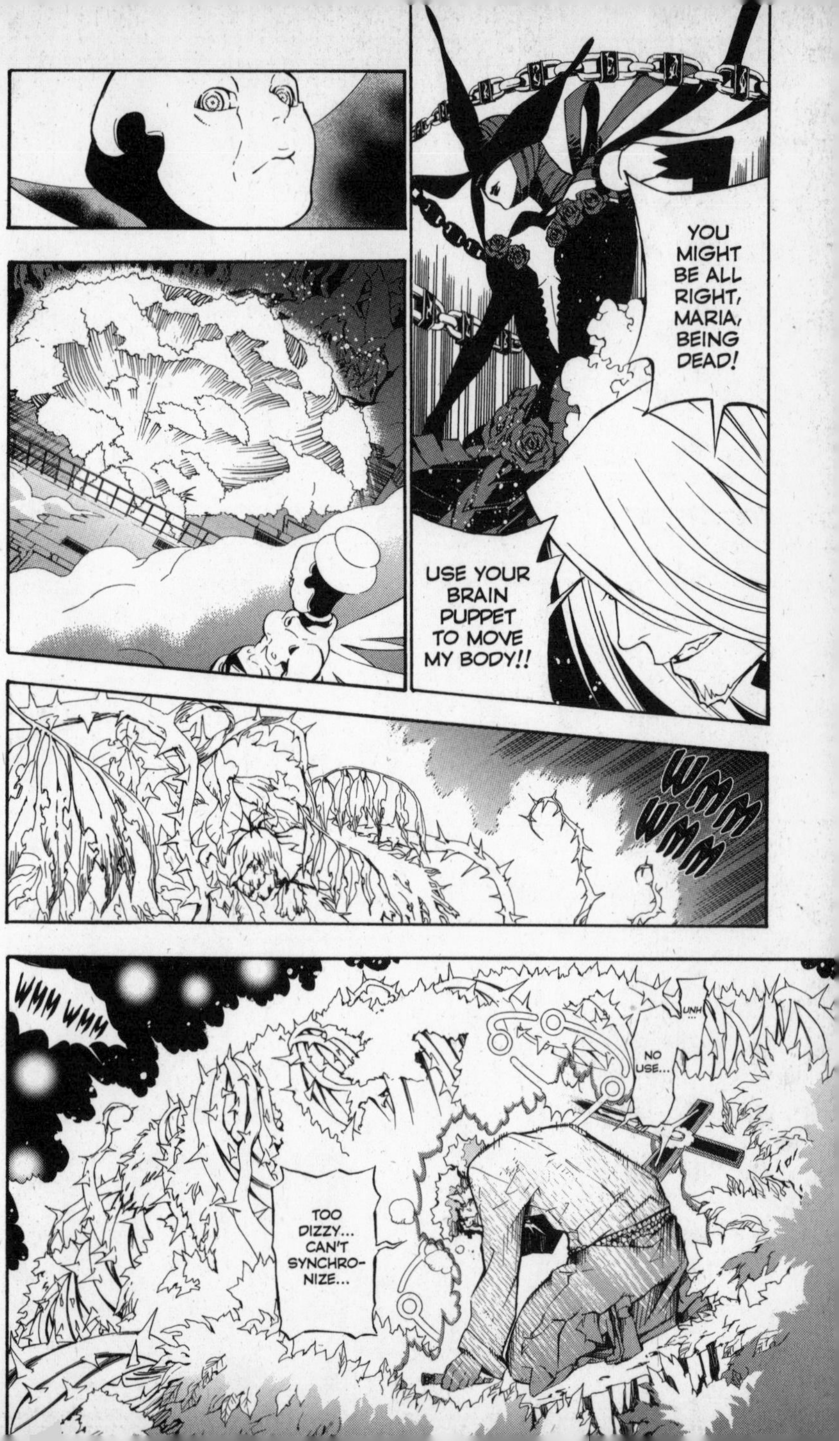
YOU MIGHT BE ALL RIGHT, MARIA, BEING DEAD!
USE YOUR BRAIN PUPPET TO MOVE MY BODY!!
WMM WMM
WMM WMM
UNH...
NO USE...
TOO DIZZY... CAN'T SYNCHRO-NIZE...

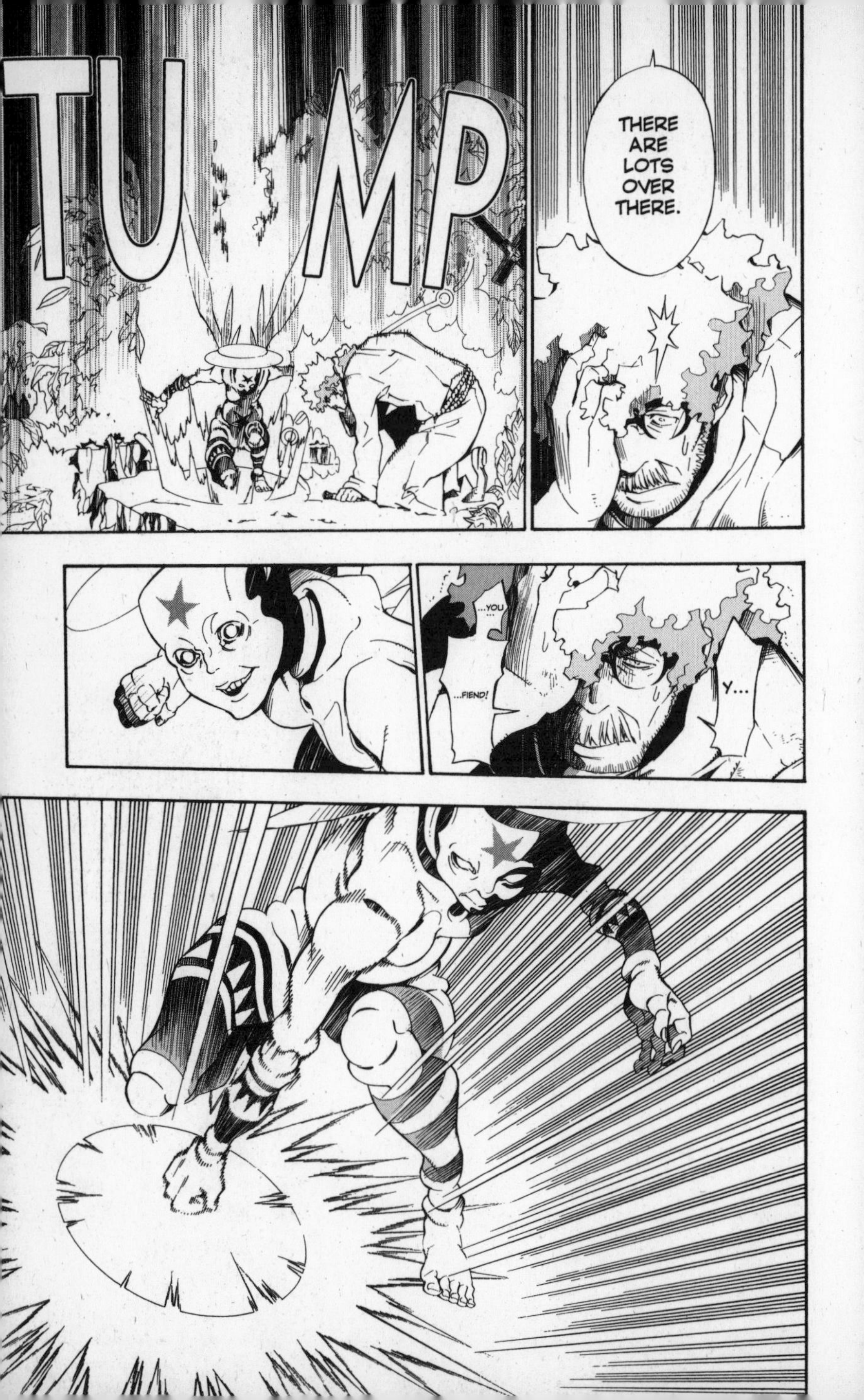
THERE ARE LOTS OVER THERE.
TUMP
Y...
...YOU...
...FIEND!

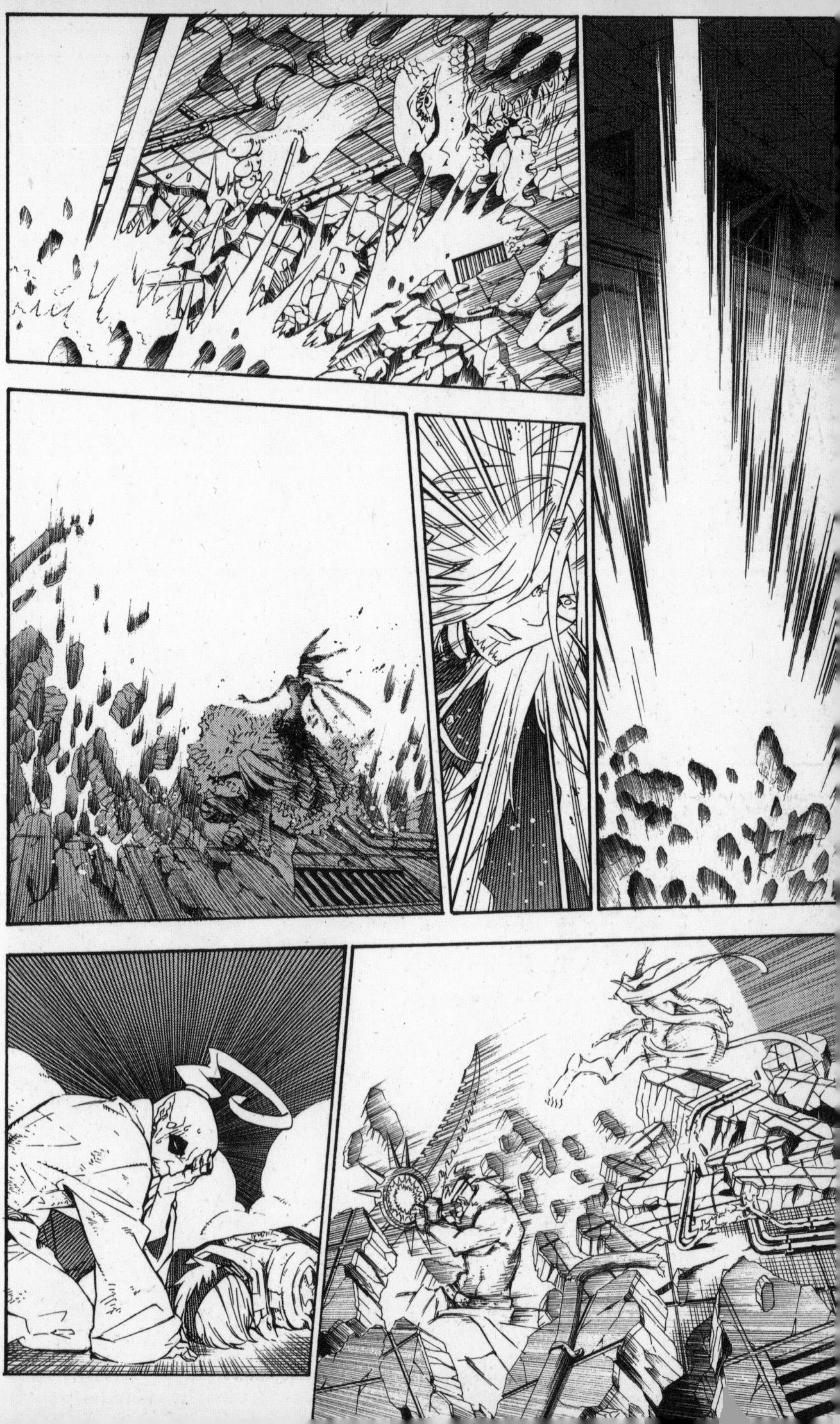

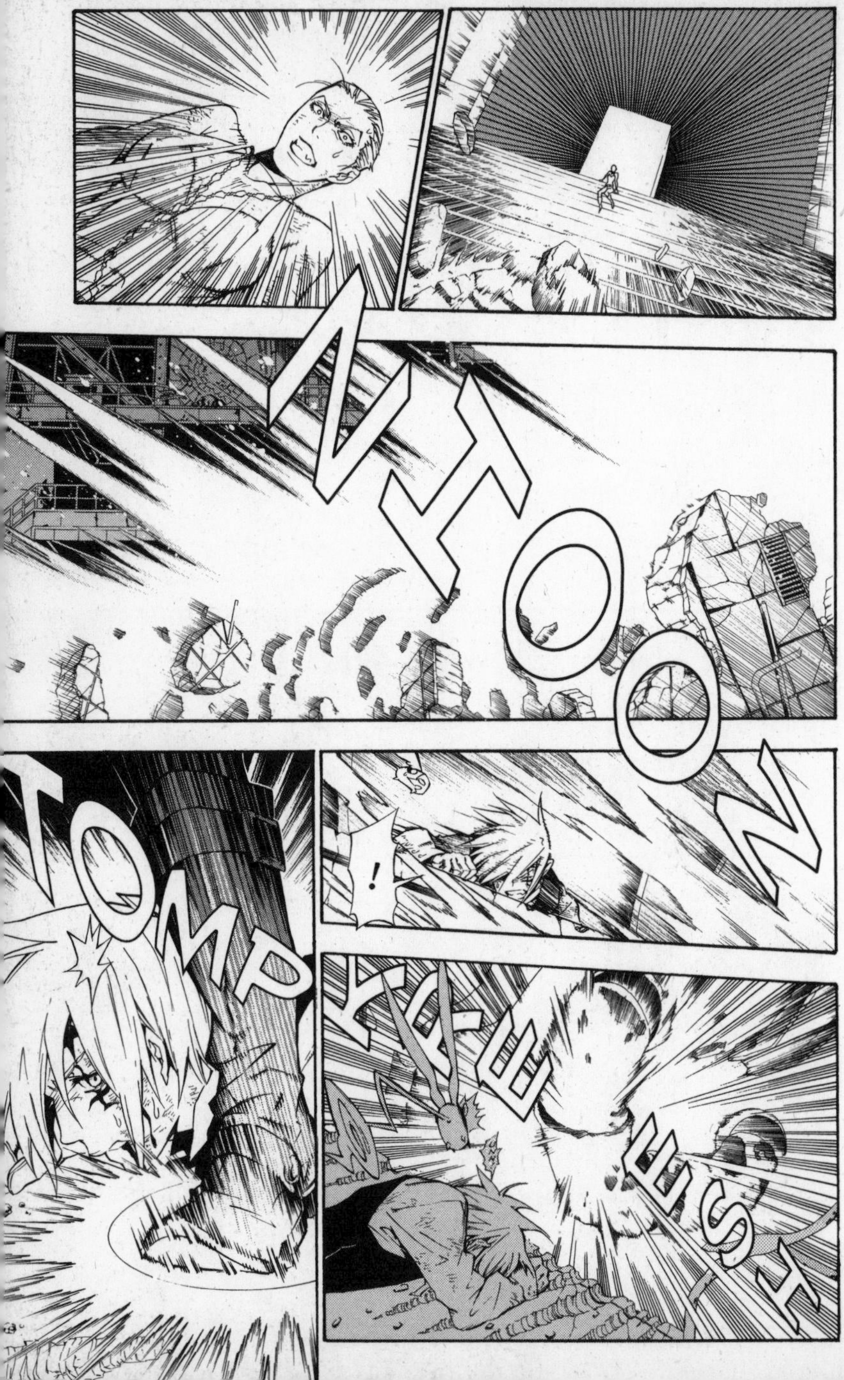
WHOOON
!
STOMP
YAEESH

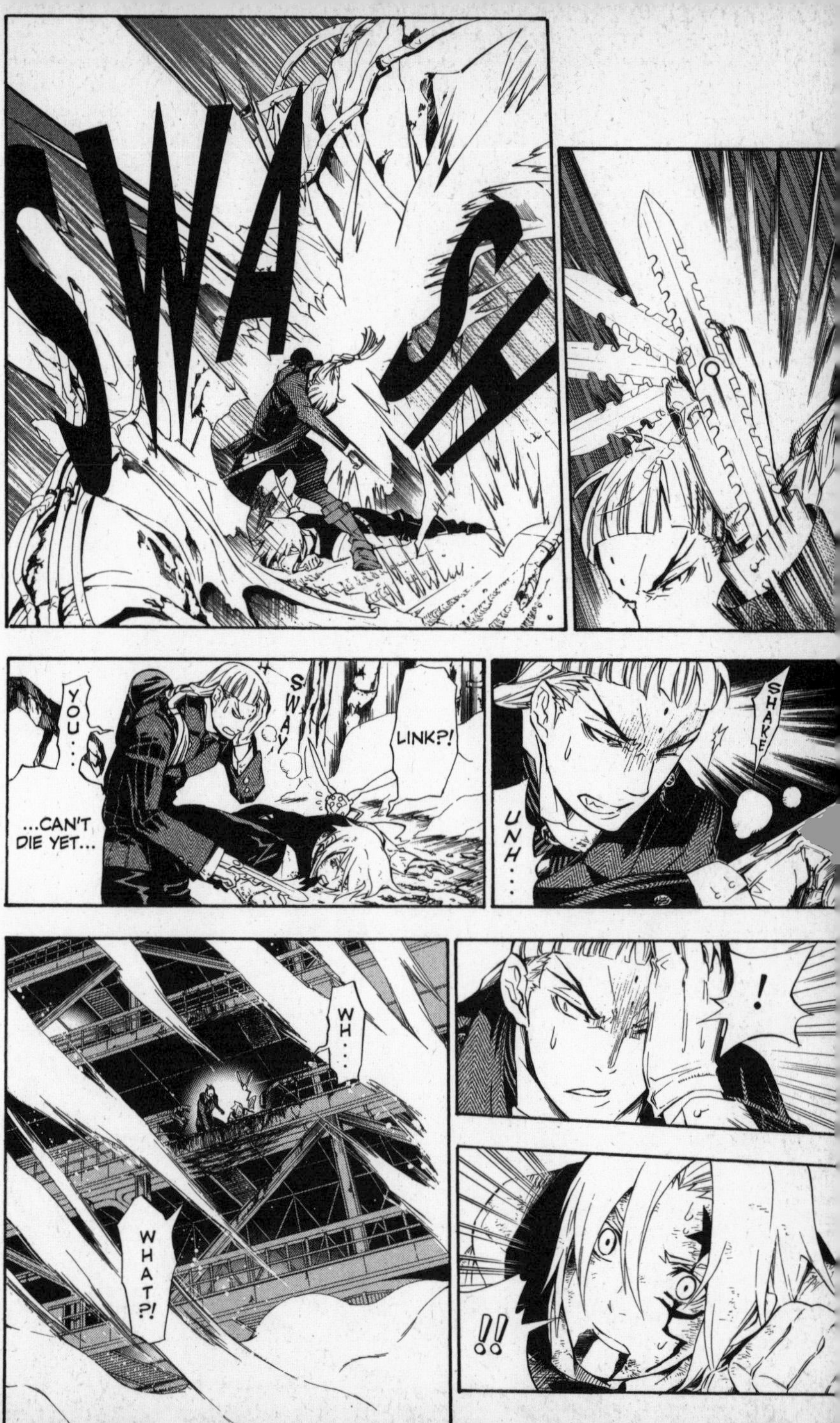
SWASH
SHAKE
UNH...
LINK?!
SWAY
YOU...
...CAN'T DIE YET...
!
!!
WH...
WHAT?!

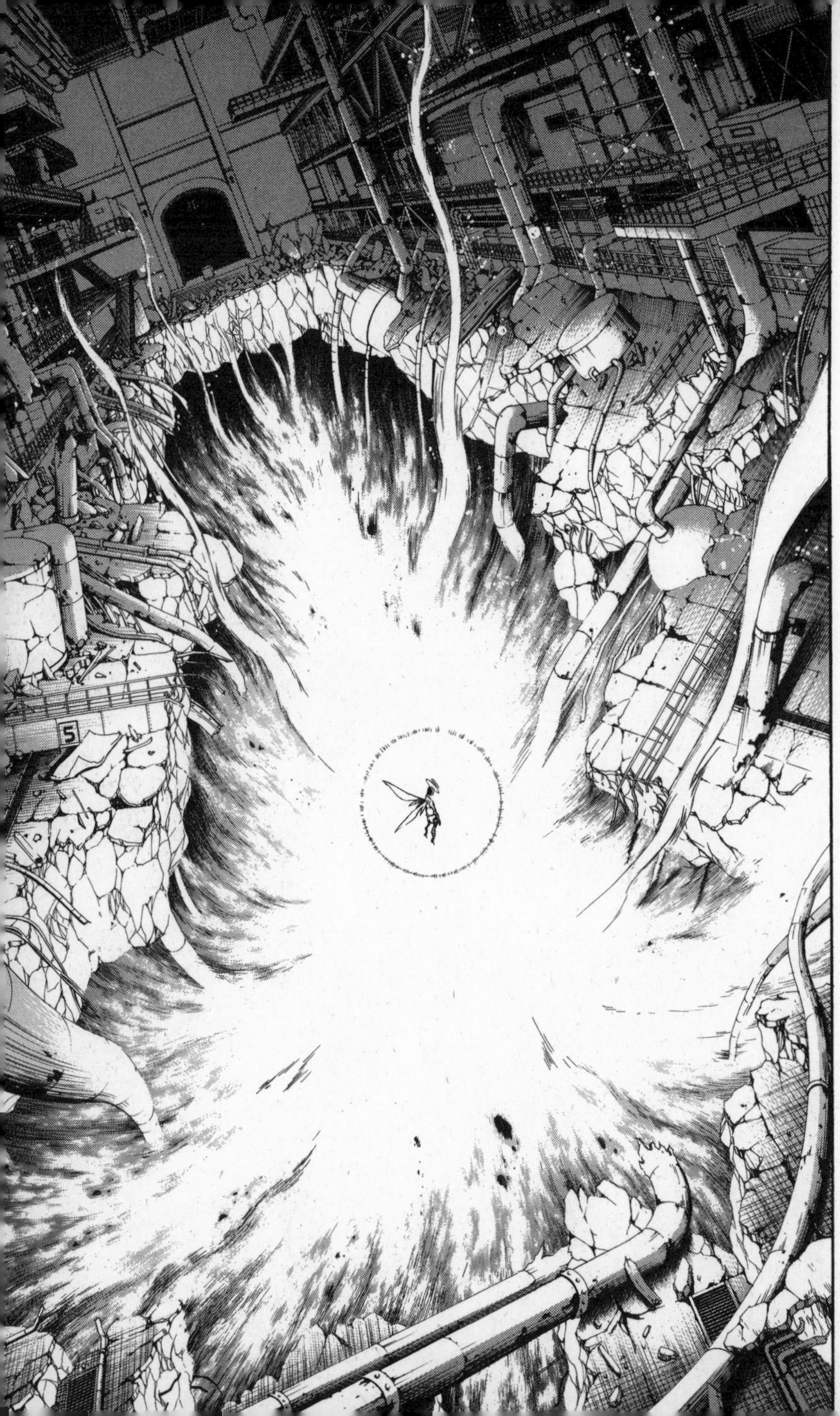

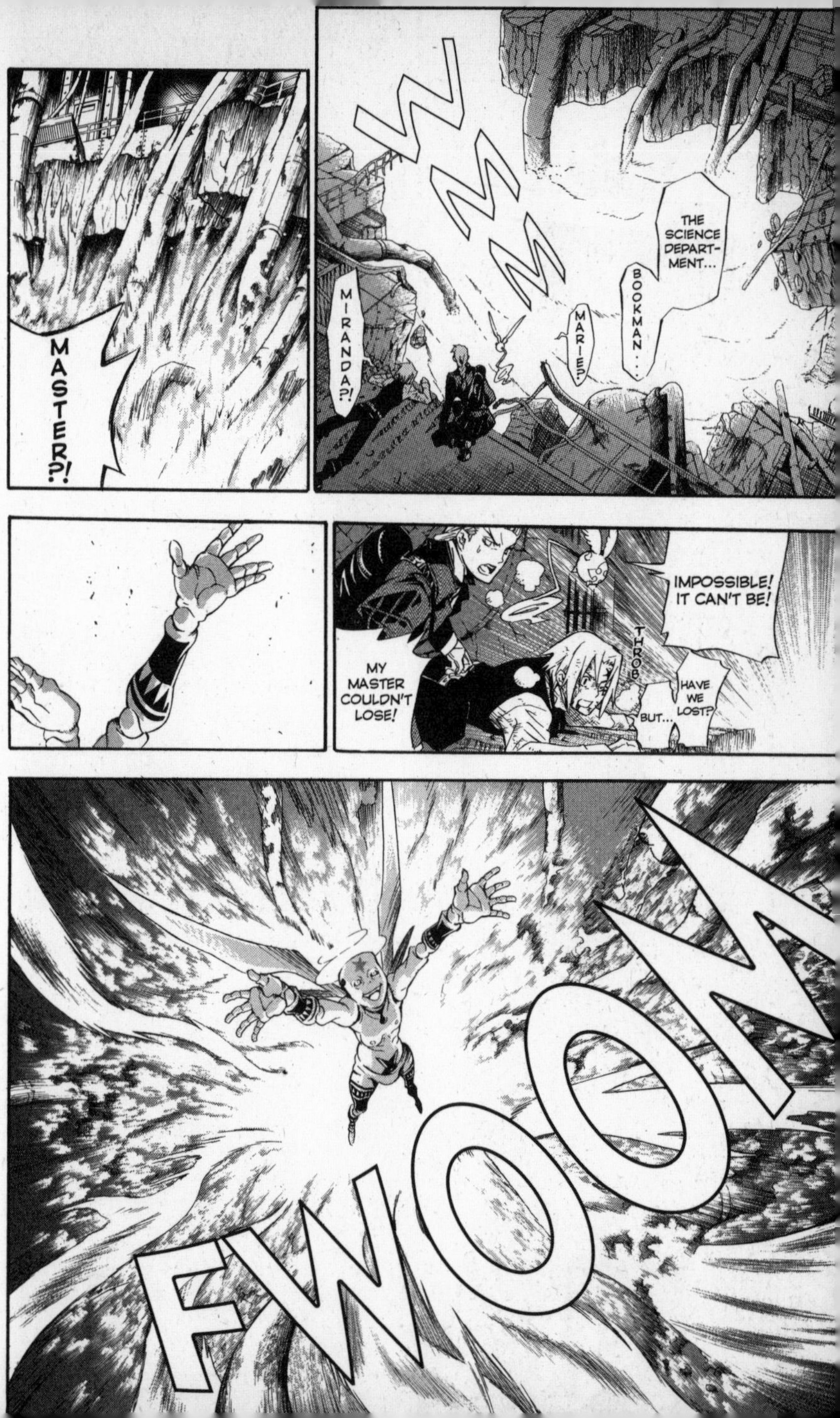
WMMM
THE SCIENCE DEPARTMENT...
BOOKMAN...
MARIE?!
MIRANDA?!
MASTER?!
IMPOSSIBLE! IT CAN'T BE!
HAVE WE LOST?
BUT...
THROB
MY MASTER COULDN'T LOSE!
FWOOM

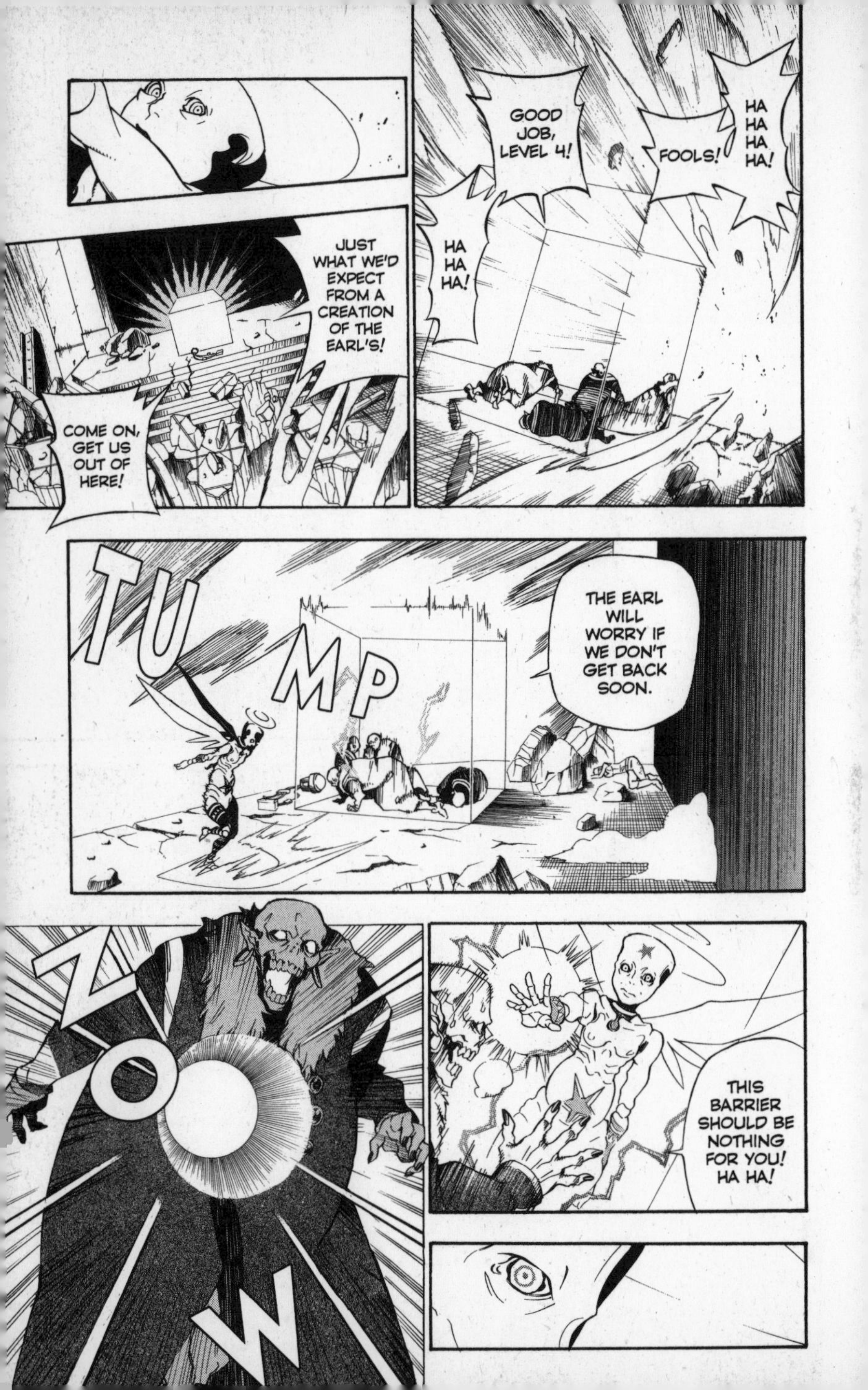
HA HA HA HA!
FOOLS!
GOOD JOB, LEVEL 4!
HA HA HA!
JUST WHAT WE'D EXPECT FROM A CREATION OF THE EARL'S!
COME ON, GET US OUT OF HERE!
THE EARL WILL WORRY IF WE DON'T GET BACK SOON.
TUMP
THIS BARRIER SHOULD BE NOTHING FOR YOU! HA HA!
ZOOW

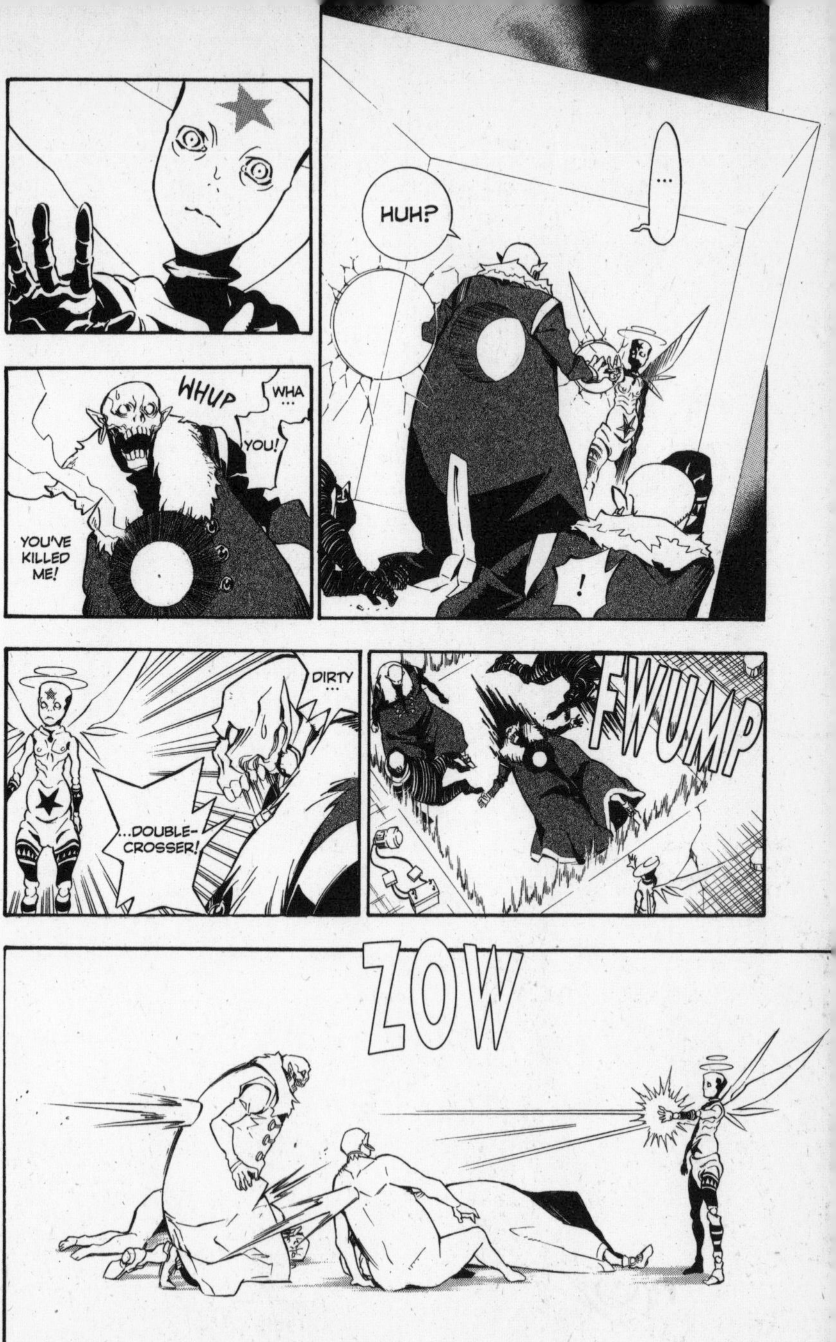
...
HUH?
!
WHUP
WHA ...
YOU!
YOU'VE KILLED ME!
FWUMP
DIRTY ...
...DOUBLE-CROSSER!
ZOW

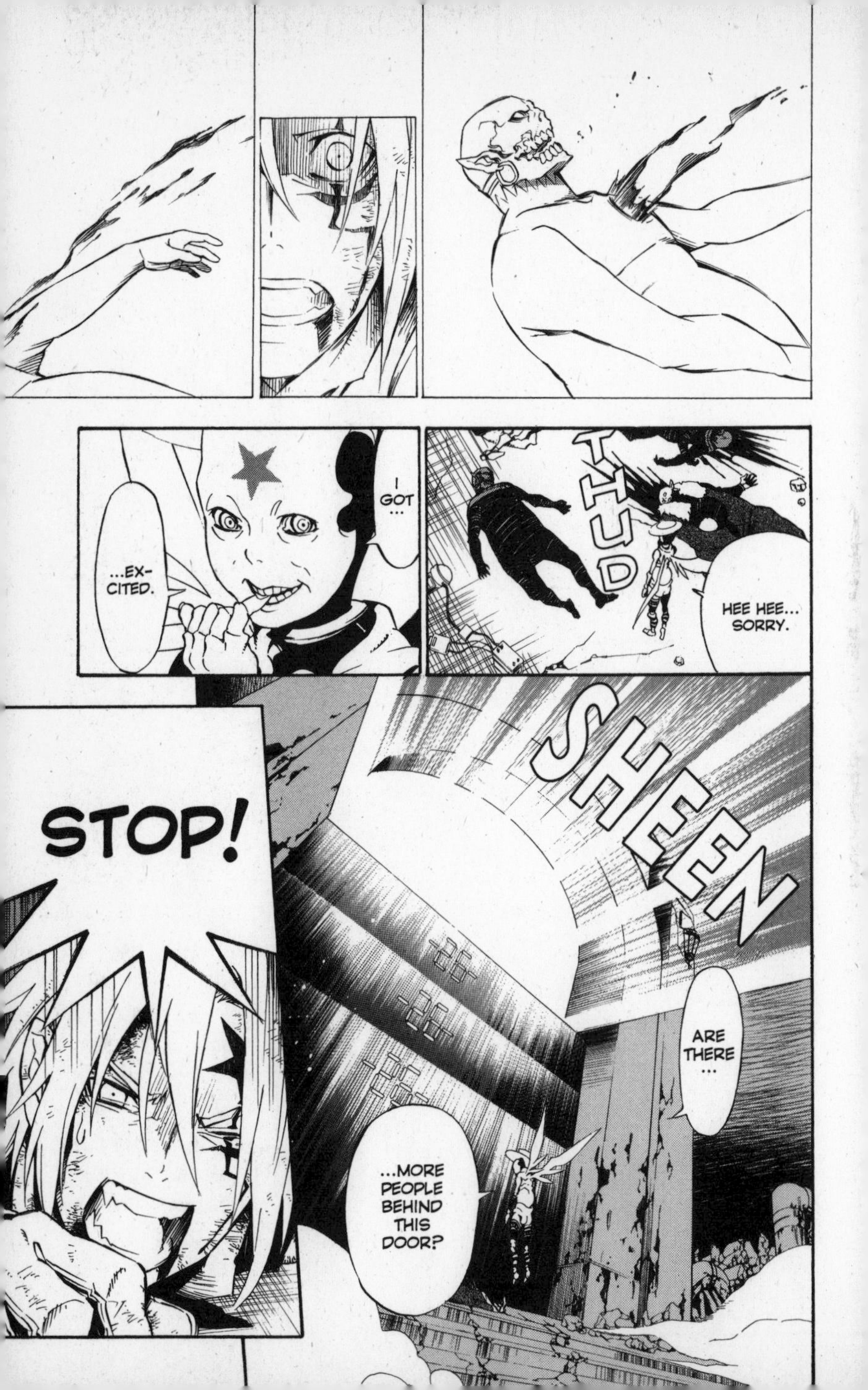
THUD
HEE HEE... SORRY.
I GOT...
...EXCITED.
SHEEN
ARE THERE...
...MORE PEOPLE BEHIND THIS DOOR?
STOP!

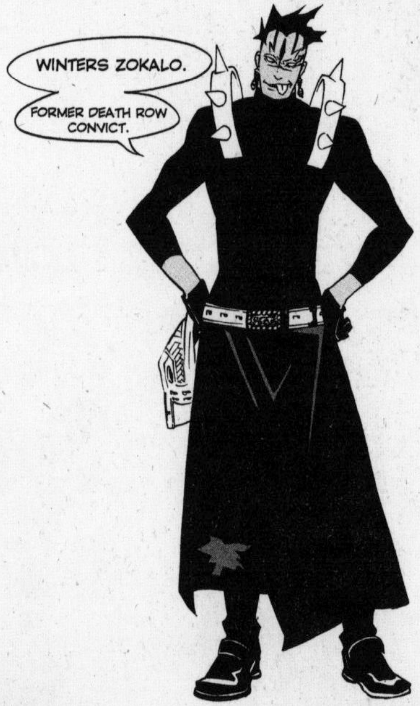
WINTERS ZOKALO.
FORMER DEATH ROW CONVICT.

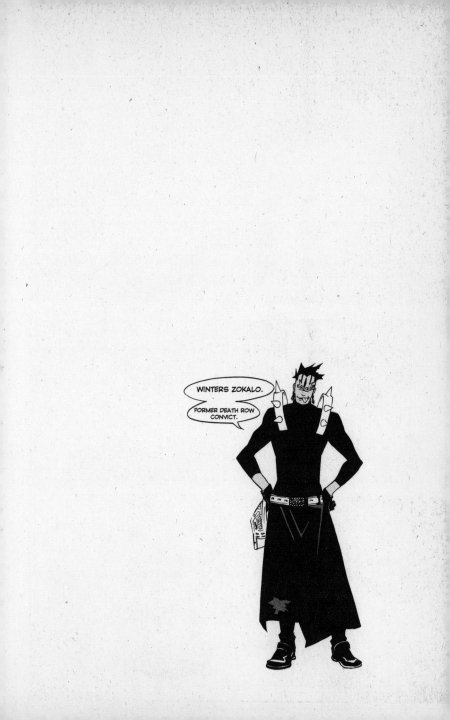

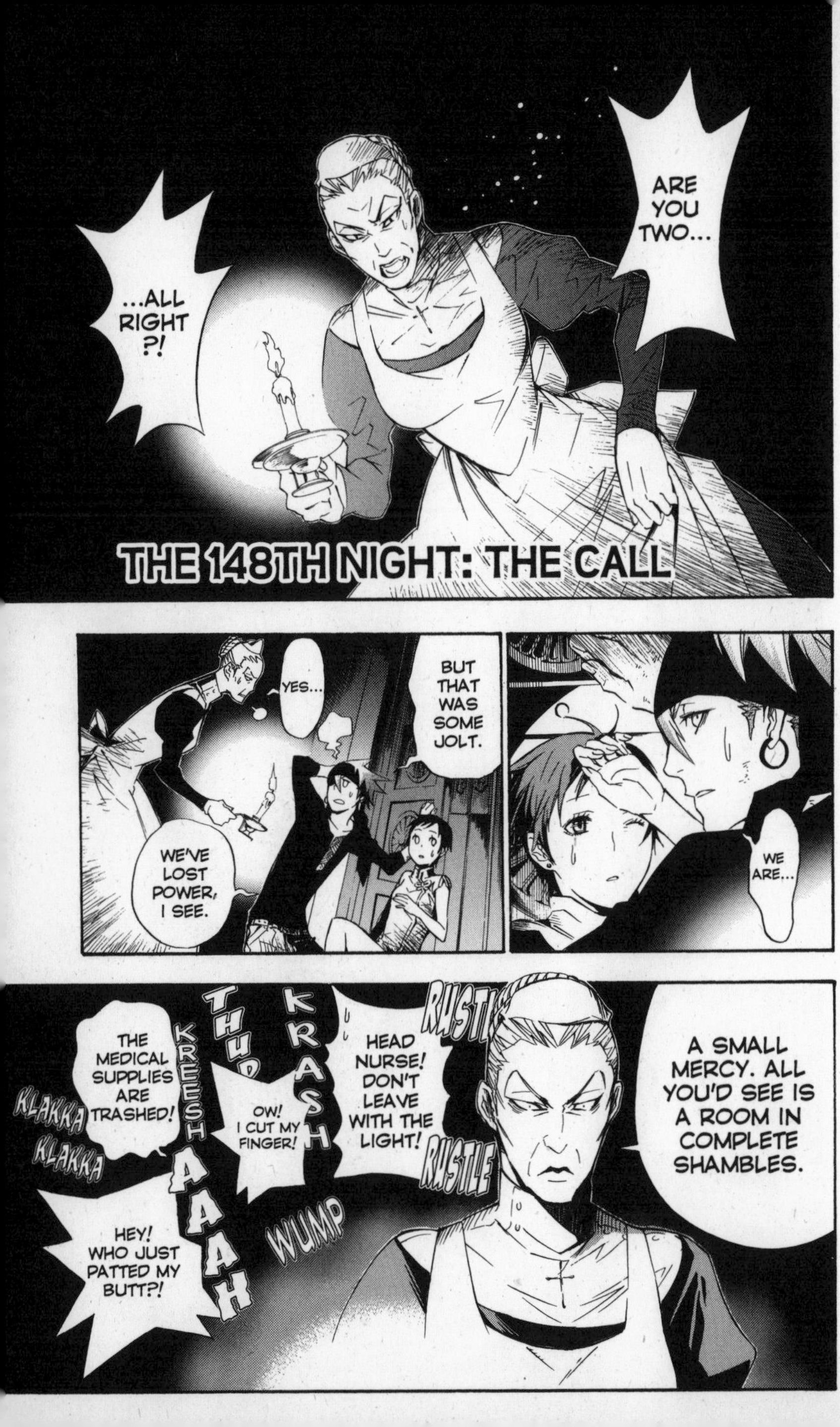
ARE YOU TWO...
...ALL RIGHT?!
THE 148TH NIGHT: THE CALL
WE ARE...
BUT THAT WAS SOME JOLT.
YES...
WE'VE LOST POWER, I SEE.
A SMALL MERCY. ALL YOU'D SEE IS A ROOM IN COMPLETE SHAMBLES.
RUSTL
HEAD NURSE! DON'T LEAVE WITH THE LIGHT!
RUSTLE
KRASH
OW! I CUT MY FINGER!
THUD
KREESH
THE MEDICAL SUPPLIES ARE TRASHED!
KLAKKA
KLAKKA
WUMP
AAAAH
HEY! WHO JUST PATTED MY BUTT?!

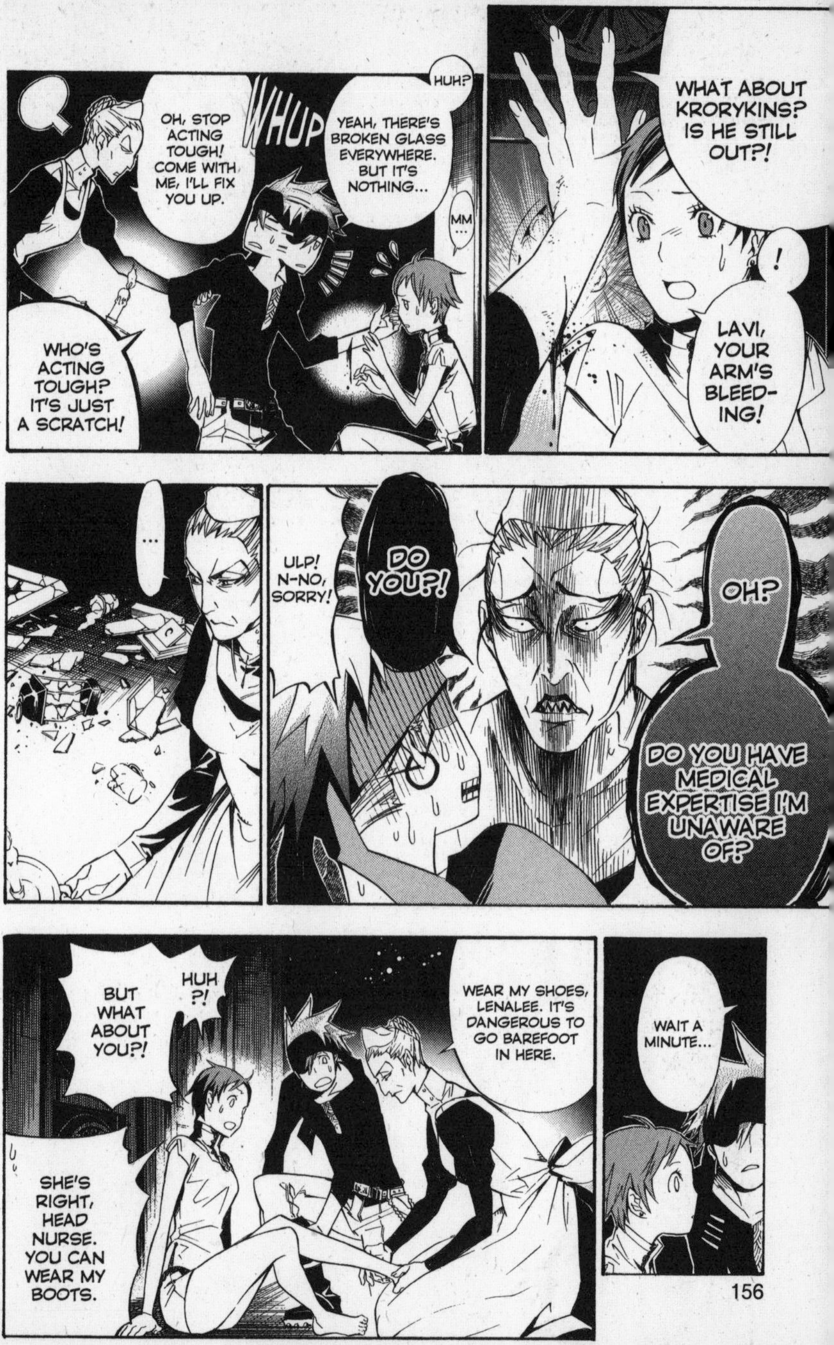
WHAT ABOUT KRORYKINS? IS HE STILL OUT?!
!
LAVI, YOUR ARM'S BLEED-ING!
HUH?
YEAH, THERE'S BROKEN GLASS EVERYWHERE. BUT IT'S NOTHING...
MM ...
WHUP
OH, STOP ACTING TOUGH! COME WITH ME, I'LL FIX YOU UP.
WHO'S ACTING TOUGH? IT'S JUST A SCRATCH!
OH?
DO YOU HAVE MEDICAL EXPERTISE I'M UNAWARE OF?
DO YOU?!
ULP! N-NO, SORRY!
...
WAIT A MINUTE...
WEAR MY SHOES, LENALEE. IT'S DANGEROUS TO GO BAREFOOT IN HERE.
HUH ?!
BUT WHAT ABOUT YOU?!
SHE'S RIGHT, HEAD NURSE. YOU CAN WEAR MY BOOTS.

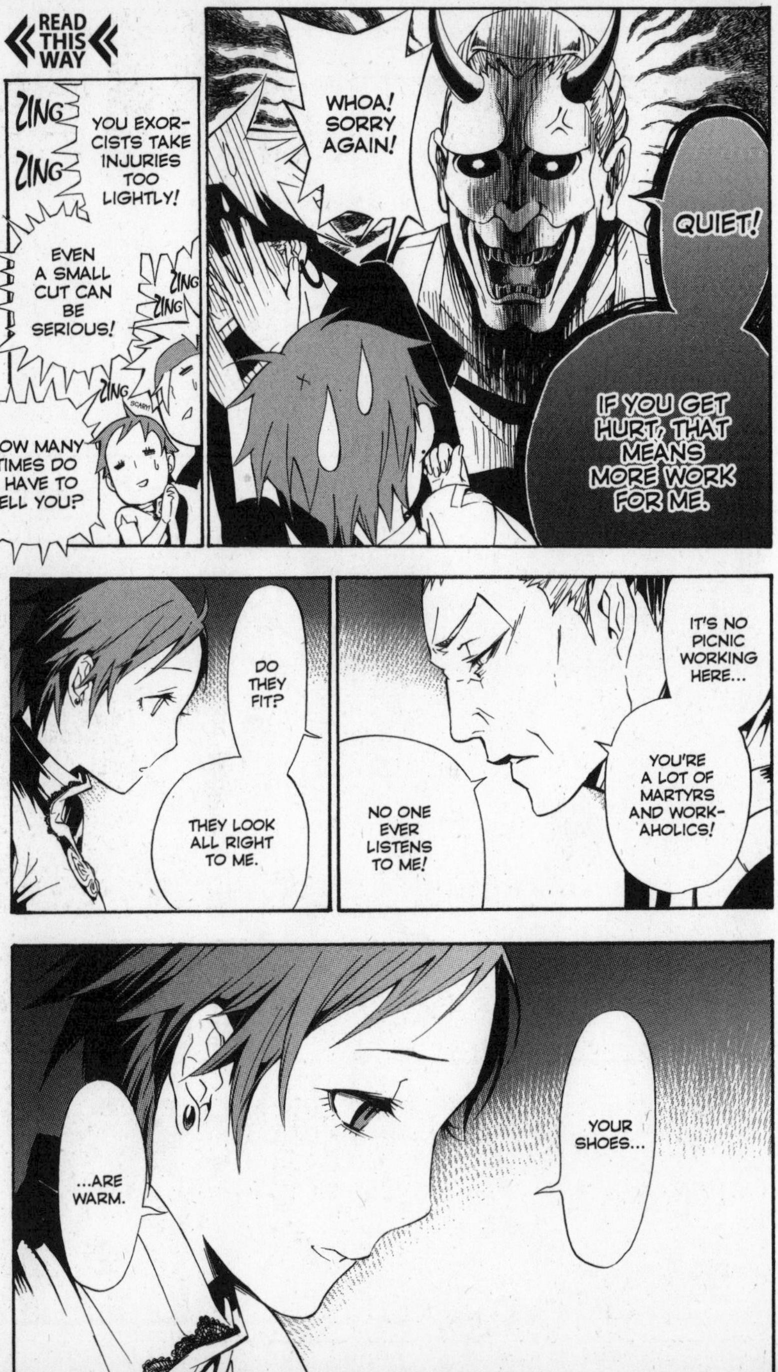
READ THIS WAY
QUIET!
IF YOU GET HURT, THAT MEANS MORE WORK FOR ME.
WHOA! SORRY AGAIN!
YOU EXORCISTS TAKE INJURIES TOO LIGHTLY!
ZING
ZING
EVEN A SMALL CUT CAN BE SERIOUS!
ZING
ZING
ZING
SCARY!
HOW MANY TIMES DO I HAVE TO TELL YOU?
IT'S NO PICNIC WORKING HERE...
YOU'RE A LOT OF MARTYRS AND WORK-AHOLICS!
NO ONE EVER LISTENS TO ME!
DO THEY FIT?
THEY LOOK ALL RIGHT TO ME.
YOUR SHOES...
...ARE WARM.

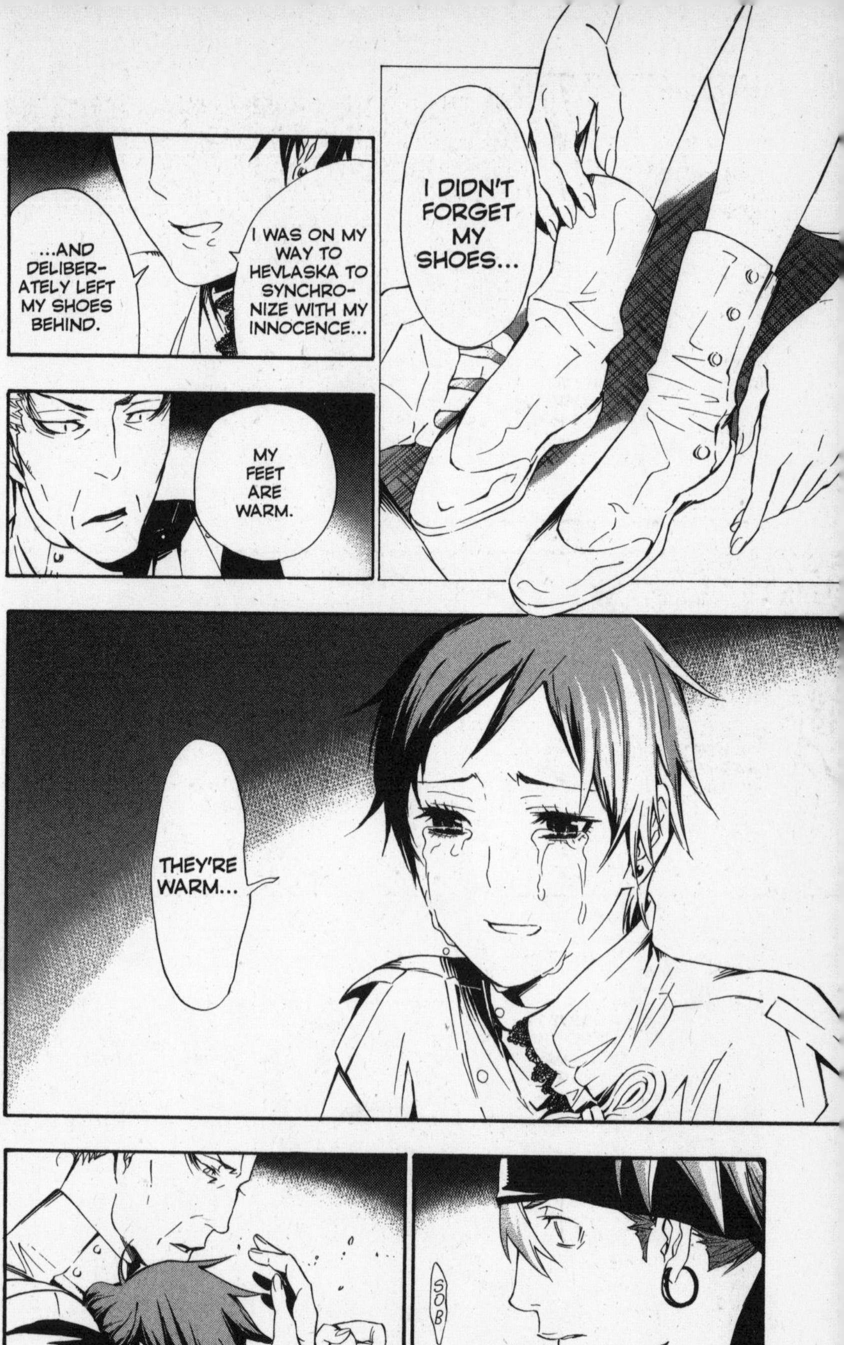
I DIDN'T FORGET MY SHOES...
I WAS ON MY WAY TO HEVLASKA TO SYNCHRONIZE WITH MY INNOCENCE...
...AND DELIBERATELY LEFT MY SHOES BEHIND.
MY FEET ARE WARM.
THEY'RE WARM...
SOB

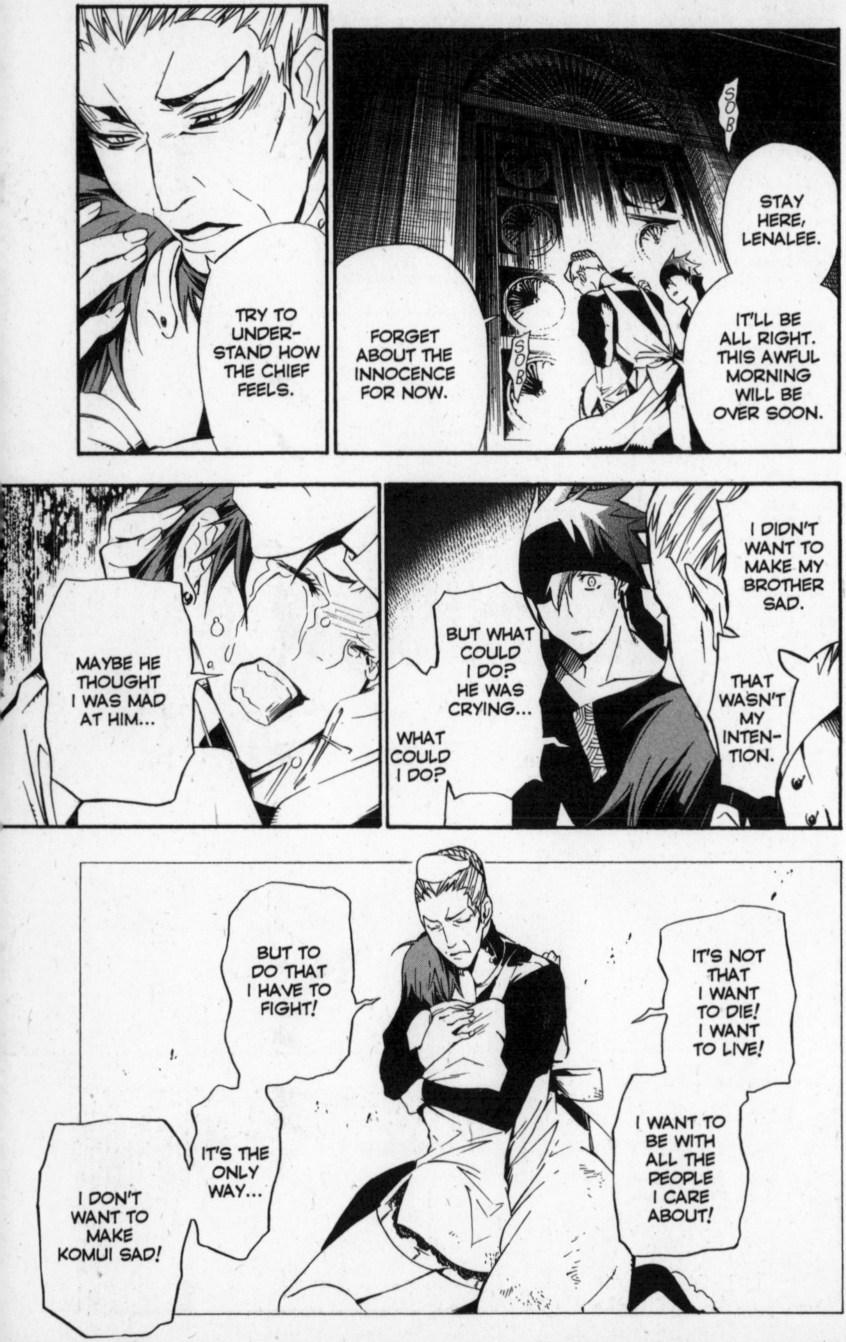
SOB
STAY HERE, LENALEE.
IT'LL BE ALL RIGHT. THIS AWFUL MORNING WILL BE OVER SOON.
SOB
FORGET ABOUT THE INNOCENCE FOR NOW.
TRY TO UNDER-STAND HOW THE CHIEF FEELS.
I DIDN'T WANT TO MAKE MY BROTHER SAD.
THAT WASN'T MY INTEN-TION.
BUT WHAT COULD I DO? HE WAS CRYING...
WHAT COULD I DO?
MAYBE HE THOUGHT I WAS MAD AT HIM...
IT'S NOT THAT I WANT TO DIE! I WANT TO LIVE!
I WANT TO BE WITH ALL THE PEOPLE I CARE ABOUT!
BUT TO DO THAT I HAVE TO FIGHT!
IT'S THE ONLY WAY...
I DON'T WANT TO MAKE KOMUI SAD!

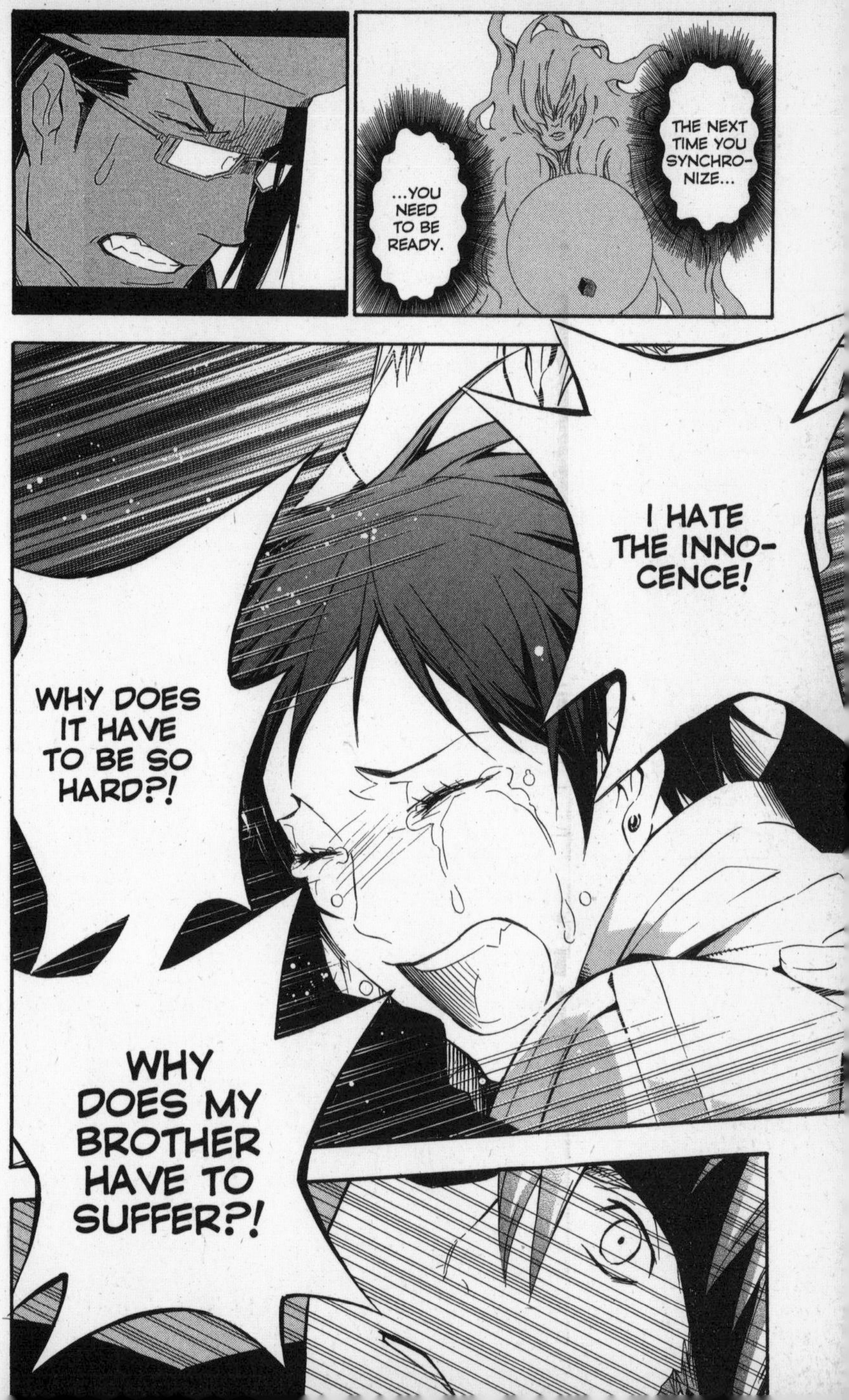
THE NEXT TIME YOU SYNCHRONIZE...
...YOU NEED TO BE READY.
I HATE THE INNOCENCE!
WHY DOES IT HAVE TO BE SO HARD?!
WHY DOES MY BROTHER HAVE TO SUFFER?!

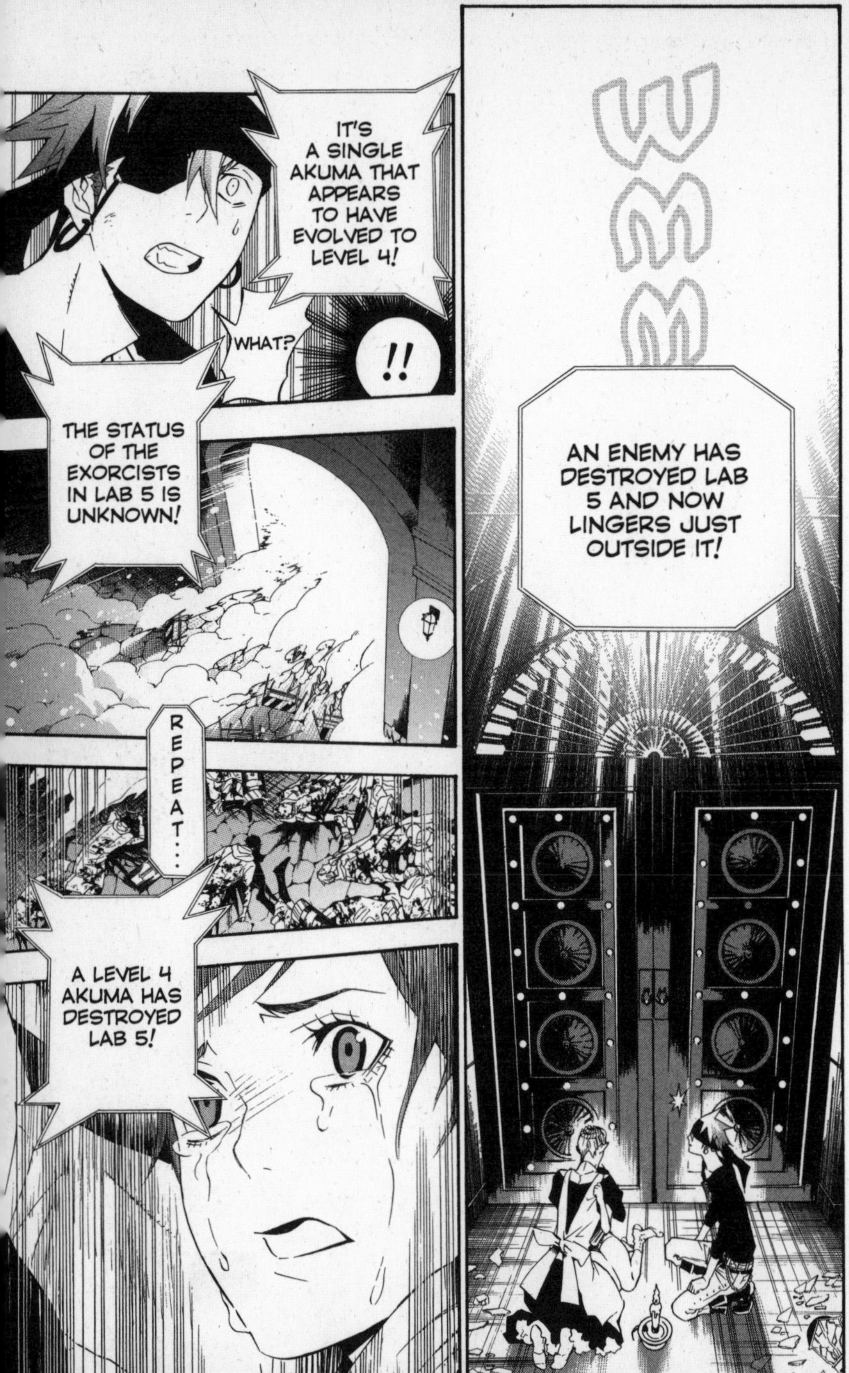
WMMM
AN ENEMY HAS DESTROYED LAB 5 AND NOW LINGERS JUST OUTSIDE IT!
IT'S A SINGLE AKUMA THAT APPEARS TO HAVE EVOLVED TO LEVEL 4!
!!
WHAT?
THE STATUS OF THE EXORCISTS IN LAB 5 IS UNKNOWN!
REPEAT...
A LEVEL 4 AKUMA HAS DESTROYED LAB 5!

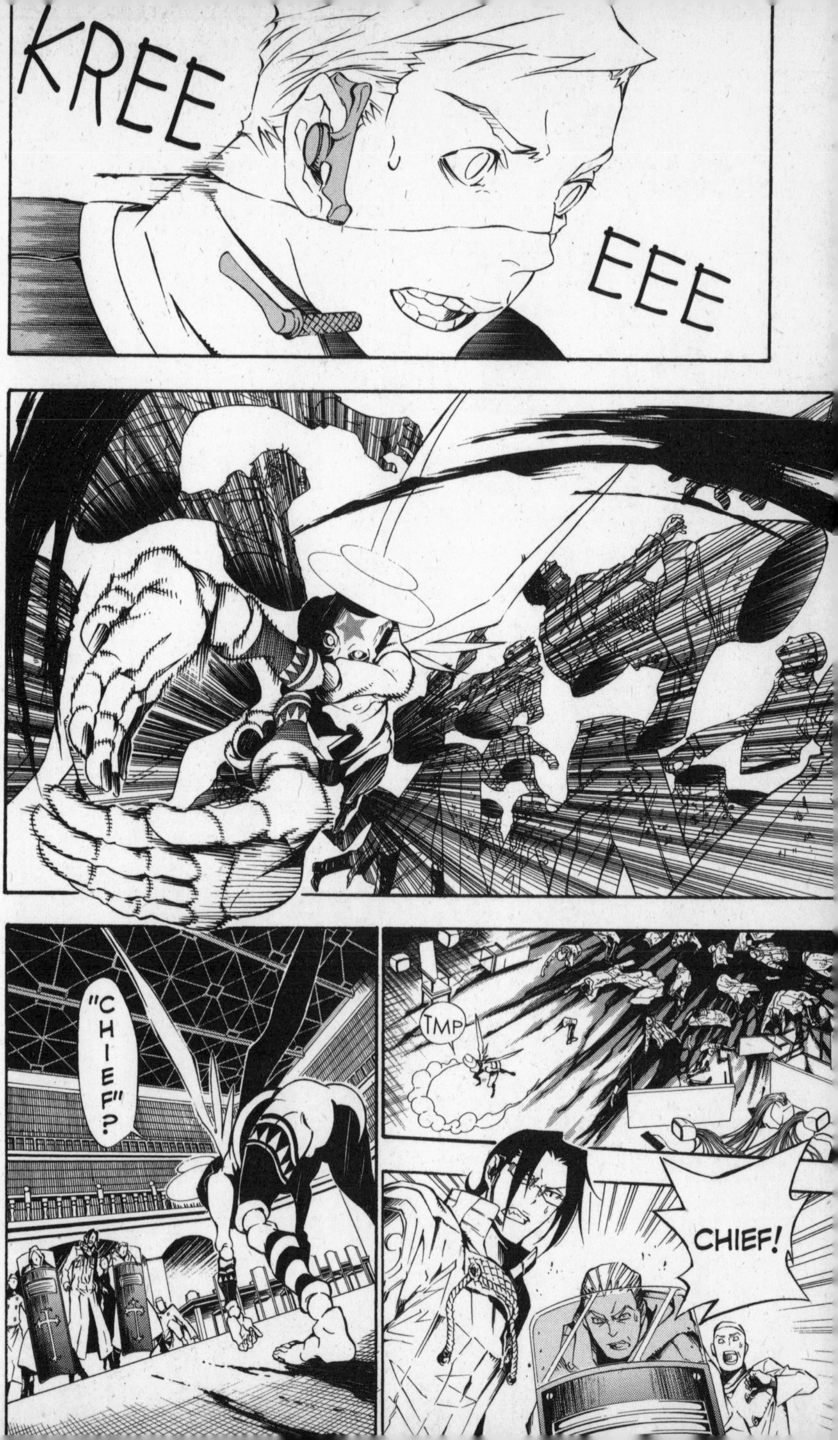
KREE
EEE
TMP
CHIEF!
"CHIEF"?

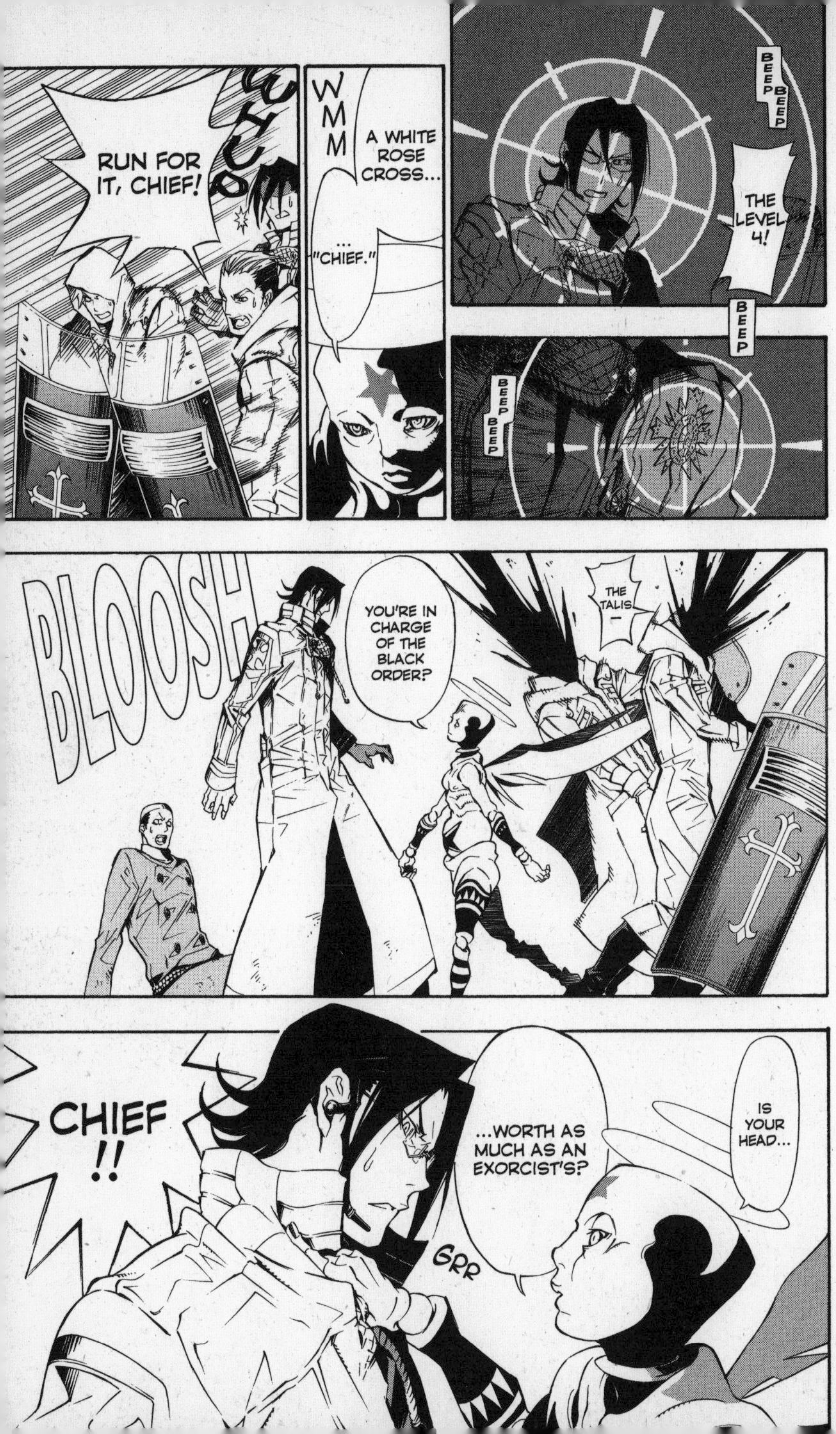
BEEP BEEP BEEP
THE LEVEL 4!
BEEP
BEEP BEEP
WMM
A WHITE ROSE CROSS...
... "CHIEF."
WHUD
RUN FOR IT, CHIEF!
THE TALIS—
YOU'RE IN CHARGE OF THE BLACK ORDER?
BLOOSH
IS YOUR HEAD...
...WORTH AS MUCH AS AN EXORCIST'S?
GRR
CHIEF !!

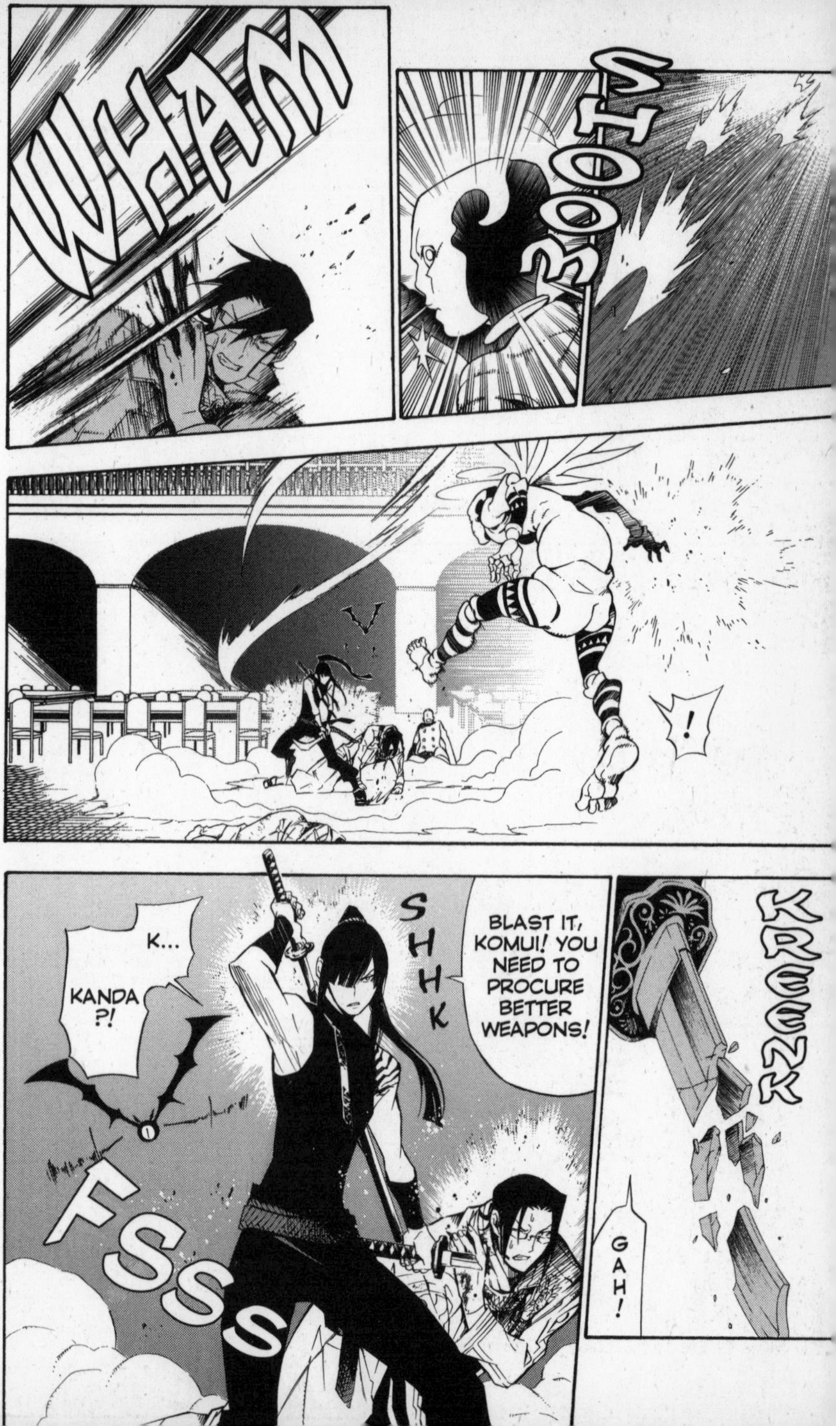
SHOOOM
WHAM
!
KRENK
GAH!
BLAST IT, KOMUI! YOU NEED TO PROCURE BETTER WEAPONS!
SHHK
K...
KANDA?!
FSSS

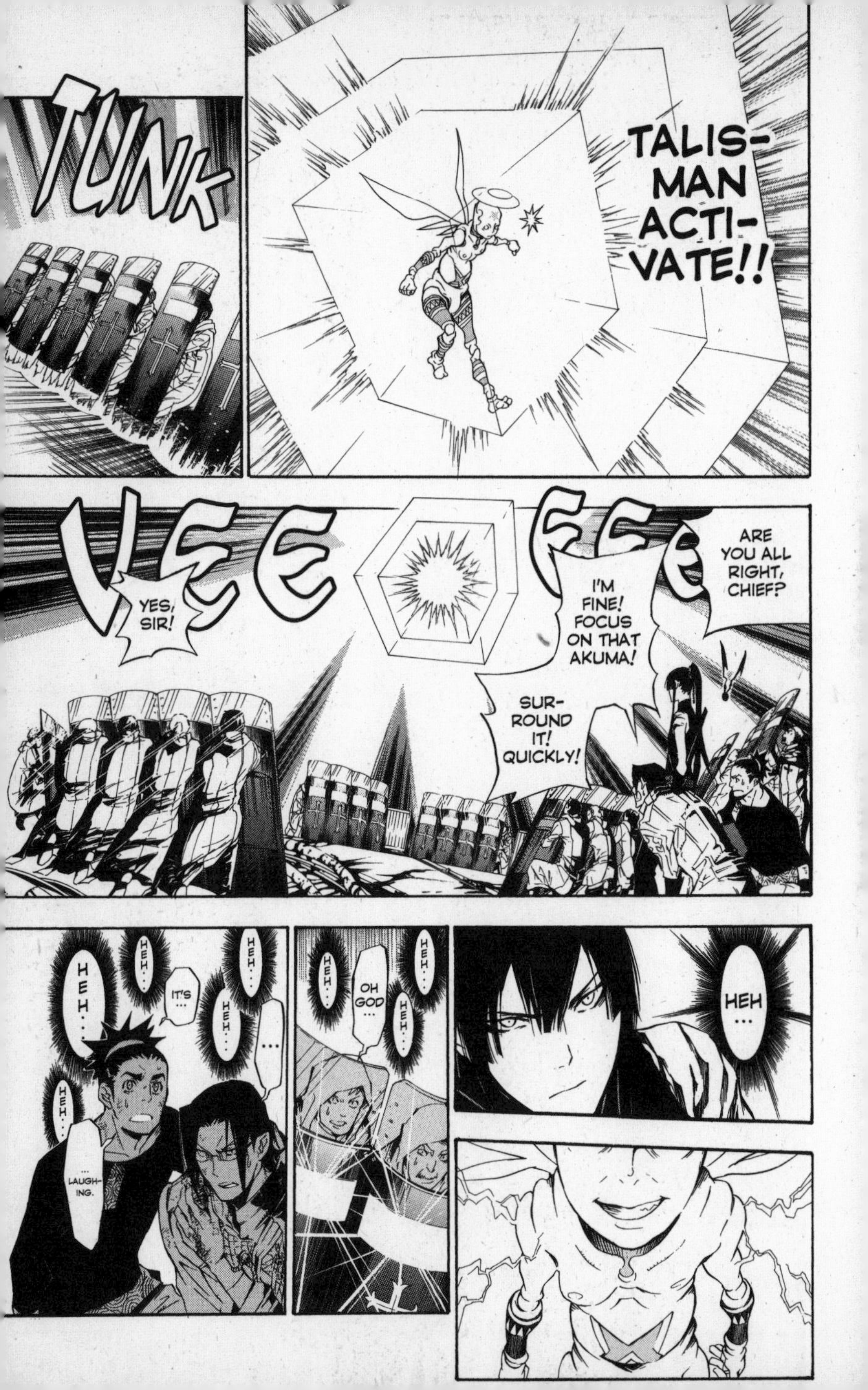
TALIS-MAN ACTI-VATE!!
TUNK
ARE YOU ALL RIGHT, CHIEF?
I'M FINE! FOCUS ON THAT AKUMA!
SUR-ROUND IT! QUICKLY!
YES, SIR!
HEH...
HEH...
HEH...
OH GOD...
HEH...
HEH...
HEH...
IT'S...
HEH...
...
HEH...
...LAUGH-ING.

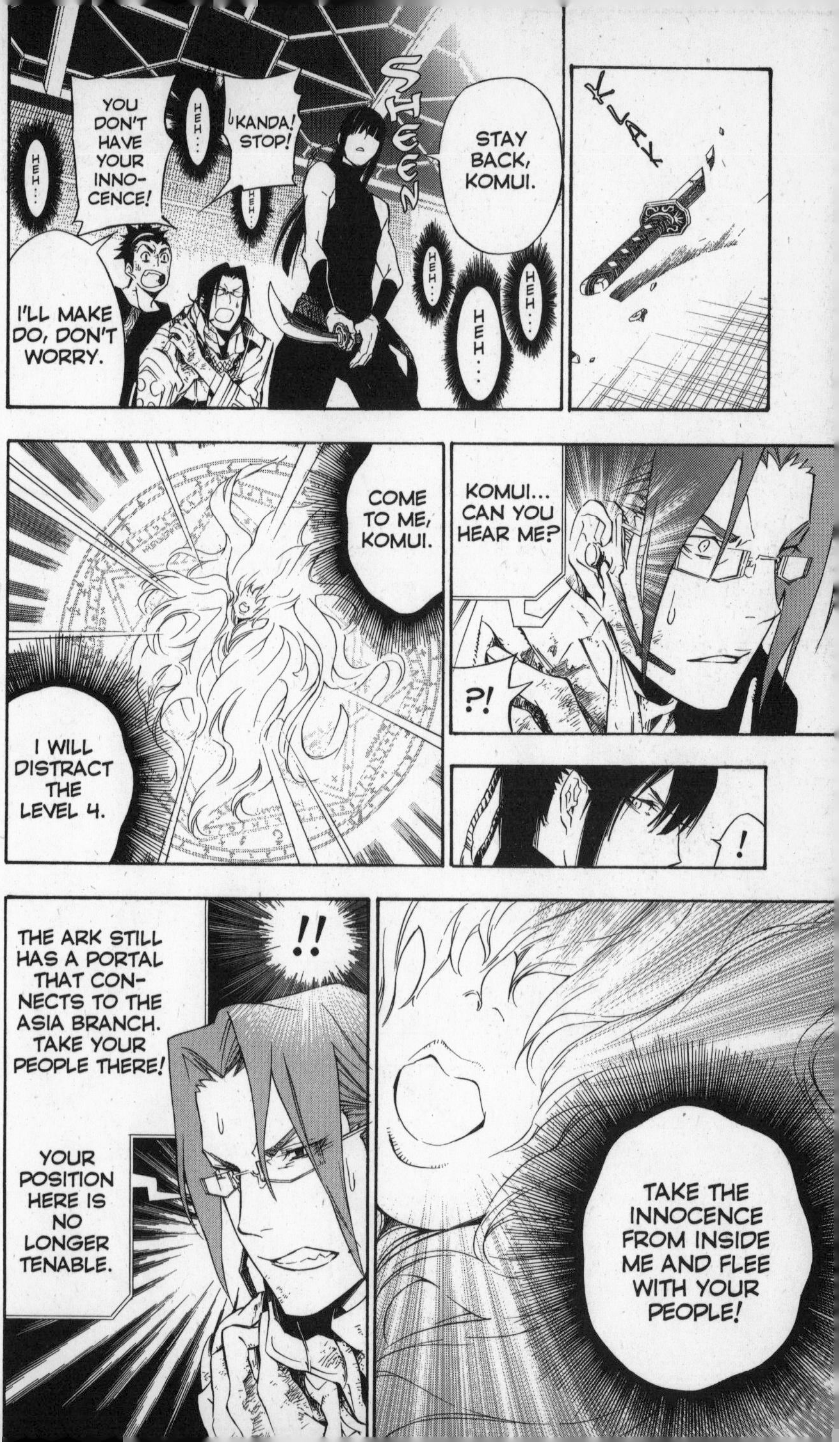
STAY BACK, KOMUI.
SHEEN
HEH...
HEH...
HEH...
KANDA! STOP!
HEH...
HEH...
YOU DON'T HAVE YOUR INNOCENCE!
HEH...
I'LL MAKE DO, DON'T WORRY.
KOMUI... CAN YOU HEAR ME?
?!
!
COME TO ME, KOMUI.
I WILL DISTRACT THE LEVEL 4.
TAKE THE INNOCENCE FROM INSIDE ME AND FLEE WITH YOUR PEOPLE!
!!
THE ARK STILL HAS A PORTAL THAT CONNECTS TO THE ASIA BRANCH. TAKE YOUR PEOPLE THERE!
YOUR POSITION HERE IS NO LONGER TENABLE.

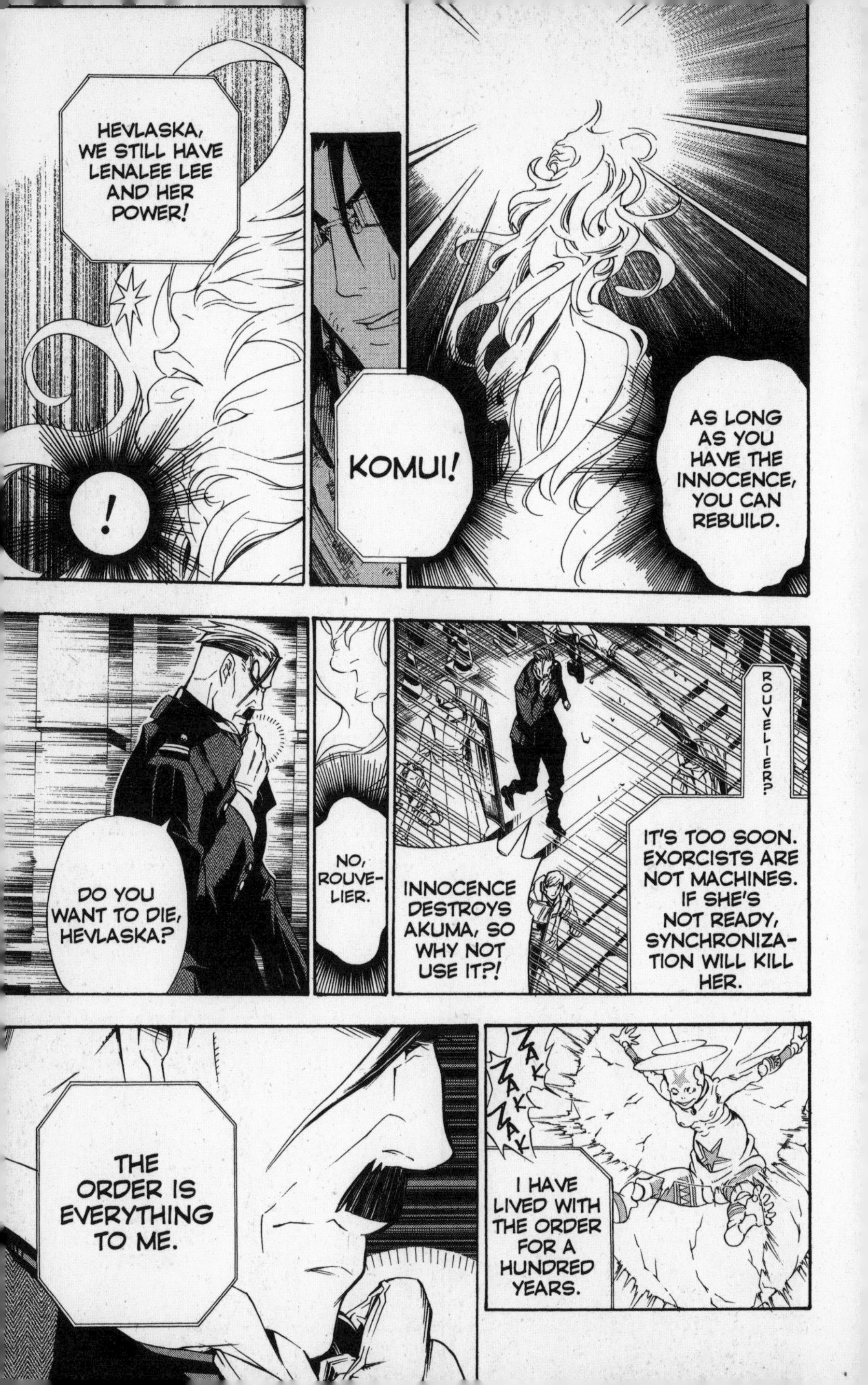
AS LONG AS YOU HAVE THE INNOCENCE, YOU CAN REBUILD.
KOMUI!
HEVLASKA, WE STILL HAVE LENALEE LEE AND HER POWER!
!
ROUVELIER?
IT'S TOO SOON. EXORCISTS ARE NOT MACHINES. IF SHE'S NOT READY, SYNCHRONIZATION WILL KILL HER.
INNOCENCE DESTROYS AKUMA, SO WHY NOT USE IT?!
NO, ROUVE-LIER.
DO YOU WANT TO DIE, HEVLASKA?
ZAK ZAK ZAK
I HAVE LIVED WITH THE ORDER FOR A HUNDRED YEARS.
THE ORDER IS EVERYTHING TO ME.

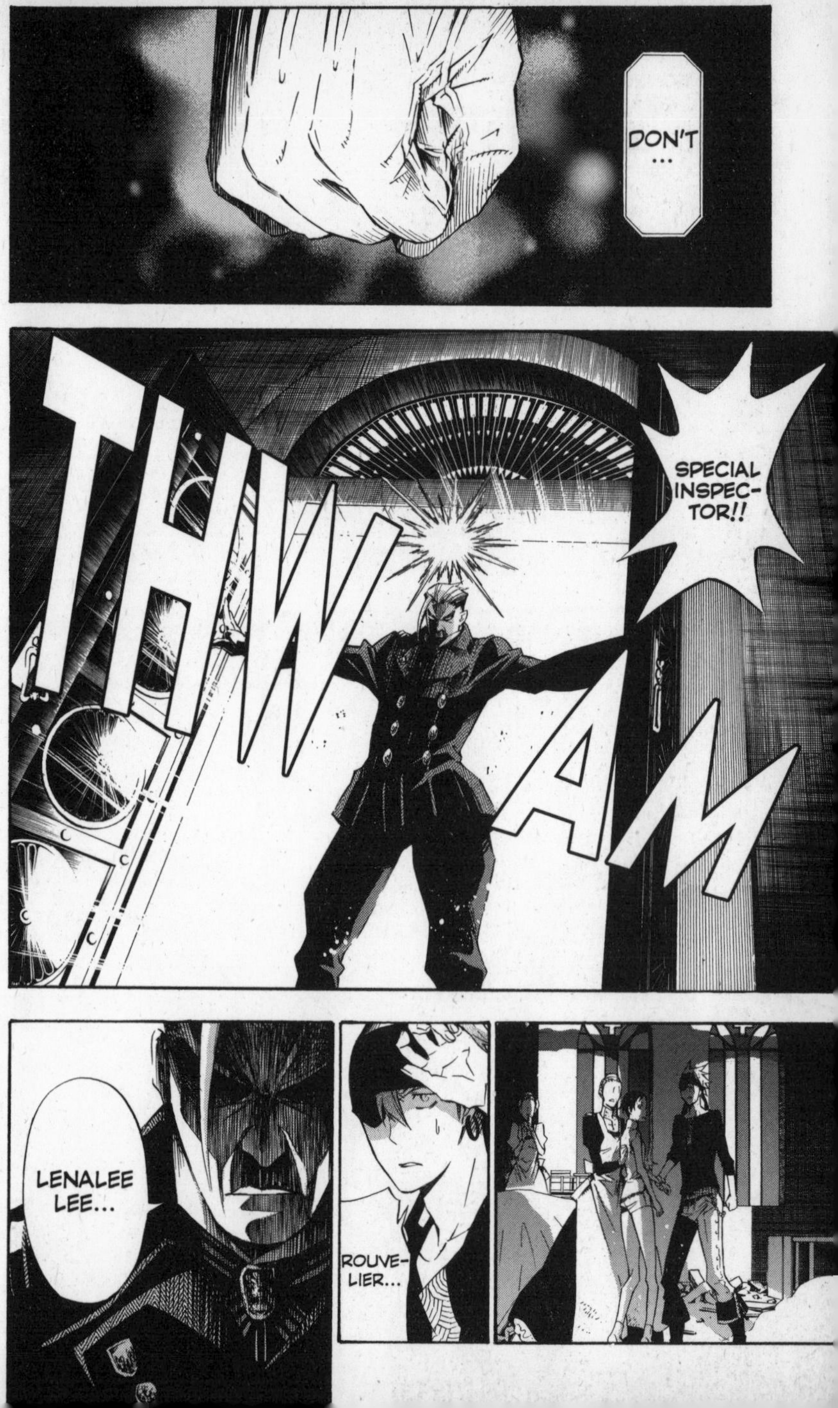
DON'T ...
SPECIAL INSPEC-TOR!!
THWAM
ROUVE-LIER...
LENALEE LEE...

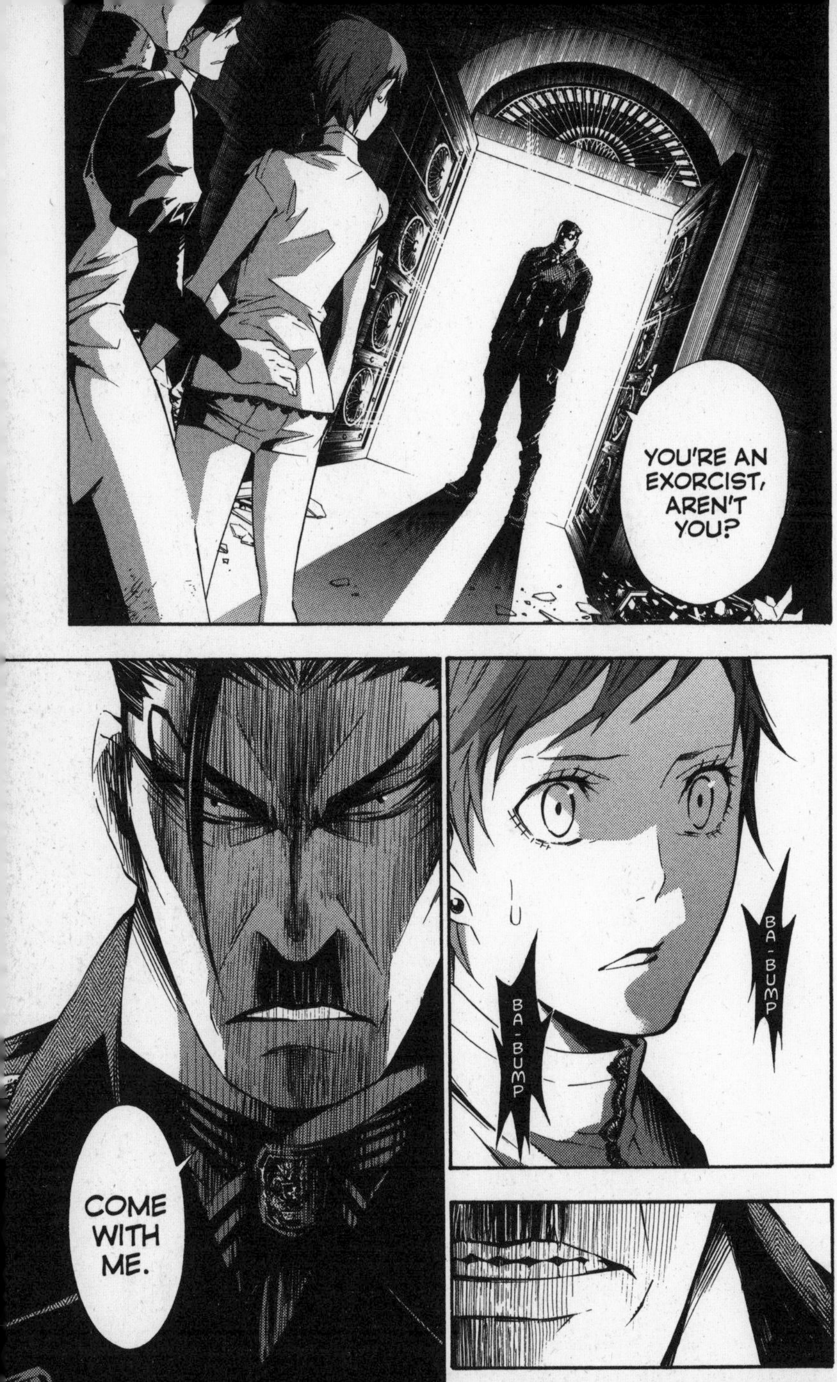
YOU'RE AN EXORCIST, AREN'T YOU?
BA-BUMP
BA-BUMP
COME WITH ME.

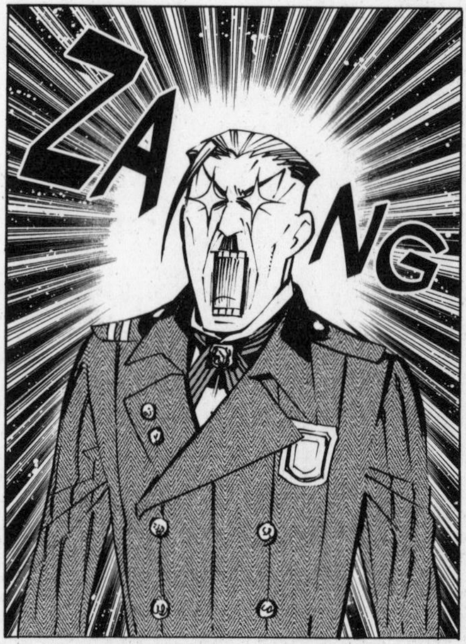
ZANG

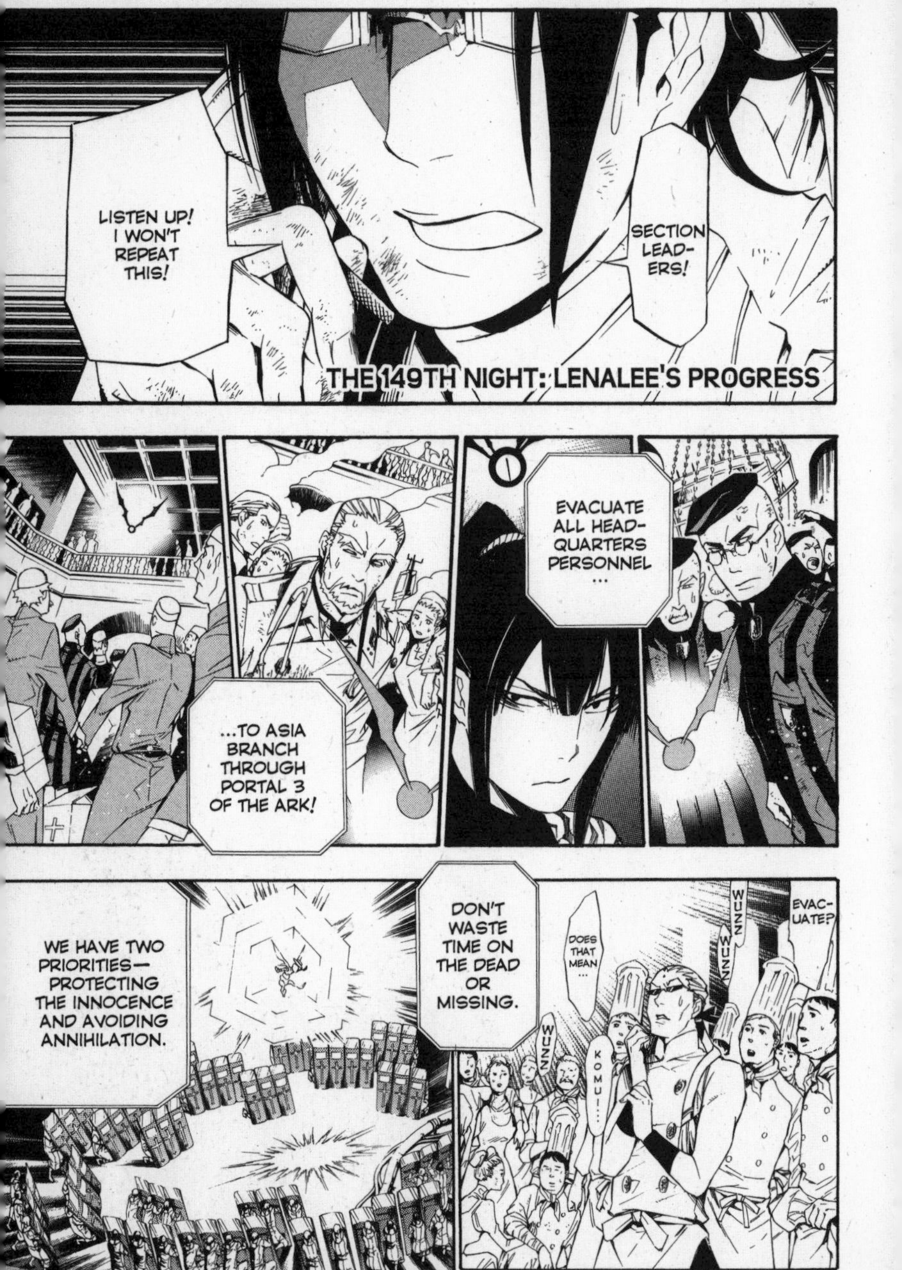
SECTION LEADERS!
LISTEN UP! I WON'T REPEAT THIS!
THE 149TH NIGHT: LENALEE'S PROGRESS
EVACUATE ALL HEADQUARTERS PERSONNEL ...
...TO ASIA BRANCH THROUGH PORTAL 3 OF THE ARK!
EVACUATE?
WUZZ WUZZ
DOES THAT MEAN ...
KOMUI...
WUZZ
DON'T WASTE TIME ON THE DEAD OR MISSING.
WE HAVE TWO PRIORITIES— PROTECTING THE INNOCENCE AND AVOIDING ANNIHILATION.

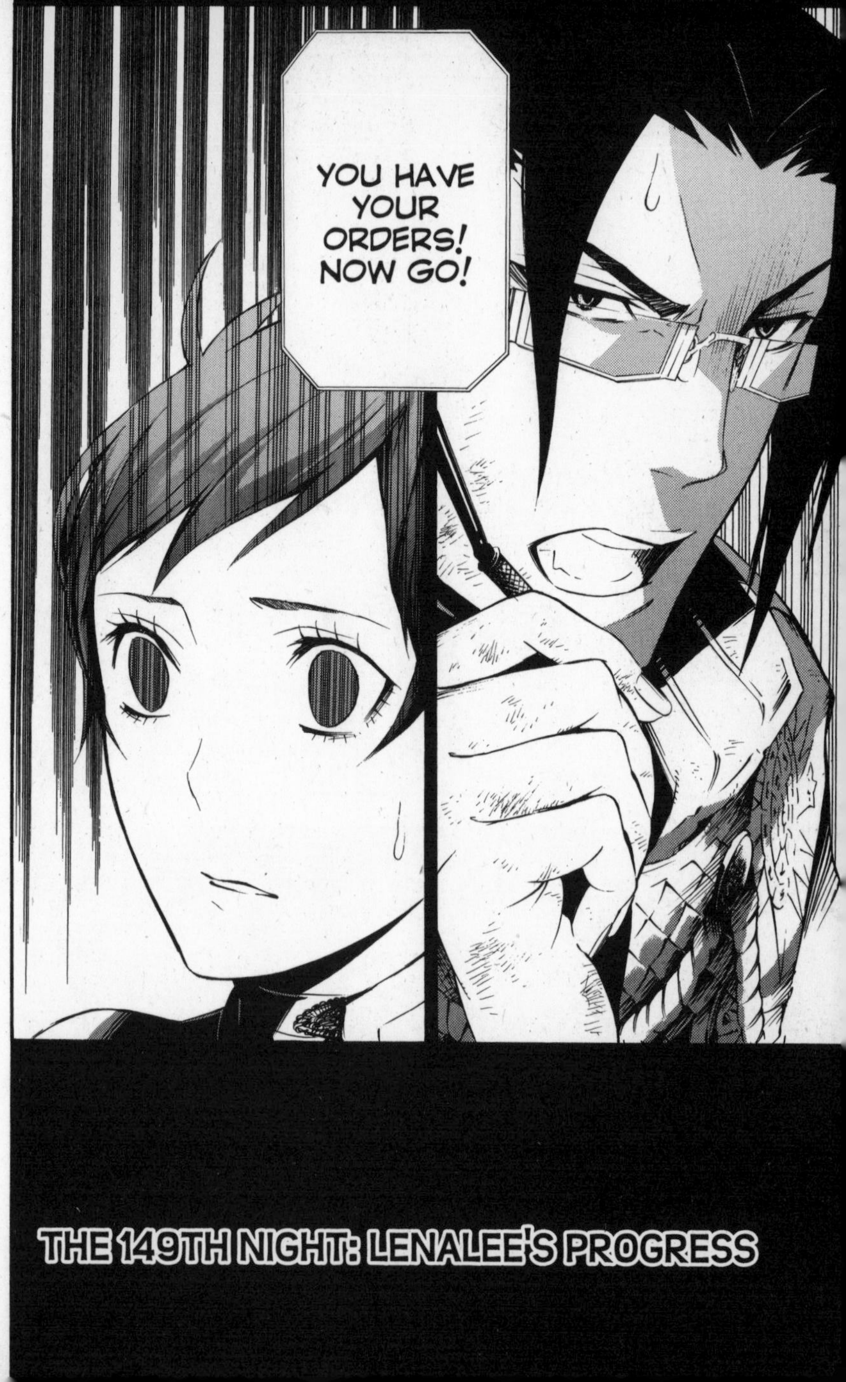
YOU HAVE YOUR ORDERS! NOW GO!

THE 149TH NIGHT: LENALEE'S PROGRESS

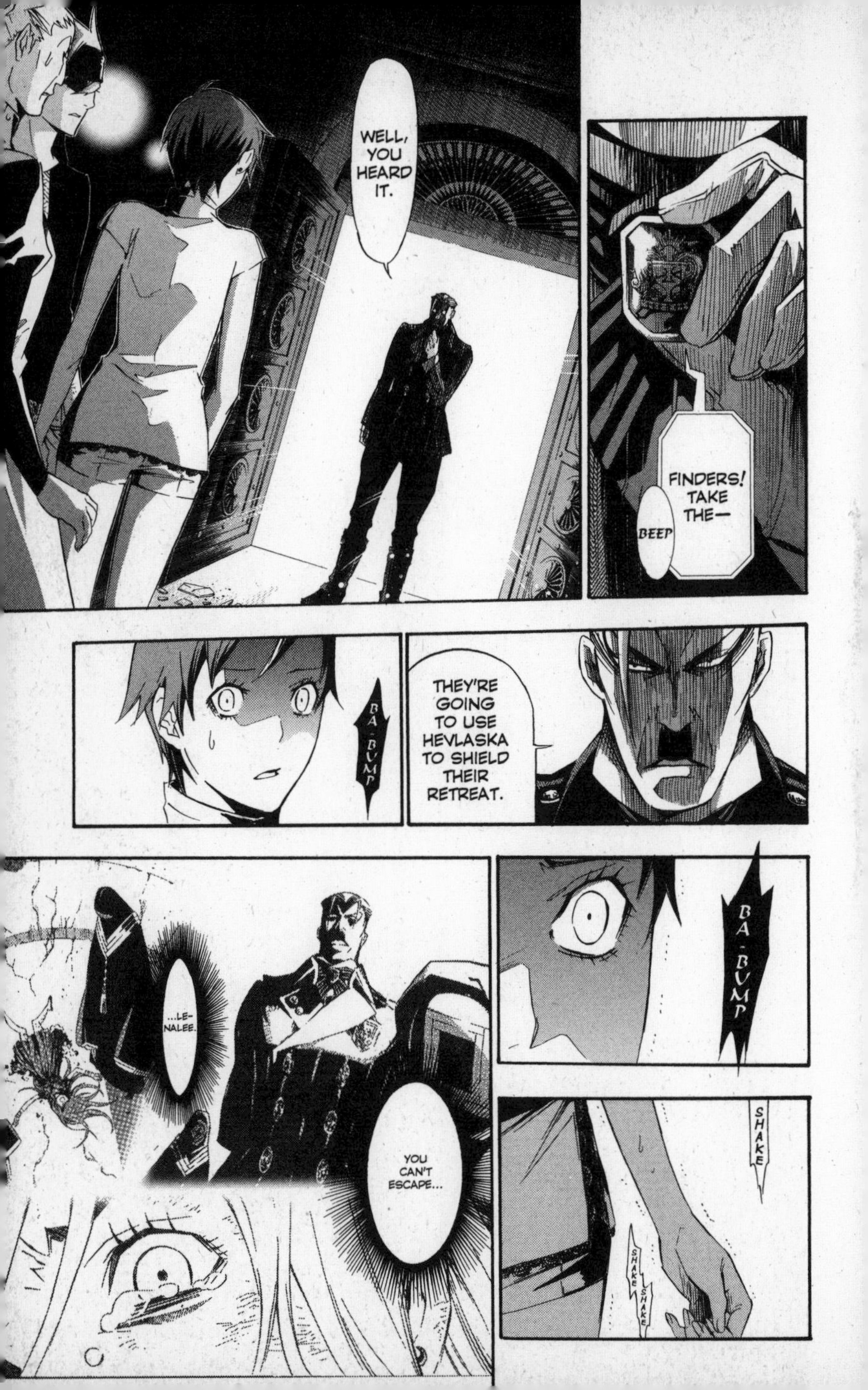
FINDERS! TAKE THE—
BEEP
WELL, YOU HEARD IT.
THEY'RE GOING TO USE HEVLASKA TO SHIELD THEIR RETREAT.
BA-BUMP
BA-BUMP
SHAKE
SHAKE
SHAKE
...LE-NALEE.
YOU CAN'T ESCAPE...

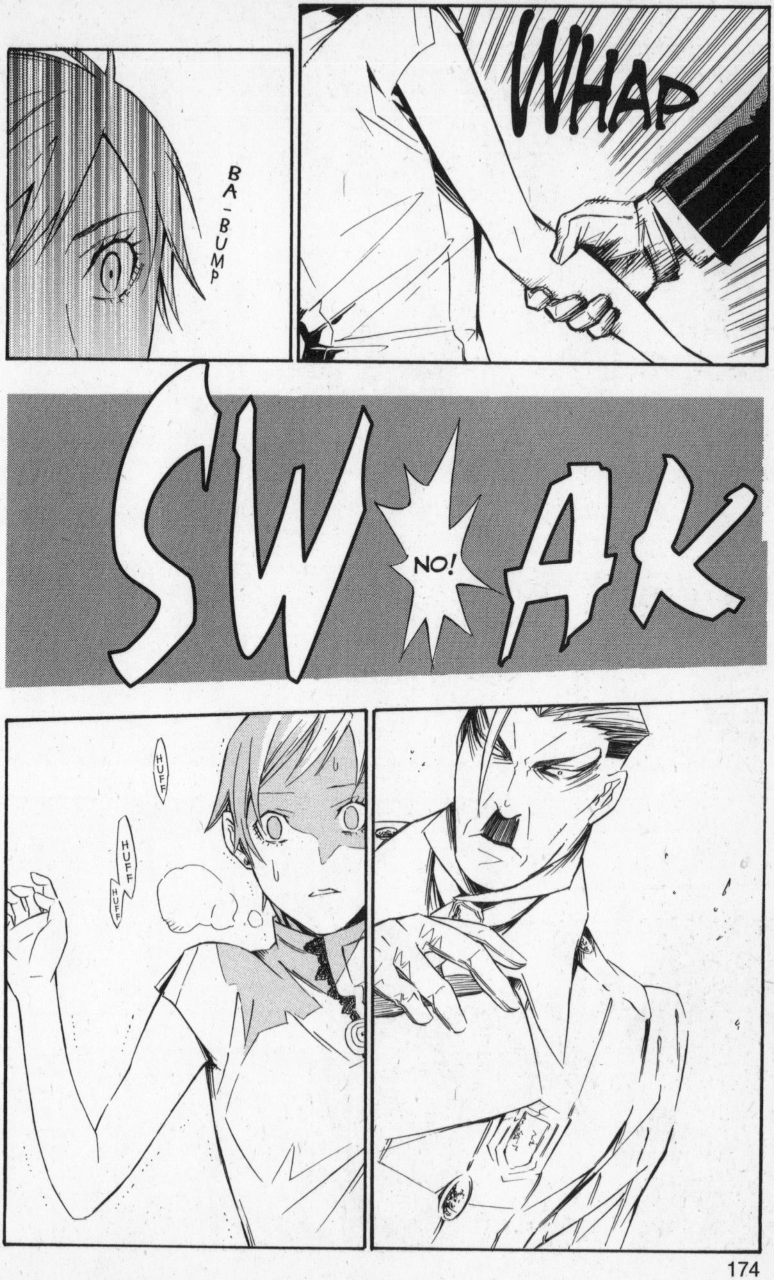
WHAP
BA-BUMP
SWAK
NO!
HUFF
HUFF
HUFF

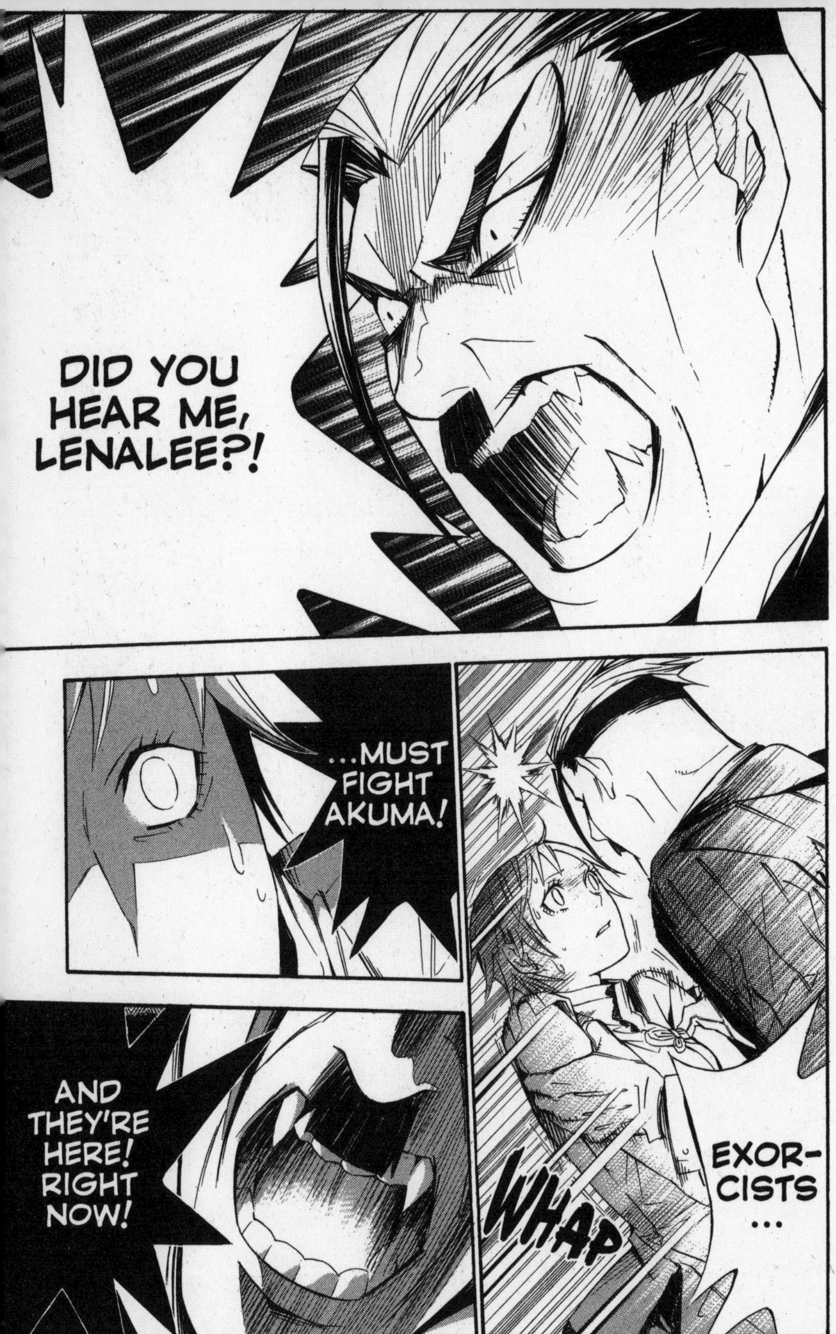
DID YOU HEAR ME, LENALEE?!
EXOR-CISTS...
WHAP
...MUST FIGHT AKUMA!
AND THEY'RE HERE! RIGHT NOW!

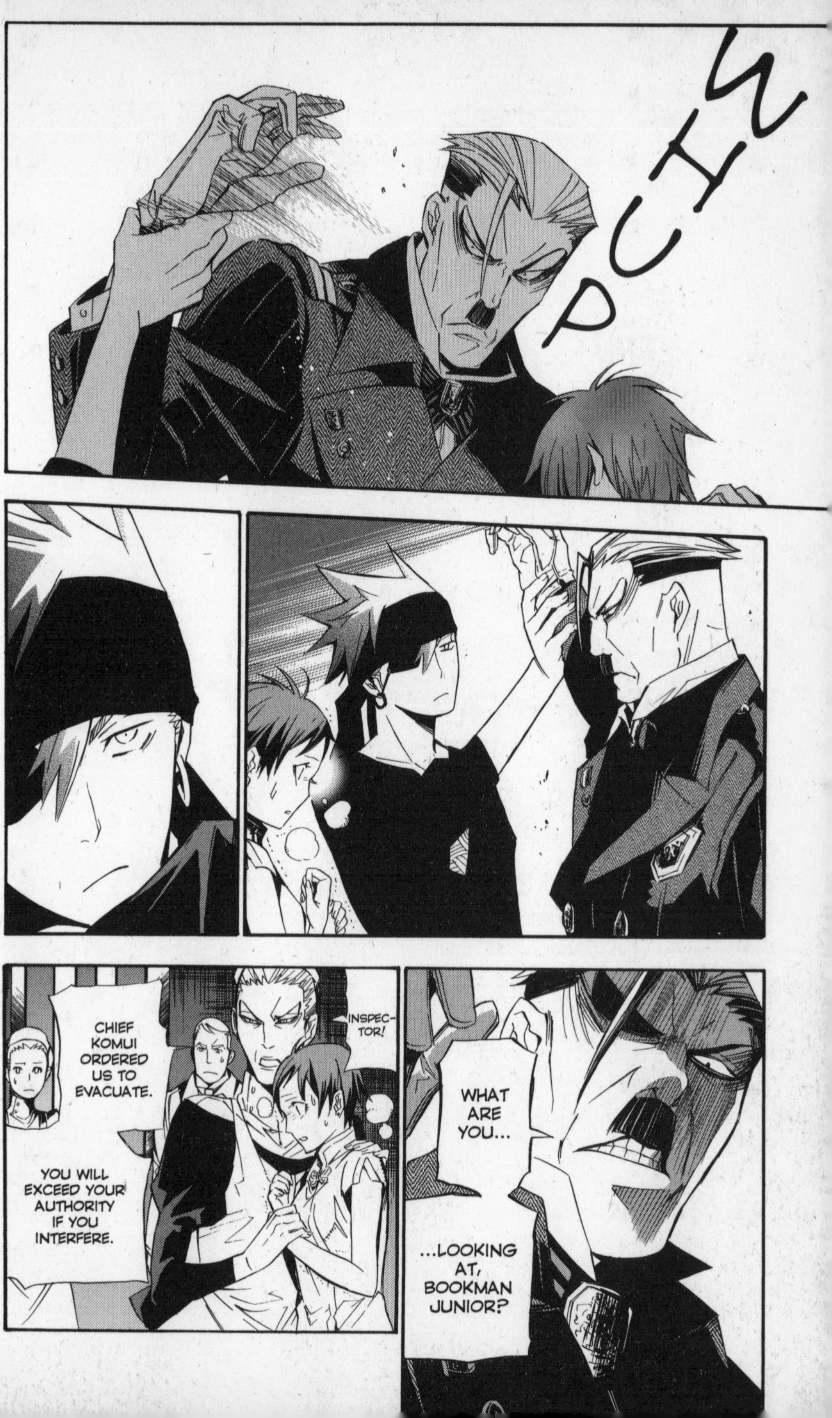
WHUP
WHAT ARE YOU...
...LOOKING AT, BOOKMAN JUNIOR?
INSPECTOR!
CHIEF KOMUI ORDERED US TO EVACUATE.
YOU WILL EXCEED YOUR AUTHORITY IF YOU INTERFERE.

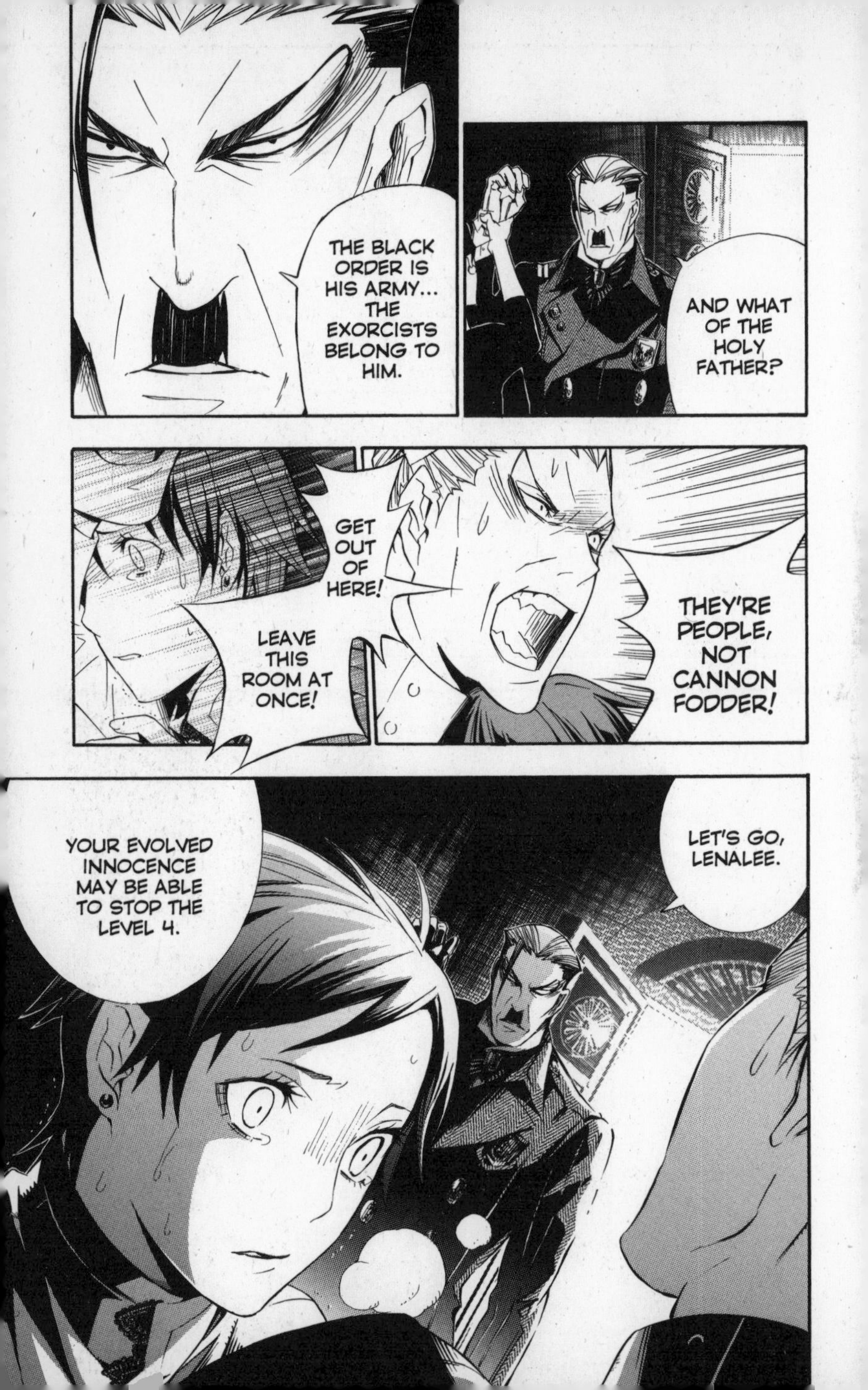
AND WHAT OF THE HOLY FATHER?
THE BLACK ORDER IS HIS ARMY... THE EXORCISTS BELONG TO HIM.
THEY'RE PEOPLE, NOT CANNON FODDER!
GET OUT OF HERE!
LEAVE THIS ROOM AT ONCE!
LET'S GO, LENALEE.
YOUR EVOLVED INNOCENCE MAY BE ABLE TO STOP THE LEVEL 4.

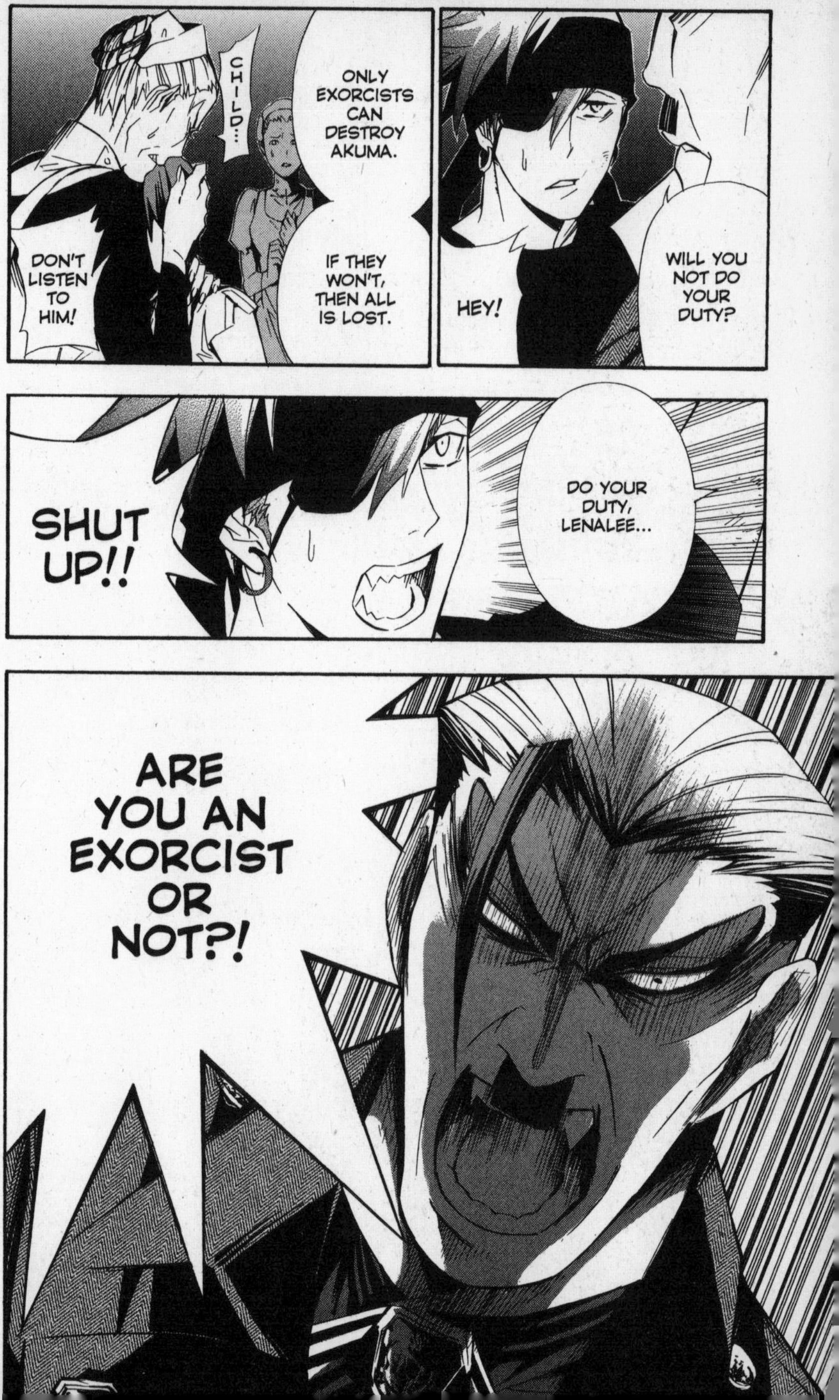
WILL YOU NOT DO YOUR DUTY?
HEY!
ONLY EXORCISTS CAN DESTROY AKUMA.
IF THEY WON'T, THEN ALL IS LOST.
CHILD...
DON'T LISTEN TO HIM!
DO YOUR DUTY, LENALEE...
SHUT UP!!
ARE YOU AN EXORCIST OR NOT?!

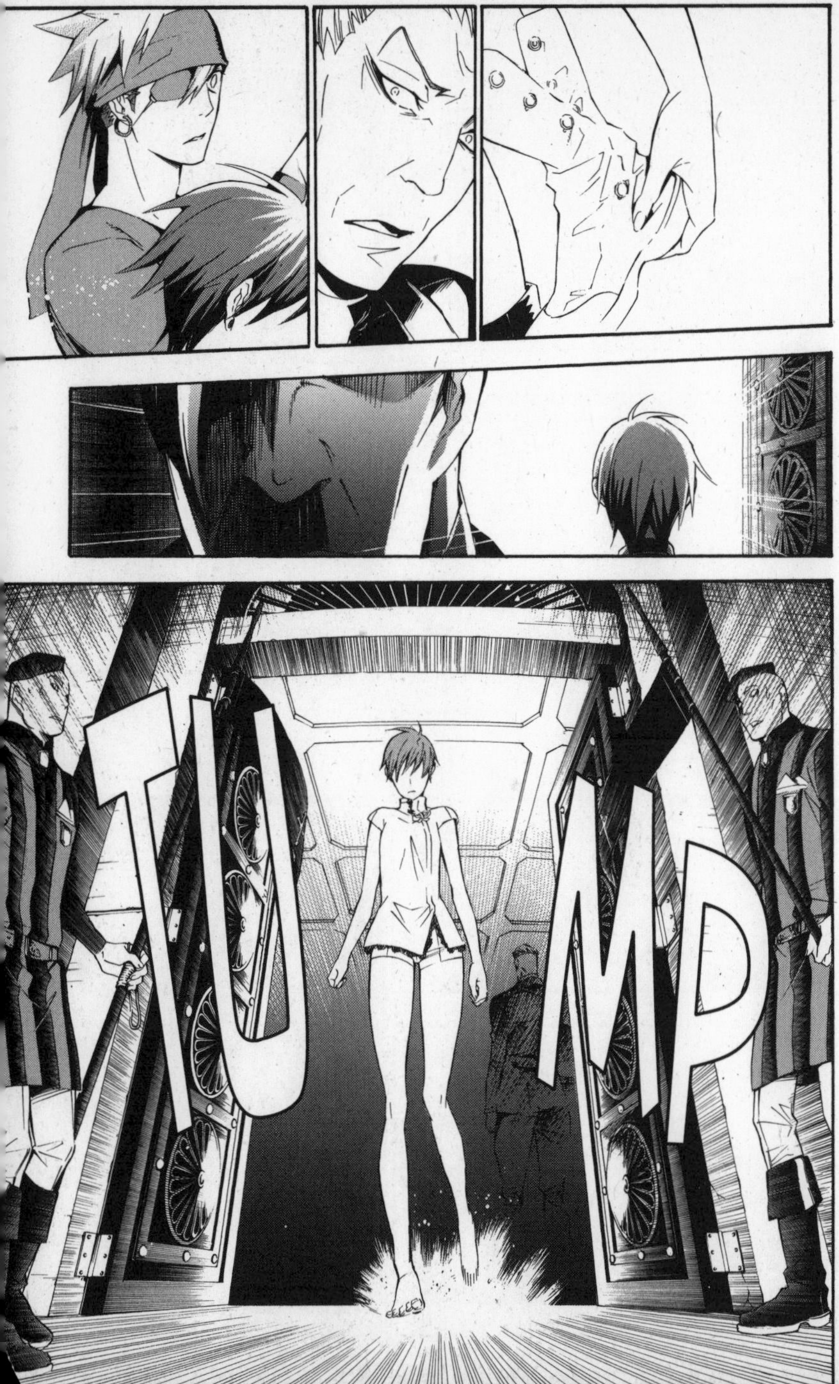
TUMP

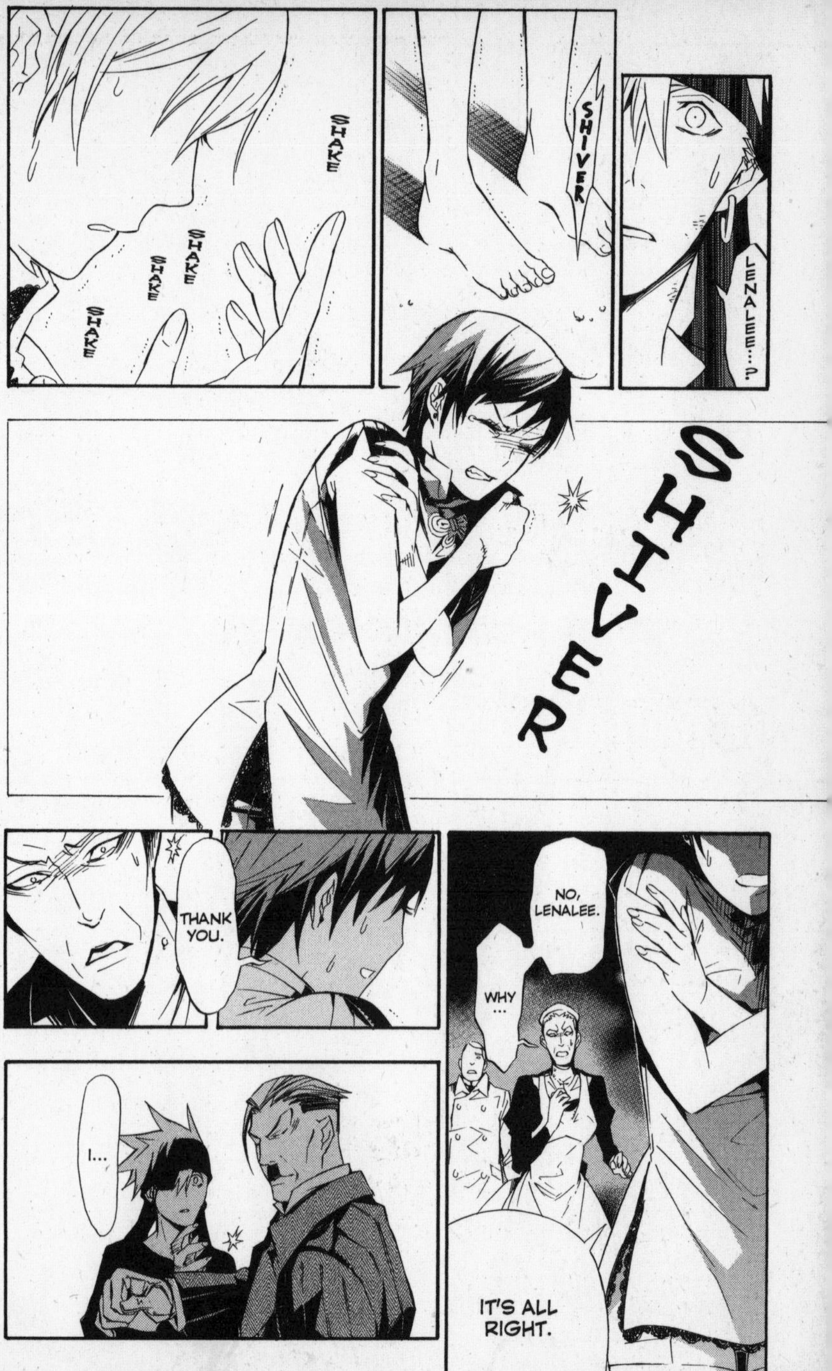
LENALEE...?
SHIVER
SHAKE
SHAKE
SHAKE
SHAKE
SHIVER
NO, LENALEE.
WHY ...
IT'S ALL RIGHT.
THANK YOU.
I...

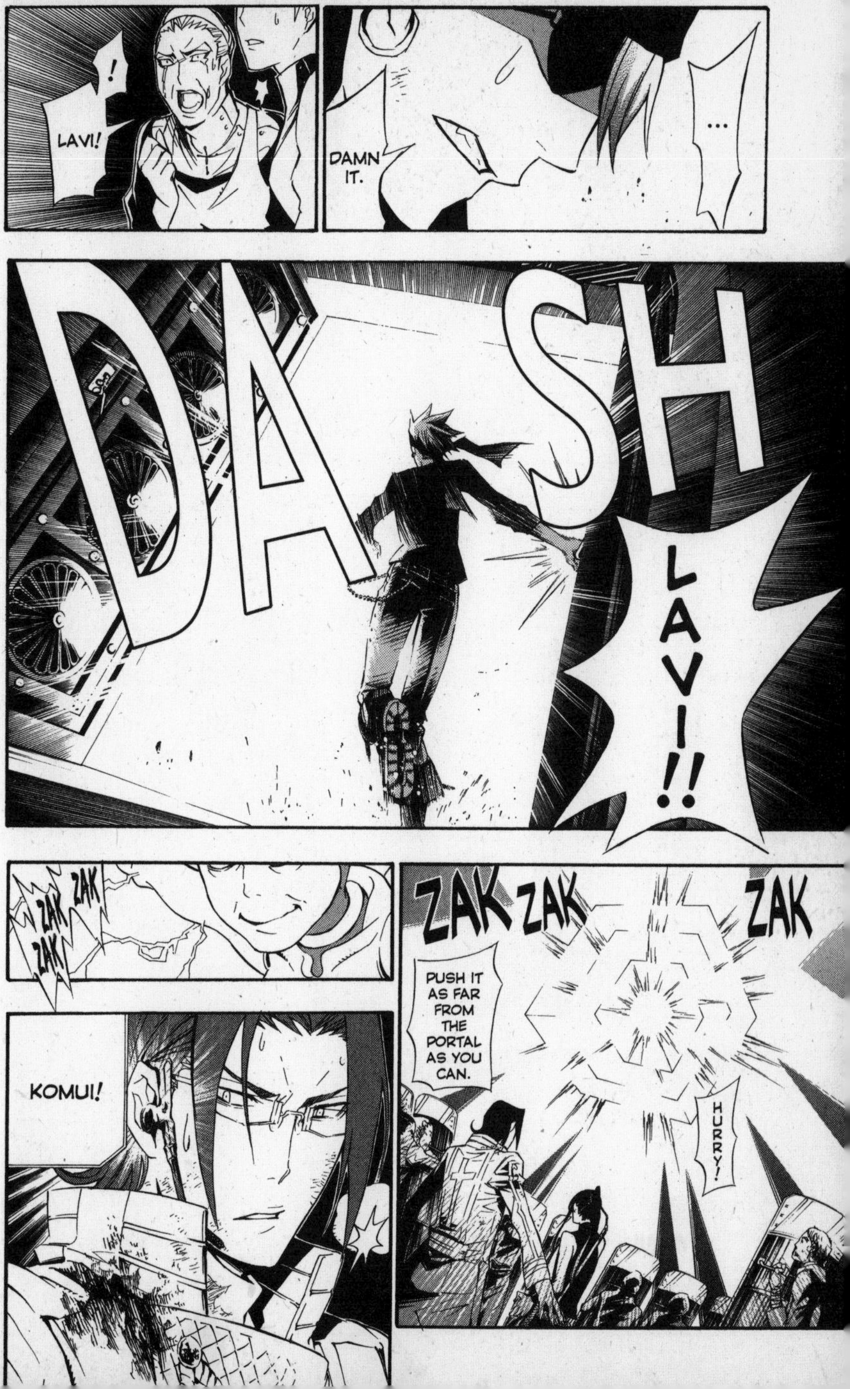
...
DAMN IT.
!
LAVI!
DASH
LAVI!!
ZAK ZAK ZAK
HURRY!
PUSH IT AS FAR FROM THE PORTAL AS YOU CAN.
ZAK ZAK ZAK ZAK
KOMUI!

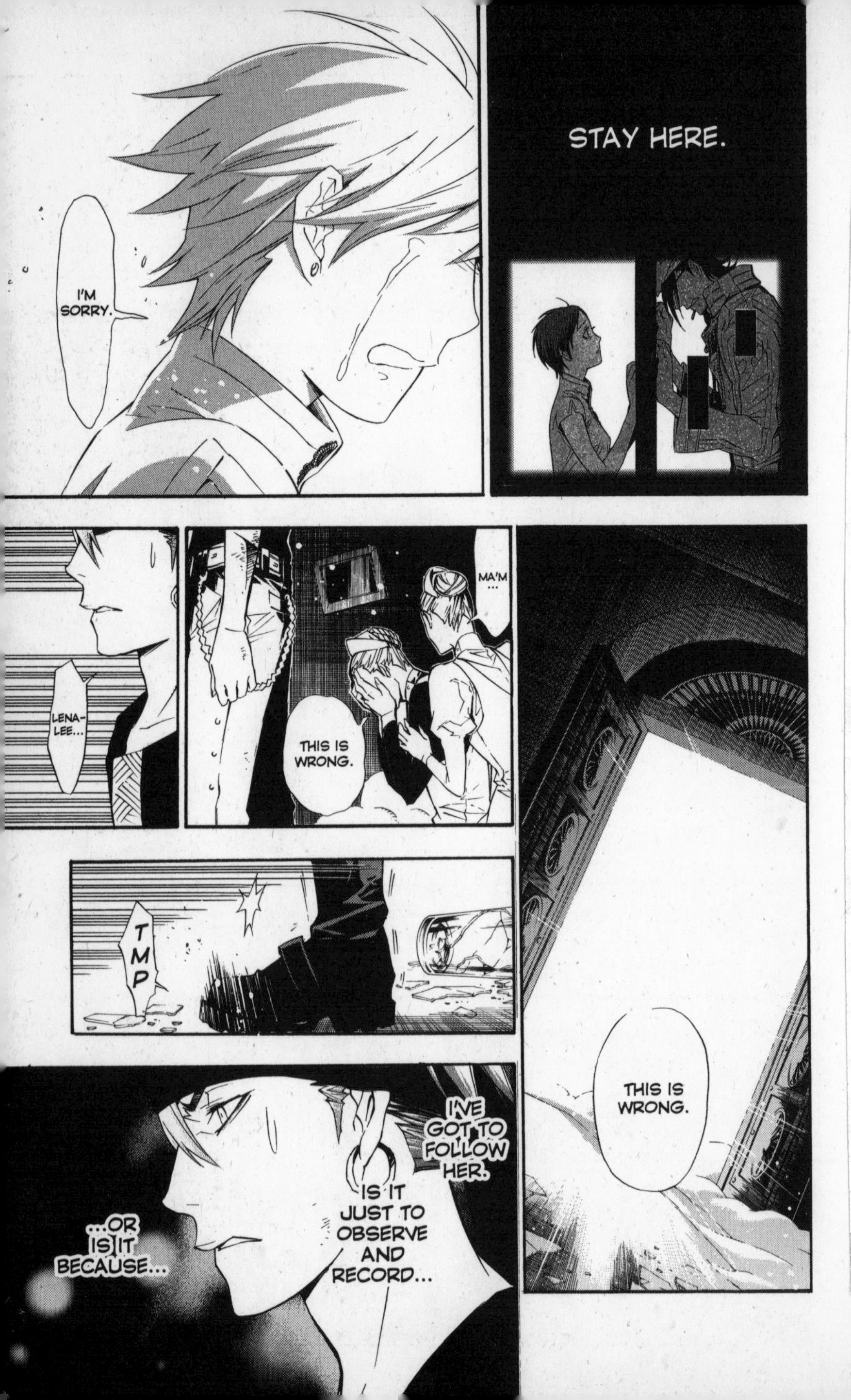
STAY HERE.
I'M SORRY.
THIS IS WRONG.
MA'M ...
THIS IS WRONG.
LENA-LEE...
TMP
I'VE GOT TO FOLLOW HER.
IS IT JUST TO OBSERVE AND RECORD...
...OR IS IT BECAUSE...

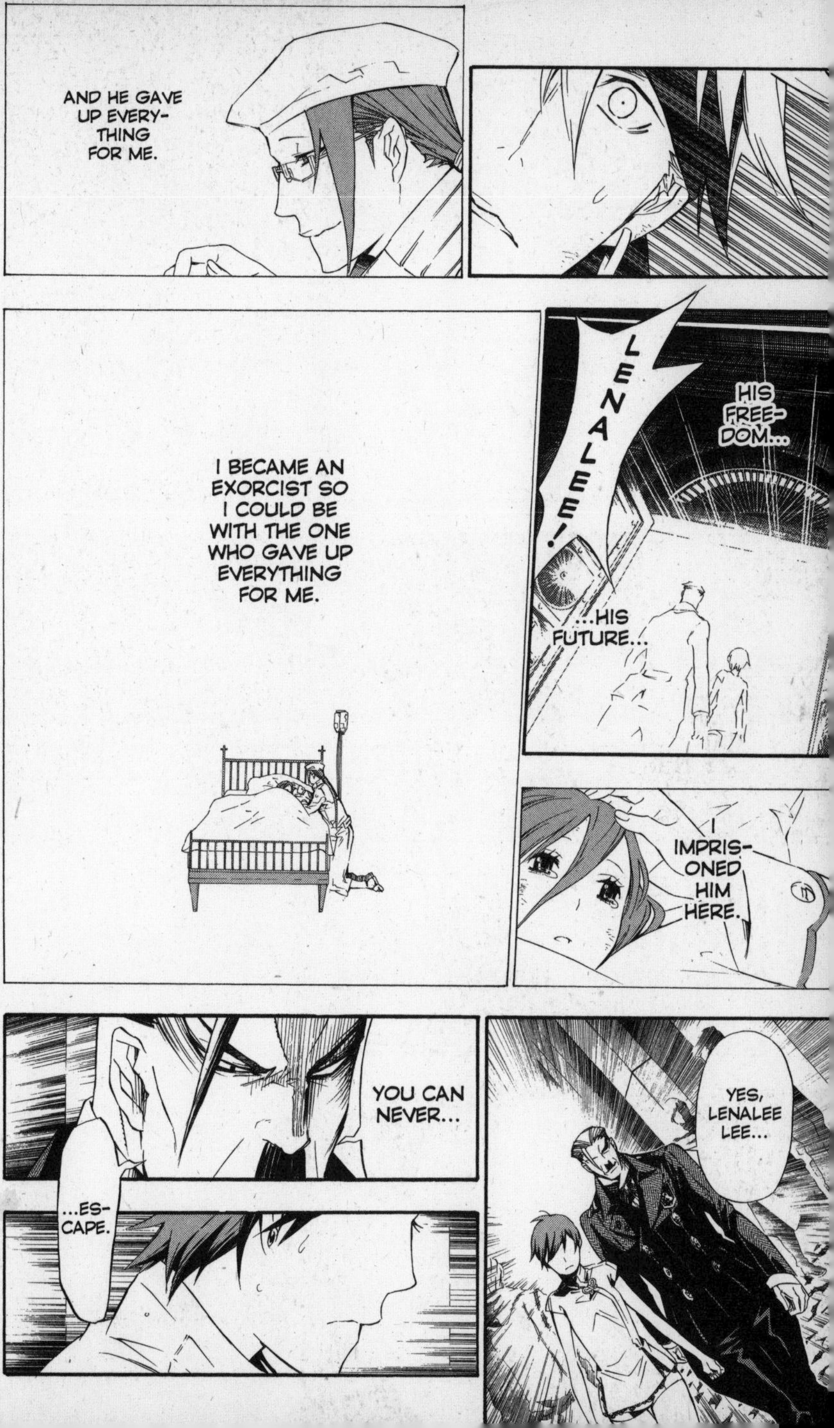
AND HE GAVE UP EVERY-THING FOR ME.
LENALEE!
HIS FREE-DOM...
...HIS FUTURE...
I IMPRIS-ONED HIM HERE.
I BECAME AN EXORCIST SO I COULD BE WITH THE ONE WHO GAVE UP EVERYTHING FOR ME.
YES, LENALEE LEE...
YOU CAN NEVER...
...ES-CAPE.

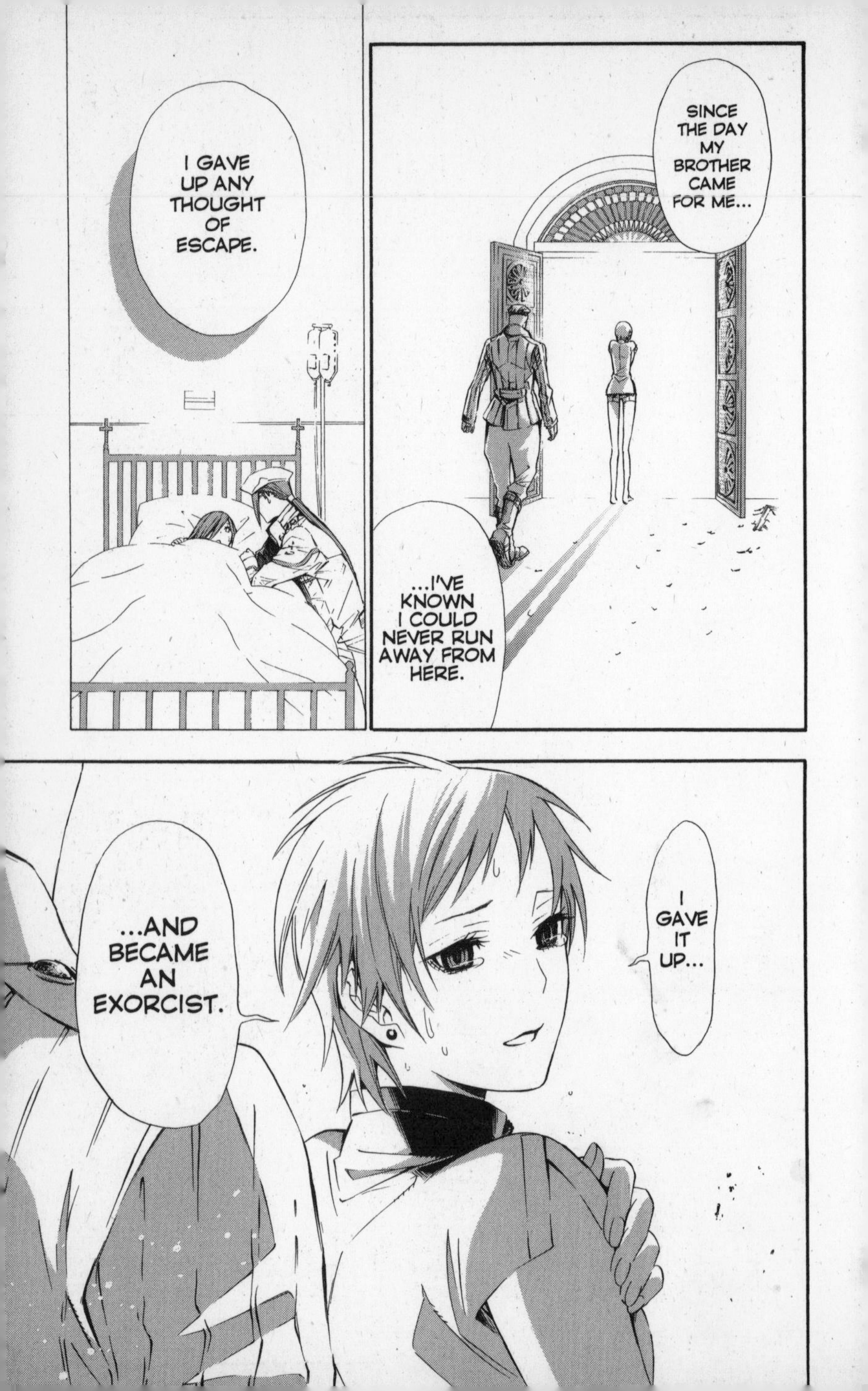
SINCE THE DAY MY BROTHER CAME FOR ME...
...I'VE KNOWN I COULD NEVER RUN AWAY FROM HERE.
I GAVE UP ANY THOUGHT OF ESCAPE.
I GAVE IT UP...
...AND BECAME AN EXORCIST.

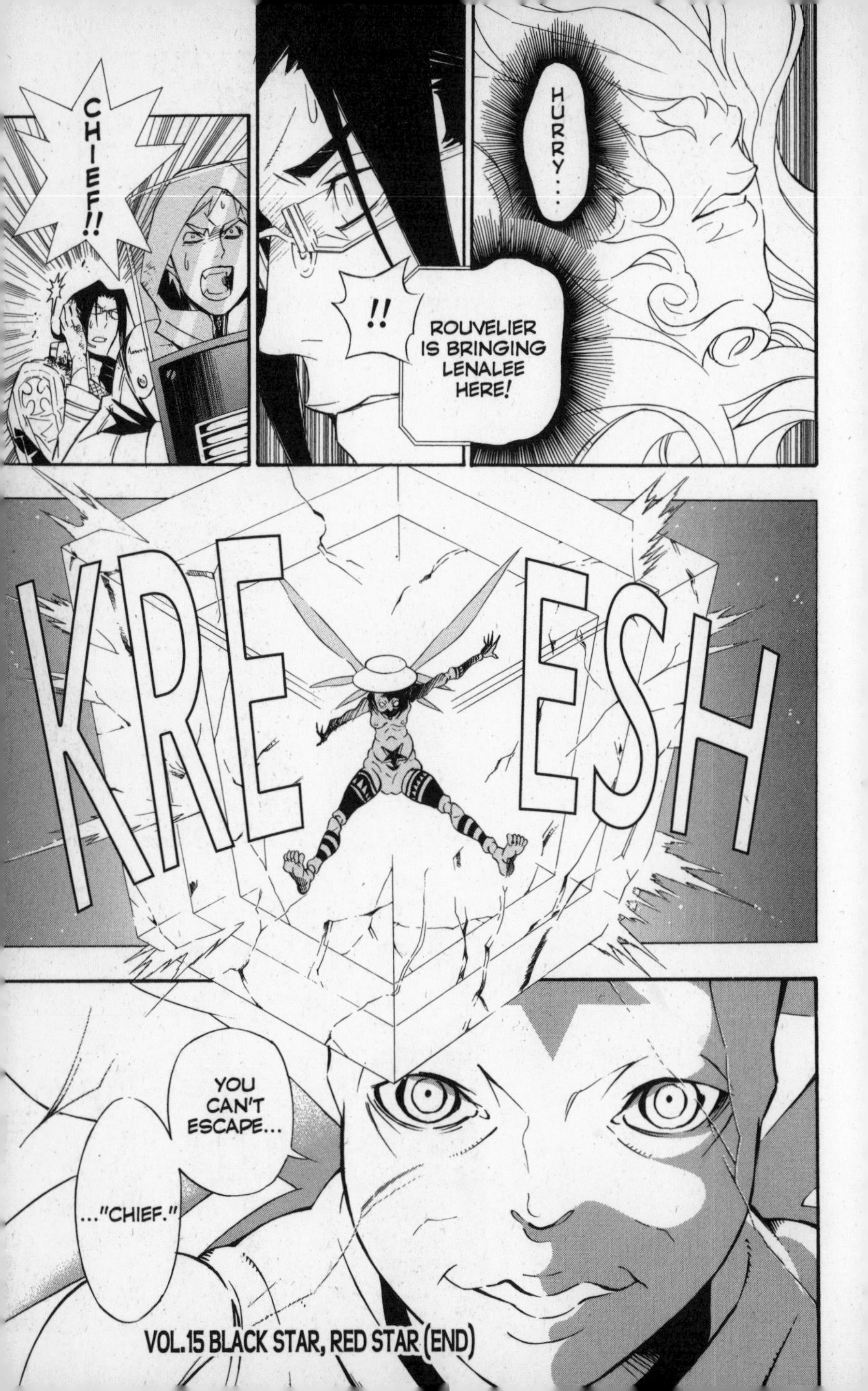
HURRY...
ROUVELIER IS BRINGING LENALEE HERE!
!!
CHIEF!!
KREESH
YOU CAN'T ESCAPE...
..."CHIEF."
VOL.15 BLACK STAR, RED STAR (END)

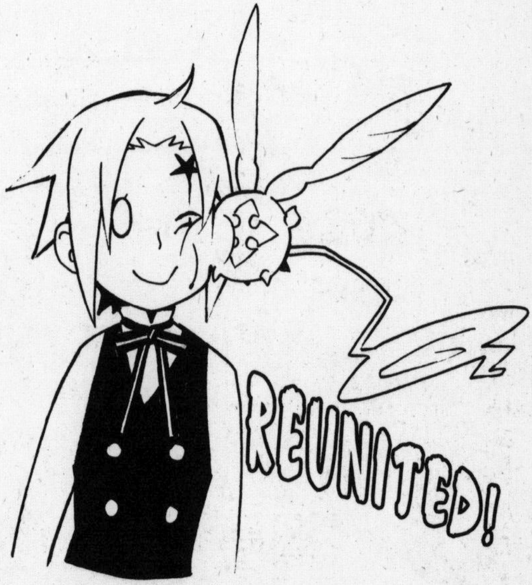
REUNITED!

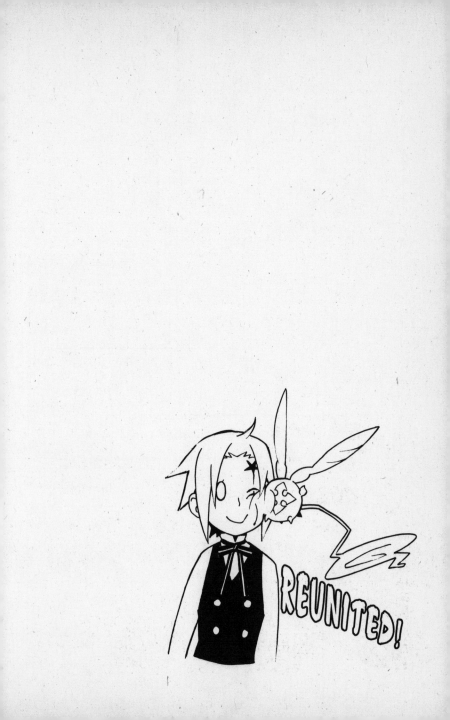

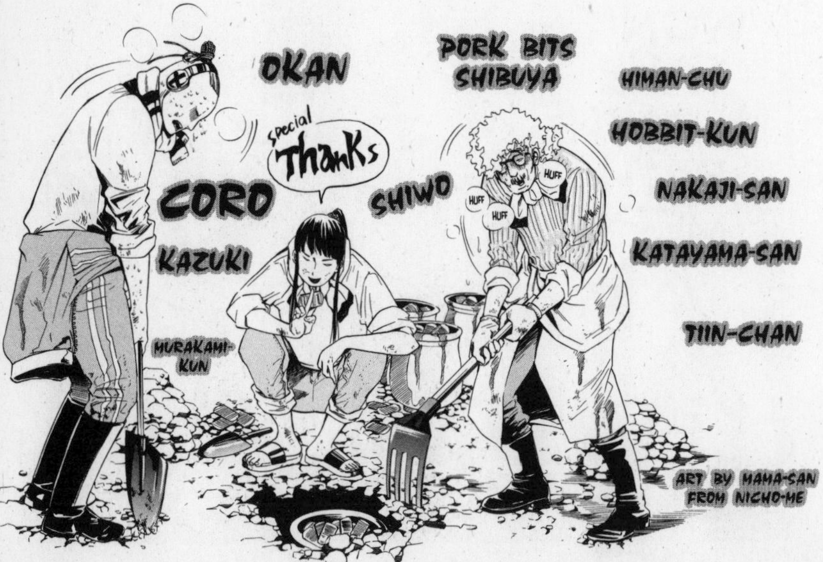
special Thanks
OKAN
PORK BITS SHIBUYA
HIMAN-CHU
HOBBIT-KUN
NAKAJI-SAN
KATAYAMA-SAN
TIIN-CHAN
CORO
SHIWO
KAZUKI
MURAKAMI-KUN
HUFF
HUFF
HUFF
ART BY MAMA-SAN FROM NICHO-ME

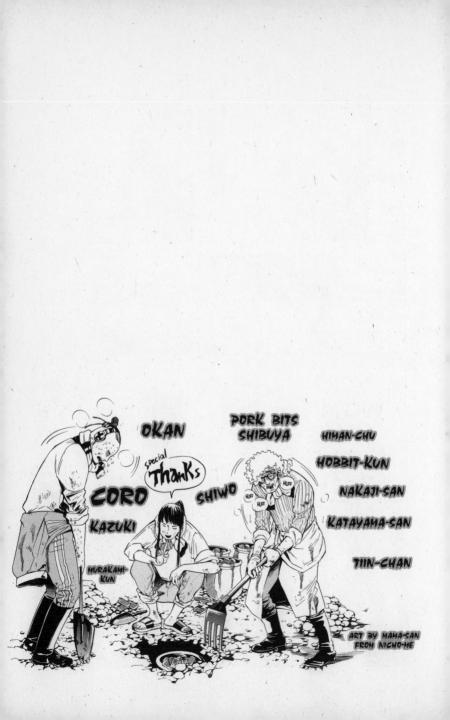

THE PEOPLE OF D.GRAY HOUSE: THE LONELY FATHER

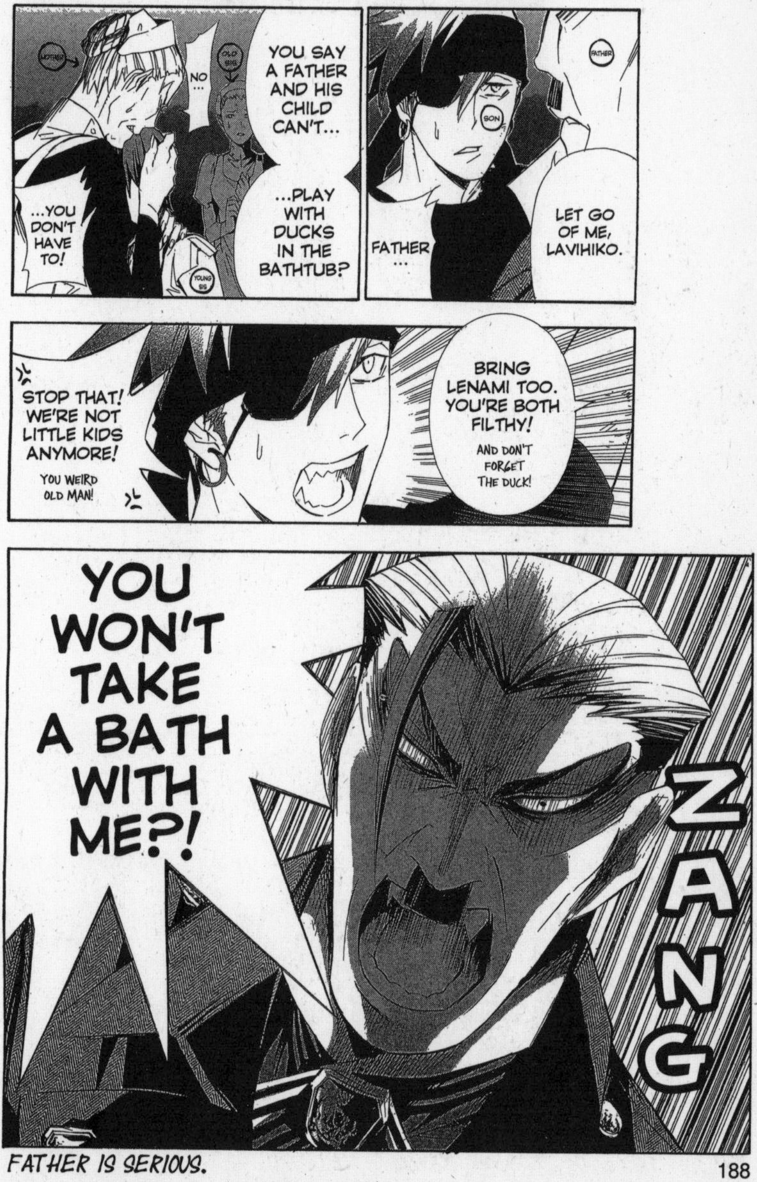
FATHER
SON
LET GO OF ME, LAVIHIKO.
FATHER ...
MOTHER
OLD SIS
YOUNG SIS
YOU SAY A FATHER AND HIS CHILD CAN'T...
...PLAY WITH DUCKS IN THE BATHTUB?
NO ...
...YOU DON'T HAVE TO!
BRING LENAMI TOO. YOU'RE BOTH FILTHY!
AND DON'T FORGET THE DUCK!
STOP THAT! WE'RE NOT LITTLE KIDS ANYMORE!
YOU WEIRD OLD MAN!
YOU WON'T TAKE A BATH WITH ME?!
ZANG

FATHER IS SERIOUS.

BIG BROTHER ARRIVES

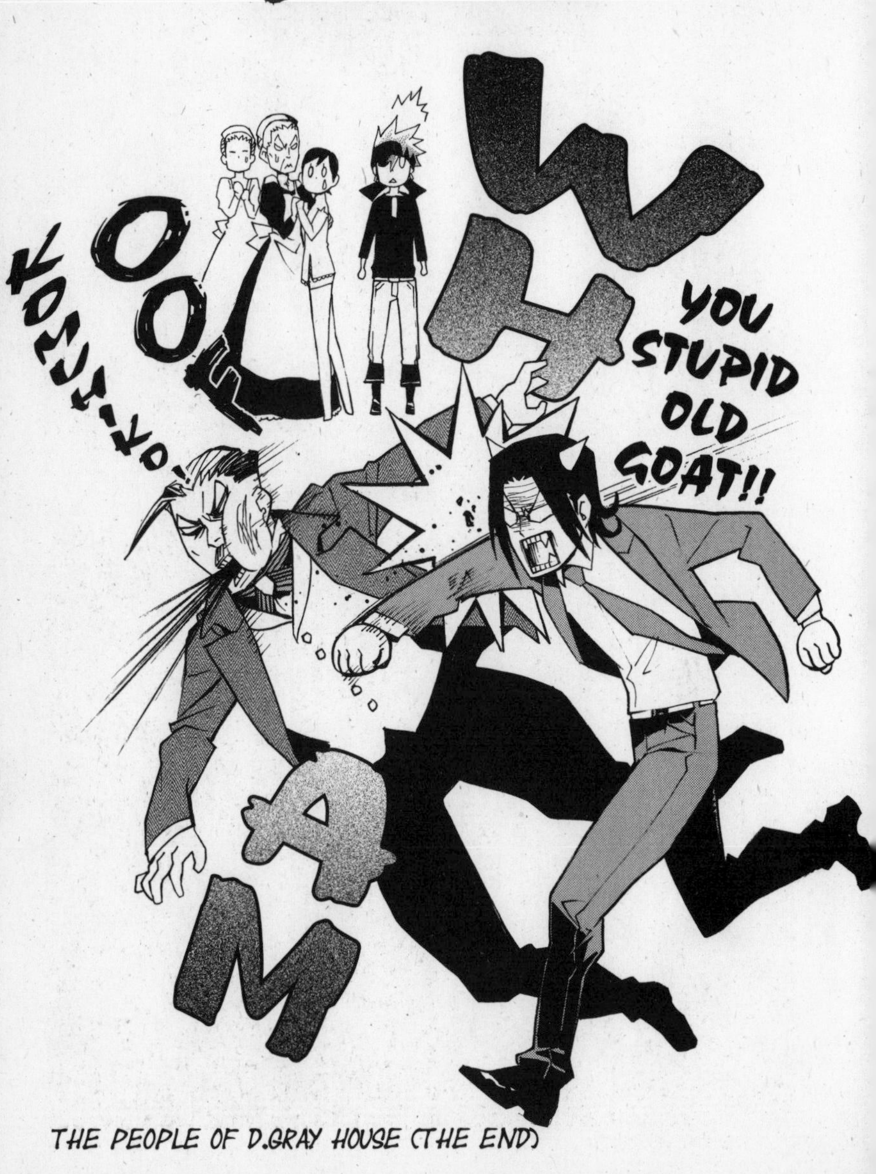
YOU STUPID OLD GOAT!!
WHAM
KOMUI-KO!
OO

THE PEOPLE OF D.GRAY HOUSE (THE END)

IN THE NEXT VOLUME...

While the Level 4 akuma threatens all who remain at Black Order headqua
Rouvelier hustles Lenalee to a meeting with Hevlaska. Komui, consumed b
Lenalee, tries to follow, but that only causes the Level 4 akuma to come a
surviving Exorcists do all they can to stop the Level 4, but their best effor
to be enough to even slow it down!

Available February 2010!

Cuyahog
Libra
Cuyahoga Fa